PLATO'S SOCRATES

PLATO'S SOCRATES

Thomas C. Brickhouse
and
Nicholas D. Smith

New York   Oxford
OXFORD UNIVERSITY PRESS

Oxford University Press

Oxford   New York
Athens   Auckland   Bangkok   Bombay
Calcutta   Cape Town   Dar es Salaam   Delhi
Florence   Hong Kong   Istanbul   Karachi
Kuala Lumpur   Madras   Madrid   Melbourne
Mexico City   Nairobi   Paris   Singapore
Taipei   Tokyo   Toronto

and associated companies in
Berlin   Ibadan

First published in 1994 by Oxford University Press, Inc.,
198 Madison Avenue, New York, New York 10016

First issued as an Oxford University Press paperback, 1995.

Oxford is a registered trademark of Oxford University Press, Inc.

Library of Congress Cataloging-in-Publication Data
Brickhouse, Thomas C., 1947–
Plato's Socrates / Thomas C. Brickhouse and Nicholas D. Smith.
p.   cm.
Includes bibliographical references and index.

ISBN 978-0-19-510111-9

1. Socrates.   2. Plato—Views on Socrates' philosophy.
I. Smith, Nicholas D.   II Title.
B317.B69   1993   183'.2—dc20   92-38865

8 10 9

Printed in the United States of America
on acid-free paper

Preface

This book consists of six inter-related essays on controversial topics in Plato's early dialogues. Each essay is intended to stand on its own, although references to arguments developed in other sections of the book are frequent. For those who wish to read the entire book, we have tried to minimize repetition.

We discuss a wide variety of questions which arise within six general subjects. These subjects are, in order, Socratic method, Socratic epistemology, Socratic psychology, Socratic ethics, Socratic politics, and Socratic religion. We do not claim that these are the only interesting subjects in Plato's early dialogues, nor do we claim to have exhausted each subject we examine; we claim only that the topics we study are interesting ones. In part, we selected these topics because they have become very controversial. We hope our book will add further fuel to the relevant controversies, and we are well aware of how unorthodox many of our conclusions are.

In chapter 1, we consider Socrates' manner of doing philosophy. Socrates says he tests or examines people, and usually may be seen to be seeking to refute them. In Plato's early dialogues he almost always succeeds in doing so. Scholars have become accustomed to referring to Socrates' way of doing philosophy as reflecting a certain method, which is called the *elenchos* or the elenctic method. We argue that Socrates does not regard himself as having a specific method at all. He does not do what he does—in his eyes, at least—*methodically*. He just asks questions, and he never suggests that he has a specific methodology by which he undertakes his examinations of others or chooses the questions he asks them. Instead, he claims only to follow the lead his interlocutor provides. We go on, however, to show how Socrates' examinations of others provide a potent and constructive way of doing philosophy. Some important scholars have denied that what Socrates does can have constructive philosophical results. We disagree, and provide a novel account of how Socrates reached positive results.

In the second chapter, we contrast Socrates' notorious profession of ignorance with his occasional claims of knowledge, and with his frequent expressions of great confidence in what he believes. We argue that insufficient attention has been paid to the fact that what Socrates actually disclaims is not knowledge of any sort, but rather knowledge of a very special sort—a sort that makes its possessor wise. Others have also argued that Socrates may have two different sorts of knowledge in mind when he disclaims knowledge in many passages and also claims knowledge in others. The differences between the two sorts of knowledge, according to some, is the degree of certainty possessed by each sort: one is certain; the other is not. Our view differs from others' in regarding the important difference as— most importantly—a difference in powers of judgment. In short, we characterize the relevant difference in terms of a sort of knowledge that makes its possessor wise, and a sort of knowledge that may be completely certain, but which leaves its possessor "in truth of no account in respect to wisdom" (*Ap*. 23b3–4). We then turn to one of the most vexing questions of Socratic philosophy, namely, the relation in Socratic epistemology between knowledge of definitions and knowledge of examples. We offer a comprehensive study of the texts which have been argued to commit Socrates to a "Socratic fallacy," and show that none requires a reading that commits Socrates to the fallacy in question. Although our position is in substantial agreement with those of a few other scholars, ours is conditioned by the novel conception of Socratic epistemology we offer in the first part of the chapter. We conclude this chapter with an examination of the Socratic conception of wisdom itself, and its central place among the virtues.

In the third chapter, we consider Socrates' paradoxical attributions of psychological states—both cognitive and affective—to those who would vigorously disclaim being in such states. We show how good sense can be made of Socrates' attributions—despite their apparent perversity—as reflecting a reasonable theory of what ensures the regularities Socrates finds in the results of his elenctic examinations of others. We show how this same theory helps us to understand what is, perhaps, the most notorious paradox in Socratic philosophy: the denial of *akrasia*—actions in which one does what is wrong despite one's knowledge that the act in question is indeed wrong. We know of no scholar who has treated Socrates' psychological views in such comprehensive form, or who has even attempted to provide a unified psychological theory to Socrates.

In the fourth chapter, we consider Socrates' ethical views. Ethics—in particular, virtue—is the main focus of Socratic philosophy. Accordingly, an entire book could be written on this subject alone, with whole chapters devoted to Socrates' treatments of each of the individual virtues he identifies, and a number of additional chapters devoted to various other subjects of profound ethical significance, such as friendship, the good life, and happiness. We cannot attempt such a detailed study here. Instead, we consider a number of general features of all of Socrates' ethical discussions, specifically, the relations between goodness and happiness, virtue and happiness, and goodness and virtue. In our discussions of these topics, we agree with some (but not all) scholars that Socrates is an "eudaimonist," that is, one who construes goodness in terms of the promulgation, attainment, or maintenance of happiness. Contrary to all other scholars, however, we deny that Socrates regards virtue as both necessary and sufficient for happiness. Indeed, we deny *both* of the relevant conditionals: we argue that Socrates holds virtue to be, of itself, neither sufficient nor necessary for happiness. We do not deny that Socrates regards virtue as a treasure of inestimable value to its possessor, however, and show how it can be of such enormous value even though it does not hold the place in Socratic philosophy that others have argued for it. Part of our argument derives from recognizing the significance of Socrates' own characterizations of himself: for example, he says he is a "good man," but, lacking wisdom, he cannot be a virtuous man. He makes plain, however, that under certain favorable circumstances such a man as he is could be happy.

In the fifth chapter, we examine Socrates' political views, which scholars seem to have placed at every conceivable position in the political spectrum. Such great diversity of opinion among scholars is the result of the complexity of the relevant issues and the peculiarities of the evidence available. In order to get clear on what the texts really do tell us about Socrates' political views, we undertake a close and patient study of these texts, insisting always on interpretations of them which provide as obvious a sense to them as can be given, as well as a consistent picture of the political views motivating them. We conclude that Socrates was committed to a remarkably inflexible conception of the authority of civil law. We also argue that the texts alleged to document Socrates' hostility towards democracy and democratic leaders betray no partisan political bias, and cannot rightly be construed as favoring any of the political factions of his time. One very controversial consequence of our argument is that we find no reason to believe that his ultimate trial and execution were motivated by partisan political concerns.

The specific formal accusations against Socrates were explicitly religious ones, though this fact has been dismissed as misleading by scholars who attributed political motives to Socrates' prosecutors. In the sixth chapter, we argue for a much more straightforward understanding of Socrates' trial and the motives of his prosecutors than has become fashionable among scholars. We first argue that, in fact, the accusations do reflect religious prejudices, and we go on to argue that the prejudices themselves are represented quite accurately by Socrates himself in Plato's *Apology*. Each of these positions is controversial, but the second one has been explicitly or implicitly denied by every contemporary scholar who has written about the trial. Despite the obvious charity of the view that Socrates is completely open and honest in this matter, we find ourselves alone in arguing that the evidence strongly favors the view that Socrates in no way misrepresents either the real nature of the charges or the motives of those who accused him. In order to make this argument, however, we need to look closely and carefully at Socrates' religious views and at the arguments of those who have seen dangerous unorthodoxy in them. One consequence of our view particularly pleases us: we find Socrates utterly innocent of the charges against him. Those who find Socrates in some sense evading or misrepresenting the charges imagine that he does so because he is actually guilty of them.

Whose Philosophy Is This?

The entire field of Socratic studies has been a busy one lately, stimulated to a large degree by the attention called to it in the work and teaching of Gregory Vlastos. Although we rarely agree with Vlastos's specific positions, our debt to him and our recognition of the great significance of his work will be obvious from our many references to his work, and from the extensive critical attention his views receive in our own arguments. No doubt, our very selection of topics re-

flects Vlastos's influence; these are all topics on which his work has been widely
and rightly regarded as breaking important new ground.

Perhaps the most important quality of Vlastos's work is that it has provided
grounds for treating the philosophy of the character, Socrates, in Plato's early
dialogues as a serious special subject for investigation. Scholars have not always
accepted this conclusion, nor do they all accept it even now. But whether or not
we agree with Vlastos that Plato's Socrates in the early dialogues is the historical
Socrates—or a reasonably close facsimile of the historical Socrates, perhaps as
close as we can hope to find—Vlastos's work shows that it makes sense to talk
about the Socrates of Plato's early period dialogues as having, arguing for and
from, a certain philosophically rich and subtle point of view.

We do not, in this book, intend to answer the question of whose philosophy
we are actually interpreting. The title, *Plato's Socrates,* reflects that it is Plato's
portrait of Socrates we wish to explore. In some sense or senses the philosophy
we are attempting to bring to light is both Platonic *and* Socratic: Platonic at least
insofar as Plato is the author of those texts in which this philosophy is expressed,
developed, and explained, and Socratic because it is the character, Socrates,
whose words this philosophy motivates and expresses. It might be a philosophy
that both Socrates and Plato accepted, at some time or times in their lives. It
might be one that neither ever—or ever fully—accepted. We claim only that a
distinct philosophy can be found consistently portrayed as Socrates' in Plato's
early dialogues, and that the philosophy so portrayed is itself consistent. Both of
these claims have been matters of controversy. We hope our book provides some
additional ground for accepting both claims.

From the fact that we are agnostic about whose philosophy (if anyone's) is
accurately represented in Plato's early dialogues, it does not follow that historical
facts about the life of Socrates are irrelevant to interpreting our texts. In choosing
to name his principal character Socrates, and by carefully situating this character
in a number of settings that call to mind various events in the historical Socrates'
life, Plato invites his readers to see his character in the light of what they independently know about Socrates. It does not simply follow from this, of course, that
Plato was trying to be historically or even philosophically accurate in his portray-
als of Socrates, though it is certainly possible that he was. But whatever his specific motive in identifying this character as Socrates, it is appropriate, in our attempt to understand Plato's character, to apply what we know about the historical
Socrates' life. Plainly, where Plato selects a well-known person and puts him into
very specific historical contexts, it makes good sense for us, Plato's readers, to
understand Plato's character in a way that makes sense of *that* character speaking
and acting within the particular setting of the dialogue. Dismissing the facts of
ancient Greek history, therefore, as irrelevant to Plato's art is to dismiss an important aspect of Plato's art itself; surely part of Plato's supreme artistry is evident
in his representation of the words of famous (and infamous) men in settings where
their words have special poignancy.

For the above reasons, we may occasionally argue in ways that pay unusually
close attention to some one or more specific facts about the historical Socrates, or
about Athens and its institutions. And we occasionally fault rival interpretations

for readings that ignore such facts or require us to dismiss them as irrelevant to the claims Plato's Socrates makes. We believe that our insistence on accuracy in these matters has led us to a number of conclusions that are strikingly different from received interpretations. Our readers will see clearly when such issues are at stake.

Abbreviations, Texts, and Translations

With a few obvious exceptions, we have employed abbreviations for names and works in the form listed in the *Oxford Classical Dictionary*. Whenever we had only a few texts to cite, we have done so by simply listing our citations in parentheses. Where further comment was needed, or more texts were to be listed, we have given these in the notes.

The passages cited from Plato are those of the Oxford Classical Texts, using the standard form of citation—Stephanus page, letter, and line numbers. All translations, unless otherwise noted, are our own. We have always provided translations for cited Greek words and phrases. When we refer frequently to a certain Greek word or phrase, we first list it in the original Greek and then offer a direct transliteration. We then use the transliterated form for all subsequent citations.

Acknowledgments

We have received various forms of assistance as we worked on this book. The National Endowment for the Humanities provided various kinds of funding to each of us for projects whose results are included in this book. We were graciously permitted the use of a number of libraries as we worked on these topics, including the Bodleian Library and the libraries at Stanford University, the University of California at Berkeley, and the University of Virginia. Nicholas D. Smith is also grateful for the extensive support provided to him by the Department of Philosophy and the library at the University of Hong Kong during his visit there in the spring of 1991. By far the greatest support for our work, however, has come from our home institutions, Lynchburg College and Virginia Polytechnic Institute and State University, which accordingly deserve our special thanks.

We are indebted to many people, moreover, whose criticisms of drafts of this book or some parts of it have helped us to correct innumerable mistakes and confusions. Even where we did not follow others' advice, their criticisms often made us more aware of the implications of our views and prepared us to answer criticisms we might not have anticipated otherwise.

Those who have read and criticized drafts of one or more sections or chapters of this book include (in alphabetical order) Julia Annas, Hugh Benson, Mary Whitlock Blundell, Richard Bodéüs, Robert Bolton, John Bussanich, Darrel Colsen, Joseph DeFilippo, Daniel Devereux, David Gill, Laurence Goldstein, Daniel Graham, Charles Griswold, James Haden, David Halperin, Anna Maria Ioppolo, Yasuo Iwata, David Keyt, James C. Klagge, Richard Kraut, Mark McPherran,

Harlan B. Miller, Teruo Mishima, Debra Nails, Christopher New, Charles M. Reed, David Reeve, George Rudebusch, Jose G. T. Santos, Henry Teloh, Katsutochi Uchiyama, Gregory Vlastos, Roslyn Weiss, Shigeru Yonezawa, and Charles Young. Many of the above have also generously provided samples of their own work for us to study, and have spent time in correspondence or conversation with one or both of us on some of the issues we raise in this book. Our public and private correspondence with Mark McPherran and Gregory Vlastos on the topic of Socratic religion has been especially useful and detailed. We would not have dared to write this book had it not been for so many others' willingness to criticize our initial efforts. Our critics and those whose work we criticize herein are, in many cases, our best friends. We would not want it any other way.

We have presented various sections of this book, in some form or other, at a number of conferences and seminars. We have benefited immeasurably from criticisms we have received at such meetings, and wish we could here acknowledge by name all of those who paid us the compliment of questioning our views. Nicholas D. Smith had the privilege of attending three meetings that deserve specific mention: the Second International Association for Greek Philosophy meeting on Samos in August 1990, organized by Konstantin Boudouris; the meeting of the Association for Greek Philosophy in Kyoto in March 1991, organized by Katsutochi Uchiyama and Shigeru Yonezawa; and the Seminar of the Association for Greek Philosophy in Tokyo in March 1991, organized by Teruo Mishima. Each of these meetings allowed us to benefit from comments we would not likely otherwise have received.

Various sections of this book are revisions of published articles. Some have undergone extensive revisions, including modifications of their main theses; others have been changed only slightly. All have been at least somewhat changed. We are grateful to the following journals and their editors and publishers for allowing us to revise these materials for inclusion in this book.

"*Hē Mantikē Technē: Politicus* 260e1 and 290c4-6," which is forthcoming in *Polis,* has been revised herein as sections 6.4.2–3.

"The Socratic Doctrine of 'Persuade or Obey,' " which appeared in *The Philosophy of Socrates,* ed. K. Boudouris, Kardamitsa Pub. Co., Athens (1991), 45–62, has been revised herein as section 5.2.

"Socrates' Elenctic Psychology," which appeared in *Synthese* 92.1 (1992), 63–82, has been revised herein as sections 3.1–4 and 3.6.

"Socrates' Elenctic Mission," which appeared in *Oxford Studies in Ancient Philosophy* 9 (1991), 131–59, has been revised herein as sections 1.2–3.

"What Makes Socrates a Good Man?" which appeared in *Journal of the History of Philosophy* 28 (1990), 169–79, has been revised herein as section 4.5.

"A Matter of Life and Death in Socratic Philosophy," which appeared in *Ancient Philosophy* 9 (1990), 155–65, has been revised herein as section 6.5.

"Socrates the Anti-utopian," which appeared in *Utopia e Modernita. Teorie e prassi utopiche nell' eta moderna e postmoderna,* ed. G. Saccaro Del Butta and A. O. Lewis, Gangemi editore, Casa Del Libro, Rome (1989), 717–25, has been revised herein as section 5.3.5.

"Socrates on Goods, Virtue, and Happiness," which appeared in *Oxford Studies in Ancient Philosophy* 5 (1987), 1–27, has been revised herein as sections 4.1–4 and 4.5.11.

Lynchburg and Blacksburg, Virginia   T.C.B.
May 1993   N.D.S.

Contents

PLATO'S SOCRATES

1

Socratic Method

1.1 Did Socrates Have a Method?

1.1.1 The Socratic Method of Teaching

One often hears of teachers employing the "Socratic Method." This term refers to someone who teaches by asking his or her students leading questions—compelling them to think their way through to the correct understanding of the subject matter. The Socratic method of teaching is contrasted with lecturing, and is often regarded as superior to lecturing precisely because the students of Socratic teachers are required to think for themselves, rather than allowed to listen passively while their non-Socratic teacher simply tells them all they need to know. The Socratic method of teaching no doubt got its name because Socrates is always asking questions. The questions he asks are, moreover, always "leading" questions; we never see Socrates asking questions when he does not at least appear to have some answer already in mind.

But however tempted we might be to see Plato's Socrates as the paradigm of a Socratic teacher, at least three important facts about the Socrates of Plato's early dialogues require us to resist this temptation. (1) He claims not to know—not to have wisdom regarding—the subjects about which he asks his questions.[1] So-called Socratic teachers typically ask their questions and lead their students to the right answers precisely because they *do* know their subjects and, hence, *do* know the right answers to their questions. Many scholars have simply rejected Socrates' famous profession of ignorance as ironical or strategic, and thus eliminate the problem.[2] We shall explain our own view of Socrates' "ignorance" in detail in chapter 2, but for now it is worth noting that if he really does have the knowledge he claims to lack, he is remarkably good at hiding it. Of the fifteen dialogues generally regarded as early or transitional in Plato's career as a philosophical writer, more than *half* end up with the discussants in a state of confusion or perplexity which the Greeks called ἀπορία

---

1. See *Ap.* 20c1–3, 21d2–7, 23b2–4; *Charm.* 165b4–c2, 166c7–d6; *Euthphr.* 5a7–c5, 15c12, 15e5–16a4; *La.* 186b8–c5, 186d8–e3; 200e2–5; *Lysis* 212a4–7, 223b4–8; *Hip. Ma.* 286c8–e2, 304d4–e5; *Grg.* 509a4–6; *Meno* 71a1–7, 80d1–4; *Rep.* I.337e4–5.

2. See, for example, Gulley [1968]; Shero [1927]; Vlastos [1971b], 7–8 (though Vlastos changed his mind about this).

(aporia).[3] And even in those that are not aporetic Socrates frequently professes ignorance and invariably fails to support the dialogue's positive conclusions with a full moral theory. Moreover, if the Socrates of the early dialogues really does have the very knowledge to which his questions are supposed to lead his interlocutors, Plato, for some reason or other, has chosen to portray him as a *terrible* teacher of what he knows: Socrates' students are often depicted as being confused by and annoyed at him; rarely if ever can they be said to have really *learned* anything. We conclude that whatever Plato's Socrates is doing, it is not leading his interlocutors in the way the Socratic teacher leads his students—precisely because Socrates is not, and freely acknowledges that he is not, qualified to be an expert guide.

(2) No doubt because he does not regard himself as having the knowledge or wisdom he would need to guide students in the relevant way, Socrates often explicitly denies that he is a teacher or that he has any knowledge to teach.[4] It may be, of course, that this is irony, a part of Socrates' strategy as a teacher. But, if so, it is again odd that we never see Socrates come out from under this alleged cover of strategic irony and that we never see his students completely succeed in learning the "lesson" Socrates is allegedly teaching.

(3) Teaching by what is now termed the Socratic method is constructive, designed straightforwardly to make the student progress from ignorance of a subject to knowledge or understanding of that subject. Plato's Socrates seems, on the contrary, invariably to be doing something that is at least partly destructive; although he sometimes disguises his real goals by feigning interest or respect for another's opinions, we always discover that, in fact, Socrates is seeking somehow or other to refute the one he is questioning. Socrates even claims that he has a "mission" undertaken on behalf of the god of Delphi to show people who think they are wise that they are not (*Ap.* 23b4–7).

In this chapter, we shall argue that there is a sense in which his interlocutors do indeed have something to learn from Socrates. But, in our view, Socrates, as Plato depicts him, is not a teacher at all; he is a seeker after moral wisdom who encourages others to engage in the same search. Socrates' interlocutors are invited to join him in the pursuit of wisdom, rather than to be passively "instructed" in whatever Socrates has already learned himself. We cannot provide an exhaustive study of Socrates' goals in just this chapter, however, for his conception of his activities is supported by a variety of views he holds: about the nature and accessibility of knowledge; about human nature and human potential; about the real goals of inquiry in generating value in human life; about the role of the individual in society; and about the relationship between religion and reason. Because we shall discuss each of these views in the succeeding chapters, there is a sense in which this entire book is about the Socratic method. We shall concentrate in this chapter

---

3. Eight dialogues are plainly "aporetic": *Charmides; Euthyphro; Hippias Major; Hippias Minor; Laches; Lysis; Protagoras; Republic* I. Some commentators treat all of the early dialogues as aporetic—see, for example, Benson [1990a], 141–44.

4. *Ap.* 19d8–e1, 20c1–3, 23a3–b4, 33a5–b8; *Charm.* 165b5–c1, 167b6–7, 169a7–8, 175e5–176a5; *La.* 186a3–c5, 186d8–e3.

only on identifying how Socrates goes about his philosophizing, and what he takes
to be its scope and limitations.

1.1.2   The Ἔλεγχος (Elenchos)

Elenchos would ordinarily be translated as "refutation," but sometimes only
means something like "examination" (see, for example, *Ap.* 39c7, 39d1). Certainly, Socrates' interlocutors appear to be defeated by the arguments he constructs, and Socrates often acknowledges that he is attempting to refute his interlocutors (see *Charm.* 166c8, 166e1–2), although he always goes on to claim that
this does not exhaust his purpose (see *Charm.* 166c7–d6). Whether rightly or
wrongly, then, Socrates' style of philosophizing has come to be known among
scholars as the "method of *elenchos*" or "the elenctic method."[5] But Socrates
himself only says that he "examines" (ἐξετάζω), "inquires" (ζητῶ, ἐρωτῶ,
συνερωτῶ), "investigates" (σκοπῶ, διασκοπῶ, σκέπτομαι, διασκέπτομαι),
"searches" (ἐρευνῶ, διερευνῶ), "questions" (ἐρέω), or simply "philoso-
phizes" (φιλοσοφῶ).[6] Socrates has no special word for his "method," nor does
he ever refer to what he does as reflecting a method.[7]

If we are to decide whether Socrates actually regarded himself as having a
method, we must attend both to what Socrates thinks can truly be called a
"method" in the early dialogues and also to what we actually find Socrates doing
and what he says about what he is doing. We shall follow the scholarly tradition
in referring to what Socrates does as "performing" or "practicing" the *elenchos*.
This is not to say, however, that we believe Socrates thought he had a distinct
method. Indeed, we shall argue that he did not see himself as employing a specific
methodology. Later in the chapter, however, we shall show how his manner of
examining others—even if Socrates himself would not regard it as a specific
method—was nonetheless well designed for Socrates' own philosophical goals.

1.1.3   Craft and Expertise

It is no doubt tempting to think that Socrates must have self-consciously employed
a method, because his questioning or examining others seems so invariably to lead
to the same result: his interlocutors are revealed to have contradictory beliefs,
whereby the interlocutor's initial claim or hypothesis is shown to conflict with one
or more of the interlocutor's later admissions. How would Socrates characterize
his ability to do this so dependably? Would he say that his ability to reduce his
interlocutors to perplexity was comparable to a cobbler's ability to make good
shoes, or some other craftsman's ability to practice his craft (τέχνη/*technē*) and

---

5. Gregory Vlastos briefly discusses the history of scholars' uses of this term—and the fact that
Socrates never actually names his method ([1983a], see esp. 27–28).

6. Instances of each term and its cognates are too frequent in the early dialogues to list.

7. This is also mentioned by Vlastos [1983a], 28 and n.5, who notes that the word, "μέθοδος"
(method), was coined by Plato, but only *after* the early period (its first occurrence is at *Phd.* 79e3;
see also 97b6).

produce his craft's product (ἔργον/*ergon*)? In short, is Socrates' ability to refute others a craft?

The early dialogues are consistent in treating all knowledge as if it were craft-knowledge (about which we shall have more to say in chapter 2) and in regarding virtue as if it were a kind of craft whose goal is the production of a good life. But nowhere in the early dialogues does Socrates offer a comprehensive account of what conditions must be met for something to qualify as a craft. Such conditions have to be gathered up from various references to crafts scattered throughout the early dialogues. At least the following conditions may be found:

Rationality/Regularity: The craftsman goes about doing his work in an orderly, purposive, and rational way—he does not go about his business "at random" (*Grg.* 503e1–504a5) or by conjecture. Rather the craftsman is guided by knowledge (*Grg.* 464c6). Moreover, just as the craftsman's method is orderly, the results of his craft are regular and orderly (504a7–b9).

Teachability/Learnability: For something to be a craft, it must be *teachable*, and it must be *learnable*. Although it can happen that someone can become skilled in a craft without having had a teacher (*La.* 185e7–9, 186b1–5, 187a1), ordinarily, a craftsman will have been taught his craft, and will be able to teach it to others (*Grg.* 514a5–b3; *La.* 185b1–4, 185e4–6; see also *Prt.* 319b5–c8). To have learned a particular craft is to have become a craftsman of that craft (*Grg.* 460b1–5).

Explicability: The craft-expert can teach his craft because he can explain what he does by giving an account of the nature of its objects and their causes (*Grg.* 465a2–6; see also 500e4–501b1). The account of the nature of the object explains what the object is; the craftsman can give such an account of that about which he is an expert (*La.* 189e3–190b1).

Inerrancy: The craft-expert does not err in his work or in his judgments about the subject matter of his expertise; his knowledge is so exact that his judgments—even if they may seem inappropriate or even altogether mistaken to non-expert observers—are matters of complete confidence (*Euthphr.* 4e4–5a2; see also *Euthyd.* 279d6–280b3, on identifying craft with wisdom). When the non-expert attempts to do the work of experts, he has a far greater chance of failure (*La.* 186b5–7, 187a8–b4).

Uniqueness: The craftsman is a specialist whose special abilities are unique to him and other craftsmen who specialize in that craft. "The many" are usually distinguished from the craftsman merely by virtue of the fact that the former lack the specialized knowledge possessed by the latter (*Ap.* 24e4–25c1; *Cri.* 47a2–48c6; *Grg.* 455b2–c2; *La.* 184c9–e9). Thus, carpenters will be among "the many" with regard to shoemaking, and shoemakers will be among "the many" with regard to carpentry.

Distinctness of Subject Matter: Each craft has a distinct subject matter, which can be used in such a way as to distinguish that craft from other crafts. This subject matter is to be identified with whatever it is that *technē* serves to produce (*Grg.* 452a7–d4, 453c4–454b1, 455d2–3; *Ion* 531a1–532c8, 536e1–542b4). Within the same broad category of subject matter, however, there may be more than one craft doing its work; thus, for example, under the general heading "tending to (or productive of) the health of the body," we find two crafts: gymnastic, which is prophylactic, and medicine, which is curative (*Grg.* 464b3–c3).

Knowledge/Wisdom: The craftsman *knows* his subject matter, is *wise* regarding it (*Ap.* 22c9–d4; *Grg.* 459b1–3, 464c6). It is in virtue of this knowledge or wisdom that the craftsman is inerrant and can teach his craft (*Prt.* 361a5–c2). It actually seems as if "knowledge," "wisdom," and "craft" are often used interchangeably, although as we shall argue in chapter 2, there is a sort of knowledge that is not identical to nor even partially constitutive of wisdom.

1.1.4 Elenchos *and Craft*

If we apply these standards to Socrates' *elenchos,* we will see that he would not regard himself as having a craft. The work of the craftsman is always orderly; he never goes about his business "at random," or by "conjecture," and his products are always themselves orderly. Now, Socrates does not ask his questions *purely* "at random"—he obviously has a variety of standards to which he appeals in making his examinations of others: his interlocutors must say only what they believe;[8] the discussants must seek adequate definitions of the relevant terms of their inquiry before attempting to discern the applications and extensions of these terms;[9] lists of examples will never qualify as proper definitions;[10] and so on. But Socrates plainly would not regard such rules of thumb as sufficient to elevate his style of philosophizing to the status of craft. As he begins his defense before the jury in the *Apology,* for example, he explicitly says an unplanned style of speech is customary for him (*Ap.* 17c6–18a3). Moreover, it is plain that what the *elenchos* accomplishes, though predictable, does not manifest the sort of regularity and order that the products of the crafts of shipbuilding or architecture do. It is predictable, perhaps, that Socrates' interlocutors will be perplexed by the time they have been thoroughly examined; but perplexity can hardly be regarded as an orderly outcome (see, for example, *Euthphr.* 11b6–e1; *Meno* 79e7–80b7; see also Socrates' own expressions of perplexity at *Hip. Mi.* 372a6–e6, 376b8–c6).

Moreover, because Socrates does not have the wisdom so many of his interlocutors suppose they have, he does not satisfy the knowledge/wisdom criterion. Without such knowledge, Socrates cannot explicate what he is looking for, and he cannot teach what he does not know. Socrates occasionally says that he does not know the answers to his own questions (*Charm.* 165b5–c1; *Rep.* I.337e4–6, 354c1–3; see also *Hip. Mi.* 372a6–e6, 376b8–c6). So he must proceed, when he does not know, "by conjecture" (see also *Meno* 98b1). And because he cannot teach, he can offer no guarantee that those who interact with him will turn out well—as he says of himself in the *Apology* (33b2–6), "I put myself forward to ask questions for the rich and poor alike, and if anyone wishes, he may answer

8. See *Euthphr.* 9d7–8; *Cri.* 49c11–d1; *Prt.* 331c4–d1; *Rep.* I.349a4–8; *Grg.* 458a1–b1, 495a5–9, 499b4–c6, 500b5–c1.

9. See our discussion of the priority of definitions in sections 2.3 and 2.4.

10. See *Euthphr.* 6d9–e1; *La.* 191e9–11, 192b5–8; *Meno* 73c6–8, 75a4–5, 77a5–9. For discussion, see Benson [1990b].

and hear what I have to say. And whether any of them turns out well or not, it would not be just to hold me responsible, for I never promised them anything nor did I teach them anything." In fact, a substantial number of Socrates' interlocutors in Plato's dialogues are people who we know turned out very badly. Accordingly, the results of his examinations are also neither regular nor orderly, nor can Socrates claim to be inerrant. Much to his surprise, Socrates sometimes finds that the *elenchos* produces a conclusion he finds difficult to accept (see, for example, *Hip. Mi.* 376b8–c6; *Lys.* 218c4–8).

It is also clear that Socrates does not regard his own ability to examine people as unique. Already there are young men who are able to imitate him and get similar results (*Ap.* 23c2–7), and Socrates is convinced that after he has been executed, there will continue to be others who can do what he has done (*Ap.* 39c6–d3). Socrates even seems to suppose that the jurors themselves could take Socrates' role in "troubling" Socrates' sons after Socrates is gone just as he has troubled those who have stood as his judges (*Ap.* 41e1–42a2). Although in section 1.3.6 we shall have more to say about how readily Socrates thinks others can do what he has done, nowhere does he suggest that his ability to examine others constitutes a craft by which he can be distinguished from other men.

Finally, it appears that the *elenchos* does not have a distinct subject matter. We never see Socrates examining others to find out if they really possess knowledge of carpentry or medicine, for example; rather, we see him almost invariably attending to moral questions (see Aristotle, *Metaph.* A, 987b1–4). But in the *Ion* Socrates uses the *elenchos* to show that the rhapsode does not possess a craft. And in the "slave-boy" episode in the *Meno* (82b9–85b7), Plato shows how the elenctic approach may be used in geometrical reasoning. Of the seven criteria by which crafts are distinguished from non-crafts, therefore, it looks as if the Socratic *elenchos* meets none.[11] Plainly, then, Socrates would deny that, in practicing his *elenchos*, he practices a craft.[12]

---

11. It might be thought that Socrates' remarks at *Grg.* 521d6–8 indicate that Socrates thinks that there is a craft of using the *elenchos* after all and that he possesses that craft. But in fact Socrates does not say that he actually possesses the craft. All he says is that he "alone among the Athenians attempts the real political craft." As Irwin notes ([1979], note on 521d, 240–41), this remark is consistent with Socrates' not possessing any craft-knowledge at all.

12. In Brickhouse and Smith [1984d], we offer a detailed criticism of Gregory Vlastos's account [1983a] of the *elenchos*. To the many arguments we offered there, we can now add one other: Vlastos's account of the *elenchos* would appear to give Socrates a method which satisfied all of the seven criteria by which crafts might be identified. In Vlastos's view, the *elenchos* is driven by Socrates' own consistent and true moral (and morally relevant) beliefs. Accordingly, his elenctic arguments must indeed be *rational* and *regular,* and *inerrant.* Vlastos's Socrates obviously *knows* what he talks about, and can prove that each of his beliefs is true. And because Socrates knows—or is in a position to know—all moral truths, certainly he could *teach* them (or a sizable number of them) to others. Socrates could *explain* what he does by revealing the moral and non-moral axioms that guide his *elenchos,* and then showing—as per Vlastos's account—how one could unerringly identify and explain other truths in terms of these axioms. Vlastos's Socrates is *unique* in being able to guide arguments in this way, for obviously Socrates did not believe that his fellow Athenians held all and only true moral beliefs (as Vlastos says Socrates himself does). Vlastos also appears to believe that even the distinctness of subject matter condition is satisfied: he insists that Socrates would employ his *elenchos* in searching "only for truth in the moral domain" ([1983a], 32). It would appear to follow, then, that

1.1.5 The Alternatives to Craft

Many things are explicitly contrasted with craft in the early dialogues. Not counting pure ignorance, which could also be contrasted to craft, Socrates identifies a number of things by which people are able to achieve various results, but which nonetheless fall short of being a craft: flattery (*Grg.* 463a6–b1, 464c5–465b6, 466e13–467a1); divine power (*Ion* 533d2, 534c5–6, 535e9), divine lot (*Ion* 534c1, 535a4, 536d3, 542a4), or inspiration (*Ap.* 22b9–c1; *Ion* 533e4–534a7, 536a8–c6); and experience or routine[13] (*Grg.* 462b6–e1, 463b3–4, 465a2–6, 500e4–501b1; cp. Polus' remarks at *Grg.* 448c4–7, which show that he does not recognize the distinction between craft and experience).

But Socrates would not characterize his philosophical questioning in any of these ways. Plainly it is not flattery, which seeks only to please (*Grg.* 464c3–465b6, 501c2–5, 502b1–c4, 513d1–e4). Socrates' ability to conduct the *elenchos* is also not the result of divine power, lot, or inspiration. He does regard his examinations of others to be a mission given him by the god (*Ap.* 23b4–c1, 28d6–29a4, 29d3–30a7, 30e1–31b1, 33c4–7). It does not follow from this, however, that he has some special talent or inspiration that guides him to ask the questions he asks. The god has ordered him to pursue his mission, but does not necessarily assist him as he carries it out. Nor does Socrates' divine monitor (δαι-μόνιον/*daimonion*) appear to be of much assistance in Socrates' examinations. For all of the evidence we have of the *daimonion*'s activity,[14] not once do we find Socrates adjusting the path of his questioning of another on the basis of a signal from his *daimonion*.

Socrates also makes it quite clear that one does not need experience in order to make use of the *elenchos*. Instead, Socrates exhorts one and all to lead examined lives; and even young and inexperienced men can examine others and reveal ignorance (see *Ap.* 23c2–7). Thus, although Socrates' remarkable ability to reduce his interlocutors to perplexity is no doubt bolstered by experience, it is not itself what Socrates calls "experience," nor does it have "experience" as a necessary or sufficient condition.

Even if we are able to throw light on what Socrates would say about his own special skill in constructing elenctic arguments, we have nevertheless been unable to identify any category of talent, gift, skill, or craft under which anything we

---

Vlastos's analysis of the *elenchos* would give Socrates a very potent craft, or something very like a craft. But any suggestion that Socrates actually possesses a craft of morality simply fails to cohere with the numerous passages referred to previously (1.1.4) in which Socrates implies that he possesses no such thing. We would do well, then, to seek an alternative to Vlastos's account. In section 1.2, we offer our own account.

13. These two—experience (ἐμπειρία) and routine (τριβή)—are always treated together, as if they identify the same category. Routine is referred to independently from experience only at *Phaedrus* 260e2–5. In the only other reference to routine in that dialogue—later at 270b5–6—the two are paired. Nothing in this one exception forces us to distinguish between routine and experience, at least for our present purposes.

14. See *Ap.* 31c8–d1, 40a4–6, 40c2–3, 41d6; *Euthphr.* 3b5–7; *Euthyd.* 272e4; *Rep.* VI.496c4; *Phdr.* 242b8–9; [*Theages*] 128d2–131a7; [*Alc.* I] 105d5–106a1. For a discussion of the *daimonion*, see section 6.3.

might identify as the Socratic method would fall. We conclude from this failure that Socrates would not regard himself as having anything so systematic as a method at all. He asks his questions—just as others can—seeking, investigating, and examining others and what they say in the hopes that he might discover something of value. Because he has spent so much of his life in elenctic argument, we are sometimes tempted to infer that Socrates knows more than he is letting on about the subject matter at hand. But Socrates has no method, if by "method" we mean to identify an orderly procedure which follows patterns that must be learned and mastered before one is able to achieve effective results. There is no "cookbook" for the Socratic *elenchos,* nor could a step-by-step procedure ever be set forth. Any of us *could* do what Socrates does, although, of course, not as well; and, according to Socrates, *all* of us *should* do what he does. The fact that we would get better at it with practice should be no impediment to our undertaking Socratic examinations right away and for the rest of our lives. Accordingly, we have nothing to learn before we employ Socrates' method. It follows from these considerations that Socrates thinks there is no method to learn.

1.2   Socrates' Elenctic Mission

1.2.1   What Does Socrates Do, and How Does He Do It?

Thus far we have argued that Socrates' *elenchos* is not a craft. It is nonetheless true that Socrates does what he does with remarkable and obvious facility. He asks his questions, and inevitably reduces his interlocutor to perplexity. In fact, the interlocutor always ends up abandoning his original position. What is puzzling is exactly how Socrates achieves this effect: elenctic arguments appear only to demonstrate the inconsistency of the interlocutor's initial moral claim with those of the interlocutor's other beliefs that serve as the premises of the argument.[15] At the conclusion of the *elenchos,* then, it would appear that it is incumbent upon the interlocutor only to revise at least one of his expressed beliefs, either the moral hypothesis itself or one of the beliefs from which the negation of the hypothesis has been deduced. Yet both Socrates and his interlocutor often act as if the moral hypothesis must be discarded because it has been refuted and its negation established. This reaction is made all the more puzzling by the fact that Socrates' questioning seems merely to draw out various of the interlocutor's other beliefs which then serve as the premises of the *elenchos.* Typically, Socrates neither questions those beliefs nor argues for them. In the absence of independent reasons for accepting the premises of the *elenchos,* why do Socrates and his interlocutor abandon the moral hypothesis at issue and accept its negation because of an argument that only shows its inconsistency with those premises?

Most scholarly treatments of the Socratic *elenchos* have been limited to at-

---

15. For a discussion of those who have held the view that the *elenchos* can only demonstrate the inconsistency of his interlocutor's beliefs, see Vlastos [1983a], 44–46. Vlastos himself once accepted this view ([1976], vii–lvi). More recent expressions of this position may be found in Stokes [1986], esp. 1–35 and 440–43; and Benson [1987], [1989], [1990a], [1990c].

tempts to answer this question.[16] But scattered throughout the *Apology* and other early dialogues are a surprising number of passages in which Socrates and his interlocutors specifically refer to the distinct philosophical goals Socrates pursues. Yet in spite of the number of such passages, nowhere in the early dialogues does Socrates state explicitly why he thinks elenctic testing provides an appropriate way to achieve those goals.[17] Since he uses this single style of argument, not only must any adequate account of Socrates' philosophy answer the narrow question of whether elenctic arguments demonstrate only the inconsistency of his interlocutors' beliefs, but it must also examine the degree to which Socrates might be justified in thinking that the *elenchos* furthers each of the variety of philosophical goals he says that he pursues. In this section, we shall attempt to accomplish both of these tasks.

1.2.2 How Ought One to Live?

In the *Apology,* Socrates tells the jury that he tests all who claim to know "the things of greatest importance," "young or old, foreigner or fellow citizen" (*Ap.* 30a2–4). What is of greatest importance to Socrates is the answer to the question "How ought one to live?" Thus, in *Republic* I, for instance, we find him telling Thrasymachus: "The argument is not about an ordinary matter, but about how we ought to live" (*Rep.* I.352d5–6). Similarly, in the *Gorgias* Socrates tells Callicles:

> This inquiry is the noblest of all, O Callicles: concerning those things about which you have rebuked me—what sort of man should one be and what should he do and how much, when he is old and when he is young. (*Grg.* 487e7–488a2)

These remarks, then, suggest that at least a part of what Socrates takes himself to be doing in his elenctic examinations is pursuing an understanding of how people ought to live.

Socrates stresses that one aspect of his service on behalf of the god is destructive. The god, he says, has commanded him to free his fellow humans from their

16. One exception to this tendency among Socratic scholars is Paul Woodruff's treatment [1987] of the *elenchos*. Although we think that Woodruff is correct in pointing out that the Socratic method is intended to achieve a variety of goals, we disagree with Woodruff insofar as he thinks that Socrates employs different sorts of elenctic arguments to achieve those goals. If we are correct, the view we advance in this section can—and Woodruff cannot—account for the fact that Socrates never seems to abandon one distinctive type of argument. We also believe, as our argument will show, that there are more uses for the *elenchos* than the three identified by Woodruff: that of exhortation, which we explore in some detail below; that of interpretation, which we discuss in section 3.2.4, and which is a species of our "constructive" use); and that of a disproof of knowledge (roughly the same as our "destructive" use). Woodruff does not see the *elenchos* used constructively in such a way as to establish generally applicable moral truths, except when used in interpretations of poetry, oracles, and the like.

17. The fact that Socrates does not discuss the *elenchos* per se is treated in detail in Vlastos [1983a], 27–28. We do not claim that the *elenchos* is the only tool Socrates employs in the pursuit of his mission; his mission has a number of goals and he pursues them through a number of techniques, including direct exhortation and by offering himself as an example for others to follow. But we shall attempt to show that the *elenchos* contributes to each of the explicit goals of Socrates' mission, and how it does so.

pretense of real wisdom by showing them that they do not know what they think they know. Thus, though he says that he will talk to anyone who cares to do so (*Ap*. 33a6–b3), he especially seeks out those who claim to understand some moral term or issue in dispute (*Ap*. 23b4–7, 29e3–30a2). What such people mistakenly think they know is how one ought to live if one is to have virtue (ἀρετή/*aretē*). So one of the things Socrates intends, through his examination, is to undermine certain of his interlocutors' beliefs regarding the good life.

But Socrates does not just seek to call into question his interlocutors' false beliefs about how one ought to live; he also hopes to make substantive and constructive progress towards developing a correct understanding of how one ought to live. Socrates reveals this interest in the *Gorgias:*

> If we do these things, it is necessary that we all be contentious with regard to
> knowing what is true concerning what we are discussing, and what is false. For
> it is a common good for all that this be revealed. (*Grg*. 505e3–6)

A similar claim is made in the *Charmides*. Socrates asks Critias, "Or do you not think that it is a common good for all men for it to become evident how each thing is?" (*Charm*. 166d3–6). The "how each thing is" that Socrates wishes to discover is of course, the right account of what moral views are to be adopted if one's life is to be well lived, for Socrates is convinced both that the best life requires the acquisition of virtue and that becoming virtuous requires one to come to know what virtue is. Thus, unless he has some other way to achieve his goal of understanding, Socrates must think that the *elenchos* can lead to the discovery of moral facts, if he has any hope of actually making constructive progress in moral inquiry.[18]

1.2.3 *Examining Lives and Not Merely Propositions*

If Socrates is to succeed in freeing persons from their pretense of wisdom regarding how best to live, he must use the *elenchos* in some sense to diminish the appeal of false moral beliefs. Thus, one might think that in examining the various claims made by his interlocutors, Socrates is merely trying to demonstrate the falsehood of certain propositions the interlocutor has endorsed.

Nevertheless, there is good reason to think that by his testing, Socrates sees himself as doing something more than just attempting to display the falsehood of his interlocutors' propositions. Consider, for example, what Nicias tells Lysima-chus in the *Laches:*

---

18. In a number of his papers, Benson has argued against the idea that the *elenchos* can have a constructive function ([1987], [1989], [1990a], and [1990c]). But his arguments have invariably been against those (mainly Vlastos [1983a]) who have suggested that *individual* elenctic arguments may be supposed to establish clear constructive results. We, too, have argued against the specific way Vlastos conceives of the *elenchos* (see especially Brickhouse and Smith [1984d]). Our argument in this section *does* conceive of the *elenchos* as having a constructive function; it *does not* do so, however, by construing individual elenctic arguments as establishing the constructive results in question. Hence, although our view is a "constructivist" one, it is not the sort of "constructivist" view that Benson's arguments have opposed.

You do not seem to me to know that whoever is closest to Socrates and draws near into a discussion with him, if he would but begin to discuss something else, will necessarily not stop being led around by him in the discussion until he falls into giving an account of himself—of the way he is living now and of the way he has lived in the past. (*La.* 187e6–188a2)

Similarly, in the *Gorgias*, believing full well that he will refute Callicles' view of the value of justice, Socrates tells him at the outset:

If you allow (what I say) to be unrefuted, by the dog, the god of the Egyptians, Callicles will not agree with you, O Callicles, but will be in conflict with your whole way of living. (*Grg.* 482b4–6)

What Nicias reports and what Socrates asserts, then, is that through the *elenchos* Socrates examines the manner in which his interlocutors live (see also *Ap.* 39c7: ἔλεγχον τοῦ βίου).[19]

This aspect of Socrates' description of his mission has received virtually no attention in scholarly accounts of the *elenchos*.[20] Other commentators typically see only that Socrates employs the *elenchos* on propositions, demonstrating the incompatibility of his interlocutors' beliefs, and (on some accounts) showing others to be more justified. But Socrates does not say that he examines what people say or even what they believe; he says he examines *people* (e.g., *Ap.* 21c35, 23b4–6, 23c4, 28e5–6, 29e4–5, 38a5), and as we have said, by this he means examining the ways in which they live (see esp. *Ap.* 39c7). Socrates docs not say that untested propositions are not worth believing or that unexamined beliefs are not worth holding; he says that the unexamined *life* is not worth living (*Ap.* 38a5–6). Of course, he examines lives by getting his interlocutors to express the values according to which they live in propositions that may then be examined. But as he tells us in the passages from the *Gorgias* and the *Laches* quoted above, Socrates is interested, not merely in the truth or falsehood of these propositions, but rather in the lives whose values these propositions characterize.

We can now see why Socrates insists that his interlocutors say only what they

---

19. The discussion of the use of "βίος" (life) in Greek moral contexts has been limited primarily to Aristotle's use of the term; see, for example, Cooper [1975], 159–60; and Keyt [1978], 145–46. Keyt makes a persuasive case that the term, at least as Aristotle uses it, can signify *either* a person's total life, as, for example, the life of the temperate person as opposed to the life of the intemperate person, or an aspect or phase of one's life, as, for example, the intellectual life as opposed to the moral life. In the latter signification, it makes sense to speak of a single person living two or more lives synchronously. When Socrates says that he examines a person's life he cannot reasonably be employing the latter sense, as *La.* 187e6–188a2 and *Grg.* 482b2–6 make clear. Rather, he wants to know what we would now call a person's "conception of the good," since that will inform everything else that person does and values and, hence, will illuminate the general kind of life a person thinks he should live.

20. One recent exception to this tendency is to be found in Seeskin [1987], chap. 2 (see esp. 35–37). No doubt there are other analyses of the *elenchos* which allow agreement on this point. But scholars have typically failed to address this aspect of the *elenchos* explicitly. Hence, a number of philosophically interesting uses to which Socratic argumentation may be put are neither claimed on its behalf nor explained.

truly believe.[21] Only if the interlocutors answer his questions with their sincerely held beliefs can Socrates be confident that he is really testing an aspect of how they think they should live. Indeed, the demand that the interlocutor say only what he truly believes is so important to the *elenchos* that Socrates frequently invites the interlocutor to withdraw or amend what has been said if the interlocutor is not fully satisfied that his beliefs expressed in response to Socrates' questions have been represented accurately.[22]

It would be a mistake, however, to think that Socrates uses the *elenchos* to test only his interlocutors' lives. In the *Apology* he tells the jury that he has been commanded by the god to examine *himself* as well as others (*Ap.* 28e4–6), and since "the unexamined life is not worth living" (*Ap.* 38a5–6), we must assume that Socrates' life also needs examination. Now one might suppose that two separate sets of elenctic arguments must be employed in order for Socrates to examine both his interlocutor's *and* Socrates' own lives. But, with only two exceptions (*Prt.* 338c7–339d9 and *Grg.* 462a1–467c2), nowhere in the early dialogues does Socrates submit to questioning himself. So it must be that in the process of examining others Socrates regards himself as examining his own life, too. This is why, in the *Charmides,* for example, Socrates tells Critias in the most emphatic terms that he, Socrates, expects to benefit from having Critias submit to elenctic testing.

> How, I said, can you think, if I am trying most of all to refute you, that I do so on account of anything other than the fact that I would wish to understand what I say, fearing that I might overlook something, thinking I know something when I do not? Therefore even now I say I am doing this; I am investigating the reasoning most of all for my own sake, but perhaps also for my other friends. (*Charm.* 166c7–d4)[23]

1.2.4 Must Socrates Agree with All of His Premises?

It might be thought that if Socrates is to derive a benefit from the *elenchos* along with his interlocutors, he himself must share the beliefs which form the premises

---

21. See *Euthphr.* 9d7–8; *Cri.* 49c11–d1; *Prt.* 331c4–d1; *Rep.* I.349a4–8; *Grg.* 458a1–b1, 495a5–9, 499b4–c6, 500b5–c1. Socrates occasionally seems willing to dispense with this condition, e.g., with Callicles in the *Gorgias* (at 499b4–c6, and in letting pass Callicles' professed lack of commitment at 501c7–8, and from 505c5 on) and with Thrasymachus in *Rep.* I (see *Rep.* I.349a9–b1 and from 350e1 on). We do not think this vitiates the rule that the interlocutor must say what he believes in order to maximize the benefits of the *elenchos*. For one thing, it is clear that when Socrates continues the inquiry after Callicles and Thrasymachus have become passive, the products of it derive plainly from what they had already asserted *before* they became passive. Thus, even if the argument were pursued in such a way as not necessarily to reflect either of the participants' beliefs, it might still be that something is to be learned about the sense of the position under examination. This may be all that can be claimed for the discussion of a view attributed to "the many" at *Prt.* 351c2 ff., since neither Socrates nor Protagoras explicitly endorses it. It may be that Protagoras is merely being cautious in his refusal to commit himself with "the many."

22. See *Euthphr.* 11b2, 13c11–d3; *Cri.* 49d9–e2; *Prt.* 354b7–355a5; *Grg.* 461c8–d3, 462a3, 482d7–e2; *Rep.* I.348b8–10; [*Hipparch.*] 229e3–230a9.

23. See also *Prt.* 348c5–d5; *Grg.* 486d2–488b1; *Rep.* I.336e2–337a2, 348a7–b4.

of the *elenchos*. If so, by deducing the negation of the moral hypothesis proposed by an interlocutor, he would have reason to think not only that the total set of his interlocutor's beliefs elicited in the discussion is inconsistent, but also that the negation of his interlocutor's moral hypothesis would have been proved. This negation, then, would be "a good common to all." [24]

Socrates plainly believes many of the propositions he uses as premises in elenctic arguments (e.g., "Virtue is always beneficial" or "All men pursue what they think is good for them"). No doubt Socrates often accepts each of the premises of a given argument. For example, in his argument with Polus regarding the relative value of being unjust with impunity as opposed to being unjust and paying the penalty (*Grg.* 466c3–481b5), it is entirely likely that Socrates accepts all of the premises from which the conclusion they reach follows. But from the fact that he himself sometimes (or even frequently) accepts the truth of the premises, Socrates could hardly think that the outcome of one *elenchos* would reveal moral truths applicable to all people, which, as we have seen in the *Gorgias,* he proclaims he is seeking. All Socrates can infer from those cases in which both he and his interlocutor agree about the premises is that *they* regard the conclusion as being true. [25]

It is also plain that Socrates does not always accept the truth of the premises he uses. For example, in the *Euthyphro* Socrates employs Euthyphro's belief that the gods quarrel and disagree (6b7–c4, 7b2–4, 7d8–8b6)—a premise about which he has already expressed skepticism (6a6–8)—as a part of an *elenchos* designed to show that piety is not to be defined as "loved by the gods." There are, moreover, good reasons for rejecting the notion that Socrates thinks that elenctic success *necessarily* depends upon *his* acceptance of the premises. First, no argument is offered for the premises of most elenctic arguments. This is not, however, because he thinks these premises are always either endoxical [26] or self-evident. [27] In fact, he explicitly rejects mere appeals to common opinion as a means of establishing the premises (or conclusions) of his arguments (*Cri.* 44c6–48a10; *La.* 184d6–186b9), and a proposition such as "virtue is always noble," which is certainly a candidate for an elenctic premise, is hardly self-evident to the likes of Callicles or Thrasymachus. Far from relying on premises that are either endoxical or self-evident, Socrates tells Polus in the *Gorgias* (472b6–c2) that in fact he

24. This view has been advanced by Kraut [1983a]. A somewhat similar view of the positive results of the *elenchos* can be found in Davidson [1985].

25. Vlastos [1983b] recognizes this point as a problem with his and others' attempts to show how Socrates could expect to generate constructive results from the *elenchos*.

26. For a discussion of why Socrates does not take the premises of the *elenchos* to be *endoxa,* see Vlastos [1983a], 40–44. A contrasting account may be found in Bolton [1993]. Certainly most of the premises of Socrates' elenctic arguments are endoxical. We shall argue that what matters, however, is that they be premises the interlocutor sincerely accepts. See especially *Cri.* 49c11–d5, where Socrates cautions Crito not to agree unless he sincerely believes the premise in question—a premise Socrates explicitly characterizes as one which few accept. We believe that many other similar examples can be found in various arguments in the early dialogues.

27. For this view, see Gulley [1968], 43–44; for a discussion of why Gulley's view should be rejected, see Vlastos [1983a], 42–44.

needs only one witness—the interlocutor himself—to establish the premises Socrates uses in his arguments. Whether others would share the same beliefs is of no consequence whatever (see also *Cri.* 49d2–5).

Second, in some elenctic arguments the moral hypothesis in question itself serves as a premise such that when it is conjoined with other premises its negation is deduced.[28] It is obvious that Socrates himself does not antecedently endorse the refutand of an *elenchos.* One might think Socrates believes that he furthers his goal of discovering generally applicable truths only with those elenctic arguments whose premises do not include the targeted moral hypothesis, and that he employs those elenctic arguments whose refutand also serves as a premise merely to demonstrate the inconsistency of his interlocutor's beliefs.[29] But nowhere does Socrates give the slightest indication that he uses two distinct types of elenctic arguments to do different sorts of logical work against his interlocutors.

If this is correct, and despite what we might have expected given Socrates' belief that he himself also benefits from his elenctic examination of others, we may conclude that the premises of some elenctic arguments need express *only* the interlocutor's sincerely held beliefs.[30] The elenctic questioner, then, simply follows the interlocutor wherever the interlocutor leads (*Euthphr.* 14c3–4).

1.3 Deriving the Benefits of the *Elenchos*

1.3.1   Why the Destructive Aspect of the Elenchos *Is Beneficial*

According to the claims about the nature of the *elenchos* and its uses, we can easily see how Socrates could reasonably expect the *elenchos* to achieve the goal of freeing an interlocutor from the pretense of wisdom and why Socrates would

28. Robinson [1953], 15, terms an elenctic argument of this sort an "indirect" *elenchos,* as opposed to a "direct" *elenchos,* where the refutand does not serve as a premise from which its negation is deduced.

29. This way of treating the "indirect" *elenchos* is defended by Vlastos [1983a], 39–40. Vlastos takes this view regarding the "indirect" *elenchos* because he rightly sees that it could only be a demonstration of the inconsistency of his interlocutor's beliefs. But, according to Vlastos, in the *Gorgias* Socrates claims to be offering a proof of the truth of the negation of the moral hypothesis under scrutiny ([1983a], 44–57, esp. 46–47). Thus, he argues, Socrates cannot be using the "indirect" *elenchos* to generate any positive results. If the account of the *elenchos* we are offering is correct, however, Socrates generates positive results from his repeated use of the "direct" and "indirect" *elenchos,* since in our account the mere inconsistency of an interlocutor's beliefs is in itself of great significance to Socrates' search for how best to live. In fact, we simply deny that there is any important difference between elenctic arguments that do, and those that do not, include the refutand as a premise.

30. This is surely the case in the first refutation of Euthyphro, in which Socrates employs as a premise Euthyphro's supposition that the gods fight and disagree—a premise Socrates explicitly doubts (*Euthphr.* 6a6–c7, 7b2–4, 7d8–8b6). It does not follow from this that Socrates can be directly deceitful. When asked directly, Socrates must say only what he thinks (see *Grg.* 495a7–b3). But he may let pass premises or fallacious inferences within an elenctic examination of another's views with which he does not agree, so long as in doing so he maintains a fair representation of his interlocutor's views. Thus, we deny that Socrates ever engages in eristic disputation, as some have argued (see, e.g., Klosko [1979]), or that Socrates ever styles his arguments in such a way as simply to confuse his opponent (see, e.g., Teloh [1986], 36).

count that as important. If elenctic arguments are to attain the positive results he sometimes says he is seeking, Socrates must first ensure that the interlocutor's prior prejudices not bar the way to open inquiry. Thus, if he is to make progress, Socrates must first attack the beliefs that hinder inquiry, thereby inducing in the interlocutor an openness to reconsider what he thought he already knew. Each time Socrates argues in such a way as to reduce a formerly confident interlocutor to *aporia,* we have an instance of how the *elenchos* can be used to achieve its "destructive" goal.

An additional and decidedly constructive use of the *elenchos* can be brought to light by recognizing its special role within the testing not only of moral propositions but of lives. Each time Socrates refutes an interlocutor, he does so by showing that the interlocutor's own beliefs are in conflict. The incoherent set of beliefs is not just any set: it is the set of beliefs held by the interlocutor about how to live. Accordingly, each such belief is accompanied by an inclination to live in the relevant way. If one's beliefs about how it is best for one to live are inconsistent, one cannot consistently follow all of one's relevant inclinations; in such a condition, one will be doomed, at least to some degree, to a life of frustration and inner conflict. Recognizing this, Socrates is convinced that all people—if only they thought about it—would want their beliefs about how is it best for them to live to be consistent.

In showing that an interlocutor's beliefs are inconsistent, Socrates shows that the set of the interlocutor's beliefs about how to live (or some subset of it) is inconsistent. So the interlocutor can be fully assured that his pursuit of the good life is likely to be or has actually been in some substantial way self-defeating. The interlocutor's own beliefs, Socrates has shown, would direct the interlocutor both to pursue and to shun some of the same activities. Although the interlocutor may not know which of his beliefs is best given up in order to be relieved of this conflict, he can be assured at least that some change is necessary. Before conversing with Socrates, the interlocutor may have felt no particular need to mend his ways. But the *aporia* that results from Socratic questioning gives the interlocutor an important reason to pursue the examined life: the recognition that one is seriously confused about how best to live. By pursuing the examined life, one may reasonably hope to make progress in deciding in any given case which of one's conflicting beliefs should be abandoned.

1.3.2   *The* Elenchos *and Self-Knowledge*

When Socrates' interlocutors are refuted, they should recognize at least that something is lacking in what had before seemed obvious to them. Socrates has shown them that the principles or opinions by which they were leading their lives are inconsistent. Because Socrates has not introduced anything into his elenctic conversations that his interlocutors did not themselves accept, his interlocutors have been given grounds for supposing that their confusion owes entirely to their own opinions. One cannot seek to resolve one's confusion until one recognizes that one suffers from it.

In bringing the interlocutor's confusion to light, Socrates also encourages the interlocutor to reflect more deeply upon what the interlocutor really believes. One occasionally sees Socrates not only revealing his interlocutor's confusions but also attributing to his interlocutors beliefs which, at the time of attribution, the interlocutors themselves would disclaim having. For example, at *Gorgias* 472b6 and following, Socrates shows that Polus had failed to grasp what he, Polus, really believes about the value of justice. Why Socrates believes the *elenchos* justifies so remarkable a conclusion is something we shall take up in chapter 3. But for now we simply note that Socrates thinks that in "refuting" Polus, Socrates shows Polus something Polus did not know about himself. For Polus, the benefit is self-knowledge.[31]

Of course, it is most unlikely that a single conversation with Socrates will offer so much to an interlocutor. So long as the interlocutor does not continue to pursue philosophy, whatever ground he gained from arguing with Socrates may be lost. Unless one lives the examined life—that is, unless one receives the benefits of elenctic examination on a regular basis—one may never be in a position really to know oneself.

1.3.3 Establishing Generally Applicable Moral Truths

Unless our considered opinions are somehow better than our unreflective ones, however, Socrates cannot rightly claim to be doing something good by encouraging one and all to prefer the former to the latter. It is certainly conceivable that the beliefs Socrates reveals in his interlocutors are false, and that what they should believe—if they are to lead happy lives—is what they had unreflectively supposed before Socrates clarified their real commitments. So if leading the examined life is to be beneficial, examination must not only clarify what one really believes but must also reveal beliefs that are right and not wrong.

Earlier in their discussion in the *Gorgias,* Callicles had scoffed at Socrates' claim that injustice with impunity is always worse for the wrongdoer than for the person wronged. After subjecting Callicles' objections to the *elenchos,* Socrates shows that, indeed, it is Callicles who has turned out to be ridiculous, like all the others who have argued for the view Callicles attempted to defend (*Grg.* 509a4–7). This passage strongly suggests that Socrates' confidence in his own view derives at least in part from the fact that he has previously examined others who were initially inclined to deny what he has come to believe. The result, he says, is always the same: they ended up looking ridiculous. Certainly Socrates has had the opportunity to examine many different people who happen to hold the same view. He has no doubt frequently met people who, like Callicles, supposed they could consistently reject Socrates' view of the relative merits of doing and suffering injustice. Given Socrates' desire to examine *all* who claim to know how best to live and his view that by means of the *elenchos* he is somehow examining his interlocutor's life, it is not unreasonable to think that the others whom he has examined pursue a wide variety of lives. If so, Socrates can inductively infer that

31. See also *Prt.* 319d6–7, where Socrates attributes to the Athenians the view that statecraft cannot be taught. For further discussion of this phenomenon, see sections 3.1.1–3.3.2.

anyone who, like Callicles, rejects Socrates' view of the value of injustice has an inconsistent conception of how to live.[32] To put the point another way, Socrates can inductively infer that no one who rejects Socrates' own view can maintain a coherent conception of how to live. Because he is not in a position to know *how* his generalization is correct, however, Socrates must continue to examine others to see whether anyone can hold an opposing view consistently with his other beliefs. To get additional confirmation that the generalization is correct, Socrates needs only to be confident that the premises of the *elenchos* express his interlocutor's sincerely held beliefs. Socrates may, of course, happen to share some of the beliefs expressed by his interlocutor and which serve as the premises of the *elenchos*. But Socrates' own beliefs *need not* enter into the *elenchos* as premises at all.

Moreover, we can see why Socrates would place such importance on his interlocutors' freedom to withdraw their assent from any of the premises to which they have given their assent. If an interlocutor fails to withdraw one of the premises, Socrates can confidently conclude at the completion of the *elenchos* that on reflection even the interlocutor, given *his* own judgment of *his* life, really does share Socrates' controversial moral belief, despite the interlocutor's initial denials. And where the interlocutor had initially proposed an opposing opinion, even in those instances in which Socrates does not share his interlocutor's belief in one or more of the premises of the *elenchos*, Socrates can fairly claim that he has *refuted* his interlocutor. After all, he has demonstrated that the interlocutor, in the light of the interlocutor's own other considered beliefs, actually rejects the opposing proposition.

Even if the above account of the constructive aspect of the *elenchos* is correct, however, it remains unclear how Socrates can think that elenctic arguments might achieve the goals of furthering an understanding of how one should live. From the fact that Socrates can infer inductively, for example, that the negation of his own view of the value of justice is inconsistent with every person's life, he obviously cannot infer that his own view of the value of justice is sufficient to render a person's life consistent. After all, even if one holds the Socratic view of the value of justice, one may still hold other inconsistent beliefs.

Nevertheless, from the fact that he is always able to demonstrate that anyone who holds an opposing view has inconsistent beliefs, Socrates is in a position to draw an extraordinary conclusion regarding his own view of the value of justice. To the extent that he has generated inductive evidence through previous elenctic examinations for the necessity of his own view for a coherent life, Socrates can claim to have established a general truth applicable to all.

32. Irwin [1986b] reaches a somewhat similar conclusion regarding what we call the "constructive" use of the *elenchos*. According to Irwin, the *Gorgias* was written relatively late in Plato's early period. Moreover, Plato never tips his hand as to how he thinks the Socratic *elenchos* generates positive results until writing *Gorgias*. Irwin argues that when faced with the fact that he holds contradictory beliefs, Callicles abandons his commitment to hedonism and thereby "agree(s) to the crucial claims that define the outlook of a rational agent" (70). While Irwin may be right that Callicles' agreement does reflect the choice of a rational agent, it is not clear that choice reflective of rational agency will always explain the selections of interlocutors in other dialogues. Our view relies on no such hypothesis.

Before he has examined many interlocutors who happen to hold the same thesis, however, Socrates is not in a position to make any claims about what it is necessary to believe in order to have a coherent life. And before he has examined a number of people who hold the same view, nothing prevents Socrates from having an opinion about that view, although until he has an opinion for which he has built up a store of elenctic evidence, he cannot reasonably hold his opinion with great confidence. Our argument is only that repeated elenctic examinations can confirm the untenability of the opposed view and thus give Socrates grounds for claiming that leading the examined life has constructive doctrinal consequences.

When Socrates says that he is looking for how humans ought to live, we should not be misled into thinking that he is searching for one single activity in which all men should engage to the exclusion of all others. He does not think that there is anything inherently wrongful or misguided about a life centered around agriculture, for example, or the love of friends and family. He never even condemns a life of making money, unless it should involve valuing money more than virtue. What he does think about the relationship between the right moral views and the rest of one's life is stated bluntly in the *Apology:* "Virtue does not come from wealth, but from virtue comes wealth and all other good things for human beings both in private and in public" (*Ap.* 30b2–4).[33] For Socrates, then, what is crucial about the attainment of happiness ($\varepsilon\dot{\upsilon}\delta\alpha\iota\mu o\nu\iota\alpha$/eudaimonia) is not the specific life one chooses, but rather that one first develop virtue. Without attaining virtue, one is always at risk that the life one chooses to pursue will end up in disaster.

But because Socrates, for the reasons we have given, believes that a number of his own moral beliefs are necessary for a consistent conception of how to live, and because he takes one's specific desires invariably to follow one's practical beliefs, Socrates has what he considers good reason to think that one must come to accept a number of the beliefs Socrates himself has come to accept if one is ever to attain happiness.[34] This result of the repeated use of the *elenchos*, however, is available only to those who, like Socrates, lead the examined life. Only

---

33. Some translators, puzzled by the apparent implication that virtue will make people wealthy, have avoided this appearance by making Socrates' claim only that wealth *becomes good* through virtue (see, for example, Reeve [1989], 124–25, n.21, following Burnet [1924], 204, note on 30b3). This is plainly Socrates' meaning, and we interpret the passage accordingly. But we cannot accept Burnet's suggestion that this is merely a problem of *translation.* The text reads as we have rendered it; the problem must be resolved through interpretation.

34. Seeskin recognizes that the Socratic *elenchos* tests not merely propositions, but how interlocutors think they ought to live. Moreover, Seeskin understands—rightly in our view—that Socrates has reason to think the *elenchos* will yield positive results only if he believes "it is impossible for someone to hold a consistent immoralism" ([1987], 36). But Seeskin sees this point as warranted only by the theory of recollection introduced in the *Meno* and other later dialogues. (Benson [1987] also argues that the possibility of constructive results from Socratic questioning is a notion introduced for the first time in the *Meno.*) We are convinced this is mistaken. (See Smith [1987].) In our view, Socrates arrives at this conclusion by induction. Thus, he can defend the claim by citing the fact that those he has examined who tried to maintain an immoral view have always ended up looking "ridiculous" (see *Grg.* 509a7 and our discussion in section 1.3.3).

one who "examines himself and others" frequently and skillfully can engage in enough elenctic arguments with a sufficient variety of people to draw the important inductive conclusions we have just identified. Moreover, only by leading the examined life is one able to uncover those inconsistent beliefs one holds which frustrate one's own ultimate goals. Of course, the process may never be complete; even Socrates continues to be confused and to err on a number of important issues.[35] But regarding those issues on which he has had clear and repeated elenctic results, he enjoys a much better moral position than do those whose souls abound with unrecognized conflicts.

Socrates' use of the *elenchos* to reach constructive results is not unrelated to his conviction that he has been divinely commanded to question others. The inductive evidence he gains by repeated arguments thus enjoy a kind of divine sanction, for they are dependably borne out by a style of inquiry endorsed by the god. The god would not command Socrates to ask questions whose answers always end up being the same, but nonetheless quite mistaken and evil. Moreover, in the *Apology* (31d3–4) Socrates tells the jury that frequently when he has been about to undertake something evil, his *daimonion* has "turned him away." The fact that his pursuit of his elenctic mission has never itself been the subject of daimonic alarms, then, gives Socrates additional reason to believe that his examinations produce only benefit.[36] Thus, even though Socrates gains only inductive evidence through the employment of each *elenchos*, he has special reason to trust his results. We may conclude, then, that Socrates has good reason to think that propositions whose negations are continually defeated by the *elenchos* are moral propositions which everyone would be better off believing.

1.3.4   Testing Definitions

We have already outlined some of the ways in which the *elenchos* might be used to gain a better understanding of moral questions. But there is another aspect of Socrates' elenctic examinations, frequently in evidence in the early dialogues, according to which its use may promote the wisdom he finds so lacking among his fellow Athenians. He believes, of course, that if one is to be morally virtuous, one must know what virtue is, and that if one truly knows what virtue is, one can correctly express its definition.

Nowhere in the early dialogues do we find Socrates using the *elenchos* to arrive at what he is willing to countenance as knowledge of virtue; indeed, it is a matter of controversy as to whether or not Socrates can succeed in gaining even a

---

35. See, e.g., *Hip. Ma.* 304c1–2; *Hip. Mi.* 372b1–e1; *Lys.* 218c4–8. The very fact that Socrates' *daimonion* is always opposing him because he is about to do something wrong amply demonstrates that Socrates' judgment is fallible (*Ap.* 40a4–6). These passages plainly present problems for Vlastos's view [1983a] of the Socratic *elenchos*, according to which all of Socrates' moral beliefs are consistent.

36. For a discussion of how the *silence* of his *daimonion* can provide Socrates with important information, see Brickhouse and Smith [1989b], sec. 5.5 (237–57). It is possible, of course, that in individual arguments the *daimonion* may stop Socrates from pursuing a certain line of thought or questioning. We do not know of an instance, however, in which Socrates actually structures his specific questions in response to a daimonic alarm.

part of any of the definitions for which he and his interlocutors seek.[37] For the reasons we have already given concerning other Socratic views and the support for them he believes he gets from the *elenchos,* we believe that Socrates would see the parts of definitions whose negations are repeatedly rejected in elenctic tests as having a strong claim to being worthy of acceptance. Of course, the results of some of the definitions Socrates tests are purely destructive, and the point of such tests is merely to show the interlocutor his own ignorance. But as we have said, insofar as Socrates has notions of what must be a part of any such definition, notions that have been supported by their negations' consistent inability to survive elenctic scrutiny, he may suppose he gains some warrant for ever greater confidence that his own notions are correct.

There are instances, moreover, in which Socrates actively engages in the test in a more positive way. For example, Euthyphro has been fully reduced to *aporia* by *Euthyphro* 11b6, yet Socrates continues his search for the definition of piety by contributing one of what certainly appears to be his own views. He proposes that piety is part of justice (12c10–d4; cf. also *Grg.* 507b1–3, 523a7–b4). Socrates' own contribution to the search is never discarded later; only when Euthyphro is once again engaged does the emerging definition again falter. So Socrates does not test definitions only in order to bring his interlocutor to abandon a faulty definition. The *elenchos* allows Socrates to have an interest in his interlocutors' proposed definitions, an interest that is independent of his destructive motives.[38]

In sections 2.3 and 2.4, we shall take up the role of definitions in Socrates' conception of wisdom. But this much about the role they play in Socratic philosophy is clear: Socrates believes that only with knowledge of the definition of a virtue, for example, may one know (i) why a given instance of that virtue is an instance, and (ii) in every case what course of action would instantiate or exemplify the workings of that virtue.[39] We have argued elsewhere that Socrates has considerable confidence in judging the value of some instances of virtue.[40] But unless one knows *what* the virtue is, one will not in every case be able to tell what is virtuous from what is not. So Socrates sometimes tests definitions in pursuit of the wisdom necessary for a fulfilling life.[41]

---

37. Examples of such controversies may be found in regard to Socrates' pursuit of a definition of piety in the *Euthyphro.* For examples of various sides of the debate, see, e.g., Allen [1970], 56–58; Robin [1935]; and Shorey [1933], each of whom denies that anything positive can be found in the later arguments of the *Euthyphro.* Against the specific view that *Euthphr.* 14a1–2 expresses part of the Socratic conception of piety, see Reeve [1989], 64, n.74. An extended discussion of our view may be found in Brickhouse and Smith [1989b], 91–100. For those who are inclined to agree that a definition partially acceptable to Socrates can be discerned by a careful interpretation of the *Euthyphro,* see, e.g., Adam [1908]; Arnim [1914]; McPherran [1985]; Rabinowitz [1958].

38. A contrasting view of this passage is offered in Benson [1989] 598, n.16.

39. The most recent—and also the most thorough and careful—discussion of this issue may be found in Benson [1990c]. Benson argues for an even stronger interpretation of the ''priority of definition'' than we have identified here, which we cannot accept. For our own view, and a thorough response to Benson, see sections 2.3 and 2.4.

40. Brickhouse and Smith [1984b]. See also our defense of this view in chapter 2.

41. Paul Woodruff ([1982] and [1986]) also mentions the role of the *elenchos* in testing definitions. Woodruff drops this function in his most recent paper on the subject ([1987]—see n.16.).

In fact, we do not believe the *elenchos* could ever fully achieve the goal of making its practitioner wise. If the god's own gift, Socrates himself, a man who has led an exemplary life of examination, continues to be ignorant of (for example) the nature of justice, it seems most unlikely that anyone could become wise in the way Socrates claims not to be. This is not to say, however, either that there is no sense in testing definitions of virtues or that leading the examined life is without benefit. By testing definitions, one can gain ever clearer conceptions of the virtues in question. Over the many years that Socrates has examined interlocutors, he has seen that certain conceptions are bound to conflict with other things people happen to believe. We may fairly assume that Socrates has also found a variety of propositions bearing on the nature of virtue, which all those he has examined, upon reflection, admit they believe and cannot contradict. If so, Socrates himself can confidently express certain truths about virtue, even if he is never able to offer what he knows to be a completely accurate conception. So by leading the examined life, Socrates is surely in a better position than Euthyphro to judge what is and what is not pious, even though neither can give the correct definition of piety. The ground for the advantage Socrates has in judgment is not the knowledge Euthyphro lacks, but rather a clearer conception, born of a life of reflection on what virtue requires. Through reflection on virtue, one comes to understand better what virtue is, without necessarily ever coming to understand completely what virtue is. So complete understanding, though sufficient, is not a necessary condition of good judgment. On our view, the great benefit of the examined life is thus not the wisdom Socrates professes to lack, but rather the good judgment that he manifestly possesses.[42]

1.3.5   Fighting for What's Right: Deliberation and Exhortation

Thus far we have been concerned primarily with various logical features of the *elenchos* that would allow Socrates reasonably to think both that he "refutes" his opponents and that he, at the same time, makes progress towards the acquisition of moral truth. There is yet another aspect of Socrates' mission that cannot be found in standard accounts of the *elenchos*, given their emphasis on *propositions* or *beliefs* and not, as we have emphasized, on the testing of *lives*. Socrates repeatedly reminds his jurors in the *Apology* that the things he does include not only testing people, but also reproaching them (30a1, 30e7), urging and persuading them of various things (30a8, 30e7, 36c5), and rousing them to action, as a gadfly rouses a sleepy horse by stinging (30e4–5). He offers "great proofs" (32a4) that, as one who "really fights for what's just" (32a1), he has never given in to any evil, no matter how powerful and dangerous its proponents may have been (see 32a6, 33a3–4), and that he has always taken extreme care never to be unjust or impious (32d2–3). These—and we believe other—passages demonstrate that at least one part of Socrates' mission in Athens is to be active in some way in the practical sphere (without, however, pursuing involvement in institutional politics—see *Ap.* 31c4–33a3 and our discussion in chapter 5). Socrates, thus, does

42. For further discussion, see sec. 4.5.

not merely try to persuade people to believe certain things and to disbelieve others; he seeks to get people to *do* certain things, and *not to do* others. Can the *elenchos* also be used to serve these ends, or for these, must Socrates resort to more standard forms of exhortation, such as oratorical rhetoric?

The *elenchos* may be used as an aid to deliberation about how to act and in that way serves a practical function. Though we believe this function is evident in the *Laches, Protagoras,* and perhaps the *Euthyphro,* as well, the clearest example of a deliberative *elenchos* is Socrates' discussion with Crito. When employed in deliberation, the principal goal of the *elenchos* is to test whether or not a certain proposed course of action is compatible with those principles that Socrates or his interlocutor, or both, either already accept or come to agree upon in the course of the discussion. In the *Crito* Socrates and Crito engage in the deliberation jointly. Crito says Socrates should escape from prison; Socrates and Crito engage in an *elenchos* that shows that escape would be incompatible with principles to which they are both committed (see esp. 47a2–6, 49a4–e2). They conclude that Socrates ought not to escape. This is not merely a destructive use of the *elenchos;* the point is not to relieve Crito of his pretense of wisdom regarding some general view of how best to live. Nor is it constructive, at least not in the standard way; that Socrates should not escape from prison is not some moral view he has come to adopt through the repeated failure of others to be able to maintain their contrary view. Just as plainly, no definition is at stake. By testing the consistency of Crito's belief that Socrates would be better off escaping against their other beliefs, Socrates is using the *elenchos* to test the moral acceptability of a particular proposed course of action, given some specified moral principles.

As we have seen, Socrates need not always accept the premises of an elenctic argument; we have shown that even in cases where he accepts the conclusions he and his interlocutor reach, the premises may reflect only his interlocutor's beliefs. But plainly, in a deliberative discussion such as the one with Crito, Socrates' own acceptance of the conclusion cannot be derived from premises that only Crito or some other interlocutor—but not Socrates himself—accepts. Socrates' own acceptance of the conclusion of a piece of deliberation must flow from his acceptance of the premises of that deliberation. So it might be thought that the arguments of the *Crito* are not elenctic at all, but rather constitute a straightforward chain of argument—from principles that Socrates believes to be true[43]—against Crito's proposal that he should escape from prison. Why do we call this deliberative argument "elenctic," since it seems not to differ from any other philosophical argument aimed at convincing an opponent of the truth of a proposition?

First, as we would expect, when he is about to work an *elenchos,* Socrates is careful to remind Crito that he must say only what he thinks most reasonable (46c6, 49a1–2). More importantly, he continually asks Crito whether he still agrees with each of the premises of the argument (e.g., 46b–47a, 48b11–c2) and reminds him that he is free to reject any of them (e.g., 49d1–2). Nothing whatever is said about the need for questioning any of the premises or for offering additional

43. This, presumably, is the way Kraut [1983a] would characterize the formal aspects of the arguments of the *Crito.*

arguments for truth. Their continued agreement is sufficient to warrant the use of the premises in the argument. Given that the premises rest only on the fact that Socrates and Crito continue to hold them, it is more reasonable to conclude that Socrates has only shown that leaving prison is inconsistent with their long-standing principles and that remaining in prison is consistent with those principles. Like any other elenctic argument, then, the acceptance or rejection of the initial claim under examination—in this case, that Socrates should leave prison—turns on whether or not it *contradicts* beliefs that are more basic to both Socrates' and Crito's conception of how best to live. How Socrates and Crito resolve the issue before them tells us something about what is central to their conceptions of how it is best for anyone to live: is it prudent for anyone to commit an injustice in order to preserve one's own life?

There are yet other elenctic examples of Socrates' "fight for what's just." We argued in section 1.2.3 that elenctic arguments examine some aspect of how people live. Socrates fully expects those who claim to know the most important of things to feel great shame as a result of his elenctic proofs that some of their beliefs about such things must be confused. As Nicias says in the *Laches,* one is reminded in the process of being examined by Socrates of past and present misdeeds (*La.* 188a6–b1). But given the goals of his mission Socrates articulates in the *Apology,* the point of interrogating all who think they know is not merely to shame them, but also to encourage them to seek the best sort of life. This is not a *logical* consequence either of the *elenchos* or of the shame the interlocutor feels after the *elenchos* has been worked upon him; but it is a natural *psychological* reaction to the position in which the interlocutor finds himself. The shame one feels at having one's ignorance brought to light should provide a powerful incentive for one to rectify the deficiency. So Socrates hopes to shame his interlocutors into positive action. Some, such as the general Nicias, recognize that conversing with Socrates forces the interlocutor to reflect on one's life (*La.* 188b1–4). Socrates' tactic does not always work, however; many of his interlocutors just become angry (*Ap.* 21d1, 21e1–2, 22e6–23a2, 23c7–d2).

But Socrates says he reproaches and exhorts his fellow Athenians for another reason as well: he also reproaches people who are engaged in or are likely to commit an evil action, due to ignorance or to false and evil convictions, and he does this in an attempt to dissuade them from the evil they would do. In these and other cases he exhorts people to *do the right thing.* Let us call this use of the *elenchos* the "hortative" use, for the goal of it is to get people to do the right thing, and not merely to recognize their own ignorance or to believe or disbelieve some proposition or propositions. Socrates can use the *elenchos* in this way, for as we have already said, the *elenchos* can bring the interlocutor to the position of seeing that, on reflection, the interlocutor does not believe the view he began by endorsing. Because, in Socrates' view, one's actions invariably follow one's beliefs, the interlocutor who is brought by the *elenchos* to recognize what the interlocutor *really* believes, upon reflection, will now desist from the course of action he was earlier inclined to pursue, and will pursue instead that course of action he has, on reflection, come to see he regards as preferable. Several examples illustrate this aspect of Socrates' *elenchos.*

1. When Socrates questions Meletus in the *Apology*, there are a number of things he hopes to accomplish. First, he wishes to show that Meletus brought the indictment against Socrates out of "exceeding insolence, licentiousness, and rashness" (26e9). Moreover, as we have argued elsewhere,[44] Socrates also uses the interrogation as part of his refutation of the formal charges against him. He also wishes to expose the confusions in Meletus' prejudices because Socrates (no doubt rightly) supposes that these same confused prejudices are to some degree shared by the jury. Plainly definitional issues are not at stake here; nor is Socrates constructively generating or defending some general positions about morality. Nor is Socrates' interrogation of Meletus purely destructive, for the point is not just to relieve Meletus and the jury of their pretense of wisdom. Instead, Socrates is using the *elenchos* here to reproach the wicked (Meletus) for doing something evil (attempting to harm Socrates) and to exhort others (the jurors) to *do the right thing* (acquit him).

2. When Socrates engages Euthyphro in discussion, it is true that the topic is piety, and the two seek a definition. But surely this is not all there is to it. There is a destructive aspect as well: Euthyphro is plainly guilty of the kind of pretense to wisdom Socrates takes himself to be divinely commanded to assail. We think Diogenes Laertius was correct in pointing out (see 1.29) still another aspect of the discussion, one that cannot be accounted for without identifying a hortative aspect to the *elenchos*. The problem with Euthyphro is not just that his pretense of wisdom needs to be cleared away to prepare him to learn; it is that his ignorance is leading him to do something evil: he proposes to prosecute his father, contrary to the (appropriate) outrage of the rest of his family.[45] So one thing, perhaps the most important thing, on Socrates' agenda in the discussion with Euthyphro is getting the latter to *do the right thing* and desist from his prosecution.[46]

There are almost certainly other instances of this aspect of the *elenchos*, as well. For example, part of what Socrates does in the *Protagoras* is intended to dissuade the impulsive and impressionable young Hippocrates from becoming a pupil of the Sophists, for example, signing up for their lessons, risking the welfare of his soul, and throwing his money away (see 311a8 ff.). But the two examples above suffice to make the point. It is an explicit aspect of Socrates' mission that he reproaches and exhorts people, and this reproaching and exhorting is directed

44. Brickhouse and Smith [1985]. See also Brickhouse and Smith [1989b], 112–24.

45. *Euthphr.* 4d5–6; see also Socrates' response at 4a11–b2, and his challenge to Euthyphro to defend his actions at 9a1–b3.

46. It might be thought that the text does not rule out the possibility that Euthyphro might already have presented his indictment to the King-archon by the time he and Socrates talk (though we are inclined to take Diogenes' reading as much more likely to represent Plato's apologetic interests). But even so, Socrates might still be interested in dissuading Euthyphro from continuing to pursue the prosecution, however far it had already gone. Certainly it is clear that Socrates finds Euthyphro's case dubious on moral grounds, and based wholly on Euthyphro's unwarranted confidence in his knowledge of the nature and requirements of piety. It is not surprising that Socrates' tone with Euthyphro is reproachful, for Socrates hopes that by pointedly scorning such ignorance he will instill in Euthyphro a sense of urgency about the pursuit of the truth. A detailed analysis of how Socrates' arguments in the *Euthyphro* contribute to this practical goal (among other things) can be found in Weiss [1986]. Another view similar to ours may be found in Heidel [1900], esp. 166.

not only at what people believe as a matter of theory, but also at what they pursue as a matter of practice. Any characterization of the *elenchos*, therefore, that conceives of it as only prescribing or proscribing beliefs is thus too narrow to accommodate all that Socrates hopes to do with the *elenchos*.

It follows that the *elenchos* is a tool for normative persuasion intended to make a real difference in the actions people undertake. Thus, it is not merely intended to further one's understanding of moral concepts. So the claim that Socrates investigates lives means that he investigates those propositions which guide people's lives. But this also includes Socrates' practice of passing judgments on what individuals do, and reproaching and exhorting individuals to engage in certain actions, which partly constitute their lives. This feature of Socrates' use of the *elenchos* only makes sense if, as we have argued, Socrates believes he is in a position to discern moral truths that are generally applicable to all people. If he were not, he would have no reason to trust his own judgment of the moral issues in question over that of those he reproaches and exhorts. The very fact, then, that Socrates feels justified in reproaching and exhorting others provides solid evidence that his practice of the *elenchos*—his having led the examined life—has given him better moral judgment than he finds in others, despite what he says is his complete lack of wisdom.

1.3.6   How to Lead the Examined Life

In the *Apology* Socrates tells the jury that much of the enmity that has arisen against him derives from the fact that a number of rich young men imitate him by going around practicing the *elenchos* on those who pretend to possess real wisdom. His imitators, he believes, succeed at least in discovering by their examinations of others that a great many people think they know something when in fact they know little or nothing (*Ap.* 23c2–7). Later he exhorts his judges to imitate him also, telling them that engaging in arguments about virtue as he does is the greatest good for men (*Ap.* 38a2–3). After the jury has condemned him, Socrates confidently prophesies that other, younger men will come along to examine their lives as Socrates has, though perhaps more harshly (39c3–d9), and his last request to the jury (41e1–42a2) is that they "harass" his sons as he has "harassed" his fellow Athenians (presumably, elenctically).

Socrates' own sense of mission is, perhaps, unique. He may be the only one devoted to practicing it as an act of piety; it may indeed be pious for others to pursue it,[47] but those who do pursue it may do so only out of amusement or purely intellectual interest. To some degree, then, the others who imitate Socrates may be less committed to the examined life, and thus less effective at championing it in Athens. Socrates never says, however, that his mission was given to him uniquely; his final analysis of the meaning of the oracle to Chairephon is that the

---

47. It would appear to follow from Socrates' view of the oracle and the proper response to it that anyone who undertook his philosophical pursuits in Athens would be acting piously. For discussions of Socrates' view of the connection between piety and the practice of philosophy, see Anderson [1967]; Heidel [1900], 174; McPherran [1985], 306–9; C.C.W. Taylor [1982], esp. 113–18.

god "is speaking of Socrates, using my name and making me an example, as if he were saying, this one of you, O Athenians, is wisest who, like Socrates, recognizes that he is really of no worth as regards wisdom" (*Ap.* 23a8–b4). Only a few Stephanus lines later Socrates first mentions the young men who imitate his service to the god. Though, again, there is no suggestion that in doing so they recognize their practice as a religious mission, there is equally no suggestion that in imitating Socrates they inevitably somehow fall significantly short of obtaining the same results he had obtained. We conclude that, though Socrates may think that only he has been "commanded by the god" (*Ap.* 33c4–7) to examine others, what Socrates does can be done by others. Neither his exhortations, therefore, nor his examinations of others, nor even their beneficial results, are unique to Socrates himself. If they were, his death would be a horrific evil indeed, for nevermore would the benefits he bestowed upon Athens be available. Because all of the benefits Athens has been given by Socrates were bestowed through his elenctic testing of others, and because Socrates is certain, by the end of the *Apology,* that his death will be no evil, we can infer from these passages that the *elenchos* can be used by all people, and will in fact be used by a number of people surviving Socrates.

In our interpretation, many of the benefits of elenctic examination can be achieved only if one is patient enough to pursue it through conversation after conversation, and clever enough to find the premises that will lead his interlocutors into the right kinds of difficulties. Even the most casual reading of Plato's early dialogues will reveal the subtlety of Socrates' reasoning. But surely not everyone is acute enough to practice the *elenchos* as well as Socrates. How then can everyone be expected to lead the examined life, if the examined life presupposes examination through *elenchos?*

Socrates' famous admonition to lead the "examined life" leaves room for different ways in which this might be done.[48] First, by exposing themselves to Socrates' examinations, Socrates' interlocutors make some progress towards leading examined lives. In fact, the same benefits of repeated elenctic encounters as we found available to the elenctic questioner appear to be equally available to one who would be examined repeatedly and in a variety of ways—in the *Meno,* we are told that

> If someone will ask him [the slave boy] these same things often and in a variety
> of ways, you know that in the end he will know these things as accurately as
> anyone. (*Meno* 85c10–d1)

So one need not practice the *elenchos* oneself to lead an examined life; one need only to have one's life examined by others. Interlocutors benefit from being examined, especially so long as they obey the rule that they must say only what they really believe. Those who are intellectually incapable of employing the *elenchos* to examine themselves and others can still actively and regularly solicit its employment upon them by others who are capable of doing so. Thus, even those who cannot perform the *elenchos* can live examined lives, so long as there

---

48. The following discussion owes much to Mark McPherran's work [1986].

are enough other people who are actually capable of performing it on them. And this is assured by the fact that others who also employ the *elenchos* lived during Socrates' time, as his remarks at *Ap.* 23c2–7 and his prophecy at *Ap.* 39c3–d9 show. Other people may be capable of conducting an elenctic examination although they no doubt will not be as talented or dedicated as Socrates. But so long as one is willing to subject one's beliefs to elenctic examination by any examiners at all, one can remain relatively safe from the sort of smug ignorance Socrates condemns. Moreover, not all practitioners of elenctic examination need to be especially talented. But one must *routinely* submit to examination. After all, the mere fact that the *elenchos* fails to bring an inconsistency in the interlocutor's beliefs to light would not induce the right-minded interlocutor to accept some falsehood unquestioningly. If one is dedicated to engaging regularly in philosophy, one would soon enough find that the objectionable belief is in conflict with one's other beliefs.

1.3.7 Conclusion

In this chapter we have addressed one of the most fundamental, yet one of the most vexing, aspects of Socratic philosophy. If our account of Socrates' use of the *elenchos* is even approximately correct, Socrates does indeed have reason to believe that each of the various goals of his religious mission can be accomplished by the repeated employment of only one sort of argument, the *elenchos*. If we are right, his elenctic examinations generate both positive and negative results. But in our account of the *elenchos*, moral philosophy for Socrates is not merely a matter of demonstrating which propositions in the moral sphere are true and which false. Rather, it is a rich and complex enterprise in which one must purge others of their pretense of wisdom, undertake to determine what kinds of things all human beings must believe about how to live if their lives are to be happy, test and refine definitions of the virtues, deliberate about right action, and when the nature of right and wrong action is clear enough, exhort others to pursue what is right and shun what is wrong. It is testimony to Socrates' genius as a moral philosopher that he turns the elenctic process into a vehicle by which his entire moral mission, in all its complexity, may be pursued.

2

Socratic Epistemology

2.1 The Paradox of Socrates' Ignorance

2.1.1 Some Questions about Socratic Ignorance

Socratic scholars have often expressed puzzlement at what Socrates says about human epistemic possibilities and his own epistemic states.[1] Their puzzlement is understandable, for the texts themselves are quite confusing. On the one hand, Socrates frequently proclaims his own ignorance;[2] on the other, he occasionally, but quite explicitly, claims to know something and even more often appears to assert opinions with the utmost confidence. Socrates claims both that he is the wisest of men (*Ap.* 23b2–4) and that he is "wise in no way great or small" (*Ap.* 21b4–5). It is possible that the apparent incoherence of Socrates' various claims is quite real; even the most careful philosophers sometimes err, if only by overstating their position. Perhaps Plato is not always careful to provide Socrates with a consistent position. Perhaps Socrates gets caught up in his own rhetoric and exaggerates his real view. Perhaps he is occasionally confused. But one should not too easily be discouraged by the appearance of paradox; something important might be at work beneath it, which once seen would both dissolve the appearance of inconsistency and edify the one who got beyond that appearance.

One thing about the apparent conflict should strike us as especially peculiar: though the apparent inconsistency in his claims seems perfectly obvious, not once does one of his interlocutors call Socrates' attention to the problem. This cannot be because his professions of ignorance and his expressions of confidence are never made within the same conversation, for they are. Perhaps the most notorious example of the two claims' juxtaposition appears at the end of Socrates' discussion with Callicles in the *Gorgias*. Socrates first boasts of having absolutely assured reasons for accepting a certain position, but in the next breath disclaims knowledge:

> These things which have been made apparent to us in our earlier arguments, as I say, are held down and fastened, if I may put it in a somewhat boorish way, by reasons of iron and adamant; so at least it seems so far. And if you, or someone

1. Vlastos [1985] provides a review of the many positions scholars have taken.
2. *Ap.* 20c1–3, 21d2–7, 23b2–4; *Charm.* 165b4–c2, 166c7–d6; *Euthphr.* 5a7–c5, 15c12, 15e5–16a4; *La.* 186b8–c5, 186d8–e3, 200e2–5; *Lysis* 212a4–7, 223b4–8; *Hip. Ma.* 286c8–e2, 304d4–e5; *Grg.* 509a4–6; *Meno* 71a1–7, 80d1–4; *Rep.* I.337e4–5.

more vigorous than you, doesn't release them, no one who speaks in a way other than I now speak can speak well. What I say is always the same, that I do not know how these things are, but of those I happen to meet, just as now, no one has been able to speak otherwise without being ridiculous. (*Grg.* 508e6–509a7)

We have discussed this passage already in section 1.3.3. But now we must pose a few new questions. If Socrates has reasons of iron and adamant, why does he say, "I do not know how these things are"? Why does he not continue his boast by saying that he knows perfectly well how things are and that Callicles, like everyone else who had tried to say the opposite, did not overturn Socrates' opinion because one cannot refute a proven truth? And why does the resourceful Callicles not seize the obvious opportunity to scold Socrates for the inconsistency of his position?

In this chapter, we shall answer these questions by a review and interpretation of the pertinent texts. In essence, our view is this: Socrates considers there to be two general sorts of knowledge, one which makes its possessor wise and one which does not. Socrates, and others too, can confidently and quite correctly claim to have a number of instances of the latter sort; but no human being can rightly claim to have the former sort, since no human being has ever attained the wisdom Socrates himself disclaims having when he professes ignorance. We shall also argue that the distinction between these two sorts of knowledge would be so evident to Socrates' interlocutors (and Plato's intended ancient readers) that what appears paradoxical to us would not have appeared paradoxical to them. Hence, when Callicles, for example, neglects to charge Socrates with inconsistency in replying to what Socrates says in the passage quoted previously, we may suppose that Callicles' forbearance only results from his recognition of the two sorts of cognition: one was at work in Socrates' boast, the other in Socrates' disclaimer.

We shall present our argument in stages. First, we shall consider Socrates' profession of ignorance and attempt to make clear what it is that Socrates disclaims when he professes not to know. We shall then turn to Socrates' expression of a number of moral propositions of whose truth Socrates appears resolutely convinced and show why these, too, do not violate the professions of ignorance as we have interpreted them. After we have provided this interpretation, we shall look at Socrates' conceptions of the epistemological and methodological priority of definitions, and show how these conceptions work within Socratic epistemology. We shall conclude with a discussion of the role of knowledge of definitions in the good life.

2.1.2 Is Socrates' Profession of Ignorance Sincere?

Socrates' repeated profession of ignorance is one of the best attested and most notorious features of his discussions with others. We find it reported throughout the early dialogues, as well as in a variety of other ancient sources.[3] But for

---

3. Arist., *Soph. El.* 183b6–8; Aisch. Soc., *Alc.* 10C (Dittmar); Aelius Aristides, *Oration* 45.21 (W. Dindorff, II, p. 25); Antiochus of Ascalon *ap.* Cicero, *Acad.* 1.4.16; Arcesilaus, *ap.* Cicero, *Acad.* 1.12.45; Plut. *Adv. Col.* 117D.

someone who claims to be ignorant himself, Socrates has an astonishing capacity to discern ignorance and confusion in others. As a result of his critical capacities, Socrates has come to be known as a great ironist, disclaiming knowledge most vehemently at precisely those times when he seems most certainly to exemplify having it. Of course, Socrates himself never admits to being an ironist; only his annoyed interlocutors make that charge against him,[4] a charge which a number of modern commentators think is nevertheless correct.[5] On this view, Socrates feigns ignorance merely to bait his interlocutors into answering his questions—questions he knows perfectly well would lead his interlocutors into confusion and self-contradiction. Socrates knows that his interlocutors will give the wrong answers— that is, answers that will lead them into difficulty—precisely because Socrates himself knows the right answers to his question. But he is also confident that in their ignorance his interlocutors will offer what Socrates knows to be the wrong answers. Unless Socrates really knows precisely what he insists he does not, how could he be so supremely confident that through examination each of his interlocutors will inevitably be refuted and thereby further Socrates' attempt to "give aid to the god and show that he [the interlocutor] is not wise" (*Ap.* 23b6–7)?

The view that Socrates' profession of ignorance is insincere, if accepted, would neatly resolve the paradox. When Socrates feigns ignorance, we should not be taken in; when he claims knowledge, we could simply accept his claim without paradox. But recent scholarship rejects this solution,[6] and we think rightly.[7] First, dismissing the profession of ignorance as insincere puts other Socratic assertions in serious jeopardy. How much can we trust Socrates' other proclaimed views if one of the opinions he most often expresses—that he is ignorant—is not to be believed? If Socrates can dissemble about this, why should we suppose that he does not dissemble about other things as well? The standard answer to these questions—that Socrates dissembles as an enticement to argument—does not work, for Socrates also repeatedly professes his ignorance to his jurors in the *Apology*, none of whom, under the circumstances, is in a position to be seduced into arguing with Socrates. Unless there is some other answer to be given, we might as well despair of reconstructing a "Socratic philosophy" from the many arguments and assertions we find him making, for these, too, might only be expressed ironically.

2.1.3   In Professing Ignorance, What Does Socrates Disclaim?

If we assume, then, that his profession of ignorance is sincere, what precisely does Socrates disclaim? Let us look more closely at one of the most notorious

---

4. See, for example, *Ap.* 38a1; *Grg.* 489e1; *Rep.* I.337a4–7; *Symp.* 216e4–5, 218d6–8. An interesting recent discussion of Socrates' "irony" may be found in Vlastos [1991], ch. 1. For a critique of Vlastos's account, see Brickhouse and Smith [1993].

5. See, for example, Gulley [1968], 69; Shero [1927], 109; Vlastos [1971b], 7–8 (Vlastos has changed his mind about this, however—see next note).

6. See, e.g., Austin [1987]; Irwin [1977], 39–40; Lesher [1987]; Vlastos [1985]; Woodruff [1990].

7. We have offered an extensive argument against the view that the profession of ignorance was ironical in Brickhouse and Smith [1984a]; see also Brickhouse and Smith [1989b], 37–47, 100–108, 133–37.

instances of his disclaimer. In the *Apology*, Socrates tells his jurors that a Delphic oracle started him on his philosophic mission in Athens (20e–23c).[8] Socrates' friend, Chairephon, went to Delphi and asked if there was anyone wiser than Socrates, and the Pythia answered that there was no one wiser. But Socrates found this answer extremely puzzling, for, as he says, "I am aware of being wise in no way, great or small" (21b4–5). Socrates proceeds to investigate the meaning of the oracle by examining others who have a reputation for wisdom. He discovers some who know nothing that is fine and good (21d3–4), and some who were divinely inspired but nonetheless lacked wisdom (22b8–c2). Still others—the craftsmen—"knew many fine things" and hence had some wisdom (22d2–4). In possessing knowledge of their crafts, they were indeed wiser than Socrates (22d4–6). But they were not wiser than Socrates *all things considered*, for they suffered from a kind of folly that greatly outweighed the knowledge and wisdom they possessed. They knew their crafts, but they were foolish—thinking they knew what they did not know—about "other, most important things" (22d7–8), whereas Socrates was better off: although he lacked their wisdom, he also lacked their folly (22e1–5). So Socrates turns out to be wiser than all of them precisely because he alone recognizes that he "is in truth worth nothing in respect to wisdom" (23b3–4).

In this passage, we get perhaps the most detailed explanation of Socrates' ignorance. Socrates does allow (at 20d6–9) that he has a kind of wisdom, which he calls "human wisdom." But his investigation of the meaning of the oracle shows him that "human wisdom is of little or no value" (23a6–7). What would be of great value, if only he had it—namely, real wisdom—Socrates and all others lack. The greatest wisdom for human beings, as we have just seen, is the recognition that we are "in truth worth nothing in respect to wisdom" (23b3–4). Unlike human beings, "the god is really wise" (23a5–6). So in professing ignorance, Socrates disclaims having the kind of wisdom the god has. Socrates does not deny having "human wisdom"; indeed, of this, no other human has more than he. But this wisdom is also a trifling thing. What, then, is the wisdom Socrates lacks?

It is clear in this passage that not just any knowledge gives its possessor real wisdom, although a number of scholars seem to have missed this point.[9] Socrates does not disclaim having any knowledge whatever, only knowledge of anything "fine and good" (21d4), including the craftsmen's knowledge of their crafts,[10] which he allows is a "fine thing" (22d2). Socrates knows at least this: he knows that he lacks real wisdom.[11] In this small piece of knowledge lies Socrates' "human" wisdom.

8. On how the oracle could have provided Socrates with a religious mission, see Brickhouse and Smith [1983], and [1989b], 87–100.

9. We can think of no other reason Irwin, for example, would insist that Socrates has *no* knowledge, but only true belief ([1977], ch. 3, 37–41, and 294, n.4). Other expressions of this view may be found in Burnyeat [1977], esp. 384; Santas [1979], 120 and 311, n.26; Woodruff [1982], 140.

10. Socrates' claim to lack ἐπιστήμη (knowledge) is contrasted directly with the craftsmen's having it.

11. *Ap.* 23b2–4. Socrates does not merely *think* or *believe* that he lacks knowledge; he *knows* it— "ἔγνωκεν" denotes nothing weaker than "knows." See Austin [1987]; Woodruff [1990], n.3.

In what, then, would real wisdom consist? Socrates later makes clear what he thinks is most important.

> I go about doing nothing else than prevailing upon you, young and old, not to care for your bodies or for wealth more than for the perfection of your souls, or even so much; and I tell you that virtue does not come from wealth, but from virtue comes wealth and all other good things for human beings. . . . (*Ap.* 30a7–b4)

Nothing, then, is more important than virtue; yet in regard to virtue, no one is wise. We conclude that when Socrates professes not to be wise and when he proclaims that no others are wise regarding "the most important things," he means that whatever other knowledge anyone may have, neither he nor anyone else he has ever questioned has knowledge of virtue.

2.1.4 Socratic Ignorance versus Skepticism

This observation helps us to see how it is that Socrates does not violate his profession of ignorance when he occasionally claims knowledge or makes confident assertions on other topics. For example, in many of the dialogues Socrates searches in vain for a correct definition of virtue, or of one of the several virtues. And because he does not know these definitions, he makes his profession of ignorance.[12] But Socrates never once shows the slightest hesitation in stipulating the conditions of proper definition to interlocutors whose attempts appear inadequate to him.[13] Indeed, when the thing to be defined is not a virtue, Socrates may well know the definition. It is plain that Socrates has not the slightest doubt that he knows the definitions of "quickness" (*La.* 192a8–b3) and of "figure" (*Meno* 76a4–7), for example. But, as we have seen, it is clear Socrates would not view this sort of knowledge as a very worthy thing, as something truly "fine and good" (*Ap.* 21d4), for plainly knowledge of such things is not knowledge about "the most important things."

Nor do we ever see Socrates evincing the least doubt about matters whose epistemological status eventually became matters of great controversy in philosophy: the evidence of the senses, knowledge of other persons, theoretical objects, scientific theories, induction, deduction, and so forth. Some of these things, it is clear, are not of interest to Socrates at all; he says he never even discusses natural scientific issues (*Ap.* 19d1–7).[14] Socrates also never considers epistemological

---

12. See, e.g., *Lys.* 223b4–8; *Meno* 71a1–7, 80d1–4; *Rep.* I.337e4–5; *Prt.* 360e6–361a3.

13. See, e.g., *Euthphr.* 6d9–e1, 9c7–d5, 11a6–b5; *La.* 191c7–e2; *Hip. Ma.* 287d6–289d5, 292c3–293d6. See Austin [1987]; Woodruff [1990].

14. Socrates does allow that science is an area of inquiry in which the accomplishment of knowledge might yield a wisdom greater than human (*Ap.* 20d9–e2; see 19c2 ff.). Others have sought wisdom in this area, and Socrates' "first accusers" (*Ap.* 18a7–c1, 19a8–c9, 23d2–8) have said that he, too, does so. Socrates insists, on the contrary, not only that he knows nothing of such matters at all (19c9), but also that he does not even discuss them (19d1–7). So when Socrates professes ignorance at *Apology* 19c1–7, he disclaims knowledge of natural scientific subjects. These cannot, however, be "the most important things" of which Socrates says no human has knowledge, for it is surely not an immodest and misguided *natural scientific* confidence that renders the craftsmen more foolish than

problems regarding "ordinary knowledge claims" and their corrigibility, claims based on memory or perception. No doubt, his own knowledge of the definition of "quickness," for example, has its source in ordinary experience and ordinary language. He never claims ignorance of such things; he never accuses others of supposing they have knowledge of such things when they do not. But he certainly would not class knowledge of these sorts as being something "fine and good" or as having a place among "the most important things." They are, after all, *ordinary* knowledge claims.

2.1.5 Some Socratic Convictions

But if "the most important things" pertain to virtue, and if to know something truly "fine and good" is thus to know something morally significant, it would appear Socrates does have a class of convictions that are indeed "most important" and that are indeed "fine and good." The conclusion of the argument with Callicles in the *Gorgias,* which we quoted at the beginning of this chapter, is perhaps one example of such knowledge. But Socrates does not make his claim to having reasons of "iron and adamant" as categorically as one might wish, which leaves the *Gorgias* passage quoted above (508e6–509a7) somewhat less than decisive. One might worry that Socrates' reasons of "iron and adamant" cannot be quite so secure if he must follow this description of them with qualifiers like "so at least it seems so far" and if he allows that it is possible that they are nonetheless reasons that "you [Callicles], or someone more vigorous than you" might undo. These may be only reflexive expressions of Socratic modesty, but they may also show us something important about the degree to which Socrates takes his arguments to achieve certainty. Might it be, then, that Socratic ignorance is due to his inability to be absolutely certain of any of his own beliefs?[15]

The problem with such a suggestion is that some of Socrates' claims of moral knowledge do not receive the same qualification as does his claim to the "reasons of iron and adamant" in the *Gorgias.* Twice in the *Apology* we find unqualified and explicit claims of moral knowledge: at 29b6–7, Socrates unequivocally claims to "know that it is evil and disgraceful to do wrong and disobey my superior, whether he be god or man." For good measure, he adds the strong suggestion that there are other such things he knows: "So I shall never fear or flee from those things which I do not know whether they are good or bad rather than *evils which I know are evils*" (29b7–9). And at 37b2–8, when he is asked to offer a counter-penalty, it is clear that he knows that some of the options to which the jurors' votes might be attracted are evil:

> Since, then, I am convinced that I have wronged no one, I certainly do not need to wrong myself, and to say of myself that I deserve anything evil, and to propose any penalty of that sort for myself. Why should I? So that I not suffer the penalty

Socrates, all things considered. Plainly, many of the craftsmen would happily concede that of natural science they "had no knowledge great or small," in which case they would not be Socrates' inferiors with respect to wisdom.

15. See Vlastos [1985]. Reeve ([1989], 37–52) adopts a strategy similar to Vlastos's.

that Meletus proposes, about which I say that I do not know whether it is a good
thing or an evil? Shall I choose instead of that something *which I know to be
an evil?*

The fact is that although Socrates explicitly claims moral knowledge quite rarely,
he makes a number of moral claims in the *Apology* and elsewhere with the unqualified conviction and without the least epistemic qualification (see, for example,
Euthyd. 283c4–5, and esp. 296e8–297a1, where Socrates claims to have known
"long ago" that good people are not unjust). Similarly, having pointed out that
the practice of philosophy in Athens was assigned to him by the god, Socrates
compares his persevering in philosophy to a soldier's remaining at his post despite
even life-threatening consequences. In making this comparison, Socrates betrays
not the slightest doubt that his (or the soldier's) actions are proper. But again,
though these convictions may indeed qualify in Socrates' mind as knowledge, he
claims to possess no wisdom. Hence, the possession of such knowledge does not
make Socrates wise. What, then, does the wise person have that Socrates lacks?

   We believe the important difference between the wise person and Socrates
cannot be characterized in terms of fallibility with regard to *each particular* judgment, as some have claimed,[16] but must rather be conceived in terms of general
fallibility in whole areas of judgment. Socrates says that the wise person is able
to judge all *bona fide* cases of a given moral quality (*La.* 199c3–e4). But Socrates
himself lacks this ability; indeed, he explicitly acknowledges his own capacity for
confusion and error.[17] Even if one had absolutely infallible justification for claiming to know one or a few particular propositions, it would not follow that one
would be free from confusion and error on other—even closely related—issues.
This, we contend, is the difference between the wisdom Socrates lacks and the
knowledge he and others have.[18] After all, Socrates believes he has divine sanction direct from the god of Delphi for some of the claims he makes with such
confidence in the *Apology*. But Socrates knows only a number of particular truths,
whereas the wise person would know any of the particular truths relevant to his
or her field of wisdom. The wise person's wisdom would consist (in part) in the
knowledge that permitted him or her to judge *all* pertinent cases, namely, knowledge of moral definitions and their applications—knowledge, that is, of what it is
for an instance of virtue to be virtuous. Since no one, including Socrates, has *that*
knowledge, however, no one can be said to be truly wise.

2.1.6   Being a Good Judge

Socrates offers an excellent assessment of the kind of knowledge he and others
have at *Ion* 532d8–e3. He characteristically (and ironically) praises Ion and others

   16. See note 15.
   17. See Socrates' expressions of perplexity at *Hip. Mi.* 372a6–e6, 376b8–c6, and *Lys.* 218c4–8.
The fact that his *daimonion* so often troubles him (see *Ap.* 40a4–6) amply demonstrates Socrates'
susceptibility to error.
   18. A similar argument is made by Lesher [1987]. A distinction similar to the one we are about to
attribute to Socrates may be found expressed by Aristotle at *An. Post.* 1.13. See also *An. Post.* 2.1–2.
Bolton [1993] also notices this distinction in Aristotle and applies it to Socratic epistemology. For
further discussion of this distinction, see section 2.2.

like him for their possession of wisdom, which allows them to say wonderful things. But he says of himself

> I, on the other hand, have nothing to say but the truth, in the manner of an ordinary person. Accordingly, concerning what I asked you just now, notice how trivial and commonplace is what I said, that which anyone could know (γνῶναι). . . .

The subsequent discussion shows why Socrates is so confident that the general proposition about which Ion has been asked is one that "anyone could know": it is the conclusion of a straightforward induction from a series of instances that are themselves obviously true. Thus, once the premises of the induction have been stated, Ion can hardly deny that he too knows the general proposition induced without flying in the face of the plainest common sense. By employing everyday experience judged by common sense, as he so often does with his inductions from obvious examples, Socrates recognizes that he and any other person can come to know all sorts of truths. Such knowledge seems a small thing to Socrates. Socrates has it; so do ordinary people. But such knowledge does not make them wise, for it provides them with no special expertise of the very sort Ion claims to have (and Socrates claims he and Ion lack).[19]

Some confirmation of this view can be gained from considering those cases where he does grant others their claim to *wisdom*. The only cases where Socrates without irony sanctions claims to wisdom are those involving the crafts. The craftsmen, he allows, do have a kind of knowledge that Socrates himself lacks, which gives them a kind of wisdom that Socrates also lacks (22d3–4). So the kind of knowledge that makes one wise is comparable in some way to craft-knowledge.[20] At the heart of this comparison, we believe, is Socrates' conviction that wisdom is a power: wisdom is the sort of thing that makes one able to judge and to act rightly in the appropriate circumstances. The knowledge that a certain particular proposition is true, no matter how secure, does not give one this power. Such a one is fit to be a judge only of those precise cases to which the proposition refers—perhaps one single case. The true cobbler is not the one who is able to make one good pair of shoes, or even a few good pairs. To be a true craftsman, the cobbler must understand *what it is* for a pair of shoes to be a good pair of shoes, and also *be able to employ* that knowledge in *making* and *judging* all sorts of good shoes. Some of us might be able to recognize a good pair of shoes now and again; with a little patience and a lot of luck we might even be able to put together a pretty good pair. But we would not be good craftsmen because we

---

19. See *Euthyd.* 293b7–8, where Socrates claims to know "many things, but slight ones," and *Meno* 98b2–5, where Socrates says he does not know much, but he does know that there is a difference between knowledge and belief. (See also *Euthyd.* 293c2, 295b2–3.)

20. See, for example, *Euthyd.* 292c7–9 and 294b3–4, where crafts are Socrates' first examples of knowledge. On what constitutes craft-knowledge, see section 1.1.3. The connection between Socrates' conceptions of knowledge and craft is explored in admirable detail in Woodruff ([1990], 18). Woodruff has little to say, however, regarding the connection between knowledge and wisdom with which we are so particularly concerned in this chapter. Another analysis similar to ours, from which we also learned a great deal, may be found in Reeve [1989], 37–45.

would not have the skill, the *technē*, to do it with any assurance or any regularity. Our occasional and specific ability to do the right thing here or there in shoemaking or shoe judging is not general enough to make us wise in the way of the skilled cobbler. And even if one were in cognitive possession of some complete list of all pertinent propositions about shoes and shoemaking (as if the idea of such a list even makes sense!), such possession would not provide its possessor the skill by which he or she could reliably make good shoes.

Wisdom, then, consists in the kind of knowledge by the possession of which one is able to perform the right acts and to judge the proper instances pertinent to the field of endeavor in which one is wise. One aspect of such knowledge is not propositional: it requires that one have the ability to do the right things at the right times in one's field of expertise. Another aspect—to which we shall return in chapter 3—has to do with the control knowledge gives its possessor over his or her own inclinations: the wise person never pursues inclinations conflicting with his or her good. But to these, we must add still another condition: the wise person can always provide an account of his or her judgments.[21] If one cannot provide such an account which explains *why* one's judgment is correct, one does not have the kind of knowledge Socrates claims to lack. None of Socrates' claims of knowledge or conviction requires that he also be able to give the proper account of what he knows. So as convinced as he may be of the truth of any number of moral propositions, he is equally convinced of his inability to account for their truth. As confidently as he may hold them, none of his convictions will count as knowledge that would make him wise. Without an account, what he knows is "in truth worth nothing in regard to wisdom" (*Ap.* 23b3–4), as he tells the jury in the *Apology*.

2.2 Knowing How Something Is

2.2.1 How It Is That Socrates Does and Doesn't Know

The interpretation we have proposed distinguishes between the kind of knowledge that is constitutive of wisdom and a kind (or some kinds) of knowledge that is (are) not. We began our discussion, however, puzzled by why it is that the paradox never seems to have occurred to Socrates' interlocutors, whom Socrates often chastised for their own inconsistencies of belief. Surely, if the paradox was so apparent, one of them would have been bright enough to see it and throw it back at Socrates; surely Plato himself was intelligent enough to see it and expose it (or else resolve it explicitly) in his dialogues. If our solution is right, then, it must have been patent to Socrates' interlocutors (and to Plato and his readers). But if so, where does Socrates make the distinction we say he relies upon?

For the answer, let us return again to the *Gorgias*. Immediately after claiming to have his arguments of iron and adamant, Socrates makes his profession of ignorance. But the language he uses is peculiar. He says, "What I say is always

---

21. See, e.g., *Grg.* 465a2–5, 500e4–501a3.

the same, that I do not know *how these things are*" (οὐκ οἶδα ὅπως ἔχει—*Grg.* 509a5). What does it mean to deny knowing of a thing ὅπως ἔχει (how it is)?[22]

We have already explained why we do not believe that Socrates' profession of ignorance disclaims merely knowing that some statement about right and wrong is true. In this case, Socrates is saying that he does not know *how it is* that the claim for which he has such good arguments is true; he does not have the sort of knowledge by which he could *explain* the proposition's truth and by which he would qualify as an expert concerning such issues.[23] He only has good reason to think *that* his conviction is true.

2.2.2 Does This Distinction Make Sense?

There are a number of ways in which Socrates might come to know those things he claims to know. We shall argue in chapter 6 that he might come to know something through divination. In this chapter, we have already noted how some of Socrates' knowledge claims seem to have been generated through ordinary experience. In chapter 1 we showed that Socrates can come to know something through repeated elenctic testing. Plainly, what he comes to know through divination need not also come with the relevant sort of account by which he could explain *why* what the gods have revealed is true. The gods could presumably provide the explanation, but they need not have given this to Socrates; perhaps they only told him what the truth of the matter happens to be. So knowledge gained through divination that some proposition (p) is the case does not bring with it knowledge by which the truth can be explained—the knowledge of *how it is* that p is true. Divinatory experience can itself perhaps be defended to others who believe in gods, whose views can be revealed through divination. So Socrates can be justified in claiming knowledge without being able to explain *how* what he knows to be the case is true. Again, he can have a conviction for which he has absolutely compelling evidence (viz. its having been affirmed by a god who cannot say anything false—see *Ap.* 21b6–7) without in addition being able to account for *why* or *how* his conviction is true.

The same conclusion follows in cases where Socrates' knowledge comes from

22. In Vlastos's account [1985], Socrates here simply denies certain knowledge of the truth of the proposition he has been disputing with Callicles—that it is better to suffer than to do evil. Socrates has "reasons of iron and adamant" for claiming that the proposition is true, but still lacks the kind of evidence that would give him certainty. Hence, in one breath he claims to have extremely powerful reasons for accepting the proposition; in the next, according to Vlastos, he disclaims certainty that the proposition is true. Vlastos does not consider the possibility that Socrates might be disavowing something other than *that* what has been established in the argument with Callicles is true, though he translates the passage correctly (see p. 4). Woodruff's translation simply begs the question: "I do not know *that* these things are so" ([1990], 5).

23. The distinction we are here attributing to Socrates between knowing *that* something is the case and knowing how it is that such and such is the case is explicitly drawn by Aristotle (*Metaph.* 981a28–30). It is also worth noting that Aristotle says that persons of experience "know the that" (τὸ ὅτι ἴσασιν). Thus, Aristotle finds nothing to prevent him from speaking of someone knowing that such and such is the case, though the person does not know why it is the case.

everyday experience. Everyday experience tells one many things, but experience alone cannot tell one *why* the world operates as it does, *why*, that is, what one comes through experience to know is true. One comes to know many things, but the regularities of experience come without explanation. The explanations must be discovered. If indeed Socrates believes that some moral claims can be sufficiently secured by common experience as to become known, then, such knowledge remains "trivial and commonplace," for without an explanation of the truth of such moral claims, their knowers remain wholly without moral wisdom.

But it was neither through divination nor everyday experience that Socrates came to have the "reasons of iron and adamant" to which he refers in the *Gorgias*. It was rather through repeated elenctic examinations that Socrates came to the conviction that it is better to suffer than to do evil. Why do such arguments not assure knowledge of *how it is* that Socrates' conviction is true? We can imagine Socrates, in case after case, arguing what comes to be his conviction against a variety of interlocutors, each of whom ends up, as Socrates says, seeming "ridiculous" and unable to continue the defense of his contrary position. As we said in chapter 1, after many such arguments, Socrates might quite reasonably become convinced that his interlocutors all failed to defend the contrary position precisely because it is indefensible. On the basis of his repeated elenctic arguments with a variety of interlocutors, Socrates can fairly conclude that no one can defend the view that it is better to do than to suffer evil. No matter how strongly the interlocutors seem to believe that doing is better than suffering evil, in the end they all seem prepared to abandon that view in favor of its contrary. Socrates' elenctic examinations consistently come to this; he regards his practice of the *elenchos* as having been willed by the god; and the god wills all and only good things for men.[24] Hence, this result of his *elenchos* seems assured: it is better to suffer than to do evil.

This account explains why Socrates was quite convinced, as if by "reasons of iron and adamant," that a certain point of view is true: his elenctic arguments show that no one can believe the contrary of what those arguments show. It does not follow from this, however, that he has come across anything that will tell him *why* this elenctic product is true. All he knows is that those who assert otherwise always get caught in contradiction. Arguments by *reductio ad absurdum* do not need to provide premises by which the truth of their conclusions can be explained—they only establish that their conclusions must *be* true because the negations of such conclusions are surely false. Without a suitable understanding of the nature of justice, then, Socrates is not in a position to explain *why* it is that it is better, for example, to suffer than to do injustice. But *that* it is better may be demonstrated by repeated (and adamantine) elenctic arguments. So Socrates may know that suffering is better than doing evil without knowing *how it is* that this is true. And without knowing *how it is* that this is true, he cannot give an account

24. Socrates is convinced that his mission in Athens, which he pursues only by practicing the *elenchos*, was ordained by the god. The god is, he is certain, concerned for humans' welfare (*Ap.* 31a6–7, 41d2). Accordingly, Socrates seems entirely confident that in practicing his *elenchos*, the results he obtains can be trusted—to do so, after all, is only to trust in the goodness of the mission the god assigned to him.

of this truth. Accordingly, as he says, he can continue to "assume that these things are so" (*Grg.* 509a7–b1). Although he has decisive arguments for what he "assumes," he cannot explain it or give a general account of it. In short, what knowledge Socrates possesses is knowledge without wisdom.

In saying, then, at the end of the *Gorgias* passage that he assumes the truth of his conclusion, Socrates never suggests that he thinks the conclusion is not justified. Rather, he betrays a lack of satisfaction with the *way* in which he knows what he knows—he has come to his knowledge in a way that establishes (at most) only *that* what he knows is true. He would greatly prefer to know that which would explain *how it is* or *why* what he knows is true. This latter sort of knowledge, however, always eludes him. So he says to Callicles that he has provided decisive arguments for his view; but, as always, he remains ignorant of *how it is* that what he has established so decisively is true. There is plainly no paradox in these two claims, and Callicles sees none.

2.2.3 Can the Elenchos *Ever Close the Gap?*

But might Socrates not attempt to engage in a series of arguments by which the pertinent principles of explanation might be uncovered? In other words, might he not examine a series of interlocutors in such a way as to obtain arguments of iron and adamant about *why* or *how it is* that suffering is better than doing injustice? To do so, he would need to generate some conceptions of justice and the good whose negations would always fail to pass elenctic tests.

It seems clear that Socrates does have some basic conceptions of moral terms, which may well have derived from elenctic activities. For example, in his conversation with Euthyphro, after the latter has become thoroughly perplexed and unable to decide where next he should go in defining piety (*Euthphr.* 11b6–8), Socrates himself provides the next step (11e8–12a2). His own proposal does not lead Euthyphro to complete success; in fact, the dialogue still ends in failure. But we do not suppose that the ultimate failure of the dialogue shows that Socrates' proposal is worthless;[25] rather, the argument's failure shows that Socrates' account was *incomplete*. So though Socrates may have come to his conception by means of repeated elenctic testing, such tests have not brought him to the point of having a complete conception of piety. Might he make this final step through a careful and conscientious employment of the *elenchos?*

Nothing in the texts directly answers this question, though it is certainly some evidence against an affirmative answer that Socrates has not come to such knowledge despite his having lived a life devoted to elenctic testing. The *elenchos,* which always functions *ad hominem,* may allow Socrates over time to develop a rough-and-ready view of piety or of some other moral notion. But to complete this view, Socrates would need to explore all of the conceptual territory. But because the *elenchos* proceeds only by eliciting answers about what individuals

---

25. See, most notably, McPherran [1985], who cites our own work (Brickhouse and Smith [1983]), as well as a number of others who take a "constructive" account of the argument in the *Euthyphro*. A dissenting view of the *Euthyphro* may be found in Benson [1989], 598, n.16.

happen to believe, even if he examines a wide variety of different conceptions of a virtue, it is difficult to see how he could ever be confident that all of the ingredients necessary for an adequate definition have been uncovered. So it is unlikely that Socrates' sole way of philosophizing—practicing the *elenchos*—would ever be enough to bring him even to this much of what he would need to become wise. This is not to say, again, that the *elenchos* is of no help in refining one's account; at the very least, the *elenchos* shows that certain elements do not belong to a proper definition, as well as revealing a variety of truths a proper definition must explain. We are only claiming that Socrates cannot likely believe that his task of finding the right definition will ever be complete. If this is right, the fact that Socrates may come to know many things about virtue through the *elenchos,* his questioning of others will not likely enable him to know *how it is* that what he has come to know about virtue is true.

2.2.4   A Few More Texts

We argued earlier that Socrates' profession of ignorance is best understood *not* as a disclaimer of all knowledge, but rather as a disclaimer of wisdom. We have now argued that one way in which Socrates characterizes this lack is to say, even where he has excellent elenctic arguments for his position, that he does not know *how it is* that what he is convinced of is true. We have tried to show how this sort of ignorance is compatible with knowing *that* what one believes is true. Thus, Socrates' interlocutors do not regard his profession of ignorance regarding some subject as paradoxical despite his occasional confidence *that* something about that subject is certainly true.

We have not argued that the distinction between *whether or not* something is true and *how it is* that something is true can be found expressed explicitly in all of the relevant texts. We wish to argue only that this distinction explains what is at work in what might otherwise seem to us—and to Socrates' interlocutors—an oddity: a Socrates who often speaks with great confidence and who even occasionally claims to know, but who nonetheless always professes to be ignorant of the subject under discussion. Socrates does not always have to make the distinction we have found him making in the *Gorgias,* for in most contexts the paradox that this distinction helps to dissipate is not likely to be a problem for Socrates' interlocutors or for Plato's readers.

But, in fact, there are a number of texts in which the knowledge at issue is explicitly characterized as "knowing how it is." For example, at *Euthyphro* 4e2–3, Euthyphro characterizes his confidence as deriving from his knowledge of "*how it is* with the divine with regard to the holy and the unholy" (τὸ θεῖον ὡ˙ ἔχει τοῦ ὁσίου τε πέρι καὶ τοῦ ἀνοσίου). Socrates replies,

> But, by Zeus, do you think that you have such precise knowledge about divine things, *how they are* (ὅπη ἔχει), and about holy and unholy things, that, when those things happened as you say, you are not afraid of doing something unholy yourself by prosecuting your father? (*Euthphr.* 4e4–8)

Euthyphro and Socrates make clear that Euthyphro does not simply claim to know *that* the specific action he proposes to take against his father is holy; his claim to know this specific case is predicated upon his general claim to knowing *how it is* in these matters.

Similarly, when Critias becomes defensive in the *Charmides,* Socrates reassures him by making clear what he regards the goals of discussion to be:

> How, I said, can you think, if I am trying most of all to refute you, that I do so on account of anything other than the fact that I would wish to understand what I say, fearing that I might overlook something, thinking I know something when I do not? Therefore even now I say I am doing this; I am investigating the reasoning most of all for my own sake, but perhaps also for my other friends. Or do you not think that it is a good common to all human beings for it to become evident *how each of the things is* (ἕκαστον τῶν ὄντων ὅπῃ ἔχει)? (*Charm.* 166c7–d6)

We shall have more to say about what Socrates regards the goals and priorities of inquiry to be in section 2.4. For now, it suffices to notice that Socrates wants to discover how things are. Given what we have already said, it is clear that he would not be satisfied merely with finding out one or a few related moral truths; to seek to know "how things are" is not to be satisfied with knowledge of a few such propositions.

We believe that the passages we have discussed in this section tell us a great deal about Socratic epistemology, for they allow us to explain what kind of knowledge Socrates occasionally claims to have himself, and which he occasionally also seems willing to grant to others. But our discussion also shows that such knowledge is of relatively little worth when compared with moral wisdom, for unlike moral wisdom, particular bits of propositional knowledge cannot function as reliable guides in their possessors' pursuits of the good life.

2.2.5 A Few Final Remarks about the Two Sorts of Knowledge

Some scholars may wish not even to call the kinds of limited cognitive states Socrates occasionally claims to have "knowledge"; but perhaps most can agree that such states provide Socrates with a kind of conviction that allows him to follow some course of action or other with confidence. We cannot stress enough how completely Socrates' epistemology is suffused with a concern for action and how little concerned he is with pure theory. Because Socrates was, as Aristotle has said (see *Metaph.* A, 987b1–4), interested only in ethics, his epistemology has as its single most important characteristic that each cognition is related directly to how one acts and what one does.

In chapter 3, we shall discuss Socrates' conception of psychology and his view that we never do what we recognize as evil; for now, we should be very aware of how inappropriate it is to attempt to understand Socrates' epistemology in terms of the conception of knowledge which has received the most philosophical attention in modern times: "propositional knowledge," or knowledge *that* such and such is the case. For Socrates, because the only knowledge that concerns him is knowledge that has consequences for how we should live, his conception of knowledge cannot simply be understood as knowing *that* something or other is true, for it plainly also has as one of its components that the knower knows *how* to do something or other. This is why Socrates' paradigms for the knowledge he seeks are the crafts; it is also why the ideal of the "learned" person, who knows many facts but has no craft, is nowhere given approval in Plato's early dialogues. Even if he had recognized the possibility of such a person, Socrates would have regarded him as relatively useless.

The knowledge we have identified as constitutive of wisdom would be the most useful thing one could ever come to possess, for it would enable one to be an expert in the craft of living and it would enable one to teach others how best to live. Tragically, Socrates has never met anyone who possesses this knowledge. The knowledge Socrates possesses, as we have seen, though not constitutive of wisdom, does nonetheless have practical application. For example, when Socrates hears of the oracle to Chairephon—that there is some sense in which no one is wiser than he is—he is convinced that there is a sense in which this must be true and he acted accordingly even before he came to be in a position to have any genuine understanding of the sense of the oracle. His knowledge that it was some-how true gave him the kind of confidence he needed to risk everything in his attempt to come to understand the oracle's meaning. It would hardly be worth making so many enemies and impoverishing himself only to find out that the god had lied.

But even where Socrates has such confidence, he may be faced with choices for which such knowledge avails him nothing. To avoid such incapacities in judg-ment, Socrates thinks we must become wise. We have shown how Socrates can regard himself and others as possessing various cognitive states he occasionally calls "knowledge," even ones in which he has complete confidence in making some decisions, without regarding himself or anyone else as wise.

Scholars may wish to quarrel with our willingness to call such cognitions "knowledge," but as we have seen, Socrates himself sometimes uses the Greek equivalents of this term. But whether or not we should settle on "knowledge" as the term to identify such cognitions, we hope we have made it clear how Socrates could think that there are some states he counts as knowledge which do not qualify as wisdom. Indeed, he is so confident of the content of these states that he will offend any person and take any risk rather than act in a way contrary to the way such cognitions tell him to act. Whatever we call them, there can be no doubting Socrates' unshakable confidence about them. In our view, what Socrates lacks, when he insists he is ignorant, is not so much confidence about the truth of the propositions he claims to know, but rather the ability to explain them or to know *how it is* that they are true.

We have tried to show why his calling such cognitions by various Greek words for "knowledge" is compatible with his profession of ignorance, by identifying something else—something infinitely more valuable—as that which he professes to lack. Whether or not our terminology seems apt, we hope at least to have made a clear distinction between the sorts of cognitions Socrates and others have, on the one hand, and the wisdom, the moral expertise, the divine capacity for judg-ment in life that Socrates and all others lack, on the other. It is this latter quality—

and only this latter quality—we have argued, that Socrates disclaims having when he professes ignorance.

2.3 The Epistemological Priority of Definition

2.3.1 A Serious Challenge to Our View

At this point, someone might object that Socrates could only claim knowledge of any sort at the cost of becoming inconsistent with one of his best known views. A number of scholars [26] have argued that Socrates believes that

> (P) only if one knows the definition of some quality (F-ness) can one know whether or not any instance of F-ness is really an instance. [27]

This principle (hereinafter, P) is supposed to provide an interpretation of a number of passages that plainly do commit Socrates to the view that, in some sense or other, knowledge of definitions is epistemologically prior to other sorts of knowledge. It should be obvious from what we have already said that we do not believe that Socrates accepts P, for we have found texts in which Socrates explicitly claims knowledge of some specific things, and we are also convinced that any number of Socrates' confident claims are knowledge claims—that is, we see them affirmed and applied in the practical realm with the utmost confidence. So if Socrates does hold P, then either his many confident affirmations, including his explicit claims of knowledge, are bogus, or else his profession of ignorance is insincere. He, at least, makes inconsistent claims, if he does hold P. [28] Perhaps he is

26. See esp. Benson [1990c]. See also, Allen [1976], esp. 39; Beversluis [1974]; Crombie [1962], vol. 1, 57; Geach [1966]; Guthrie [1969], vol. 3, 352; Robinson [1953], 51. An ancient expression of this objection may be found in Plut. *Adv. Col.* 117D. Opposing views may be found expressed in Beversluis [1987]; Brickhouse and Smith [1984b] and [1989b], 101–3; Irwin [1977], 37–41 and 294, n.4; Lesher [1987]; Nehamas [1986]; Vlastos [1985], 23–26.

27. Benson ([1990c], 20, n. 2) actually distinguishes two distinct principles:

(P) If A fails to know what F-ness is, then A fails to know, for any x, that x is F;
(Q) If A fails to know what F-ness is, then A fails to know, for any G, that F-ness is G.

We shall note this distinction ourselves, in section 2.3.4.6, but shall attend specifically and systematically only to Benson's Principle (P). On "F-ness" rather than "F" (the more traditional rendering), see Benson [1990b].

28. Benson mentions but never discusses this problem ([1990c], 44, n.40). He also does not explain how Socrates can make the confident moral judgments he often makes, given his claim not to know the definition of moral terms. In Benson's view, it would appear that Socrates can claim to know neither that his judgments are correct nor that those he opposes often with obvious conviction—are false. So, for example, in Benson's view, for all that Socrates knows, the practice of the *elenchos* might well be impious, which would make Socrates guilty of Meletus' charge. In fact, given Benson's analysis of *Euthphr.* 4d9–5d5 ([1990c], 33–35), no one could ever be morally justified in any action at all unless he or she knew what virtue itself is. It would appear to follow that Socrates cannot even be *justified* in defending himself against the charge of impiety, unless he knows what piety is. This consequence condemns Socratic philosophy to something like moral nihilism: No moral view can be

completely confused. But we are also convinced that Socrates is committed to the epistemological priority of knowledge of definitions. The question we must answer, therefore, is "What sort of knowledge is knowledge of definitions prior to?"

2.3.2 Some Scholarly Controversy

Does Socrates ever really affirm P? We shall argue that Socrates affirms only that one must know the definition of F-ness before one can be in a position to judge in general which things are and which things are not F. Hence, without knowledge of the definition of F-ness, one's judgment of F things is subject to error. This does not entail that one can *never* make a correct and justified judgment in a secure way; it entails only that one cannot *always* do so. It is one thing to say that one's judgment, as a general rule, is subject to error; it is quite another to say that each and every one of one's judgments is subject to error. We believe Socrates is committed only to the former, weaker view of the corrigibility of his epistemic states. But let us look at the relevant texts and see what they say.

2.3.3 Hippias Major *304d5–e3: How to Be a Judge of Beauty*

After a long argument with Hippias, Socrates finds that they have not accomplished what they set out to accomplish, and he is dismayed by that fact. In a thinly veiled reproach to Hippias, Socrates imagines going home and having someone reproach him.

> [H]e asks me if I am not ashamed in daring to talk about beautiful pursuits, when I have been so obviously refuted about the beautiful itself. "And yet how will you know," he says, "who produced either an account, or any other matter beautifully when you are ignorant of the beautiful? And since you are in that state, do you think it is better for you to be alive than dead?" (*Hip. Ma.* 304d5–e3)

There are a number of things that should trouble us about taking this passage to express P. First, in order to do so, we would need to read the passage quite literally. But it follows from the literal reading that Socrates believes everyone is better off dead *just because* everyone is ignorant of the beautiful. Unless we are prepared to affirm this consequence, we must admit that Socrates is guilty of hyperbole.[29]

Even if we do insist on a literal understanding of Socrates' claim, it does not

---

justified without the knowledge of definitions Socrates is convinced that no one has ever achieved. Hence, no moral view has ever been justified. Whether or not one ever could be justified depends upon how optimistic we take Socrates to be about anyone's ever achieving knowledge of these definitions. The fact that Socrates himself has not, after a lifetime of examining himself and others, is certainly a good ground for profound pessimism.

29. In section 6.5, we shall argue that there is a sense in which Socrates really does believe that we all are better off dead. This consequence does not follow, however, simply from the fact that we are ignorant of the beautiful. Vlastos ([1985], 24–25) seems to think we ought to take Socrates' claim here quite seriously. Benson's rebuttal ([1990a], 152) to Vlastos is more sensible.

follow that no one can judge any case of beauty without knowledge of the beautiful. Certainly there is, in the reproach, a strong sense that Socrates' judgment is being challenged. The sense of the challenge is that Socrates is in no position to play the part of a judge, to lay claim to being able to tell what is and is not beautiful. But the question "Who are you to judge?" does not challenge one's claim to judge any case at all; it only challenges one's ability to judge in general; so "How will you know?" only challenges Socrates' general access to the pertinent knowledge. (See the similar challenge at *Hip. Ma.* 286c8–d2; see also *Ion* 531a1–532c8.)

If one did know what the beautiful is, one could, it seems, act as a judge of beautiful things. But Socrates could well answer his adversary that he is indeed in a position to know in a few cases. To his adversary's challenge "How will you know?," imagine Socrates replying, "It is true; I do not have the sort of knowledge that would always secure my judgments in these matters, and you are right to chastise me if I ever talk as if I have it. I am indeed no judge. But in this particular case, it happens that. . . ."

Now those who believe that Socrates was committed to P must suppose that Socrates could never adequately finish the final sentence of this sort of reply, for no answer that did not demonstrate knowledge of the definition would ever suffice. We disagree, but we also think their view requires us to misinterpret the condition Socrates puts in his adversary's mouth. If we imagine for the sake of argument that the final sentence can be completed in some way, it remains true that Socrates can fully concede that he (Socrates) is no judge of such matters and that he should not behave as if he has such knowledge. "But in this particular case, it happens that" Socrates *is* in a position to judge. So his adversary does not insist that there can be no exceptions to his claim—if Socrates can prove that he does indeed know one or a few isolated examples of beauty, he will not be permitted to ignore the point his adversary has made, as if it had been refuted by Socrates' counterexamples. The sense of his adversary's reproach, then, is not that Socrates cannot judge *any* cases; if it were, a single counterexample would dispel the reproach. The sense of his adversary's reproach is that Socrates lacks the understanding to be a good judge in general. Socrates' adversary, then, does not accuse him of having no knowledge; rather, Socrates' adversary accuses him of not being wise.

2.3.4 Applying Our Interpretation to a Few More Texts

Those who have attributed the belief in P to Socrates have not relied solely on the passage from the *Hippias Major* we have just discussed, however; so neither should we rest our case here. Let us look at a few more of the texts that have been cited for the position we oppose.

2.3.4.1 Euthphr. 4e1–5d1

EUTH.: [My father and my other relatives say that] it is unholy for a son to prosecute his father for murder—since they know so little, Socrates, of how it is with the divine regarding the holy and the unholy.

Soc.: But, by Zeus, do you think that you have such precise knowledge about divine things, *how they are* (ὅπη ἔχει), and about holy and unholy things, that, when those things happened as you say, you are not afraid of doing something unholy yourself by prosecuting your father?

EUTH.: I would be worthless, O Socrates, and Euthyphro would be no different from most people, if I were not to know precisely about all such things.

[. . .]

Soc.: So tell me now, by Zeus, what do you now claim to know clearly, about the nature of the pious and impious in regard to murder and other things?

A later passage, *Euthphr.* 15d4–e1, echoes this one: Socrates says that Euthyphro would not have prosecuted his own father if he did not regard himself as knowing what the holy is.[30]

Now how could Socrates be making this point against Euthyphro, without committing himself to P? If we return to our understanding of the passage from the *Hippias Major,* we will see that Socrates' point in challenging Euthyphro (in the *Euthyphro*) is exactly like Socrates' imaginary adversary's challenge to Socrates himself in the *Hippias Major:* Socrates is challenging Euthyphro to show what puts Euthyphro in the position of being able to judge cases like this one. Nothing Socrates says rules out that Euthyphro has some special and specific knowledge pertinent to this one case; he simply follows Euthyphro's lead in challenging Euthyphro to produce the precise and general knowledge of everything Euthyphro claims to be employing in the present case. It is Euthyphro, let us recall, who contrasts his relatives' poor understanding to his own precise knowledge of "how it is with the divine with regard to the holy and the unholy" (*Euthphr.* 4e2–3). When Socrates asks Euthyphro if Euthyphro has such knowledge "about divine things, how they are, and about holy and unholy things" (*Euthphr.* 4e4–6), Socrates is assuming that Euthyphro would not have proceeded with the prosecution if he did not suppose he had such knowledge. But nothing in Socrates' challenge requires that Euthyphro's action *can be* justified *only if* Euthyphro can produce such knowledge. The challenge simply assumes that this is the sort of justification Euthyphro actually claims to have. Euthyphro is free to disclaim this sort of justification, and say "It is true; I do not have the sort of knowledge that would apply to every relevantly similar case, and you are right to chastise me if I ever talk as if I have it. I am indeed no judge. But in this case, it happens that I know I should prosecute my father, for I have some specific item of knowledge that secures this particular judgment."

In section 2.2.2, we identified a number of things that might give someone such "specific items of knowledge." For our purposes now, let us imagine that Euthyphro claims "I have been commanded to do this by the god through oracles and dreams and in every way in which any other divinity commanded a human being to do anything" (see *Ap.* 33c4–7). If this had been Euthyphro's claim, Socrates' challenge at *Euthyphro* 4e4–8 might be answered without an appeal to precise knowledge of "how it is with the divine with regard to the holy and the

30. See n.28.

unholy.''[31] Accordingly, we do not see these passages as requiring Socrates to be committed to P.

2.3.4.2 Euthyphro 6e3–6

> Soc.: Well, then, teach me what this reality is, in order that by looking at it, and using it as a paradigm, I can say that of the things you or anyone else would do is holy if it agrees with it, or, if it does not, I can deny that it is holy.

This passage only says that knowledge of what is holy could be used for judging what is and is not holy. But this has nothing to do with P, which holds that knowledge of definitions is *necessary* for such judgments.[32] Moreover, surely it is plain from what we have said why Socrates would be eager to know definitions even if such knowledge were not necessary for the ability to judge examples. For without such knowledge, even if one can judge some instances, based upon special and particular knowledge that one might have, one will never be wise; one will never be able to be sure that he or she will be able to make the sorts of moral judgments that will indemnify his or her soul from the effects of moral errors.

Moreover, Socrates identifies no other way to determine *in general* which acts are holy, even if there can be cases where one might be able to know that this or that act is holy. And even these cases might not all be the product of intelligent application of some method; they may be no better than the products of a certain divinatory event, which one would be extremely fortunate to experience, but which one could not reproduce. It does not follow from one person's being exhorted by the god to perform some action that it would be right for any other person to perform that action. And unless the exhortation was to the performance of that action over and over again (as it appears to have been with Socrates and his mission), it would not even follow from a divine command to perform a particular action that the agent should perform the action more than once. So there do not seem to *be* "other ways of determining which acts are holy," even if we are right in saying that now and again someone might be in a position to tell that this or that act was holy. So Socrates has every reason to want to know definitions of moral terms; nothing else will give him the wisdom he seeks, or anything close to it. This, then, is Socrates' conception of the epistemological priority of definitions: one must know the definition of F-ness before one can be wise in regard to F-ness and examples of F-ness. That is, one must know the definition before one can qualify as an expert judge regarding F-ness.

2.3.4.3 Laches 189e3–190b1

> For if we happen to know about something, that its being joined to something else makes that other thing better, and further we are able to make this thing

---

31. We are not simply assuming that such a response would leave no room for further dispute; we are merely claiming that such a response could, in principle, qualify as an answer to Socrates' challenge. Socrates might well go on to test Euthyphro's claim to have had such experiences in this case, to see, for example, if Euthyphro had understood correctly the experiences he had, and so on.

32. Benson wonders "Why should [Socrates] be so concerned to answer his 'What is Holiness' question, if there are other ways of determining which acts are holy?" ([1990c], 29). Because Benson cannot find a satisfactory answer to this question, he concludes that this passage probably shows that Socrates is committed to P, after all ([1990c], 29–33).

become joined to the other, clearly we know the thing itself about which we are advisors regarding how it might be acquired easily and best. Perhaps you do not understand what I say, but will understand more easily in this way. If we happen to know about sight that joining it to the eyes makes them better for its having been joined to them, and further we are able to join sight to the eyes, clearly we know sight itself, what it is, about which we could give advice regarding how someone could acquire it easily and best. For if we did not know what sight or hearing is, we would hardly be advisors or physicians worth paying attention to regarding the eyes or ears and how one could best acquire hearing or sight.

As we have been arguing in regard to other cases, Socrates is here again simply laying down what would be needed to qualify one as a judge of (or in the language of this passage, and we believe equivalently, an "advisor" regarding) the benefits of eyesight (or hearing, or anything else), and how to attain it. The claim does not insist on the rule's being exceptionless; it merely asserts that one cannot be qualified to judge *in general* without the knowledge of what it is about which one is making the judgment.[33]

If our reading is correct, then even if one happened somehow to *know* something, however trivial, about certain eyes, one could hardly qualify as an expert about vision. If we pause to consider this claim, we will see that it makes good sense. Jane might well come to know that she has an astigmatism. When she noticed that she was getting headaches whenever she read, she visited a local opthalmologist, who diagnosed her problem as astigmatism. Perhaps she is extremely suspicious of opthalmologists, and so she goes to a number of different ones to see if she would get corroboration of the first diagnosis she received. Each opthalmologist she visited told her the same story. Now unless we are to adopt an extremely skeptical position with regard to the fallibility of opthalmologists—a position Socrates himself never so much as hints at with regard to qualified craftsmen's ability to practice their crafts—it seems fair to say, at least for all practical purposes, that Jane now knows that she has an astigmatism. But this knowledge does not qualify her as an opthalmologist, or as one who can now go and give advise to others about the causes and cures of eyestrain, or headaches, or anything else. In order to be in a position to give the advice she got from her opthalmologists, she needs to know opthalmology; since she does not, she is in no position to give advice about eyes or eyesight, despite her knowledge of this one case. Plainly, many such examples could be given.

If we are right, then, Socrates is not interested in delimiting the conditions according to which one can know anything at all—no matter how trivial and spe-

---

33. Benson ([1990c], 38) understands this passage as committing Socrates to what he identifies as principle F:

(F) If A fails to know what F-ness is, then A fails to both know that having it makes x better and be able to add it to x [*sic*].

If Benson were right about this passage, it would follow that, for Socrates, anyone who lacked knowledge of what sight is could not know that having sight would make some specific pair of eyes better. But the passage does not say this; it does not even address the question of specific cases.

cific—about a subject. As always, Socrates' emphasis is on the sort of knowledge that one can put to use; the sort that would make one an expert, a qualified judge, or advisor about the subject; the sort that would make one wise. If we understand him in this way, we shall not be forced to attribute to him a commitment to P—a principle which even most of those attributing it to Socrates have found quite implausible.[34] Rather, we will find nothing unlikely in Socrates' claim. We also find the claim in keeping with Socrates' emphasis on the practical, and not on the purely theoretical, aspects of epistemology.

2.3.4.4   Lysis 223b4–8

> We have made ourselves ridiculous, Lysis and Menexenus—I, an old man, and you. For those who go away will say that we think we are one another's friends—for I put myself in with you—but what a friend is, we have not been able to discover.

Those who would read this passage as endorsing P actually commit Socrates to a further, absurdly strong, claim. According to P, one cannot *know* that something is an instance of friendship unless one knows what friendship is. But Socrates never says that he, Lysis, or Menexenus has claimed to *know* they are friends. If we read this passage as an endorsement of something like P, then, the claim in question must be that Socrates, Lysis, and Menexenus have made themselves ridiculous for even daring to *think* (οἴομαι—223b6) they are friends without being able to discover what a friend is. On this reading, Socrates and his young associates should leave realizing that, for all they may *think* otherwise, they may not even *be* friends.

We think this reading cannot be correct for two reasons. First, we think that Socrates is not so foolish as to suppose that one is not even entitled to think that something is F without knowing what F-ness is. If this were true, there is little or nothing anyone would be entitled so much as to think about any moral issue or course of action. Such an extreme view does not accord with Socrates' own moral confidence, in many cases, nor do we see him attempting to get his fellow Athenians to stop thinking about moral topics; quite the reverse, in fact. Second, we do not see Socrates' claim at the end of the *Lysis* as betraying any real doubt about whether or not he, Lysis, and Menexenus are friends. Rather, he is merely pointing out that they appear ridiculous for their inability to understand what they take themselves so plainly to instantiate.

2.3.4.5   Meno 71a5–b7

> I am so far from knowing whether virtue can be taught or not, that I happen not to know at all what the thing itself, virtue, is. [. . .] Not knowing what a thing is, how can I know of what sort it is? Or does it seem to you possible for someone who does not know at all who Meno is, to know if he is beautiful, or wealthy, or well-born, or the opposite of these? Does it seem possible to you?

---

34. Benson alone attempts to defend P against the charge that it is implausible ([1990c], 29, n.20).

This text turns P around: Socrates parallels his ignorance with someone who "does not know at all who Meno is" and is asked to say whether or not Meno is beautiful, and so forth. P, on the other hand, denies that one can tell whether or not Meno is beautiful unless one knows what beauty is. In other words, P denies that one can judge that S is F unless one knows what F-ness is; this passage, if it denies anything, denies that one can know that S is F unless one knows what S is. These are very different principles. Accordingly, this passage does not support the inclusion of P within Socratic philosophy.

Moreover, this principle is a good deal more plausible than P, for unlike P, it simply insists that one must know *what* one is talking about before one can know what to say about *it*. It would be hard indeed for one to be completely ignorant of a subject (and *complete* ignorance is what this passage explicitly attributes to Socrates, regarding what virtue is, and to Meno's judge, regarding who Meno is) and yet to be in a position to judge which predicates can, and which cannot, be attributed to that subject. Now perhaps we could concoct a case in which such a thing were possible: one might have it on divine authority that something (S) was beautiful without having any idea what S is. In such a case, if we wanted to call it knowledge at all, it would remain true that the subject was in no position to represent to himself or herself so much as a general idea of what the claim means. It appears, rather, that such a case of knowledge would qualify as no better than knowing that a given sentence was true without so much as knowing what it was about. It would not be strange, then, if Socrates were simply to deny that there could be such knowledge.

However, this passage does not actually assert that such knowledge is impossible. Instead, Socrates is merely asking Meno a rhetorical question about the possibility of such knowledge. As tempted as we may be to conclude that Socrates regards the answer as obvious, this passage falls short of being decisive in committing Socrates to the view that there could be no such knowledge. Meno makes this commitment; Socrates merely solicits it. If Socrates can allow exceptions, he doesn't tell us here. In any event, such odd cases would hardly be pertinent to the conversation he is having with Meno.

A similar claim may be found at *Republic* I.354c1–3, where Socrates says that without knowing what justice is, he will not be able to know whether or not justice is a virtue or whether or not justice makes one happy. We shall return to this passage from the *Republic* in section 2.4, but for now, it is worth noticing that its logic is the same as in the above passage from the *Meno*: one must know what something is, before one can know which predicates to attach to it.[35]

2.3.4.6 Prt. 312c1–4

What a sophist is I would be surprised if you know. But if you are ignorant of this, then you do not know to whom you are handing over your soul, whether it is a good thing or an evil thing.

---

35. These passages, then, are really pertinent not to Benson's Principle P, but rather his Q; see Benson [1990c], 20, n.2 and our n.27.

This passage certainly does argue that knowing what a sophist is, is epistemologically prior to knowing whether going to one would bring benefit or harm. But is this support for Socrates' holding P?[36] We think not.

First, the logic of the claim Socrates makes in this passage is similar to what we found in the passages we discussed in 2.3.4.5; unless one knows what S is, one can't know whether some predicate (in this case, "provides benefit") is rightly attributed to S. This claim is not the same as the claim that one must know what F-ness is in order to identify examples of F-ness.

Second, this passage does not rule out the possibility of the sort of exception we have been considering. Socrates is here challenging the young Hippocrates to show what warrants his eagerness to give himself over to Protagoras for his education. Socrates wants to know what Hippocrates thinks he is doing—that is, Socrates wants to know what Hippocrates thinks he can expect to get from the sophist. In making the challenge he does, in this passage, he assumes that Hippocrates has no special and specific knowledge that would pertain to this case—for example, a direct command from Apollo to Hippocrates bidding him to learn from Protagoras. This assumption should not be elevated to the status of an exceptionless epistemological principle, however. Socrates makes his assumption because absolutely nothing suggests that he is dealing with an exceptional case of the sort we might imagine.

Instead, Socrates assumes that Hippocrates must be making similar assumptions about going to Protagoras as one would make about going to a painter or a carpenter (see Socrates' implied comparison at *Prt.* 312c7–8). One ordinarily does not go to a carpenter for some assistance without some fairly clear idea of what the carpenter is skilled at doing, unless, of course, one has some other, very exceptional ground for doing so. Socrates is not concerned here to leave room for such an exceptional case, for he has ample reason to be confident that the case with which he is dealing is not exceptional in the relevant way.

Even if we are wrong about this, however, and Socrates really is here expressing an exceptionless epistemological principle, there is nothing remarkable about the claim that one ought to know what a craftsman has to offer before one seeks to do business with the craftsman. So Socrates' claim in this passage—that without such knowledge, one is in no position to know whether good or bad would come of such a transaction—is entirely reasonable.

Would it be reasonable to suppose that Socrates would extend such a principle to moral concepts, and not just apply it to craftsmen? Let us consider a sample of such an extension:

(Q) Without knowledge of what virtue is, one cannot know whether being virtuous would be beneficial or not.

Now, in the light of passages like *Republic* I.354c1–3, which we discussed briefly in 2.3.4.5, it would appear that Socrates is sometimes willing to say things that sound like Q. We shall have more to say about passages like these in section 2.4,

---

36. Benson cites this passage in support of P ([1990c], 40–41).

but one thing is worth noting here. The substitution in Q of a moral term for a term identifying a (putative) craftsman of some sort certainly does yield one different result. In the case of the craftsman, Socrates strongly suggests that one should not pursue an association until one learns what such an association might bring. That is, one would be imprudent to engage in an association with some (putative) craftsman of some service or product, D, who will do (or make) D to (or for) one, until one knows well what D is. But Socrates would be the last to argue that one should not pursue virtue until one knows what virtue is. It is quite the reverse, in fact, for Socrates regards it as his mission to go out and exhort his fellow Athenians to pursue virtue above all else, holding any other goods as dependent on it (see *Ap.* 29e4–30b4). Yet he plainly does not believe that anyone in Athens already knows what virtue is. So the two cases are not parallel, and we should accordingly beware making inferences from passages such as *Prt.* 312c1–4 to Q.

2.3.6   Summary and Conclusion

We began this section by examining a problem for our claim that Socrates was prepared to identify certain specific cognitions about virtue or various virtues as knowledge, despite his belief that no one knows how to define "virtue," or the terms for any of the particular virtues. The problem was that, if many scholars were right, Socrates also endorsed an epistemological principle (P), according to which one could not know that some instance of F-ness is such an instance, without prior knowledge of the definition of F-ness. If Socrates really did accept this principle, he could not consistently recognize as legitimate the knowledge claims we identified earlier in this chapter.

In this section, we have considered a number of passages that are often cited in support of the view that Socrates accepts P. We have sought to discredit the attribution of this principle to Socrates partly because we think P is philosophically mistaken—insisting, as it does, that one must have final success in obtaining the end product of an inquiry before one is in a position to know that there is anything to inquire about. But we also think P is to be rejected because it yields a variety of other consequences that cannot be made consistent with what we know of Socratic philosophy. In each case, we presented an alternative reading of the text which is consistent with the actual wording of the relevant texts, but which does not entail P or any of the other problematical aspects of P.

The upshot of our review is consistent with our earlier remarks: Socrates allows that one can know a number of specific things, none of which amounts to the sort of wisdom he and all other people lack. He searches for definitions of the terms which identify moral properties because neither he nor anyone else who lacked such knowledge could be in a position to make authoritative judgments regarding any and all instantiations of those properties. Exceptional circumstances may be found, in which a person finds himself or herself able to tell what one or a few instances may be. In cases where the issue is not obvious, however, or where controversy should arise, such a person cannot play the part of a proper judge or advisor—that is, an expert on the subject—by not only identifying things correctly but being able to explain his or her identifications to others. Let us turn now to one of the philosophical consequences of Socrates' view of the importance of knowing definitions.

2.4   The Procedural Priority of Definition

2.4.1   *How to Conduct an Inquiry*

In the passages we looked at in section 2.3, we found Socrates telling his interlocutors that one could not be a qualified judge of F things unless one first came to know what F-ness is. Because the ability to be such a judge in moral matters would be so advantageous, not only for the judge, but also for anyone associated with him or her, we should not be surprised to find Socrates encouraging his interlocutors to seek to come to know these definitions. In fact, we find Socrates giving priority to the pursuit of definitions.

In the passages we are about to consider, Socrates says we should seek to define some pertinent moral term before attempting to discover anything else about it or its extension. So one should first define piety before attempting to find out what are or are not examples of piety, and before attempting to discover any other facts about piety, such as whether or not it makes its possessor happy. This is not an endorsement of P, which concerns the epistemological priority of definitions, but is instead an endorsement of a certain view as to how discussions should go; it is a *procedural* principle affirming the fundamental place of definitions within moral inquiries.

2.4.2   *One Over Many*

Our view of the epistemological priority of definitions has now been made clear. Given this, and because many of the passages identifying what we are calling the procedural priority of definitions are quite similar, we propose first to list and discuss a group of these passages, and then turn to a few texts requiring separate comment. The first group of passages simply betray Socrates' sense of how an inquiry should proceed and what its aims should be.

2.4.2.1   *How Inquiry Should Proceed*

Euthyphro 6d9–11
Remember, then, that this is not what I requested of you, to teach me one or two of the many holy things, but rather to teach me that form itself, by which all holy things are holy.

Laches 191e10–11
So try again and tell me first about courage, what it is that is the same in all of these cases.

Laches 192b5–8
So try now, O Laches, to speak about courage in the same way: what power is it, that is the same in pleasure and in pain and in all of the things in which we said it was, which is called "courage"?

Meno 73c6–8
Since the virtue of all of these things is the same, try to say and to remember what Gorgias says this same thing is, and you along with him.

Meno 75a4–5
Do you not understand that I am looking for the same in all of these things?

Meno 77a5–9
Come then and try to keep your promise to me by telling me about the whole of virtue, what it is, and stop making many things from one thing, as the jokers say whenever they smash something, but while leaving virtue whole and sound, tell me what it is.

In each of these passages, Socrates is confronted with an interlocutor who does not understand that the way to go about answering Socrates' "what is it?" questions is not to list examples of the quality in question, but rather to provide a proper definition.[37] Euthyphro and Laches offer examples of particular virtues (piety and courage, respectively), whereas Meno fails to recognize one complete and whole virtue, but instead shatters it into what Socrates calls "a swarm" of virtues (*Meno* 72a7). Socrates is convinced that the right way to proceed in each of these inquiries is first to attempt to discern what the thing at issue (piety, courage, virtue) is, and only then to go on to other questions about that thing or examples of it.

2.4.3   Socrates' Own Way

In a few other texts, we find Socrates simply insisting on doing things his way.

2.4.3.1   Gorgias *462c8–d2*

POLUS: So you believe that rhetoric is a fine thing that is able to give people pleasure?
SOCRATES: What, Polus? Have you ascertained from me what I think it is, that you ask what should follow that—whether I do not believe it is fine?

Polus has not tried to make "many things from the one thing," as other interlocutors sometimes do, but has pressed Socrates to answer what Socrates regards as a subsidiary question before Socrates has answered the "what is it?" question, which Socrates regards as the prior question.

2.4.3.2   Laches *190b7–c2*

Therefore, is it necessary first to know what virtue is? For if we do not know at all what virtue happens to be, how could we ever become advisors to anyone in order that he might best acquire it?

We have already seen (in 2.4.2.1) how Laches fails adequately to conceive of the definitional ("what is it?")' question. Only a moment before, however (in the passage quoted immediately above), Socrates had made it perfectly plain that this question is one the inquirers should pursue before going on to consider how they

---

37. A different characterization of the flaw in these interlocutors' responses to Socrates' questions is offered by Benson [1990b].

might give advice on the subject. Scholars have taken this passage to support the view that Socrates accepts P.[38] But this passage does no more than to pick up what Socrates had said only moments before (at *La.* 189e3–190b1) about what is necessary to qualify someone to act as the sort of advisor Lysimachus and Melesias seek (see *La.* 178a1–180a5). According to the principle of epistemological priority, to qualify as an expert (judge, advisor), one must first know definitions. We argued in section 2.3.4.3 that Socrates should not be seen in these passages as insisting on an epistemological principle like P. Accordingly, in this passage (190b7–c2), Socrates is not telling his colleagues what is necessary to judge any instance of courage at all, but rather he is urging them to pursue their inquiry about courage by seeking first that which would allow them to qualify as the advisors Lysimachus and Melesias have asked them to be.

2.4.4 Inconclusive Conclusions

We have argued that Socrates often claimed to know some specific thing about a given subject—for example, that it is never just to return wrong for wrong—without knowing *how it is* that what he knows is true, is true. Occasionally, however, Socrates not only claims ignorance of *how it is* that his results are true, but even *whether or not* they are true.

> We shall know clearly about this [sc. how virtue comes to human beings] when, before attempting to find out how virtue comes to human beings, we attempt to inquire into what virtue is itself by itself. (*Meno* 100b4–6)

By the time Socrates and Meno come to this point in their discussion, their argument has led them to the view that virtue comes to human beings by divine dispensation. But Socrates immediately adds that they have come to this conclusion before first finding out what virtue is. He then (in the above passage) says that they cannot "know clearly" whether or not they are right in their arguments until they find out what virtue is.

In this passage, Socrates does not claim—as he had, for example, at the end of his argument with Callicles in the *Gorgias*—to have "reasons of iron and adamant" (*Grg.* 509a1) for the conclusion he reaches; nor is there any talk, at the end of the *Meno*, about others who have held views opposed to the one Socrates and Meno have settled on. In chapter 1, we stressed that Socrates would need repeated elenctic encounters on the same thesis, with a variety of interlocutors, in order to derive what he might be willing to call "knowledge" from his elenctic encounters. What we see in the *Meno*, then, is the result of this process in its early stages.

It follows from what we have argued, however, that repeated elenctic encounters will eventually bring Socrates a far greater confidence in the truth of a proposition than he has reached after his discussion with Meno alone. But nowhere does Socrates say that the way he and Meno have proceeded is the only way they could have gone about seeking the right conclusion. He says only that they would know

---

38. See, for example, Benson [1990c], 37–38.

clearly about how virtue comes to human beings if only they would pursue the inquiry in the right way—seeking the definition of virtue first, before going on to the subsidiary question.

Wisdom, we can be sure, brings *clear* knowledge of the sorts of things Socrates and Meno have been discussing. But what kind of knowledge remains *unclear?* By now, our answer should be quite predictable: any knowledge which can only assert—even entirely confidently—that the *fact* of the matter is such and such, but which cannot account for *why* it is so, or *how it is* that it is so, might very reasonably be identified as *unclear* knowledge.

2.4.5   One Final Text

One more text, very like the one from the *Meno* we have just been examining, is worth considering. At the end of Book I of the *Republic,* having established in an argument with Thrasymachus that justice is preferable to injustice, Socrates is contrite about the way he has allowed the discussion to wander:

> Just as the greedy grab every dish that is passed along and taste it before they properly enjoy the previous one, so it seems to me that I, before discovering what we searched for first—what justice is—released that and set out to consider something about it, namely, whether it is vice and ignorance or wisdom and virtue; and when another argument came up—that injustice is more profitable than justice—I could not refrain from turning to that from the former question, so that the outcome of the discussion is for me that I know nothing. For when I don't know what justice is, I shall hardly know whether it happens to be a virtue or not, and whether its possessor is happy or not. (*Rep.* I. 354b1–c3)

This passage has been taken as decisive proof that Socrates thinks knowledge of the definition of F-ness must come before any other knowledge of F-ness is possible.[39] If so, our view cannot be correct, for we have argued that there is within Socratic philosophy a sense of "know" according to which, without knowledge of what F-ness is, one can know both that certain examples of F-ness are F and that some particular statement(s) about F-ness is (are) true.

We believe that the end of Book I of the *Republic* does not defeat our interpretation. First, we take Socrates' principal goal to be to establish a general claim about the priority of definition in inquiry. Socrates is distressed with himself because he has violated his own conception about priority of definition: he is firmly convinced that the right way to go about gaining the answers to such subsidiary questions about justice as those he came to pursue with Thrasymachus is first to get a fix on the nature of justice itself. As a general principle, then, Socrates

---

39. Others have tried to resist the evidence provided in this and the *Meno* passage (cited immediately above) for attributing Principle P to Socrates, by dismissing the theses expressed in these texts as corruptions of Socratic doctrines by the maturing Plato (see, for example, Vlastos [1985], 23 n.54, 26 n.65; Beversluis [1987], 221 n.4). We do believe that the *Meno* is a transitional dialogue, and that the later books of the *Republic* are from Plato's middle period. Although we thus agree that we should be alert, as we read the *Meno* and *Republic* Book I, for influences of the mature Plato's thought, our analyses show that there is no special reason to dismiss them categorically as expressions of Plato's (early) Socratic doctrines.

believes that before one seeks to discover whether or not F-ness is a virtue or whether or not the possession of F-ness makes one happy, one should first discern what F-ness is. Such knowledge would certainly put its possessor in a much better position to answer all the subsidiary questions—to know *clearly,* that is, *what* the right answers to the subsidiary questions are. More importantly, however, unlike those who are ignorant of what F-ness is, one who knows what F-ness is would be in a better position to know *why* its possessors are made happy or not and *why* it is or is not a virtue—that is, to know *why* the right answers to the subsidiary questions are right, and not just *that* they are right. This, then, is why one ought always to seek knowledge of what F-ness is before one becomes engaged in other questions about F-ness.

Given the testimony of Plato's early dialogues, Socrates is plainly sometimes willing to discuss what we have called subsidiary questions about virtue before he has established what the nature of virtue is. But from the end of Book I of the *Republic,* we can be sure that this is not the way he likes to do things. He would always prefer, as his principle of the priority of definition in inquiry tells him, to discuss first things first, and thereby come to the kind of knowledge that brings wisdom. This is why we find Socrates so often deflecting discussions of other issues into questions about definitions—if only he could answer *these* questions, he is convinced, he would be able to answer authoritatively many other moral questions.

After his argument with Thrasymachus, Socrates says that he does not even know what the right answers to what we have called the subsidiary questions are. He has argued for one side of the case, but he is not this time willing to accept the conclusion of his argument as confidently as he was, in similar circumstances, at the end of his argument with Callicles in the *Gorgias.* He has had no relevant divinatory experience, nor has he at this point witnessed the results of a sufficient number of elenctic arguments. Common experience certainly provides no decisive evidence. So Socrates does not always have the sort of "unclear" knowledge we have identified, which falls short of wisdom. But this is what we would expect if confidence about the outcome of a particular elenctic argument can be achieved only by having reached that same result previously with many interlocutors.[40] Socrates' final remarks to Thrasymachus, then, do not lay out a general rule of epistemological priority; rather they lay down a rule about priority in inquiry. But Socrates also expresses a frustrating personal lack. Having not followed his own principle of priority of definition in inquiry (and having no other ground on which to make a claim of knowledge), Socrates is in no position to know the answers to the questions he and Thrasymachus have discussed.

We have identified two general sorts of knowledge: one of which is constitutive of wisdom and one of which is not. Socrates' disclaimers at the end of Book I of the *Republic* extend both to knowledge of what justice is and to the knowledge

---

40. See also *Charm.* 165b5–c1, where Socrates assures Critias that he (Socrates) does not already know the answers to the questions he asks. Charmides also seems aware of his own lack of knowledge, on grounds that would appear to concede the priority of knowledge of the definition (see *Charm.* 176a6–b1).

that it is a virtue or that its possessor is happy. We have argued that there is a sense in which Socrates does not believe that one can know nothing of justice unless one knows the definition. On the contrary, he thinks one can have a kind of knowledge—the kind that does not make one wise—through divination, through elenctic examination, and through everyday experience. But these sorts of knowledge are not what Socrates disclaims when he says he is ignorant. Let us now be clear that we are convinced that there is another sense in which Socrates holds that knowledge of the definition of F-ness must precede all *(clear)* knowledge about F-ness. One cannot have any knowledge about F-ness that is tantamount to wisdom without first knowing what F-ness is—simply because knowing the definition of F-ness is required to have wisdom about F-ness.[41] Without knowledge of the definition of justice one cannot even know—in the sense of "know" that has the ability to provide an account as a condition—*that* justice is a virtue. This is not the only sense of "know" Socrates acknowledges, as we have seen, but it is the one that is, in his view, philosophically important. The other sort does not make its possessor wise; the other sort is "worth little or nothing" relative to the knowledge that makes its possessor wise. So when Socrates is contrite at the end of Book I of the *Republic*, it is not because he proceeded in a way that could not bring him any sort of knowledge; it is rather at least partly because it could never bring him the only kind of knowledge that would at last free him from his lack of wisdom. As a philosopher—that is, as a lover of *wisdom*—it is not enough to seek a "trivial and commonplace" sort of knowledge. One should always pursue wisdom, and this he failed to do with Thrasymachus, for whatever cognitive assurance he might otherwise obtain by behaving as he did, he proceeded in a way that could never make him wise.

2.5 Defining the Virtues and Being Virtuous

2.5.1 Wisdom and the Definitions of Moral Terms

We have argued that good sense can be made of Socrates' profession of ignorance together with his occasional claims that he possesses knowledge of moral significance. Despite his lack of wisdom, however, Socrates plainly considers himself a good man (see *Ap*. 41c9–d2, and our discussion in section 4.5). If we are right, over the years Socrates has consistently managed to steer away from evil. No doubt part of the reason for his moral success is that, as we showed in chapter 1, his elenctically produced convictions provide him with a number of fixed points for a theory of how humans ought to act. Thus, although Socrates lacks wisdom, he is aware of a significant number of propositions that a full theory of virtue would explain. But despite the advantages he has gained from leading the examined life, Socrates perceives his own moral knowledge as "worth little or noth-

41. We were influenced by Nehamas [1986] on this point. We need not be committed, however, to his more controversial claim that Socrates does not disallow some knowledge of justice without knowledge of what justice is. In our view, there is a sense of "knowledge" in which Socrates does deny the possibility of any knowledge without knowledge of the definition.

ing," and persistently seeks definitions of the virtues. As we noted in the last section, Socrates regards the search for definitions as an all-important first step in serious philosophical inquiry. Foremost among the virtues, according to Socrates, is wisdom. We might well ask, then, whether Socrates has reached any conclusions, however tentative and however general, about what wisdom consists in. Because Socrates thinks that wisdom is like a craft, it will be helpful to approach this question by asking whether Socrates has reached any conclusions about what product or *ergon* results from the practice of wisdom.

No doubt influenced by the emphasis Socrates places on knowledge of definitions, some commentators have argued that Socrates thinks wisdom just consists in knowing the correct *definition* of virtue (or definitions of particular virtues). But there are problems with this view, for Socrates also plainly believes that if one does possess moral wisdom we should be able to turn to him or her to resolve every moral dispute. How could mere knowledge of the proper definition of a moral term, or even all moral terms, enable anyone to resolve moral disputes such as whether or not to allow persons to live in public parks or whether or not companies should be required to have a certain number of minority employees? Even if one were somehow to *know* that wisdom is *defined* as the knowledge of good and evil, one would not by that knowledge alone be able to steer one's way through vexing issues such as the ones just mentioned.

Socrates' interest in having a guide to correct action is nowhere clearer than in a passage we have already quoted (at 2.3.4.2) from the *Euthyphro:*

> Well, then, teach me what this reality is, in order that by looking at it, and using
> it as a paradigm, I can say that of the things you or anyone else would do is holy
> if it agrees with it, or, if it does not, I can deny that it is holy. (*Euthphr.* 6e3–6)

In this passage, we find Socrates asking his characteristic "what is it?" question. It is natural to regard this question as seeking a definition. But at least one scholar, Richard Kraut, is concerned that moral definitions cannot be all that Socrates seeks, and argues that in this passage Socrates is not merely asking for a criterion by which to judge whether or not a given act is pious or not; he is setting down as a condition of adequacy that the answer serve as a "definitive guide to the solution to practical problems."[42] But this, Kraut points out, is plainly far more than a mere definition could possibly provide.

Kraut concludes that in asking "What is virtue?" Socrates is not seeking just a definition of the term but "a substantive theory, organized around a small number of core statements, that will tell us how to decide all practical questions."[43] According to Kraut, this explains why Socrates thinks he is so far from his goal of becoming "truly wise," for he is looking for "an entire moral theory, of which he possesses only elementary fragments."[44] The definitions of moral terms may even have a central place in such a moral theory. But definitions can be only part of what would make a person morally wise.

---

42. Kraut [1983b], 256.
43. Ibid., 282.
44. Ibid., 283–84.

We share this puzzlement about how any definition of virtue could provide a "definitive guide to action," and it is curious that more commentators have not been puzzled about how knowledge of a definition of virtue could be sufficient for wisdom. Nevertheless, there are compelling reasons for thinking that Socrates expects the "what is it?" question to be answered with a definition. First, Socrates' interlocutors certainly understand him to be asking for a *definition* when he asks the "what is it?" question. And when they attempt to answer by giving various definitions of the virtues, Socrates never says that they have given the wrong *sort* of answer because he is really looking for an "entire moral theory." Second, in several places in the early dialogues, Socrates volunteers examples of the sort of thing he is looking for in asking the "what is it?" question. But if Kraut were right, Socrates would be misleading Laches, for example, when he attempts to help the general see what *sort* of answer would be appropriate to the question "what is courage?"

> But if someone were to say to me, Socrates, what do you say is this which is in all things you call quickness? I would say to him that I call quickness the power to accomplish much in a little time—in speaking, and running, and all other such things. (*La.* 192a9–b3)[45]

So, in asking the "what is it?" question, Socrates really is looking for a definition of moral terms. But, then, how are we to understand *Euthyphro* 6e3–6, the passage on the basis of which Kraut concludes that Socrates is really asking for an "entire moral theory"? First, there is no reason to think that in asking for a "paradigm" Socrates is asking for a way of solving *every* moral problem; rather, he is only asking for help in judging whether or not something is pious. Second, if we look carefully at the passage, we will see that it does not commit Socrates to the view that knowledge of the paradigm will be sufficient to allow Socrates to judge all cases. This was presumably how Kraut read it. But the passage may be taken as stating only why Socrates is interested in obtaining the definition: if one knew the definition, one could use it "as a paradigm" to judge whether or not any particular action or person is pious. Such knowledge does not itself guarantee that one will know all that is needed in order to make the right judgment, however. One must, in addition, plainly know the relevant descriptions of the particulars to be judged, the causal relations between those particulars and their potential outcomes in the relevant setting, and many other things pertinent to making the specific judgments in question. Obviously, knowledge of the definition of piety would contribute significantly to one's power to judge putative instances of piety; but even that knowledge, great as it would be, is a far cry from an "entire moral theory" by which *every* moral problem pertaining to piety could be solved by applying the theory.

Perhaps an example would make the point clearer. Let us imagine that a legislator wished to determine whether some proposed statute is pious or not. The

---

45. For a second example, see Socrates' definition of "shape" at *Meno* 76a4–7. In that passage Socrates unmistakably implies that he wants to understand what virtue is in precisely the same way as he is claiming to clarify what shape is, namely, by a definition.

legislator, let us suppose, believes that Euthyphro's proposed definition of piety—
"whatever is pleasing to the gods"—is correct. He regards himself, accordingly,
as one who knows the definition of piety, and so he has the ability Socrates (at
Euthphr. 6e3–6) says such a person would have: the legislator can use his definition "as a paradigm" in judging the proposed statute. But as the legislator considers the case, he realizes that he does not really know what sorts of things do *in
fact* please the gods; and even if he did know this (let us suppose the gods are
pleased by and only by whatever gives them honor), he might not be in a position
to tell if this statute has the property referred to (so, for example, he cannot tell
if, all things considered, this statute would really give honor to the gods). He also
finds that he is at a loss to determine what the short- and long-term consequences
of the statute's passage might be; perhaps the passage of this statute will enrich
the festivals in Athens, but what about on the islands and in the colonies? And
are there any hidden costs to it? Lacking all of this information, the legislator
might well count himself as lacking the wisdom necessary to judge whether or not
the statute is pious.

The above example does not rely on the fact that the definition employed by
the legislator is not the correct one. To be sure, the definition is incorrect, as
Socrates' argument with Euthyphro shows. But the inadequacy of the definition is
not due to its inability to supply the sorts of morally relevant specific information
lacked by the legislator, all of which would be pertinent to the decision in question. In fact, a moment's reflection will show that *no* definition would by itself
provide such information. So, as useful as knowledge of the definition of piety
might be, in judging what is, and what is not, pious, knowledge of the definition
alone could never be sufficient for making all such judgments.

Many dialogues depict Socrates searching for an answer to the "What is X?"
question. On our view, this shows how well aware Socrates is that one cannot be
in a position to qualify as an expert moral judge without knowing the answers to
such questions. So, we do not dispute that knowledge of moral definitions is
necessary for wisdom. That is why, in the *Euthyphro* passage we have now considered, Socrates wants to know what piety is. Socrates says that he seeks such a
definition in order to use it "as a paradigm" in judging things. But, again, it does
not follow from this that he believes that knowledge of the definition alone would
suffice to allow him to make such judgments; it only follows that Socrates regards
such knowledge as very useful in making such judgments. So, nothing in the
Euthyphro requires that Socrates be asking Euthyphro for an entire theory of piety,
whatever that would be.

Thus far we have argued that in asking the "what is it?" question, Socrates is
asking for the proper definition of a moral term and, to that extent, we think
Kraut is mistaken. But we agree with Kraut in thinking that Socrates believes that
knowledge of definitions of moral terms alone would never be sufficient to make
a person wise. If knowledge of definitions of moral terms is only a necessary part
of the wisdom Socrates wants for himself and others, how would Socrates characterize the non-definitional constituents of wisdom? Without some guidance, even
if one could gain knowledge of the right definition of piety, for example, one
would still be in the dark with respect to where he or she ought to look for the

other items which would constitute wisdom. One might well know the definition of "medicine" and could therefore state what it is that a physician knows. But, plainly, this is only one constituent of the knowledge in virtue of which one actually *is* a physician.

Fortunately, Socrates' assumption that all wisdom can be compared to the knowledge possessed by craftsmen provides us with an important clue. When Socrates wishes to test whether Gorgias really has any special sort of wisdom, he immediately assumes that the relevant wisdom can be understood as a form of craft-knowledge and that the craft in question can be defined in terms of knowledge of how to produce some characteristic product, or *ergon* (*Grg.* 448e6 ff.). This is significant because a definition of a craft, stated in terms of knowledge of how to bring about a specific product, will tell us what knowledge is relevant to the possession of that craft. If health is the *ergon* of the physician's craft, then the knowledge in virtue of which one is a physician is knowledge of whatever is relevant to the production of health. This will of course include the definition of "medicine," since obviously the physician needs to know what his or her craft is. Moreover, it will include knowledge of what external items are needed to bring about health in each particular instance. Finally, such knowledge will include knowledge of what techniques must be employed to bring about health. So, by ascertaining the *ergon* of a craft, we can find out something about what sort of non-definitional knowledge is necessary to be an actual practitioner of that craft.

At this point, the possibility of stating what Socrates would count as wisdom may not be as remote as might have appeared at first. Surely one of the things the morally wise person knows is the full range of things by which one possesses each of the other virtues. Thus, if we were able to say with some assurance what Socrates takes to be the proper definition of the other virtues, we could say, in a general way, what sorts of things Socrates thinks wisdom encompasses. Now as we have argued elsewhere, a definition of "piety," expressed in terms of knowledge of how to produce a certain *ergon*, can be pieced together from various remarks Socrates makes in the *Apology* and the *Euthyphro*, which Socrates thinks can likely survive elenctic scrutiny.[46] We would do well, then, briefly to review the definition and the reasons which incline us to think Socrates accepts it.

2.5.2   The Socratic Conception of Piety

First, according to Plato's *Apology*, Socrates regards himself as innocent of the charge of impiety, not simply because he thinks he is innocent of each of the three accusations which have been formally made against him, but also because he undertook the very actions which have aroused the antipathy of Anytus, Meletus, and Lycon out of a sense of obedience to the god (*Ap.* 28e4–6, 29d3–4, 37e6). He says the god commanded him to do these things (*Ap.* 30a5, 33c4–7), and thus his philosophizing is no less than a mission he performs for the god (*Ap.* 21e5, 22a4, 23c1, 30a6–7), which makes him the god's "gift" to Athens (*Ap.*

46. Brickhouse and Smith [1989b], 91–96.

30d7–e1, 31a8). At the very least, Socrates is prepared to say that his philosophical activities are pious.[47]

Now, in the *Euthyphro*, Socrates professes not to know what piety is, and (no doubt ironically) invites the confident Euthyphro to teach him what it is (*Euthphr.* 5a3–4, 5c4–d5, 9a1–2, 12e1–4, 14b9–c3, 15e5–16a4). Euthyphro obviously has no idea how to give Socrates such instruction. Instead, we soon enough find Socrates taking the lead in formulating the definition (see *Euthphr.* 7c12–d1, 9c1–d5, 11e1–4, 12d5, 12e9). He even brings Euthyphro to a point where Socrates says (perhaps ironically) that Euthyphro was close to answering Socrates' question and thus completing Socrates' education about piety (*Euthphr.* 14b8–c4).

Socrates' role in the argument with Euthyphro has been a matter of controversy. Because Socrates "must follow the one questioned wherever he leads" (see *Euthphr.* 14c3–4), it may seem to follow that Socrates cannot take the lead in any examination. According to this view, the *Euthyphro* tells us nothing about *Socrates*' conception of piety; instead, the dialogue tells us only what is wrong with Euthyphro's conception.[48] We shall call this the "skeptical" interpretation of the *Euthyphro*.

A number of scholars have argued against the skeptical interpretation of the *Euthyphro*, however, concluding that Socrates' contributions to the conversation do betray his own beliefs.[49] We believe that this latter view, which we shall call the "constructive" interpretation, provides a more plausible interpretation of the text. But there is a special reason to take Socrates' contributions in the *Euthyphro* as expressing genuine Socratic beliefs: the picture of Socrates' conception of piety that we get from the remarks he makes in the *Euthyphro* allows us more clearly to understand his defense in the *Apology*. The grounds on which Socrates bases his arguments to the jurors, in our view, fit well with the hints he gives to Euthyphro. Because we take what Socrates tells his jurors as a serious representation of the Platonic Socrates' moral and philosophical commitments, we regard their fit with Socrates' contributions in the *Euthyphro* as evidence for the constructive interpretation.

2.5.3 Piety in the Euthyphro *and* Apology

Without repeating all of the arguments we previously advanced for this position, it may be worthwhile briefly to review the passage at *Euthyphro* 11e1–14c3.

47. In our understanding of Socratic epistemology, Socrates' complete confidence that his philosophical activities are pious does not present a problem for his assertions that he is not wise. As we explained in sections 2.1.4–5, Socrates' epistemology allows for the claim that one can be utterly certain that some particular activity x is virtuous without being able to say what it is about x that makes it an instance of virtue.

48. Those who think that the *Euthyphro* is entirely negative and tells us nothing about Socrates' conception of piety include Allen [1970], 56–58; Kraut [1983b]; Robin [1935], 254–55; and Shorey [1933], 78–79.

49. Those who use the *Euthyphro* to support a positive conception of piety include: Adam [1908]; Bonitz [1966], 233–34; Brickhouse and Smith [1983], and [1989b], 91–100; Burnet [1924], 82–142;

There Socrates gives aid to the confused "expert," Euthyphro, by pursuing a number of Socrates' own suggestions about piety.

The passage begins with Socrates proposing that piety is a part, but not the whole, of justice (11e2–12a2).[50] Euthyphro proposes that it is that part of justice concerning attention ($\vartheta\varepsilon\rho\alpha\pi\varepsilon\acute{\iota}\alpha$) to the gods; the remainder of justice, he says, concerns attention to human beings (12e5–8). Socrates shows no hesitation in agreeing with Euthyphro's suggestion, but suggests that the definition is not yet complete, for the notion of "attention" has yet to be explained.

Socrates then compares piety to various crafts involving attention to various things, the horseman's attention to horses (13a4–8), the huntsman's attention to dogs (13a9–b1); and the oxherd's attention to oxen (13b2–6). It appears, by these models, that each craft aims at producing some specific good or benefit. More important, Socrates specifically says that Euthyphro will complete the definition of piety by specifying the benefit produced by the craft of piety (13e10–11). Although Euthyphro agrees that piety is a craft, he finds one reason he cannot characterize it in the same way as he would the models of horsemanship, huntsmanship, and oxherding: these other crafts are concerned to improve those beings to which they attend (horses, dogs, and oxen, respectively). But no one can improve a god (13c6–d3). Once again, Socrates agrees.

So Socrates asks if perhaps Euthyphro meant something else by "attention to the gods," and Euthyphro proposes another sort of model—the attention of slave to master (13d4–6). This model avoids the problem of the earlier ones, for the slave is not supposed to improve his master, but only to carry out his master's wishes. Accordingly, the pious person does not seek to improve the gods, but only to carry out the gods' wishes.

Socrates shows no signs of skepticism about the suitability of this model, but does ask to know what "all-glorious product" ($\pi\acute{\alpha}\gamma\kappa\alpha\lambda o\nu$ $\acute{\varepsilon}\rho\gamma o\nu$) the gods wish to produce by employing the pious person as their servant (13e10–11). Euthyphro is at sea on this point and Socrates scolds him:

> You are not eager to teach me; that is clear. For just now when you were on it, you turned away. Had you answered it, I should already have learned piety sufficiently from you. (*Euthphr.* 14b9–c3)

If we take Socrates' various contributions to this discussion as genuine expressions of his own opinions, we find that Socrates sees the pious person as being like a servant regarding the gods, and like a craftsman in helping the gods to produce some "all glorious" benefit.

The specific product of piety is never revealed and thus the definition is left incomplete. But if we compare what we do get from the *Euthyphro* with Socrates' characterization of his activities in the *Apology*, we find striking similarities. He tells the jurors that he has performed as the god's servant in his philosophical mission (*Ap.* 21e5, 22a4, 23c1, 30a6–7), for the god commanded him to act as he has (*Ap.* 30a5, 33c4–7).

Friedländer [1964], vol. 2, 82–91; Heidel [1900]; Irwin [1977] 1–131; Jowett [1953], vol. 1, 303–8; Rabinowitz [1958]; Shorey [1933] 74–80; A. E. Taylor [1927], 146–56; C.C.W. Taylor [1982].

50. Socrates makes a very similar claim at *Grg.* 507a5–b4.

Moreover, in his response to the news of the oracle to Chairephon, Socrates shows that he was following the same conception of piety as the one we find him sketching in the *Euthyphro*. When he first hears of the oracle, he does what he can to understand its meaning. He expresses the urgency of this response when he says that he must assign "the god's business the highest importance" (21e4–5). And when he is satisfied that he has come to understand the real meaning of the oracle, his response is to "give aid to the god," by "undertaking a service on the god's behalf" (23b7–c1). It is plain, moreover, that he regards his mission as promoting some great benefit to the city, for he says he considers himself a "gift from the god" (*Ap.* 30d7–e1, 31a8), who deserves nothing less than the city's greatest honor as a reward for his life of pious service (*Ap.* 36b3–37a1).

But what is the "all-glorious benefit" that Socrates regards himself as promoting in Athens? Of course, an authoritative answer to this question is impossible to give, for in the very dialogues in which we might hope to gain some evidence from which to infer an answer, Socrates repeatedly professes not to know the definitions of moral terms. Because Socrates lacks wisdom, he does not possess a moral craft and thus cannot produce the "all-glorious benefit." But it does not follow from the fact that Socrates is unable to produce an *ergon* that he is has no conception of what that *ergon* is, nor does it follow that he cannot promote that *ergon* as best he can. It would be helpful to know, then, what, if anything, Socrates would say the object of the craft of piety is.

2.5.4 *The* Ergon *of Piety*

We believe that it is unlikely that Socrates is completely in the dark about how to characterize the *ergon* of the pious individual's activity undertaken on behalf of the god. Moreover, we believe that Socrates' mission is directed at the promotion of this *ergon*. But because he lacks craft-knowledge himself, Socrates cannot unfailingly produce this *ergon*, as the craftsman of piety would. Now one way of characterizing the goal of Socrates' philosophical activity is the persuasion of all who think they are wise when they are not to abandon their pretense of wisdom and to pursue real wisdom. Moreover, as we shall show in section 4.2.1, there is a perfectly straightforward sense in which real wisdom, moral wisdom, can truly be called an "all-glorious benefit," for Socrates believes that wisdom occupies a preeminent place among all other goods. So anyone who could provide or lead another to wisdom has the power to bestow the greatest benefit a human can receive.

In claiming that Socrates thinks that the product of wisdom in others is the product of the pious individual's craft, we are not asserting that Socrates *knows* the definition of piety. We are simply claiming that Socrates finds the conception of piety partially stated towards the end of the *Euthyphro* to be more plausible than any he has heard from Euthyphro and others who profess to know what piety is. Moreover, it should now be clear that even if Socrates were actually to *know* the definition of piety, he would still insist that he is not pious, for, as we have argued, knowledge of the definition of the term naming a particular craft is not sufficient to make one a practitioner of that craft. Because piety is like a craft, the pious person is able to perform his or her function unfailingly. Now if we are right, Socrates believes that the *ergon* of the craft of piety is the improvement of the souls of others. But, because the *elenchos* is the only way Socrates has of attempting to improve the souls of others, and because (as we argued in chapter 1) the *elenchos* is not itself a craft, Socrates lacks a technique through which he can unfailingly produce what he thinks the gods want produced through his mission. Plainly, then, even if Socrates would say that he knows the definition of virtue, he would still lack knowledge of *how* to produce the good at which virtue aims, and thus lack virtue.

2.5.5 Piety and the Unity of the Virtues

Thus far we have argued that Socrates believes that piety consists in the knowledge of how to give aid to the gods in promoting wisdom in other human beings. It follows that Socrates also believes that the knowledge possessed by the pious person constitutes at least part of the content of moral wisdom itself. At this point someone might object that if our view is accepted, then one would have to reject Socrates' famous commitment to the unity of the virtues, for Socrates says that piety is only a "part" of justice, and thus it would seem to follow that there is a part of justice that is non-pious. But, if so, it seems to follow from our view that Socrates thinks it is possible for someone to be just but not pious, a consequence which conflicts with the unity doctrine.[51]

It might be tempting to think that we can defeat this objection by arguing that, for Socrates, the phrase "piety is a part of justice" means that "piety" and "justice" simply have different *intensions*, the former entailing but not entailed by the latter; the *extensions* of the two terms, however, are identical. Were this what Socrates has in mind, he may grant that a person's acting piously entails that the gods are aided, whereas a person's acting justly entails no such thing, although it is nonetheless true that whenever a person acts justly the gods are, as a matter of fact, aided.

There is good reason to reject this way of escaping the objection, however. When Socrates himself illustrates what he means by saying that piety is a part of justice, he uses as examples the relationships between fear and reverence and then between odd numbers and numbers (*Euthphr.* 12c2–8). Not only do the paired terms have different intensions,[52] but they obviously have different extensions as well. Thus, unless his own examples are thoroughly misleading, it seems highly

51. A detailed review of the texts pertinent to Socrates' conception of what has come to be known as "the unity of virtues" may be found in Penner [1973]. (See also Penner [1992].) It will become obvious that we do not entirely accept Penner's own solution to the problems these texts raise. (See next note.)

52. Penner [1973] and [1992] argues that Socrates' conception of unity requires him to believe that each of the virtues is identical to each of the others. We will argue that there is *a sense* in which this is true, but this passage from the *Euthyphro* cannot be accounted for on Penner's strict identity account. If the relationship between piety and justice is like the relationship between odd numbers and numbers, it cannot be that piety = justice, for, plainly, it is not the case that odd numbers = numbers.

unlikely that Socrates thinks "piety" and "justice" have different intensions, but apply to all and only members of the same set of acts and objects.

But perhaps we need to be more careful about what is meant by the assumption, which seems to underlie the unity doctrine, that "piety" and "justice" and indeed all particular virtue names refer to the same thing. In the *Laches* (199e6–7), Socrates says that courage is "one part of virtue." In this passage it is clear that Socrates does not mean that "courage" can be used interchangeably with the other virtue names, for otherwise Socrates would not go on to ridicule the definition of courage as the "knowledge of good and evil—past, present, and future." Knowledge with this universal scope, Socrates thinks, is plainly too broad to be courage. Courage, it appears, concerns only future goods and evils (199b9–11), whereas the whole of virtue encompasses a knowledge of goods and evils—past, present, and future (199b11–c1). The implication at the end of the *Laches* is that at least one virtue, courage, differs in scope from at least one of the other individual virtues (whichever one might be said to concern past or present evils, for example). If so, we have additional reason to think that Socrates' suggestion in the *Euthyphro* that "piety is a part of justice" is precisely what he means, in spite of the implication that the extension of "justice" is broader than that of "piety." Indeed, taking the referents of some virtue terms to have broader extensions than others seems to be the only way to understand the implication of Socrates' remark in the *Protagoras* (329d7–8) that at least some of the virtues are different in size.

2.5.6 Wisdom and the Unity of the Virtues

In our account of Socrates' understanding of piety, we explored Socrates' suggestion that the definition of piety must specify its *ergon*. In our view, different parts of virtue—and different parts of one virtue—will aim at different *erga*. But, even so, it cannot be that these *erga* are produced by different psychic conditions, for that would plainly conflict with Socrates' suggestion in the *Protagoras* (329d4–8) that the parts of virtue are related to each other in the way pieces of gold are related to each other, "differing only in their greatness and smallness." If the *Protagoras* is to be consistent with the *Euthyphro* and the *Laches,* somehow it has to be shown how different virtue names can refer to the same psychic condition and still have different *erga* as part of their definitions.

One response might be to argue that virtue itself and the individual virtues are related to each other in the way that one large discipline such as economics is nothing but the collection of a number of "interconnected" subdisciplines such as welfare economics and micro-economics.[53] In this analogy, virtue would turn out to be the total collection of "interconnected" particular virtues, each of which is concerned with a somewhat different set of moral issues from the others, but which when taken with the others combine to make a unified theory of morality.

There are a number of reasons for rejecting the discipline/subdisciplines anal-

---

53. This is the analogy Kraut adopts to explain in what sense the particular virtues are "unified" ([1983b], 261–62).

ogy, however. First, there is no reason to accord any special status to any of the subdisciplines which make up the field of economics. But Socrates does seem to accord one of the individual virtues, wisdom, a special status with respect to the other particular virtues: each virtue other than wisdom can achieve its specific *ergon* only if its possessor is directed by wisdom. But, second and more importantly, the discipline/subdisciplines analogy fails to fit the gold/pieces of gold analogy endorsed by Socrates in the *Protagoras*. The gold/pieces of gold analogy strongly suggests that the moral expertise constituting piety and courage, for example, is identical. Expertise in micro-economics and expertise in macro-economics, while overlapping at key points, are hardly identical. Plainly, one could be an expert in micro-economics without being an expert in macro-economics. But, according to the *Protagoras* at least, one cannot be pious without being just, temperate, wise, and courageous.[54]

We believe that the gold/pieces of gold analogy endorsed by Socrates in the *Protagoras* can be reconciled with his claims, in the *Euthyphro* and *Laches*, that different particular virtues have different scopes. To see how, we must first keep in mind that wisdom occupies a special place among the particular virtues in that all of the other particular virtues *are* in some sense wisdom. To see what that sense is, it will be helpful to consider the relationship between wisdom and the other particular virtues as analogous to the relationship between a general discipline and the specialized applications of that discipline to different areas. Consider the various uses of triangulation, for example. Navigators in coastal waters use triangulation to fix their positions by taking bearings from various objects along the coastline. Surveyors also use triangulation in measuring land and setting boundaries. In using triangulation, coastal navigators and surveyors plainly use the same skill. But it is equally plain that they use this skill in application to different sorts of problems and in different contexts—that is why we don't call a coastal navigator "a surveyor" and why we don't call a surveyor "a coastal navigator." So we can readily distinguish surveying problems from coastal navigation problems, even though their solutions will come from applications of the very same skill, triangulation. Moreover, it is not that the surveyor uses a different *kind* of triangulation from the coastal navigator; it is not as if there are subdisciplines of triangulation, such that the surveyor uses one and the coastal navigator uses another. It is, in fact, just the very same skill each uses. Their use of this skill, however, produces different *erga:* in the case of surveying, it produces land measurements and border identifications; in the case of coastal navigation, it produces identifications of the positions of ships along coastlines.

So wisdom, on this view, stands in relation to the other virtues in a way similar to the relation of triangulation to surveying and coastal navigation. There is no surveying or coastal navigation (of the relevant sorts) without triangulation; similarly, there is no courage or temperance without wisdom. There is a sense in which surveying and coastal navigation *just are* triangulation; and there is a similar sense in which courage and temperance *just are* wisdom. But there is also a

54. Kraut recognizes that his analogy fails to fit the gold/pieces of gold analogy in the *Protagoras*. His response, however, is to suggest that "it is a mistake to press . . . the analogy too far" ([1983b], 262, n.29).

sense in which surveying is *not* the same as coastal navigation, and that lack of sameness would appropriately be reflected in their different definitions. So similarly, there is a sense in which courage is *not* the same as temperance. They are *not* the same, because even though it is the same skill/knowledge/wisdom involved, it is applied in each case in a different context, and to different sorts of problems, and its different applications produce different *erga*. Moreover, these different *erga* would be appropriately reflected in different definitions of the virtues.

If we are right, Socrates conceives of the virtuous person in a way that makes him or her like the person who knows triangulation: he or she has wisdom—knowledge of good and evil—which he or she can apply in solving very different sorts of moral problems. For example, when the problems concern what is or is not to be feared, the application of wisdom to find the solution is called "courage." When the problems concern helping the gods to benefit human beings, the application of wisdom to find the solution is called "piety." If this is correct, we can see why Socrates would think that each particular virtue name refers to the same thing, wisdom, and also why he thinks that the particular virtues have different scopes. Like pieces of gold, each of the particular virtues is really the same thing; yet the virtuous person can act justly without thereby performing an act of courage or piety or temperance.

The analogy to specialized applications of general skills also allows us to see how one can accept "unity," while insisting that the various skills or virtues can be related as parts to wholes. Notice that one might subdivide surveying into two parts: one which identifies boundaries, and one which measures parcels of land. In this case, we might use different names for each subdivision. But one can imagine an example where one would use the generic name for one such subdivision, but a different name for another subdivision: one might, for example, subdivide coastal navigation into a part which charts positions relative to seacoasts (which we might simply call "coastal navigation"), and a part which charts positions relative to riverbanks or landmarks in harbors (in which the same skill is used, but which we might call "river navigation," or "harbor navigation"). So, too, one might subdivide justice (the virtue which applies wisdom regarding good and evil in producing proper behavior relative to other morally significant beings and their interests) into a part which produces proper behavior relative to the gods and their interests (which we would call "piety"), and a part which produces proper behavior relative to human beings (which we would simply call "justice").

Wisdom, then, is what is common to all of the virtues. One who possesses this virtue will possess them all, for anyone who is wise will recognize what he or she should do in all morally relevant circumstances and contexts. Moreover, one must possess wisdom in order to possess *any* of the other virtues; one cannot be courageous or temperate without having wisdom. So it is that no one can have any one of the virtues without having all of the others. For no one can be virtuous in any way without being wise,[55] and if one is wise, one can use one's wisdom to produce all of the different moral *erga*.

55. We are indebted to Harlan B. Miller for help in formulating the examples we used in this section. He is not responsible for—and may not agree with—the interpretation we use such examples to articulate and clarify.

2.5.7   Final Remarks

Socrates sometimes says he is wholly ignorant of the subject about which he and his interlocutors speak. In saying this he means that he knows neither the definition of that subject's central term nor any other truth about the subject. Sometimes he may think he knows certain "trivial and commonplace" things about the subject. But if our argument in this chapter is right, nothing that Socrates can truly claim to know would count as making him possess that which is most precious: moral wisdom. We have explored the various ways in which Socrates expresses both ignorance and knowledge and have offered an interpretation according to which all of these expressions may be understood as consistent. In addition, we believe that the view we have attributed to Socrates makes good philosophical sense, for surely one can know a thing or two, but not be wise. We do not suppose that Socrates was unique in his acute awareness of this difference; indeed, it has been a feature of our interpretation that the distinction on which it relies would have been readily recognized by Socrates' interlocutors and by Plato and his readers. The use Socrates makes of this distinction, however, and the conclusions he drew from it, are quite another matter. His genius, after all, was always precisely this: employing only views with which even his interlocutors would agree, often "trivial and commonplace" observations, which "anyone could know," Socrates won himself a place among the pantheon of western philosophers.

3

Socratic Psychology

3.1 What One Really Believes

3.1.1 Discord in the Soul

Socrates' investigations often reduce his interlocutors to *aporia* by showing that his interlocutor's responses to his questions are inconsistent. The interlocutor must recognize and resolve the inconsistencies in his beliefs, or his whole life will be in discord. So Socrates warns Callicles:

> This son of Cleinias [sc. Alcibiades] is one who says now this and now that, but Philosophy always says the same things. She says what now surprises you. . . .
> So either refute her, as I said just now, and show that doing injustice and doing injustice without punishment are not the greatest of evils, or, if you allow (what I say) to be unrefuted, by the dog, the god of the Egyptians, Callicles will not agree with you, O Callicles, but will be in conflict in your whole way of living. But I think, O best of men, that it is better to have my lyre, or a chorus that I might produce, out of tune and discordant, and to have most people disagree with me and contradict me, than that I, one man, be discordant with myself and contradict myself. (*Grg.* 482a6–c3)

A number of things in this passage should strike us as odd. (1) Why is Callicles condemned to conflict within himself if he leaves Philosophy unrefuted? Socrates has not (or at least not yet) established that Callicles believes any inconsistent set of propositions; Callicles has just joined the conversation. For Callicles to be in discord with himself, Callicles must have inconsistent views or inconsistent impulses. Moreover, one of Callicles' beliefs must be the one accepted by Philosophy. How does Socrates know that Callicles has such beliefs? (2) Before he began talking with Socrates, Callicles was aware of no confusion or discord within his beliefs. Indeed, we never meet an interlocutor in Plato's early dialogues who comes to Socrates already aware of some confusion within his own views. The confusion becomes evident only after one has talked with Socrates for a while. Why should the interlocutor not suppose, as a number of them do, that the confusion is simply the result of the discussion with Socrates, and not some fundamental conflict they have unknowingly suffered all along? (3) What right does Socrates have to say that Philosophy herself holds the view that Callicles must disprove? Why does Socrates characterize Philosophy in terms of the *consistency* of beliefs, and how does Socrates know what Philosophy, in his personification of it, believes? Finally, (4) what does Socrates think is so awful about being

73

confused in the way he claims Callicles is? That is, why is it so destructive to hold inconsistent beliefs?

In this chapter, we shall explore these and other questions by showing how they can be linked to Socrates' conception of the Delphic injunction "Know Thyself."[1] We shall pay special attention to the attribution of psychological states that Socrates makes in a number of discussions to persons who are typically unaware of having them. We shall argue that although Socrates recognizes just how paradoxical these attributions are, he is convinced that they are accurate.[2] Accordingly, we shall attempt to show the ground for each paradoxical attribution. If we are right, Socrates thinks that the psychological states that Socratic examination uncovers are features of the very same self the Delphic god through the injunction "Know thyself" commands all men to discover.

3.1.2   Socrates and Polus: Delivering an Unexpected Offspring

At *Gorgias* 471e1, Polus accuses Socrates of being disingenuous (Callicles later echoes the charge—*Grg.* 495a7–b1). Socrates responds by turning the tables on Polus, claiming that he will produce Polus as a witness against Polus in Polus' disagreement with Socrates (*Grg.* 471e2–472c2). The cases are not really parallel: Polus accuses Socrates of mendacity, since he suspects Socrates of purposefully misrepresenting his own views to avoid being caught in a contradiction. But when Socrates turns the tables on Polus, he does not suggest that Polus is being dishonest about his own views; rather, Socrates claims that he can show Polus something about Polus that Polus does not suspect about himself. Odd as it seems at first, Socrates is claiming that Polus is misrepresenting *Polus'* view of the matter (*Grg.* 474a5–b10). The argument concludes with Polus' reluctant acceptance of Socrates' characterization:

> Soc.: Then I was speaking the truth when I said that neither I nor you nor any other person would choose injustice over suffering it, for it happens to be worse.
>
> Pol.: Apparently.
>
> Soc.: You see, then, Polus, that when this refutation is contrasted with that refutation, they appear not at all similar. Whereas everyone else agrees with you except me, you alone, being one, are enough for me, agreeing and being my witness. Having put the question to you alone for a vote, I let the others go. (*Grg.* 475e3–476a2)

3.1.3   Producing Polus as a Witness

It is often said that Socratic examination functions *ad hominem*. Strong confirmation of this comes from Socrates' own characterization of what he has done with

---

1. See *Charm.* 164d4–5; *Prt.* 343b3; *Phdr.* 229e5–6; *Phil.* 48c10; *Laws* XI.923a3–5; [*Alc.* I] 124a7–b1, 129a2–3, 132c10.

2. Contrast Irwin's remark ([1979], note on 466a9, 137) about one case of such an attribution: "Socrates states his reply in deliberately and *misleadingly* paradoxical terms." We do not deny that Socrates' statements are often deliberately paradoxical, designed to pique his interlocutor into follow-

Polus: he has begun and ended using only Polus as his witness and judge. What others might agree or disagree with in his argument is of no concern. But within his argument with Polus we find a few very general claims about all of humankind; everyone, says Socrates, *believes* that doing wrong is worse than suffering it, and that escaping punishment is worse than incurring it (*Grg.* 474b2–5), and no one would *choose* to do wrong rather than suffer it, if those were their choices (*Grg.* 475e2–6). We shall look at these features of the argument in order.

Socrates began by saying that Polus could be called as a witness to testify for what Polus vehemently denied, namely, that to suffer evil is preferable to doing it. (For the sake of brevity, let us call this position "SPD," for "suffering is preferable to doing," and the contrary position Polus initially advocated "DPS," for "doing is preferable to suffering.") How shall we characterize Polus' cognitive state regarding the position to which the argument with Socrates leads him? Did he in fact believe SPD all along, without any awareness of his belief? Or is it rather that he begins by believing DPS and then changes his mind, coming to see that his other beliefs entail SPD? Or might Polus' belief in SPD best be characterized in still another way?

Socrates makes the very audacious claim that Polus can be produced as a witness for SPD, despite Polus' incredulity. But in virtue of what will Polus become Socrates' witness? Socrates might suppose that he could lead Polus to become Socrates' witness just in virtue of Socrates' own ability to *convince* Polus of SPD.[3] This would make Socrates an extremely impressive rhetorician, for he would be convincing one who is very reluctant to be persuaded. That this is not the way Socrates construes the answers he elicits from Polus is evident from the way in which he puts the original challenge to Polus; he attributes the belief in SPD to Polus and "all other people" (*Grg.* 474b2–5). So unless we think that Socrates is insincere in making this attribution, we must suppose that he does not see himself as convincing Polus of anything that Polus does not *already* believe. To employ the midwife image, Socrates will not be delivering any offspring that is not already Polus'.

3.1.4 *Inconsistent versus Contradictory or Contrary Beliefs*

There is still another way in which Socrates might claim Polus as a witness: he might think that Polus already has within him certain beliefs from which Socrates can derive SPD.[4] From this it follows that Polus holds an inconsistent set of beliefs, for Polus claims to reject SPD and yet he is revealed as having beliefs

---

ing the argument, and perhaps to add to the interlocutor's feeling of shame when he discovers the extent of his own confusion. We would not accept the claim—though Irwin may not be making it— that Socrates ever intends to mislead his interlocutors through paradox. On this point, we agree fully with Vlastos ([1991], ch. 5). A contrasting view may perhaps be found in Teloh ([1986], see, e.g., 36).

3. See, for example, Irwin's description of the *elenchos* ([1979], note on 473b10, 152) as *inducing* belief in the interlocutor.

4. See, for example, Vlastos [1983a], esp. 52. See also Irwin's description in [1979], note on 466a, 139.

entailing SPD. It does not follow, however, that Polus *already believes* SPD. It is common enough for one to have inconsistent beliefs about a subject. This happens whenever some of one's beliefs have entailments that contradict other beliefs one holds or their entailments. Until those entailments and the contradictions they constitute are brought to one's attention, however, one might never be aware of the inconsistency within one's beliefs. And it might take some rather sophisticated reasoning to uncover the inconsistency. Most if not all of us, we may suppose, suffer from precisely this condition on a number of subjects; we are not aware of what the inconsistencies are yet, but we cannot consistently hold all of the beliefs we presently hold.

It is quite another thing to hold a pair of contradictory beliefs, or (as perhaps in this case) both of a pair of contrary beliefs. This is clearly a different condition from the ubiquitous case of holding what can in principle be shown to be an inconsistent set of beliefs. In order to hold contradictory or contrary beliefs, one must in some way be prepared to affirm both beliefs, even though both plainly cannot be true.

Socrates, as we have said, paradoxically attributes the belief in SPD to Polus, despite Polus' vehement denials. Still another way in which Socrates might do this is if he supposed that Polus does not really believe DPS at all, but only SPD, and that Polus was somehow misrepresenting his own convictions. In this case, Polus' pertinent beliefs would not be contradictory or directly contrary; they might not even be inconsistent. It is certain, however, that at this point in the argument, Polus does believe DPS (see *Grg.* 472d4, 473b1).[5] If he didn't, we would have no way of explaining his apparent willingness actually to pursue the ignoble goals he espouses.

It is important to notice that in claiming that Polus believes DPS Socrates does not deny that Polus also believes SPD. Moreover, Polus is acutely aware that DPS and SPD are incompatible claims; this is why he is incredulous when Socrates promises to produce Polus as a witness for SPD. But from the fact that Polus sincerely believes DPS, it does not follow that he does not believe SPD. He may indeed also believe SPD, in which case he has directly contrary beliefs, although he is not (yet) aware of it. Because Socrates concedes that Polus believes in DPS, but also attributes the belief in SPD to Polus, then, he is characterizing Polus as being in this very paradoxical condition—it is not merely that Polus has inconsistent beliefs; Polus actually believes both of a pair of contraries.

3.1.5   What Does Polus Really Believe?

But in what sense does Polus actually believe SPD? Given the distinction we have made between having inconsistent beliefs and having contradictory or contrary beliefs, we are in a position to see why it is not enough simply to characterize Polus' belief in SPD as identical to acceptance of propositions from which SPD

5. In fact, in neither of these cases does Socrates attribute to Polus the specific belief in DPS, but rather, those beliefs which Polus (rightly) sees as supporting his belief in DPS—that the wicked Archelaus is happy, and that Socrates had been refuted when he maintained that wrongdoers were wretched.

can be derived, as some have tried to do.[6] If this is all that Socrates means by claiming that Polus believes SPD, what Socrates is saying is not merely paradoxical; it is false, for as we have said, we often have beliefs which entail a contradiction without actually believing one or the other of the pair of contradictories. So even though, as the argument shows, Polus does believe a number of things from which SPD can be derived, there must be more to say about Polus' acceptance of SPD than the fact that he has beliefs from which SPD can be derived.

In order to get at what more there is to say in this regard, let us distinguish several different ways in which witnesses called in support of a position may prove unhelpful. A witness might be unhelpful because he is caught in a lie. Such a witness is guilty of perjury. Still another witness might be unhelpful simply because he cannot maintain a consistent story on the matter about which he is testifying; he turns out to be confused. Such a witness turns out to have nothing to offer the side he was supposed to support, but he also may provide nothing of substance to the opposing side. There is still another sort of unhelpful witness, one who actually gives testimony in support of the opposing side.

So, what sort of witness is Polus for himself? He is not caught in a lie—he did not perjure himself, for he honestly believed everything he professed to believe. But he cannot maintain a consistent story in his testimony; to that extent he is unhelpful as a witness for DPS. But there is more; Socrates actually turns Polus into a witness for SPD. Thus, it is not merely that Polus cannot consistently provide testimony for DPS; the testimony Polus gives favors SPD. Socrates has not merely discredited an initially hostile witness; he has actually shown him to be a witness for Socrates' case.

A number of scholars have noted that, logically speaking, at the end of an elenctic argument, the interlocutor is free to go back and withdraw his assent to one of the premises that led to the conclusion he tried to resist. Indeed, Socrates often invites his interlocutors to do just this (see, e.g., *Euthphr.* 11b2, 13c11–d3; *Cri.* 49d9–e2; *Prt.* 354b7–355a5; *Grg.* 461c8–d3, 462a3, 482d7–e2; *Rep.* I.348b8–10). The interlocutor is not logically required to reject the position with which he began, and which Socrates targeted for refutation.[7] But with Polus, Socrates is convinced that his witness can be shown to prefer giving up the original proposition (DPS) rather than those premises which entail the unwanted conclusion (SPD). Hence, Socrates is convinced that Polus will resolve his difficulty by abandoning his belief in DPS.

In some elenctic arguments—for example, many of those which test proposed definitions of moral terms—the issue to be resolved does not involve choosing between two competing substantive claims, but rather between whether or not a single substantive claim can be made. So when Socrates tests Euthyphro's claim that piety is to be defined as doing whatever all the gods love (*Euthphr.* 9e1–11b1), this proposed definition is not competing with any other proposed

---

6. See, for example, Irwin [1979], note on 472ab, 151.
7. See Vlastos [1971b] and [1983a], 30, 38. We do not accept Vlastos's account [1983a] of how the *elenchos* is supposed to do more than establish inconsistency, though, as we argued in 1.4.3 above, the *elenchos* can also be used constructively.

definition. So in examining Euthyphro's testimony, as it were, Socrates is not attempting to convert the witness. There is no disputed competing position to which Euthyphro can be converted. Accordingly, Socrates does not attribute the belief in a competing position to Euthyphro, as he does with Polus.

So in what sense, then, does Polus believe in SPD at the beginning of the argument, the very time at which Polus most fervently disclaims believing SPD? It is not *just* that Polus has other beliefs entailing SPD; as we have noted, were that all Socrates means, there would be little reason for him to attribute the *belief* in SPD to Polus at the outset of the argument. What is also true of Polus at the beginning of the argument, however, is that—even though he, Polus, is unaware of it—he is *already* disposed to agree with Socrates about SPD. If he were to be made fully aware of all of the pertinent beliefs he *already* has, and if he is rational, Polus would affirm SPD and abandon his belief that DPS. Thus, even at the outset of the argument, Polus is disposed to agree with Socrates without requiring any additional evidence than what he already believes, in support of SPD and against DPS. Of course, at the end of his argument with Socrates, Polus is plainly not yet ready to admit publicly that he was initially wrong about what he believes. But Polus' failure to admit what Socrates says he actually believes derives solely from Polus' failure to be rational.

3.1.6   Self-Discovery: A Benefit of the Examined Life

The recipients of such Socratic examinations, are, ideally, chastened (see *Grg.* 505c3–4). But even if they are not, Socrates has given them an invaluable opportunity: they are now in a better position to follow the Delphic injunction "Know Thyself." Before their encounter with Socrates, they were not aware that the goals and precepts by which they lived their lives were inconsistent. Now, unless they are blindly hostile, they can see that they were confused all along. Their confusion is not simply the result of conversation with Socrates. Socrates has brought the confusion to light, but he has not introduced anything into his elenctic conversations that his interlocutors were not ready to accept as true.

By engaging his interlocutors as he does, Socrates gives them both opportunity and motive for the sort of introspective reflection that would allow them to deepen their self-knowledge beyond the simple recognition that they are confused. Polus, who began by accusing Socrates of dishonesty and by disavowing SPD, ends up being shown that he is mistaken on both counts: Polus is wrong about what Socrates believes and about what he himself believes. So Socrates gives Polus a lesson in better knowing Polus.[8]

We are now in a position to answer one of the questions we asked at the beginning of this discussion. We wondered what harm Socrates thought there was

---

8. This claim is made explicitly at *Grg.* 495e1–2. See also *Rep.* I.337c9–10, where Socrates talks about what he would discover to be his belief if he reflected on the subject. Plochmann and Robinson describe the phenomenon as follows: "The aim of Socrates in the *Gorgias* is quite evident: to raise the interior awareness of each of his three opponents [. . .] involving them in the very process whereby he himself has been able to elevate his own thinking" ([1988], 289).

in having inconsistent and, as it turns out, directly contradictory or contrary beliefs. Invariably in such cases, what the interlocutor *really* believes turns out to be the opposite of what the interlocutor originally introduced into the argument. In discovering this, the interlocutor gains something of value. Though he may not yet be able to tell whether what he turns out to believe is true, the interlocutor is in a far better position to lead a life that is consistent with what he really believes is best. The right-minded interlocutor now knows that he must follow what he turns out, on reflection, to believe, rather than what he would unreflectively have followed prior to the elenctic encounter with Socrates. Before being examined by Socrates, the interlocutor was more likely to act in the opposite way; for before the examination, the interlocutor was unreflectively inclined to suppose that the best way to act was in a manner he really thinks is evil and harmful. This much can now be seen plainly: Polus has not always acted in accordance with his own beliefs. He could not do so, for his convictions have been shown to include a pair of contraries. Notice that it follows from this that people do not always act in accordance with all of their convictions. Indeed, there may be no way for them to do so, for their convictions may be in discord. This plainly has consequences for any understanding of the Socratic paradoxes concerning the relations between people's actions and their beliefs, to which we shall return later in this chapter.

Of course, it is most unlikely that a single conversation with Socrates will substantially change the interlocutor. Polus, for example, is plainly very reluctant to accept the consequence of the argument Socrates has led him through. So long as the interlocutor does not continue to test his own opinions philosophically, whatever ground he gained from arguing with Socrates may soon be lost. Without leading the examined life, and thus without additional testing by means of the *elenchos,* one may never find oneself in the position really to know oneself, that is, to know exactly what one's own real beliefs are.

3.2   What Everyone Believes

3.2.1   *Socrates and Callicles: What Does Philosophy Tell Us?*

Let us now return to the puzzling passage at *Gorgias* 482a6–c3, with which we began. When Callicles expresses disbelief in the results of Socrates' argument with Polus, Socrates tells Callicles that he and Polus have arrived at the views of Philosophy itself. And Socrates warns Callicles that unless Callicles can refute Philosophy's view, "Callicles will not agree with you, O Callicles, but will be in conflict in your whole way of living."

At the outset, we pointed out that this passage is puzzling in a number of respects. Now, however, we are in a better position to explain Socrates' claims. The first thing we asked was this: how or why is Callicles condemned to discord within himself if he leaves Philosophy unrefuted? The answer is now obvious: given his first remarks to Socrates, Callicles has shown, to Socrates' satisfaction, that Callicles is in the same condition as Polus was in. Just as Polus did, Callicles says he believes DPS, which is why he says that the conclusion Socrates reached with Polus would turn the lives of human beings upside down (*Grg.* 481c1–4).

But Socrates is convinced, as he was in Polus' case, that Callicles also believes SPD. If Socrates is right in this diagnosis, then Callicles is indeed condemned to discord in his soul if he does not become aware of—and resolve—his confusion on this matter.

We also asked why Callicles, or any interlocutor, should accept Socrates' characterization of the result of the elenctic process. Socrates says that the confusion his interlocutors find themselves in is not his doing. Certainly a number of interlocutors are at least initially under the impression that Socrates himself has somehow created the confusion.[9] If Socrates is right—and such skeptical interlocutors are wrong—it must be that Socrates has contributed none of the premises of the argument; all the beliefs expressed by which the argument progressed had to have been the interlocutor's own. The interlocutor must say only what he himself believes.[10] If the interlocutor has followed this rule, and if in looking back over the argument the interlocutor can find nothing that Socrates himself added without the agreement of the interlocutor, then the interlocutor can be assured that the resulting confusion is indeed his own. Moreover, if the interlocutor finds that the view he had initially rejected is the one that, on reflection, he would maintain in favor of the view he originally proposed, then the interlocutor can also be assured that Socrates was right to say that the surviving view is the one the interlocutor "really" believes.

We have still not established how it is that Socrates can be so confident in attributing the belief in SPD to Polus and Callicles. Of course, it turns out that Polus does indeed end up testifying for SPD, just as Socrates had predicted. And though Callicles drags his feet and disavows his final contributions to the argument, we can see that he, too, was well on the way to admitting what he had originally found inconceivable. But though Socrates' attributions of belief in SPD to Polus and Callicles have been to some degree supported, we might well wonder why these attributions were made in the first place. Let us recall one of the surprising features of Socrates' discussion with Polus. When first claiming an incredulous Polus as his witness, Socrates does not merely claim that Polus actually believes SPD; Socrates says that *everyone* believes SPD (*Grg.* 474b2–5). So Socrates would attribute the belief in SPD to any interlocutor he might encounter, presumably before he knew anything else about the interlocutor. What makes him so sure of this?

3.2.2 *Philosophical Discovery through* Elenchos

Earlier in their discussion, Socrates had characterized himself as a lover of Philosophy, who always maintained the same view without regard to its popularity. After he has won his argument with Callicles, Socrates tells him how he knew

---

9. See, for example, *Euthphr.* 11b6–d2; *Grg.* 482c4–483a7, 489b7–c1, 497a6–b7, 505c5–6, 513c4–6, 516d4–5; *Rep.* I.340c5–d1, 341a5–b2, b8–c3, 350d9–e4, 354a10–13; [*Alc.* I] 112d10–113c4.

10. *Euthphr.* 9d7–8; *Cri.* 49c11–d1; *Prt.* 331c4–d1; *La.* 193c6–8; *Rep.* I.349a4–8; *Grg.* 458a1–b1, 495a5–9, 499b4–c6, 500b5–c1; [*Alc.* I] 114d11–e9.

that Philosophy always supported SPD: he has discussed this issue before, with other interlocutors, and none has ever been able to defend the position Polus and Callicles had initially proposed "without being ridiculous" (*Grg.* 509a7).

This passage strongly suggests that Socrates' confidence in his own view about the value of justice derives at least in part from the fact that he has previously examined others who were inclined to deny his view of the value of justice, always with the same result. Given Socrates' desire to examine all who claim to know how best to live, it is not unreasonable to suppose that Socrates has examined many interlocutors on this point who reflected a wide variety of conceptions of value. But none has turned out to be able to maintain anything other than SPD "without being ridiculous," that is, without ending up, like Polus and Callicles, testifying against their original position. So through his love and pursuit of philosophy, Socrates has come to be in a position to make an inductive generalization: everyone really believes SPD, though many also (unreflectively) believe DPS. Those who attempt to deny their belief in SPD will inevitably end up "being ridiculous," if they are put to Socratic examination.

Socrates' generalization, then, explains why he was so sure that he attributed the belief in SPD to Polus and Callicles and "all other people." It also explains why Socrates attributes the belief in SPD to Philosophy itself, at the beginning of his conversation with Callicles. By leading the examined life, that is, by practicing his elenctic mission in Athens every day, he has come to be in a position to make an induction which places SPD within everyone's beliefs. Just as important, moreover, is the evidence he has gained for supposing that when the interlocutor is confronted with this evidence, he does not seem willing or able to jettison SPD; even if the interlocutor attempts to escape this consequence by attempting another line of inquiry, the result is always the same in the end. So Socrates can conclude that *everyone*, upon reflection, believes SPD. Like Philosophy itself, everyone holds SPD every time he is examined.

3.2.3 *What We Really* Should *Believe*

Unless we suppose, however, that by coming to recognize what we really believe, we will also become better judges of what is really good for us, it is not clear how good the god's "gift" really is. It is conceivable that it will turn out that what we really believe is false, and that what we should believe—if we are to lead happy lives—is what we had unreflectively supposed before we engage in elenctic examination and, thereby, clarify our real commitments. If so, we should become a good deal worse off from leading the examined life; if what we really believe is evil, we would be better off following those precepts we would likely follow prior to reflection. So it must be a feature of the examined life not just that we clarify what we *really* believe, but that in doing so we invariably settle on beliefs that will help us to lead better lives. What permits Socrates to make this inference?

The first thing to notice in this regard is that Socrates' position is no different from any other inquirer's. Why indeed should any of us suppose that the views we come to through inquiry, though cleansed (at least relatively) of confusion and inconsistency, are in the end better than those we would have followed unreflectively without benefit of inquiry? One might say that it is just assumed that reflection and inquiry lead us to better opinions. Such is the position of what has come to be called the "progressivist" in science, for example. But is this assumption warranted, or is it simply a matter of faith?[11] Does Socrates have any particular reason to think he generates better opinions in his elenctic examinations of others?

At least this much can be said: by examining a variety of interlocutors, Socrates can gain ever more compelling inductive evidence for supposing that no one can maintain a coherent set of beliefs that includes DPS. Insofar as the maintenance of a coherent set of beliefs is desirable, the belief in DPS would appear to be undesirable. And since the belief in SPD appears to be something that no one—not even the toughest cases, such as Callicles—can reflectively disavow, Socrates is in a position to conclude that all human beings, regardless of what else they believe, upon reflection, value justice over injustice.[12]

There is a final point worth making in this connection. Socrates is convinced that in bringing an interlocutor to the awareness that the interlocutor, too, actually believes something that as a matter of fact all other persons happen to believe, he is really giving aid to the god, who he says assigned him a mission.[13] Since Socrates believes that all the gods are thoroughly moral,[14] and since an essential part of his mission is to make his interlocutors realize their own commitments to what, as it turns out, all persons believe, it is certain that Socrates sees the self-knowledge he makes possible as an enormous good.

3.2.4   Socrates and Protagoras: Interpreting What Simonides Means

We have argued that Socrates has come to believe, through an increasingly convincing induction, that we all believe SPD, whether we are aware of that fact or not. So even when a recalcitrant interlocutor reacts with outrage at Socrates' affirmation of SPD, Socrates is convinced that the interlocutor only needs to come to know himself better. The interlocutor does not really need to form a belief he does not already possess. In situations such as these, the interlocutor, as we have said, always proves to be a bad witness for his own beliefs. On the one hand, the interlocutor follows the Socratic rule and says only what he is aware of believing; but on the other hand, the interlocutor disclaims what he really believes. So the interlocutor does not express his beliefs in a way that makes them clear. He says the opposite of what he really believes. It takes a Socratic examination to bring out what is really on the interlocutor's mind.

Another example of this may be Socrates' interpretation of Simonides' meaning at *Protagoras* 339a6 and following. The views he attributes to Simonides seem not only to violate the obvious sense of Simonides' poetry, but to do so by

11. For a discussion, see Laudan [1977], 123–27.
12. See *Grg.* 473b10 and Irwin [1979], note on 473b10, 152.
13. See *Euthphr.* 6a6–8, 14e10–15a2; *Ap.* 21b6–7, 30a5–7, 31a6–b5, 41c9–d2. See also *Rep.* II.379b1–c7; Xen. *Mem.* 1.4.2–18. Gregory Vlastos characterizes this in [1989a], though he greatly exaggerates the tension between Socrates' view and civic cult religion (about which, see section 6.2).
14. See *Ap.* 23c1, 28e4, 29d3–4, 30a5–7, 30d5–e1, 30e5–6, 31a7–8, 33c4–7.

liberally rephrasing the poet's actual words. It is worth noting, however, that Socrates characterizes what he is doing as telling what *Simonides* means (as opposed to interpreting what Simonides' *words* mean), and that invariably what Simonides ends up meaning is suspiciously Socratic in tone and content. The justification for such a method of interpretation may be no other than the same principle by which he attributes beliefs to interlocutors initially reluctant to affirm them. The views Socrates attributes to Simonides are Simonides' in just the same way as the views Socrates attributes to Polus and Callicles, for example, are theirs. Thus, if Simonides were present to act as an interlocutor, he could be brought to see that Socrates' interpretation correctly represents what Simonides really believes. Because Simonides is not present, however, no one in attendance is in a position to judge confidently what the poet thinks (*Prt.* 347e3–7). So Socrates' attribution of intentions to the poet looks terribly paradoxical. But Socrates attributes only those beliefs which he supposes all of us hold. The result is that the only views Socrates is prepared to attribute to Simonides are views he would attribute to anyone at all. The need for the poet's voice is thus eliminated, and so we find Socrates quick to suggest eliminating it at the end of his interpretive harangue (*Prt.* 347e1–348a6; see also *Hip. Mi.* 365c8–d1).

We are not claiming that Socrates sincerely means everything he says about Simonides and the interpretation of poetry. Our view leaves open the possibility that in this section of the *Protagoras* Socrates is completely ironical about certain claims he appears to be making. Our point is only this: however implausible Socrates' interpretation may appear to be on its face, insofar as the poet was attempting to express his own beliefs, Socrates' interpretation attributes beliefs to Simonides which the *elenchos* would expose as what the poet truly believes. Thus, when what Simonides really intended is at issue, Socrates can claim to have helped clarify the poet's meaning through a "charitable" interpretation of his poem.[15]

3.3 What We Really Hold in High Regard

3.3.1   Socrates and Polus on What People Hold in High Regard

We have established that Socrates freely attributes certain beliefs to people who might unreflectively disclaim having such beliefs. The beliefs he attributes are those which he is convinced all persons hold, and he has discovered the nature of these beliefs and our commitment to them by examining great numbers and varieties of people. But Socrates does not just attribute cognitive states to people who appear not to have them; he also attributes affective states to people who appear not to have them and, conversely, denies attributions of affective states to those who would claim to possess them. Let us first consider an example of such a denial which we find Socrates making in his discussion with Polus in the *Gorgias*.

---

15. We are indebted in these remarks to Nickolas Pappas [1989]. Pappas's paper convinced us that there is a serious principle of interpretation at work in Socrates' remarks in this passage. Pappas does not necessarily agree, however, with our interpretation.

At 466a4, Polus and Socrates embark on an extremely complex series of arguments designed to determine whether or not rhetoric is a *technē*, whether or not its master practitioners, the orators, are worthy of respect, and whether or not the orators have any power worth having. In fact, however, each step of the argument is not about what things are actually worthy, but instead about what things we *hold* as worthy.[16] Polus takes the way we hold things to be transparent to us; he simply assumes that we know ourselves in the relevant ways. But Socrates denies this; Socrates contradicts Polus in each instance because Socrates is convinced that we are not transparent to ourselves.

The first topic under dispute between Socrates and Polus, at this stage of the argument, is whether rhetoric is only flattery. Polus is amazed to hear Socrates' opinion that it is not, and first endeavors to refute it by an appeal to popular opinion:

> POL.: Then do you believe that good orators are regarded as flatterers in their cities, and, hence, base?

Socrates teasingly accuses Polus of starting a speech, but then answers:

> SOC.: They do not seem to me to be held in any regard at all. (*Grg.* 466a9–b3)

Socrates' response here is interesting, for elsewhere he might have conceded Polus' point but insisted that it counted for nothing. Socrates often says he disregards the views of "the many," or what is commonly believed (see *Ap.* 31e1–3; *Cri.* 47a2–6, c8–d1, 48a5–10; *Grg.* 459a1–6, 476a1–2). Instead, he focuses exclusively either on what his interlocutor believes (recall Socrates' calling only Polus as his witness at *Grg.* 471e2–472c2, 474a5–b10, and 475e3–476a2; see also *Cri.* 49c11–d1) or on what both he and his interlocutor believe (see *Cri.* 49e1–4; *Prt.* 331c4–d1). Yet here at *Gorgias* 466a9–b3, rather than discount the view of "the many," Socrates refuses to attribute to them a psychological state which they would almost certainly suppose they possess: "the many," he claims, do not have any regard for good orators, whereas Polus is convinced that the orators are everywhere held in high regard.

3.3.2 Finding Out What We Hold in High Regard

Unless Socrates is appealing to an extraordinary sense of "regard," when he claims that people do not have any regard for the orators, his point is not paradoxical; it is simply false. As Polus says, "even a child" could refute Socrates (see *Grg.* 470c4–5), if all that is needed to refute him is the unreflective testimony of "the many." Polus manifestly holds the orators in the highest regard, and there is reason to believe that his attitude is widely shared. We suggest, however, that

16. Irwin [1979] translates the paradox away (reading "ὡς κόλακες . . . νομίζεσθαι") as "to count as flatterers" rather than "to regard as flatterers"; the latter does, and the former does not, obviously make a psychological attribution. As we noted above, Irwin claims that "Socrates states his reply in deliberately, and misleadingly, paradoxical terms" (see his note on 466ab in [1979], 137). We shall argue that there is a sense in which Socrates means what he says in all of his paradoxical attributions of psychological states.

here Socrates is not intending simply to report the unreflective feelings of regard ''the many'' may or may not have, but rather to identify those feelings of regard anyone would or would not have *if* they reflected on the matter clearly, as Socrates claims to have done. Socrates' view, then, is that if only people would consider the question philosophically, they would find in the end that they had no respect for orators at all; none of Polus' feelings of regard for them, that is, would survive the process of philosophical examination. Moreover, those coming to this recognition would not construe the lack of regard they discovered in themselves to be an *artifact* of philosophical reflection, but would claim instead that they never really did respect the sorts of people they *now recognize* orators as being. What would seem new to them is their recognition of what sorts of people orators are. Hence, people would view their lack of regard for the orators to be something they discovered within themselves.

3.3.3 ''Know Thyself''

The dispute between Socrates and Polus on this point turns out to be similar to the one we have already discussed concerning belief. Polus begins each argument assuming that we all know perfectly well what we believe and feel: we know ourselves, for all of our cognitive and affective states are transparent to us. Socrates denies this because he is convinced that if only we would engage seriously in examining ourselves through philosophy, each of us would discover that there is both a surprising variety of psychological states we possess and a variety we lack. Thus, Socrates believes that philosophical examination reveals to us those psychological states that make up our most profound cognitive and affective commitments. When the oracle enjoins us to ''Know Thyself,'' therefore, Socrates takes it to mean not only that we should be aware of our own ignorance, but also that we must lead the examined life in order to come to know what we do and do not believe and feel—to discover what we would identify as our most deeply held cognitive and affective states. And when, like Polus, people assume that what we really believe and feel is transparent, they rob the oracle of its meaning and do a disservice to the god of Delphi.

3.4 What Everyone Desires

3.4.1 *Socrates and Polus Again*

The psychological attributions Socrates makes are paradoxical precisely because with each the person having that psychological state might well be both unaware of it and, as a result, inclined to disavow it and also act in a way contrary to it. In each case, a further feature becomes clear if only we could be shown what, on reflection, we believe, we would act according to these states rather than the ones of which we were unreflectively aware and initially inclined to follow.

We have not yet discussed the most infamous instance of such an attribution, however: soon after he denies that orators are respected by anyone, Socrates tells Polus that each of us always and only has a desire for what is really good for us;

accordingly, many people do what they really do not want to do. Polus actually
introduces the issue by confusing two states of affairs which Socrates insists must
be distinguished. Polus sees no difference between "doing what one thinks is best
for oneself," which is transparent to us, and "doing what one desires," which
Socrates argues is not always transparent to us. Socrates seeks to establish that
there can be cases in which the two do not coincide, but first he needs to establish
a general claim about the relation of goal-oriented behavior and the way we construe the goals we pursue. For this, a lemma is needed. Socrates begins by giving
examples of a certain sort of action: we take medicine for the sake of health; we
go on sea voyages for the sake of wealth; and so on. The point of these cases
is that

1. Actions properly described as undertaken for the sake of goals are never
motivated by desires to perform the actions for their own sakes (467d6-e1).[17]

The following propositions may be gleaned from the text to clarify Socrates' conception of a goal.

2. Some things are good [in themselves],[18] some are bad [in themselves],
and some are neither good nor bad [in themselves] (467e1–3).

3. The things which are neither good nor bad [in themselves] are such as to
be sometimes good and sometimes bad [in virtue of other things to which
they are related in either case] (467e6–468a1).

4. When people pursue the things which are neither good nor bad [in them-
selves], they pursue them for the sake of things which they conceive[19] to be
good [in themselves] (468a5–b2).

5. The reason for this is that everyone desires what is good [in itself] and
no one desires what is neither good nor bad [in itself], or what is bad [in
itself] (468c3–7).

6. Hence, in cases like putting people to death, or banishing them, or con-

17. McTighe says that these cases are supposed to be fully general ([1984], 204). In fact, they are
designed only to make a point about actions done for the sake of something else (ἐάν τις
τι πράττῃ ἕνεκα τοῦ, οὐ τοῦτο βούλεται ὅ πράττει, ἀλλ' ἐκεῖνο οὗ ἕνεκα πράττει —
467d6-e1). Because the cases at issue, of whose nature we are reminded repeatedly—slaughtering
people, banishing them, confiscating their property, and so on (466b11–c2, c9–d3, 468b4–6, c2–3,
d1–2, e8–9, 469a9–b6, c5–7, 470b2–3)—are precisely cases where the action in question is plainly
done for the sake of some end for which these actions are the means, Socrates never needs to consider
cases of action in which one's actions are ends in themselves, or both ends and means to something
else. In all likelihood, he would be willing to extend his account to such other cases, but he does not
do so in this argument. See also Irwin [1979], note on 468bc, 144–45. Our dispute with McTighe on
this point is anticipated by O'Brien's ([1967], 88, n.5) reply to Dodds's complaint ([1959], 235–36).
18. These are the "independent goods" we discuss in section 4.2. The bracketed material is
plainly assumed throughout the argument—if the goods in question were not conceived as goods in
themselves, they would be good only in virtue of something else, which would put them in the class
of the neutrals, or what we call "dependent goods" in section 4.2 (see *Grg.* 467e6–468a1).
19. This condition is supplied by the οἰόμενοι at 468b2.

fiscating their property [goal-oriented actions which are neither good nor bad in themselves], we do what we do for the sake of what we conceive as some good [in itself] (468b4–7).

7. But for a thing to be conceived as good [in itself], it must be conceived as [in itself] good for its possessor (468b6).

From (1), (4) and (7), it follows that

8. When one acts for a goal, the goal is conceived as something good for oneself.

But what do we say about one (e.g., the orator or tyrant) who has the capacity always to obtain his goals—all of which, as per 8, he conceives as good for him, but some of which are in fact bad for him? Polus is forced to admit that

9. It is possible for one to think it is better for one to do something that is really worse for one, and to act accordingly.

10. In such a case, one does what one thinks best (468d1–5).

11. But (given 5), since it is really worse, one does not do what one desires (468d5–7).

This consequence is an embarrassment to Polus because he admires the orators and tyrants precisely on the ground that they have the capacity to do whatever they think is best for them. But it now turns out that what gives them this capacity, rhetoric, does not assure the orator of anything good for the one exercising it, and hence (according to premise 5) what its possessor really desires.

But premise 5 is not obviously true, for do not people frequently desire what is actually bad? And even if we add (as per 7) the proviso that by "good" we mean "good for oneself," is it not sometimes the case that people do not desire what is good for them and do desire what is bad for them? This claim has been a matter of long-standing dispute among scholars,[20] but we think the correct interpretation of it becomes clear once we see it in the light of the other paradoxical attributions of psychological states we have been discussing.

3.4.2 Desire and the Good

It is insufficient to suppose that the desire Socrates attributes to everyone is desire for and only for what we *conceive* as good for us.[21] If this were the way to

20. For a summary of the various readings scholars have offered, see McTighe [1984], 195–203.
21. See, for example, McTighe ([1984], 234, as well as 206–7). Weiss [1985] follows McTighe in this, despite her criticisms of other aspects of McTighe's interpretation. In fact, however, our view is very close to Weiss's; we take from her our own understanding of what Socrates means to refer to as what we "really" desire directly—it is what we would be aware of desiring if we were not ignorant. We dispute only Weiss's allowing that Socrates would count the tyrant as really desiring what he ignorantly fails to recognize as evil. Socrates, we are convinced, explicitly denies this, and his denial

understand the attribution in question, the argument would allow no dichotomy
between doing what we desire and doing what we think is best for ourselves; *ex
hypothesi,* if we think a thing is best for ourselves, we would conceive of it as
good for ourselves and, hence, desire it. The dichotomy between what we desire
and what we think is best for ourselves is possible only if we desire only what is
really best for us, whereas what we think is best for us is not always what is
really best. It follows that the desire Socrates attributes to each of us is desire for
what is really best for us, whether or not we think it is best for us.

The converse is also clearly stated in Socrates' argument: we do not desire
what is bad for us (468c4–7). Again, the desire we are said to lack is not for what
we *conceive* to be bad for us, but rather for what is *really* bad for us. This would
explain why Socrates says we do not actually desire something that is bad for us
even if we happen to think it is good for us. So the relation between desire and
what we think is best for us would appear to be as follows: we desire only what
is really best for us, and pursue only what we think is best for us. The possible
disharmony between desire and thought can be explained as follows: because our
thinking can be mistaken, sometimes we do not do what we desire, though we
always do what we think is best for us. But what, then, do we make of the urges
of the tyrant, who does not do what he desires? The tyrant does most assuredly
act according to *some* impulse; it is not as though he feels an impulse where there
is no motive there at all. But Socrates says that he does not do what he desires.
How can this be?

3.4.3 Impulses and Genuine Desires

The distinction between the impulse the tyrant unreflectively follows and the desire to which Socrates consistently refers in the above argument is exactly like the
distinction Socrates later makes between what Polus unreflectively believes and
what Polus *really* believes. Socrates says that the tyrant desires, for example, to
banish people only if banishing people is really good for the tyrant; and the tyrant
does not desire to banish people if banishing them is not good for the tyrant. If
Socrates is right, the tyrant will really desire to banish people only when he believes banishing them was just; for whenever it was unjust to do so, banishing
people would be bad for the tyrant.

Of course, the tyrant is wholly unaware of any desire to be just. The tyrant
wants to know only one thing: would banishing the person benefit the tyrant?
Now, if he thinks that banishing the person will be beneficial to him, the tyrant
will banish the person; if not, not. So, if he did suppose, as Socrates does, that
banishing the person is beneficial only when doing so is just, even the tyrant
would not banish anyone unjustly. If so, what the tyrant really desires is typically
not what the tyrant thinks he desires.

---

relies on restricting the sense of "desire" to refer only to what we *really* desire in precisely the same
way as he tells the incredulous Polus what Polus believes, by which he means "really believes," in
the sense we have identified. The *Meno* (77d4–e4) makes the same points we find made here in the
Gorgias: "what is conceived as good" must be distinguished from "what is really good," and only
the latter is what is really desired. See next note for what we regard as a preferable construction.

We can now see that Socrates is not denying the obvious fact that we are attracted to what we think is best for us, even when what we think is best for us is actually bad for us.[22] Plainly, Socrates agrees that tyrants aggressively pursue injustices, precisely on the ground that such injustices seem to them (as they do to Polus) to be best for them. It is even a feature of Socrates' discussion with Polus that Socrates grants that such things may be pleasant. In fact, one of the grounds for Socrates' calling rhetoric "flattery" and not *technē* is that rhetoric, like other forms of flattery, aims at the pleasant in favor of what is really best (464d2, 465a2). Socrates never denies the appeal of pleasure; rather, he holds that the appeal of pleasure must often be resisted.

But the appeal of pleasure can seduce people into *thinking* that what is really harmful would be beneficial. Accordingly, the flatterer dangles pleasures in front of foolish people (*Grg.* 464d1–3) and seduces them into thinking that pursuing those pleasures is what is best for them. As a result, such people do what they think is best; Socrates construes the call of pleasure as a seduction precisely because the call is characterized by the (false) promise of benefit. The people who are thereby seduced do not do what they desire to do; for what they achieve is in fact harmful to them, and desire is only for real (and not only apparent) benefit.

If we think of a particular desire as a desire for some particular object that is really beneficial to us, many of us may have desires which we are unaware of and, indeed, which we would deny having. Instead, what we take to be our real desires may only be certain urges—urges which can give way to true desires, but not until we are in a position to see what our true desires are. In fact, flatterers often seduce by preying on our misjudgments of real benefit and thereby stimulating our urges for what we mistakenly think will benefit us. In this way we are distracted from reflecting upon what we really desire and therefore from cool reflection upon what will truly supply the benefit we really desire. Like children whipped into a frenzy by the pleasures promised by a pastry cook, we will have no patience for talk of bitter medicine and real nutrition (*Grg.* 464d3–e2, 521e2–522a7). But if we can be unaware of the desires Socrates attributes to us, how can he be so confident that we all along have such desires, and why does Polus concede the point, which is so damaging to his side of the argument?

Socrates is confident that the tyrant does not really desire something unjust, for Socrates' numerous elenctic encounters have convinced him that justice is always the most beneficial thing to do. If the tyrant ever came to recognize the inevitably greater benefits of justice, even he would find he desired only to do the just, and never the unjust.[23] Accordingly, Socrates attributes to the tyrant an af-

22. Santas plausibly distinguishes between the *intended* objects of desire (good things only) and the *actual* objects of desire (sometimes bad, but conceived as good) ([1979], 186–89). To say, then, that we do not ever desire bad things is not to deny that bad things are ever the actual objects of desire, but rather that they are ever the intended objects of desire. Socrates' claim that the tyrant really desires what is just now amounts to saying that the only way the tyrant will ever come actually to possess the intended objects of his desires is to make the actual objects of his desires only actually just things.

23. This formulation of the principle may be found in one form or another in Gulley [1968], 89; Santas [1979], 190; McTighe [1984], 232; and Weiss [1985], 317.

fective psychological state of which the tyrant himself would (prior to any elenctic clarification) be unaware. Socrates' attribution is legitimate, however, precisely because were the tyrant brought to his senses, he would recognize that his desire for justice was an instance of his antecedently held desire to obtain the good; he would not view his *desire* as something new: what is new is his *recognition* that he really believes that justice is the very thing he needs to satisfy the desire he has had all along. Simply showing the tyrant that justice is always beneficial and injustice always harmful does not *make* the tyrant desire the just; rather, elenctic examination allows the tyrant to see that in wanting benefit, it is the just he had really wanted all along—because what he really wanted all along was what was really beneficial, and never what was only apparently beneficial but really harmful. The tyrant was simply not aware, until he discovered the real values of justice and injustice, that what he really desired was justice.

3.4.4   Why the Tyrant Is Wretched

From what we have said thus far, it follows not only that the tyrant really *desires* always and only to do what is just, but also that he really *believes* that one should never do wrong. So what he really believes and really desires is the exact opposite of what he is aware of believing and desiring. The tyrant, then, granted the power to act out his every (unreflective) whim, is the most wretched of all men, precisely because he of all men is the most prone to act against what he really believes and against what he really desires. The tyrant does not know himself, and would not act the way he does if he did. The sort of examination Socrates offers to his interlocutors, therefore, does not just uncover what the interlocutor really believes; it also reveals what the interlocutor really desires. So elenctic examination helps one to know not only one's own true cognitive states, but one's own true affective states as well.

It may also be seen now that the tyrant's initial state of confusion about his desires is a direct consequence of the tyrant's confusion about his beliefs; if only his beliefs about the relative values of justice and injustice were corrected, his desires would automatically propel him toward correct behaviors. This is Socrates' "intellectualism," a conception of human psychology according to which all of one's actions flow directly from one's cognitive states.[24] It follows that proper moral training will not aim at changing our desires, but rather at educating that part of us that forms the beliefs that govern our behaviors.[25] This part sometimes

24. McTighe characterizes intellectualism as holding the very strong view that all choices are "solely intellectual" ([1984], 194, n.4). A weaker form is possible, however, according to which all choices reflect both cognition and desire, but are determined by cognition. It is this weaker form we should attribute to Socrates. So the tyrant genuinely follows an urge, but his having *that* urge—as opposed to some other urge—is to be explained in terms of his cognitive states. His cognitive states do not, however, account for his *having* urges; they only determine the content and direction of his specific urges.

25. Plainly, Plato's later psychology—and the tripartition of the soul—cannot be read into the *Gorgias,* precisely because that psychology permits what Socrates explicitly denies: the possibility of *akrasia* (see section 3.5). We mean only to characterize the consequences of Socrates' intellectualism, without attributing to him any of the metaphysical commitments we find in *Rep.* IV, or for that matter,

thinks something is good for us when it is not. Though it need not always be wrong, our moral fallibility derives solely from this part of us. Hence, it is this part of us that requires training, if ever we are to be in a position to escape the life of inner conflict and discord. As we have said, the best solution to this problem is to lead the examined life, through which we may come to know ourselves. Only in this way do we come to recognize what we really believe, and thus to pursue what we really desire.

3.4.5 Desire and "What One Thinks Is Best for One"

Socrates believes that desire always aims at and only at what is good (or beneficial) to oneself. But desire cannot itself make the judgments necessary to identify the relevant goals or objects that are actually what is best for one. This can only be accomplished by cognition (knowledge or belief). Cognition thus provides a kind of lens, which represents actions and objects to desire under the descriptions "beneficial" or "harmful." One is attracted to or repelled by, and thus will pursue or shun, only those actions and objects to which one is directed by this lens. In cases where the judgment supplied by cognition—one's thinking that some specific action or object is best for one—is correct, one will actually pursue what one thinks is best for one, and also what one desires, namely, something beneficial to one. In cases where the judgment supplied by cognition—again, one's thinking that some specific action or object is best for one—is incorrect, one will actually pursue what one thinks is best for one, but not what one desires. In both cases, the motivating force is the same (desire for the good or what is beneficial to oneself). Accordingly, in both cases, it is correct to say that the one acting is acting on the basis of a genuine motivation; one will also feel an attraction for the object or action one pursues. But in only one case does one do what one desires.

Perhaps it would help to clarify our account if we represented our interpretation of the relevant phenomena in diagram form.

Motivating Force	Cognitive Lens	Product
Doing what one thinks is best for one and also what one desires		
Desire for the good "Benefit to me" ⟶	Correct judgment "*this* is best for me" (when it *is* best)	Specific action (One does "what one thinks is best" and also "what one desires.")
Doing what one thinks is best for one, but not what one desires		
Desire for the good ("Benefit to me") ⟶	Incorrect judgment "*this* is best for me" (when it is *not* best)	Specific action (One does "what one thinks is best" but not "what one desires.")

Phaedrus 246a ff. Some sense of the middle period's division of the soul into parts can be found in [*Alc.* I] 133b7–c3.

It should now be clear why the tyrant does not do what he desires when he commits injustice. It is not that he has no motivation to do what he does; indeed, what motivates him is the very same desire that motivates the just person. Rather, his motivation has been aimed at injustice, by a faulty cognitive lens which misrepresents injustice as something beneficial to him, when it is in fact harmful to him. Accordingly, he desires what is beneficial to him, but finds himself attracted to and pursuing what is actually harmful to him; for he has made a cognitive error, judging what is actually harmful to him as something beneficial to him. Like all of us, he does what he thinks is best for him; but he does not do what he desires. It is not his desire but his thinking that has betrayed him. Were his thinking corrected, he would instead pursue only justice and never injustice. Moreover, as we argued in section 3.2, all that is needed to correct his thinking is for him to lead the examined life, by which he would come to recognize that what he really believes is that justice—and not injustice—is really what is best for him. Accordingly, by pursuing the examined life, the tyrant could replace the faulty cognitive lenses through which his desire is so often misaimed and thus frustrated.

3.5   The Denial of *Akrasia*

3.5.1   Construing the Nature of the Paradox

Because he recognizes no possibility of dissonance between what one believes and what one does, Socrates also rejects the possibility of *akrasia*, that moral failing in which one recognizes what is best for one to do but nonetheless fails to do it. Given what we have already said, it is clear that one can have an urge to do something evil (again, bad for oneself) even though one desires what is good (for oneself). And since one can have an urge to do something evil, one might well pursue it; surely Polus' tyrants and orators do precisely this. Accordingly, Socrates should not be represented as saying that no one does evil intentionally (or voluntarily).[26] Indeed, Socrates occasionally speaks in ways that clearly imply that evil may be done intentionally or voluntarily,[27] though it is clear from what we have

---

26. See, for example, McTighe [1984]. We prefer the accounts given by Santas ([1979], see 317, n.26), and Mulhern [1968]. McTighe's own proposed analysis ([1984], 230–36)—that Socrates regards the wrongdoer as "exempt from blame"—cannot account for the passages in which Socrates blames people for actions that on his own view would have been involuntary (e.g., *Ap.* 41d7–e1, where Socrates allows that his accusers deserve blame for having sought to injure him). (See Weiss's excellent critique of McTighe's suggestion in [1985], 318–22.) We are not simply overlooking, in our denial of this point, Socrates' claim that all evil is done involuntarily (see, e.g., *Grg.* 509e5–7; *Prt.* 345d6–e6). Instead, we claim only that when Socrates says one acts involuntarily, we should understand him only as saying that one acts in a way that is opposed to what he desires. This is the clear sense, in fact, of *Grg.* 509e5–7. (See, accordingly, LSJ *s.v.* ἀέκον: "opp. βουλόμενος.") Weiss's account of how this can be, with the slight exception noted above in note 22, is the most plausible we have found in the literature.

27. See *Ap.* 37a5–6 and *Grg.* 488a2–3, where Socrates claims never to have wronged anyone voluntarily; and *Cri.* 49a4, where Socrates insists that wrong should never be done voluntarily. If Socrates holds that it is simply impossible to do wrong voluntarily, it is hard to see why his claims never to have accomplished the impossible are supposed to impress anyone. It is also hard to understand why he would admonish Crito not to do the impossible. We owe this point and these references

already said that those who do evil intentionally cannot be doing what they (really) desire. And since Socrates accepts that we always do what we do for the sake of what we conceive as good, it is also now obvious what Socrates will say has happened when one actually pursues what is evil: he has misjudged the evil thing and conceived it as a good, perhaps because he has been seduced by a deceitful pleasure. So one's judgment can certainly be "overcome by pleasure."

But the denial of *akrasia* is not a denial of our fallibility in judgment; it is rather a denial that *knowledge* of something's being good for us could be "overcome by pleasure" and thereby cause us to do what is bad for us. Recall that Socrates holds that we always do what we think is best for ourselves; that is, he holds that we always act on the basis of what we represent to ourselves as the most beneficial course of action available to us. Accordingly, we can never act on the basis of what we presently represent to ourselves as worse for us. On this account there can be no *akrasia*. But this is paradoxical—it seems that people are often akratic. How can Socrates maintain his view in the face of so many apparent counterexamples?

3.5.2 A Test Case

Let us begin by stipulating that whatever Socrates means by "knowledge" in his denial, it requires at least that the person in question is not guilty of some relevant misapprehension or mistaken conception. In fact, only this much epistemology is needed for Socrates' denial of *akrasia*, for the rest can be done only with reference to the way the putative akratic conceives of things.

So let us now turn to a situation in which, if *akrasia* is possible at all, the akratic might be found. Having suffered from some ailment or other, a man is told by his physician that he must not eat sweets or he will make himself very sick. The man accepts the physician's authority, and what is more, wants very much not to be ill. But the man has a sweet tooth, and we now find him eyeing a piece of candy. There are a number of ways in which it might turn out that he eats the candy but does not show himself in doing so to be akratic:

1. He might eat the candy because he thought the candy was one of the pills the doctor ordered him to take.

This would be an obvious mistake in perception; the mistake owes to his ignorance of the nature of the thing he is eating.

2. He might eat the candy because he is momentarily unaware—due to forgetfulness, inattention, or some other lapse—of the physician's prohibition.

---

to Roslyn Weiss. See also *Ap.* 41d7–e1, where it is clear that Socrates attributes to his accusers the intention to harm him, and *Grg.* 481b2–4, where Socrates seems to contrast one who never intends to do any wrong to those who might do so.

Or,

> 3. He might eat the candy because he has somehow convinced himself that, in this case, it will not harm him.

Plainly, none of these are cases of *akrasia,* for in each the agent suffers from a misapprehension. But also,

> 4. He might be aware (a) that it is a piece of candy, (b) that this piece of candy is precisely the sort of thing the physician prohibited him from eating, and (c) that it will indeed harm him if he eats it, but might eat it anyhow because of his representing to himself another—conflicting—aspect of the situation, which he takes in this case to override the rule prohibiting eating the candy.

Just what would this case be like? Socrates discusses such a case in the *Protagoras,* in which one is imagined to miscalculate the harm an act will bring by overvaluing the pleasure at hand because it is closer and hence greater in appearance than it is in reality (*Prt.* 356c5–d7). So one could represent the pleasure one will get from eating the candy as having a greater value than the value one would attain from abstaining. One might say that in this case the value of eating the candy "overrides" the value of abstaining. If so, one could be said to recognize that this is a piece of candy, and even to recognize that eating candy is harmful to one in one's present medical condition, eat the candy and yet still not be akratic.[28] After all, such a person can still be shown to fail to recognize an important aspect of the situation, and thus to misjudge it: the person who eats the candy under this circumstance misjudges the relative merits of the two courses of action—he sees that eating the candy will harm him, but (wrongly) supposes that the good he will receive (the pleasure) outweighs the harm he will receive (detriment to his health). And he has misappraised the relative values of each outcome by taking what is near to him as being greater than it really is, and by taking what is further away as being less than it really is.

3.5.3 Pleasure and Benefit

This suggests still another way in which one might construe the case to be one in which one perceived benefit overrides another. The *Protagoras* makes its case on the basis of an assumption of hedonism that we do not believe Socrates actually holds. In fact, we believe that Socrates would not construe pleasure as such always as a benefit, for in the *Gorgias* it is plain that he takes some pleasures to be

---

28. This example requires us to amend Santas's otherwise admirable account of this paradox in [1979]. Santas never clearly identifies the sort of case we have here imagined, but could account for it on the ground that it is the greatest benefit overall one seeks. Accordingly, in the case we have in mind, one errs in judging the eating of the candy by failing to recognize that the product of doing so will be more harmful than another (available and recognized) option.

evil.[29] So a case, such as 4 above, might be constructed simply from any instance in which pleasure was taken to be a benefit that overrides some other (real) harm. Since in the case Socrates is imagining in the *Protagoras,* the pleasure being pursued is, *ex hypothesi,* not a good at all, Socrates thinks it would always be a mistake to construe it as "overriding" any real harm one might suffer. So any case of being "overcome by pleasure" would appear to be a case which Socrates would count as an instance of ignorance; for in every case of this sort, pleasure would be misconceived by the one "overcome" as something it was not—a benefit. Where there is misconception, there is lack of knowledge.

The misconception involved in 4, moreover, can be characterized not just as a misperception of something external to us, but as a misperception of something within ourselves. Given what we have already said, it is clear that Socrates would contrast our urge for some pleasure with our desire for what is truly good for us, and would attribute to each of us the (reflectively available) belief that detrimental pleasure is not really a benefit. So if we could only be made aware of what we really believe, we would no longer have the urge to pursue the detrimental pleasure. Such self-knowledge would not be enough to be inerrant, of course; we would have to know a good deal about the external world over which our choices ranged to accomplish such perfection. But self-knowledge would allow us to avoid doing those things we judge to be evils, such as choosing some harmful pleasure over some real benefit. Since Socrates believes that such errant choices are frequently the cause of wrongdoing, it follows that many evils could be avoided if only we all followed the Delphic injunction and attempted to come to know what is always within us, but of which we may only become aware through the psychological therapy of philosophical examination.

3.5.4   Concluding Remarks about Socrates' Denial of Akrasia

Now it might be supposed that what motivates Socrates' account is the connection he makes between knowledge and wisdom, where wisdom is conceived as having practical significance.[30] Although we are obviously sympathetic to such accounts of Socratic epistemology, we are also convinced that this is not what is at issue in Socrates' denial of *akrasia.* Insofar as Socrates ties knowledge to practical wisdom, he certainly is right to suppose that one cannot be both wise and akratic. But the point of Socrates' denial is not to make a point about inerrancy of wisdom. If this were all he had in mind, Socrates' denial of *akrasia* would be trivial, for no one is wiser than Socrates, and Socrates himself is wise only in recognizing that he is not wise (*Ap.* 21a4–23b4). Thus, "no wise person does evil" is true simply because there are no wise people in existence. Moreover, because Socrates also identifies moral knowledge and wisdom with virtue, the denial of *akrasia*

---

29. *Grg.* 474d5 ff. might be supposed to allow pleasure as an object of desire independent of benefit. But Socrates himself can hardly accept such a claim. Instead, it is more likely that he is merely showing how such a view leads to trouble for some thesis that an interlocutor has put forward and which Socrates has targeted for refutation.

30. See, for example, Gould [1955], ch. 1.

construed as simply the denial that wise persons ever do what is evil becomes the
tautology that no one does evil virtuously. Because Socrates takes his denial of
akrasia to signify something more controversial than this, its meaning must not
be construed as relying upon his conception of the knowledge he takes to be
constitutive of wisdom and virtue. In fact, we can see that the denial requires
no richer sense of "knowledge" than the one we identified above—the correct
representation to oneself of all of the features of the case relevant to one's judgment. True and sincerely held belief would be sufficient to generate the cases
under dispute.[31]

The heart of Socrates' account can be found in his collapsing of all drives into
the desire for benefit, and construing benefit in such a way as to rule out that there
could be competing and incommensurable benefits. According to Socrates' account, we always and only do what we conceive as best for us. Thus, when we
are "overcome by pleasure," it must be that in some way we are conceiving of
the anticipated pleasure as more beneficial to us than what would be gained by
pursuing any other course of action. So Socrates construes the one who is "overcome by pleasure" as representing pleasure to himself as something it is not, a
benefit. But why must we suppose that one who acts for the sake of pleasure
conceives of pleasure under the heading "benefit"? Why instead can we not have
a drive for pleasure that is not construed as a benefit but only as pleasant? Or,
alternatively, why can we not construe pleasure as a benefit which is independent
of, and incommensurable with, other sorts of benefits?[32]

Because Socrates sees every instance of wanting something as a case of construing what is wanted as a benefit, he is convinced that one who seeks a harmful
pleasure over some available and recognized (and, for Socrates, genuine) benefit
has made an error of judgment. But this is a mistake if we can be motivated to
do or obtain something without always or in every way construing the thing we
are motivated to do or obtain as a benefit to us, or if the class of benefits can
contain competing and incommensurable goods. Our wanting it, that is, might not
require us to see it as a benefit to us, or as a benefit commensurable with all other
sorts of benefits. Socrates discounts both possibilities, and thus regards apparent
akratic acts as errors in judgment. *Akrasia* is indeed impossible if every putative
akratic act can be shown to involve some misapprehension or other, including
most notably the misapprehension of costs and benefits. But nothing prevents the
possibility of *akrasia* so long as we can apprehend all costs and benefits correctly,
but allow some other motivation—as, for example, our drive for pleasure *qua*
pleasure to motivate action. Alternatively, nothing prevents the possibility of *akrasia* if the class of benefits includes incommensurable goods, the pursuit of some
of which can "overcome" our pursuits of others. Socrates treats our drive for
pleasure (and other drives we may have, such as those stemming from emotion)
as if they were all to be subsumed under the category of "drive for benefit." He
also does not see pleasure as itself one of the benefits we might pursue. But either

31. Santas also makes this point ([1979], 192–93).
32. Irwin makes a similar objection to the one we are making in [1979], note on 467e–468b, 142.

of these ways of construing pleasure might be possible, so Socrates' account is questionable at best.

It is not hard to see how one could become convinced of a view like Socrates', however. Socrates might well ask what it is to have a drive, if not (perhaps among other things) to represent to ourselves the thing to which we are driven as something we would be better off having than lacking. Accordingly, we sometimes characterize our own and others' motivations as irrational when we suppose that acting on such motives would be self-destructive. Put this way, construing all such drives as equally drives for benefit is, perhaps, not *obviously* wrong. And because the pursuit of pleasure can easily be shown to be self-destructive in some cases, it is not hard to see why one might be inclined to exclude pleasure from the class of benefits. But the fact remains that the most troublesome sorts of inner conflict typically derive from the fact that we have drives which value goals in incommensurable ways. Conflicts of such drives cannot simply be reconciled by reminding ourselves of some single value under which all other values can be subsumed and made commensurable, and according to which we might calculate the relative values, measured by this one standard, of pursuing each of the drives we find within us.

If we deny the Socratic reduction of all drives into the one single and commensurable one, we may easily explain how *akrasia* is possible: for example, one way to be akratic is simply to choose pleasure over good (or benefit); another is to choose pleasure over some other good. Choice of one object of desire over another may not reflect any judgment whatever of which of the two is fundamentally preferable, for choices do not always presuppose some common ground for rational preference and, hence, need involve no error of judgment due to a misperception or misapplication of grounds. Rather, choice may often only derive from impulses which are formed in us without directly calculative rational influence, impulses which are often in opposition to what reason would dictate.

It is, however, perhaps not difficult to see why Socrates was attracted to an intellectualistic reformulation of all of our motives. Socrates' interlocutors, when questioned, invariably assume that there is a single goal—happiness—at which we *always* aim, and which can be adequately explained. If so, *akrasia* is impossible, for to go wrong, one would always have somehow to judge the harmful action in relation to that goal. The possibility of *akrasia,* then, serves to give the lie to any such unified psychology, intellectualist or otherwise.

3.5.5 *Are There Two Theories of Motivation in the* Gorgias?

In the *Gorgias,* Socrates disagrees with Callicles' identification of the good with pleasure. Once he has shown that even Callicles himself does not, upon reflection, believe that all pleasures are good, Socrates states that "ruling over oneself" is necessary if one is to be happy. When asked by Callicles what he means by that expression, Socrates replies: "Nothing intricate, but just as the many think: being temperate and having control over oneself, ruling over the pleasures and appetites one has" (491d10–e1). Later, Socrates explains that this is why the most misera-

ble person of all is the "completely undisciplined creature" Callicles had touted
earlier in the discussion, for the undisciplined soul lacks the "order and harmony"
which result when temperance "restrains [the soul] from its appetites" (505b3).
To save oneself, Socrates concludes, one must equip oneself with the power always to forgo wrongdoing of any form.

Some scholars[33] claim that by the time Plato wrote the latter part of the *Gorgias*[34] he had become convinced that the conception of motivation Socrates employs in the discussion with Polus (and the other early dialogues) is mistaken. In
their view, the discussion with Polus relies on an affective psychology that recognized only one form of motivation, desire for what is good (or beneficial). The
latter part of the *Gorgias* is said to reflect instead what these scholars characterize
as Plato's new found conviction, elaborated in detail in the middle period dialogues, that some motivations have objects other than the good of the agent.[35]
These purportedly new motivations (appetites) aim only at pleasure and not benefit. It makes sense to speak of the need to "discipline" an appetite, they argue,
only if it is possible for that appetite to have as its object something other than
what the agent takes to be beneficial to him.[36]

One obvious problem with this interpretation, of course, is that it imputes to
Socrates two flatly contradictory theories of motivation *within a single dialogue,*
for Socrates relies on the assumption that *all* desires are actually "good dependent" (467c1–468e5) in gaining Polus' acceptance of the proposition that one can
do what one thinks is best without doing what one desires.[37] Thus, Plato suddenly
and radically altered in mid-dialogue the most basic motivational assumption of
his earlier Socratic writings and he did so without giving the audience any explicit
warning whatever that the Socratic theory is being jettisoned or why it is necessary
to do so. What is perhaps worse, the character Socrates—the man so devoted to
philosophical consistency (see *Grg.* 482a7–b1)—is made to appear not to recognize the incompatibility of the theories of motivation his refutations of Polus and
Callicles assume.

33. See Cornford [1933], 306–7 and 317; Irwin [1979], note on 507b, 222, and [1977], 123–24.
More recently, Charles Kahn has also endorsed the view that the moral psychology assumed in the
Gorgias fits the one developed in *Rep.* IV and thus is incompatible with the view of desire required
by the Socratic paradox ([1988], 89–90). Because Kahn takes the *Gorgias* to be written *earlier* than
the *Protagoras*, he argues that in writing the dialogues that defend the "Socratic paradox," "Plato has
deliberately suppressed all doctrinal references that depend on good-independent effect" ([1988], 89).

34. Contemporary commentators generally place the *Gorgias* towards the end of the dialogues
making up the early period. But even those who think that the *Gorgias* was written earlier in Plato's
career, perhaps even earlier than the *Protagoras*, would agree that it was written before Books II
through X of the *Republic*. Kahn ([1988], n.6, 70–71) offers a review of commentators who have
taken the *Gorgias* to have been written relatively early in the early period.

35. The Leontius anecdote in Book IV of the *Republic* (439e6–440b7) indicates that Plato, unlike
Socrates, thinks that desires can conflict with one's conception of what is best, for he tells us that
what the anecdote illustrates is that anger (ὀργή) and appetite (ἐπιθυμία) are sometimes at war with
each other and that anger always takes the side of reason whenever "appetite constrains someone
contrary to reason" (440a5–b7).

36. Irwin [1979], note on 505bc, 218.

37. Indeed, Irwin himself underscores the inconsistency within the *Gorgias* itself. See Irwin
[1979], notes on 468ab (143) and 507b (222).

It might be argued that the confusion scholars have found in the *Gorgias* is not unusual in the early and transitional dialogues. Plato was obviously not averse in writing the middle dialogues to putting doctrines into the mouth of a character named Socrates, which the Socrates of the earlier dialogues would not have endorsed. There can be no guarantee that Plato would not have seen fit suddenly to introduce a distinctly novel view in the *Gorgias*. Indeed, commentators have been virtually unanimous in holding that this is precisely what occurs with the introduction of the doctrine of recollection in the *Meno*.[38] Moreover, at the conclusion of the *Hippias Minor,* Plato describes Socrates as seeing no way to avoid the conclusion that morally upright persons have the power to do what is wrong voluntarily, even though such a view plainly contradicts a doctrine otherwise deeply entrenched in the philosophy of the early dialogues. Finally, in the *Protagoras,* Socrates is described as actually taking up contradictory views during the course of a single dialogue. He first argues that virtue cannot be taught, but later argues that virtue must be a kind of knowledge and, hence, must be teachable.

The atypical features of the three dialogues just mentioned, however, are importantly different from the one we are now considering in the *Gorgias*. First, there is nothing in the *Meno* that makes the dialogue internally inconsistent. Even if the Socrates who speaks in the other early dialogues never shows any sign of accepting the theory of recollection, his endorsement of this theory in the *Meno* does not result in a portrayal of Socrates as promoting two distinct and contradictory points of view in the *Meno*.

Moreover, when Socrates is portrayed as shifting positions, as he is in the *Hippias Minor* and the *Protagoras,* Plato is careful to describe Socrates as troubled by the fact that he finds himself driven to conflicting views and unable to resolve the inconsistency (see *Hip. Mi.* 376b8–c6 and *Prt.* 360e6–361d6). This is not to say, of course, that in each of the other early dialogues Plato's Socrates is always consistent. But it is doubtful that Plato could have been unaware that, in the arguments he attributed to Socrates in a single dialogue, he was relying upon incompatible theories about something as fundamental as the relationship between cognition and conation. Thus, if those who see Plato abandoning the Socratic theory of motivation at the end of the *Gorgias* are right, the *Gorgias* is unique among the early dialogues in attribution to Socrates of two distinctly undesirable features: (a) the holding of crucially important but inconsistent views about human motivation and (b) apparent ignorance of the fact that he is doing so.

We believe that our account of Socrates' conception of the relationship between cognition and desire allows us to explain why in the *Gorgias* Socrates claims that certain appetites must be "disciplined" if a person is to be happy. First, as we noted in 3.4.3, even in the earlier discussion with Polus, Socrates never denies that there are impulses that would lead the unreflective person in the opposite direction from what the person really desires. This is exactly how Socrates was able to characterize the tyrant as motivated to do what he does not really desire to do. All Socrates ever denied in the earlier discussion was that such urges could lead one to pursue what one did not recognize as beneficial, precisely be-

38. See Seeskin [1987], 35–37.

cause anyone who followed such urges would, in Socrates' view (mistakenly) conceive of the objects of such urges as benefits to themselves. This, we said, was Socrates' account of the seduction of pleasure: it seduced the foolish into pursuing the pleasant as if it were a benefit.

Callicles presents Socrates with a whole new set of challenges, not only with his advocacy of unbridled hedonism, but with his rejection of the conventional views about justice which were instrumental in Socrates' examination of Polus. But there is nothing about either Callicles' conception of the good or about his motivational assumptions that would *require* the abandonment of the view of desire Socrates promoted in his earlier argument with Polus. Callicles does say that it is best to let one's appetites "grow as great as possible and not to restrain them" (491e9–492a1). It does not follow from this, however, that he thinks that a point can be reached when one would desire an object without regard to whether or not the agent thinks the object is good, which is what would have to be the case were Plato interjecting a new theory of the relationship between cognition and desire. Callicles may simply be saying that nothing is truly good—and, hence, truly desired—unless it provides the most intense feeling of pleasure and that it is the nature of some appetites, over time, to require increasingly intense pleasures in order to be sated.

According to the view we have defended in this chapter, there is good reason for Socrates to claim that temperance brings "order and harmony" to the soul because it "restrains the appetites." Earlier in this chapter, we quoted Socrates' warning to Callicles that unless he could refute Socrates' view of the value of justice, "Callicles will not agree with you, O Callicles, but you will be in conflict in your whole way of living" (482b5–6). The reason for this, we have argued, is that, in spite of his protestations to the contrary, Callicles really believes that justice is always more valuable than injustice and, thus, he holds contradictory beliefs and hence contradictory impulses about the most important of all things— how best to live. As we have noted, no one can expect to fulfill contradictory impulses. Only by coming to see that he really believes that justice is supremely valuable can Callicles achieve "harmony"—consistency—within his beliefs and thereby ensure that he effectively pursues what he always desires, happiness.

Now when Socrates says that he agrees with "the many" about the value of "having control over oneself, ruling over the pleasures and appetites" (491d10–e1), he obviously need not agree with another view held by "the many" and expressed in the *Protagoras* that knowledge of what is best can be "over-come" by an appetite for pleasure. Socrates may simply mean that he agrees with what most people think, that it is always better not to be the sort of foolish person who pursues urges that lead him away from what is really best. This is precisely why Socrates thinks that anyone has need of temperance to "rule over our plea-sures and appetites"—not to eliminate them or to restrain them by frustrating them, but instead to identify correctly for them those objects that bring genuine satisfaction.

We have argued that, for Socrates, we are always inclined to pursue what we perceive as a benefit, and the perception of the object as a benefit is to be ex-plained in terms of some belief the agent has about the good. Thus, although an agent's cognitive states explain what objects he pursues, they do not explain why the agent has motivations at all.[39] Until someone, such as Callicles, who believes that ignoble pleasures are good, is made to see by means of the *elenchos* that this particular belief conflicts with what he really believes about the good, he can be expected to pursue ignoble pleasures. Indeed, he is quite literally powerless to control his appetites, for he is totally unaware that the pleasures he seeks are not good and, hence, not what he desires.

Moreover, this is why Socrates is confident that the *elenchos* is, by itself, sufficient to turn Callicles away from the violent and lawless life he so admired at the beginning of the discussion. Were Plato at the conclusion of the *Gorgias* suddenly to abandon the Socratic theory of motivation, then, as some commentators have claimed, Plato's Socrates would have no reason to think that the outcome of the *elenchos* would be sufficient to turn Callicles from his unjust pursuits. If the view we oppose were right, even if Callicles were brought to recognize his "good dependent" desire for the life of moderation and lawfulness, it would not assuredly follow that his "good independent" appetite for lawless pleasure would not "overcome" him. But Socrates expresses no such worry, and this is what we would expect from the Socratic theory of motivation. Because the proposition "justice is always better than injustice" has been the product of every elenctic examination of others he has undertaken on this topic, Socrates can be confident that Callicles will pursue justice, if only he will attend to what he really believes.

3.6 The Self

3.6.1 The True Self

We have shown how Socrates attributes the desire for genuine benefit to all of us. F. M. Cornford has tied this paradoxical attribution to what he calls the "true self," whose

> particular form of desire, always directed at the good it can perceive, he called by a special name, 'wish' ($\beta o \acute{\nu} \lambda \eta \sigma \iota \varsigma$). When we act wrongly, we do what we like, but not what we wish; the insight of the true self is for a moment obscured.[40]

The *Gorgias* never explicitly refers to a "true self."[41] But if what we have argued is correct, Cornford was right to suggest that the Socrates of the *Gorgias*

---

39. See note 24.

40. Cornford [1933], 306. See also Cornford [1932], 51. McTighe rightly faults Cornford for claiming that the *Gorgias* offers a theory of $\beta o \acute{\nu} \lambda \eta \sigma \iota \varsigma$, pointing out that the "text only has the verb $\beta o \acute{\nu} \lambda \varepsilon \sigma \vartheta \alpha \iota$" ([1984], 195, n.7). Others who have one way or another shared Cornford's view include Adkins [1960], 305, 309; Cushman [1958], 185, 194–95; Dodds [1959], 235–36; Gould [1955], 47–55; Moline [1981], 71–73. See also O'Brien [1967], 217–18, n.15.

41. See [*Alc.* I] 129b1–131a1, where the person is identified with his soul. Socrates' discussions of the afterlife in the early period plainly show that he does not conceive of personhood as entailing possession of the body. There could be no personal survival of the death of the body if the surviving soul did not continue to be identical to the person whose body died (see *Ap.* 40e4–41c7; *Cri.* 54c6–7; *Grg.* 523a1–527a4; also *Phd.* 115c4–116a1). Another text often cited in regard to the "true self" is *Rep.* X.611b9–612a3, in which the "true nature of the soul"—as distinct from its appearance when

had a conception of a "true self," which each of us can discover only through the sort of reflective introspection Socrates takes his *elenchos* to promote. This "self" is the one Socrates believes the Delphic injunction exhorts us to know. It is the self that believes what Polus originally supposed no one could sincerely believe; the self that intends what Socrates attributes to Simonides; the self that has only contempt for orators; the self that desires only good things. Cornford is right to suggest that the true self has insights that can be obscured, though these insights are not perceived by desire, as Cornford suggests, but rather by that within us which really believes a number of moral truths.

3.6.2   Discovering Who We Are

We have argued that Socrates rejects Polus' supposition that we are psychologically transparent to ourselves in favor of a view of our psychology according to which what is most importantly true of us may be hidden to us if we do not lead the examined life. What we are is brought to light by Socratic examination, which reveals what we really believe, intend, regard, and desire. If Socrates does not explicitly call such beliefs, intentions, regards, and desires states of our "true self," it is nonetheless clear that he attributes them to us. It is also clear that he regards them as states of ourselves which may more truly be predicated of us than those more superficial states of which we are transparently aware, but which would vanish if only we would come to know ourselves. If Socrates does not explicitly contrast the "true self" with any other self in the *Gorgias*, it may only be because he regards the "true self" as truly the only self. This, perhaps, is why when Socrates attributes psychological states to his interlocutors, he persists in attributing only those we believe are states of the "true self." The Delphic inscription "Know Thyself" makes its exhortation in oracular fashion: its meaning is obscure because it refers darkly to a self of which we might be unaware. But proper interpretation of the exhortation shows that it does not exhort us to know one of our selves, as if there were many,[42] but rather our *only* self. Socrates piously follows what he regards as the true meaning of the inscription. His famous paradoxes, then, are oracular in the interpretive puzzles they present and in the way they reflect their Delphic source.

---

in communion with a body—is discussed. Numerous other texts from the middle period clearly distinguish the soul from the body and affirm the personal survival of death. Although the conception of the afterlife Plato provides in the middle period is noticeably different from those options Socrates identifies in the early dialogues, it does not follow that the middle period's clear identification of the person with his soul is an innovation. Socrates persistently emphasizes the special value of care for the soul in the early period (see, for example, *Ap.* 29e1–2), as opposed to care for the body (see, for example, *Ap.* 30a8–b4; *Cri.* 47c1–48a4; *Grg.* 477a5–e6, 511c9–512b2; [*Alc.* I] 131b10–12). Given his suggestion (in the *Euthyd.* 279a1–281e2) that the good of the body—health—is only valuable to the person when in the service of wisdom (by "unity of virtue," the good of the soul), Socrates' emphasis on the good of the soul strongly suggests that he identified the person with his or her soul.

42. The plurals at [*Alc.* I] 134d8 and e6 presumably refer not to multiple selves within Alcibiades, but rather to Alcibiades' self and the state's "self" (see 134d1–2). We also see no reason to attribute to Socrates a theory of levels of self such as that conceived by Plochmann and Robinson ([1988], 286–93). In our view, only the "true self" is truly the self.

4

Socratic Ethics

4.1 Some Problems in Socratic Ethics

4.1.1 Principles and Definitions

At the heart of Socratic ethics may be found a version of what has come to be known as "eudaimonism," according to which the value of something is always to be construed in terms of its connection to *eudaimonia* (happiness). Specifically, to be an eudaimonist is to be committed to what we shall call the "Principle of Eudaimonism" (PE):

>(PE) A thing is good only insofar as it is conducive to happiness.

There is no trace of pure duties in the Kantian sense in Socratic thought. What is good is good simply in virtue of its contribution to one's happiness. But there may be many varieties of eudaimonism. One may count many things or only a few as good or goods. Things may be called good only if they are both necessary and sufficient for happiness, or if they are just sufficient, or if they are at least necessary, or even if they are neither necessary nor sufficient but merely contributory. There may be only independent or both independent and dependent goods. Hence, each of these needs to be defined.

>A thing is good in itself (or an independent good—IG) if and only if it is a good in virtue of nothing other than itself.

Given this, the definition of dependent goods is predictable:

>A thing is a dependent good (DG) if and only if it is a good in virtue of its contribution to or employment by some good other than itself.[1]

The next two definitions are also obvious:

>A thing is a necessary good (NG) if and only if there can be no happiness without it.

---

1. It follows that an IG can never be an evil, for its goodness does not depend upon anything else; but a DG can also be an evil, if it contributes to or is employed by an evil. Examples follow.

A thing is a sufficient good (SG) if and only if its possession alone ensures happiness.

4.1.2   Is Virtue a Sufficient Good?

In recent years there has been vigorous and instructive debate over how Socrates conceives the relationship between virtue and happiness.[2] Scholars have worried, for example, about whether or not Socrates thought that virtue was intrinsically valuable or only instrumentally valuable, that is, valuable purely as an instrument for achieving something else. At least this much is already obvious: according to PE, only happiness is intrinsically good, and virtue can thus be an intrinsic good, properly speaking, only if happiness is to be defined in terms of virtue or virtuous activity, and the latter are not simply conditions of its achieving happiness. Otherwise, virtue will be an instrumental good, and only because it contributes to what is intrinsically good, happiness.

But whatever their disagreements on other issues, we find one feature common to the various positions scholars have taken: the attribution to Socrates of the doctrine that virtue is both necessary and sufficient for happiness.[3] T. H. Irwin sums up the doctrine as follows: "being virtuous is not simply our best prospect for happiness, but in itself ensures happiness; the virtuous man will not fail to achieve happiness for reasons beyond his control."[4] In this view, Socrates believes that virtue alone will absolutely secure every benefit necessary for happiness. Thus, although the vicissitudes of fortune and the injustices of others may strip the virtuous person of everything but virtue, virtue alone provides an absolute immunity against such losses ever destroying the virtuous person's happiness.

4.1.3   Trouble in the Texts

The attribution to Socrates of the doctrine that virtue is both necessary and sufficient for happiness has at least an initial air of plausibility. The testimony of Plato

2. Santas [1979] and Vlastos ([1984b], revised as [1991], chap. 8; all further references will be to the more recent (revised) discussion in [1991]) argue that Socrates thinks of complete happiness as consisting in a variety of components, of which moral virtue is the most important. Because they see virtue as a part of happiness, Santas and Vlastos commit Socrates to the view that virtue is of intrinsic value. Irwin ([1977], ch. 4) maintains that Socrates endorses hedonism and, hence, that virtue is of instrumental value only. Most recently, Zeyl [1982] argues a view like that proposed by Vlastos, but adds to it that Socrates also believes that virtue is good for its consequences. We do not wish to argue for one side or another in this particular debate, and thus have avoided the terms "intrinsic" and "extrinsic" (or "instrumental") in our discussion. Rather, we wish only to discuss goods in terms of whether or not they are conducive to happiness through their own agency (such things are IGs), or only through the agency of something else (such things are DGs).

3. For examples, see Irwin [1977], 100 (see also his [1986a]); Vlastos [1984b], esp. 191–213 (see also [1978], 230–31, and [1980], esp. 318–23); Zeyl [1982], 225–38; Burnyeat [1971], 210–11; Gulley [1968], 200. Santas [1979] and Vlastos [1991], ch. 8, provide a hierarchy of the levels of happiness one might obtain, but believe that virtue is sufficient for at least the minimal level.

4. Irwin [1977], 100.

is uniformly supported by other ancient writers in revealing Socrates' relative lack of concern for what his fellow Athenians regard as life's most important trea- sures.[5] Wealth and its trappings, the esteem of others, and political power obvi- ously do not impress him. Unlike other Athenians, who scramble after what they mistakenly think will make them happy, Socrates is concerned only with living a good life and making his soul as good as he can make it. Thus, whether on the battlefield or on trial for his life, Socrates considers only what is just, oblivious to the dangers that swirl around him.

But the view that Socrates holds virtue to be sufficient for happiness has a very high cost, for the doctrine cannot be made consistent with Socrates' various remarks on how a person could be harmed in spite of his or her virtue. In this chapter, we shall explain Socrates' view of the value of virtue by offering an account that not only shows the various texts to be consistent with one another, but also forms a defensible position regarding the choiceworthiness of virtue over vice.

We shall begin by looking at what Socrates says about the various goods. Then, in the next section, we shall draw what we argue is a Socratic distinction between virtue, considered as a condition of the soul, and virtuous activity. We undertake to show how Socrates takes only good or virtuous activity to be neces- sary and sufficient for happiness; the virtuous condition of the soul, we shall argue, however valuable it is according to Socrates, is not sufficient for happiness. We shall go on to draw a distinction from Socratic philosophy between relative and absolute goods and evils in order to explain Socrates' claims in the *Apology* that a worse person cannot harm a better one and that no evil comes to a good person. Our general thesis is that a coherent account of Socrates' view of the relationship between virtue and happiness requires that he conceive of happiness as achieved only through good or virtuous activity. But, we argue, because such activity can be thwarted by events which the virtuous person may be powerless to prevent, Socrates believes that even the virtuous person, under certain conditions, may judge his or her life to be wretched and not worth living.

Having argued that virtue is not sufficient for happiness, we shall conclude by considering the case of Socrates himself. Socrates clearly says that he lacks the wisdom necessary to be virtuous. Yet in the *Apology* (41c9–d2), Socrates shows that he considers himself to be a good man. In the final section of this chapter, we shall consider how, on Socrates' view, one can be good without being virtu- ous. But because Socrates believed that such a good but not virtuous man could be happy, we conclude that the virtuous condition of the soul is not even a neces- sary condition of happiness.[6] Lest our argument that virtue is neither necessary

5. Perhaps the most descriptive testimony in this regard is to be found in Alcibiades' speech in the *Symposium,* esp. at 216a8–e5, 219b3–220b8. Although the *Symposium* is generally regarded as a middle period work, the speech of Alcibiades is regarded by most contemporary Socratic scholars as compatible with the Socrates portrayed in the early dialogues.

6. In denying the necessity of virtue for happiness, we change our position from the one we expressed in Brickhouse and Smith [1987b], where we argued that virtue was necessary but not suffi- cient for virtue. Now, we argue that it is neither necessary nor sufficient.

nor sufficient for happiness appear to leave one with no reason for pursuing virtue, we shall conclude with a few observations about why Socrates would regard virtue a priceless treasure for the one who could obtain it.

4.2 Goods

4.2.1 A Look at the Euthydemus

Irwin believes that an argument in the *Euthydemus* commits Socrates to the sufficiency of virtue by eliminating all of the other alternatives. Irwin writes: "In the *Euthyd*. Socrates' attitude to the popular candidates for happiness is highly critical. He agrees with the popular view that it must include all the goods there are; but he claims that wisdom is the only good, and that it is therefore necessary and sufficient for happiness." [7] Since the "unity of the virtues" doctrine identifies wisdom with virtue, Socrates must think, according to Irwin, that virtue is necessary and sufficient for happiness. Hence, on Irwin's reading of the *Euthydemus*, there is only one good, virtue, and it is an IG that is both an NG and an SG. There are no DGs, in this view, nor are there goods that are NGs but not SGs, or SGs but not NGs.

It is beyond dispute that Socrates thinks that virtue is always good (see, e.g., *Charm*. 161a2–10), and that it is always the most important good (*Prt*. 313a6–b1; *Cri*. 47e6–48a4; *Grg*. 512a5–6). But the latter claim at least suggests, though it does not entail, that Socrates thinks there are goods other than virtue. Now Irwin is certainly right in claiming that in the *Euthydemus* Socrates is highly critical of what most of his fellow Athenians would take happiness to be. And it is clear that there Socrates thinks wisdom is the only thing that is *always* good. But is Irwin right in claiming that in the *Euthydemus* Socrates endorses the view that wisdom is the only thing that is good?

The passage in question begins with Socrates and young Cleinias agreeing that all people wish to be happy (278e3–279a1), and that happiness requires the possession of "many good things" (279a2–3). They then proceed to list a number of things commonly held to be good: wealth, health, good looks, good birth, public honors, the moral virtues, and good fortune. But good fortune, Socrates argues, at least construed as a good to be pursued,[8] is best understood as wisdom, since, with the latter, one "could not make a mistake, but is necessarily correct in what

7. Irwin [1986a], 91. Irwin's inference here is actually invalid, unless he is presupposing a strengthened version of PE. One might consistently believe that PE is true, and that wisdom is the only good, but also that wisdom is still insufficient for happiness. "The only thing conducive to happiness" does not entail "the only thing sufficient for obtaining happiness." Hence Irwin's inference in this case must rely upon the assumption of some version of PE that strengthens "conducive to" to something like "necessary and sufficient for." We believe, however, that the way we have worded PE is the best way to express the commitment to eudaimonism, since a stronger version begs a number of important questions.

8. As we shall subsequently argue (see n.31), we do not take this passage to establish that wisdom *always assures* good luck, but rather only that good luck, insofar as it can be assured, would best be assured by becoming wise.

he does and in what happens'' (280a6–8). So far, then, Socrates has reduced one of the list of goods to wisdom. He cannot, and does not (yet, at least) conclude from this achievement that wisdom is the *only* good.

If wisdom is to be shown the only good in this passage, then, Socrates must go on to show either that all of the other apparent goods in the list (wealth, health, good looks, good birth, public honors, and the other virtues) can also be reduced to wisdom, or else that these others are not really goods. In fact, Socrates does neither of these things; instead he goes on to show that everything in the list except wisdom[9] is a DG, dependent upon the uses to which wisdom would put them. Socrates' first summation of the argument is instructive and worth quoting in full:

> It seems likely that with regard to the whole group of things we first called goods, the argument is not about how they are in themselves by nature goods, but rather, it seems it is thus: if ignorance leads them they are greater evils than their opposites, insofar as they are more able to serve an evil leader. But if understanding and wisdom lead them, they are greater goods, but in themselves neither sort is of any value. (*Euthyd.* 281d2–e1)

It would appear from this argument, then, that Socrates believes that only wisdom is an IG. All other goods are DGs, dependent upon the one IG, wisdom.

4.2.2 Do Other Texts Support This Understanding?

This way of understanding Socrates' point in the *Euthydemus* gains strong support from the *Apology* where Socrates emphatically states that some things other than virtue, including even money, can be good. As part of his explanation of the nature of his philosophical mission, he tells the jury:

> I go about doing nothing else than prevailing upon you, young and old, not to care for your bodies or for wealth[10] more than for the perfection of your souls,

---

9. The other virtues are dropped from this discussion in the *Euthydemus*, though this would have given Socrates an excellent opportunity to argue for the unity of the virtues, as Irwin takes the passage to suggest ([1977], 87–88, and n.57, 301). We prefer Ferejohn's explanation ([1984], 105–22, esp. 114–20). Ferejohn argues that wisdom is the only IG. The other virtues are DGs, for their value to their possessors depends upon their possessors' additionally having wisdom. Ferejohn concludes ([1984], 117) that the other virtues may be said to be "invariably beneficent" (that is, always good for their possessors), and that no goods other than the virtues are invariably beneficent, but only wisdom is "value-independent" (our IG). The "trick" to this, in Ferejohn's view (see [1984], 119), is that wisdom is a necessary condition of the rest of the virtues, so one would never realize any of them without in addition realizing wisdom. Since for the purposes of the rest of this paper we shall be discussing *realized* virtue, that is, with the achieved necessary condition of wisdom (we believe that this is also presumed in most Socratic discussions of virtue—see, e.g., *Grg.* 507b5–c5), we shall construe (all of) virtue as an IG.

10. Burnyeat [1971] translates the word "χρήματα" as "valuables" rather than as "wealth," in part to save Socrates from the claim that a material possession could be a good. But there are a number of reasons for rejecting Burnyeat's rendering. First, although "χρήματα" can mean "valuables," it still strongly connotes material things. It would be odd Greek, then, for Socrates to use the word to refer to strictly psychic benefits rather than tangible assets of some sort. Second, Socrates is chastising his fellow citizens for their misplaced values, and he clearly thinks that they have foolishly placed the

or even so much; and I tell you that virtue does not come from wealth, but from virtue come wealth and all other good things for human beings. . . . (*Ap.* 30a7–b4)

Socrates is obviously not claiming that being good always produces financial rewards, as if it were good business sense.[11] His own lack of wealth is testimony to that (see *Ap.* 31c2–3). But if we place the passage in context, Socrates' view of the relationship between virtue and wealth comes into focus. First, he explains that part of his mission is to rebuke his fellow citizens for caring more about such things as "wealth, reputation, and honor" and caring nothing for "wisdom, truth, and the perfection of the soul" (*Ap.* 29d7–e2). By so doing, he says, they mistake what is of lesser value for what is of greater value (*Ap.* 30a1–2). So, Socrates' rebuke has to do initially with the relative value of various goods; he is not claiming that what most people take to be the greatest goods can never be of any value. The passage quoted provides Socrates' *explanation* of why his fellow Athenians are mistaken. Their error, he thinks, is not simply that they have mistaken what is of lesser for what is of greater value; they also have the wrong conception of what virtue requires. They think that money and other worldly goods will give them virtue, whereas, for Socrates, true virtue consists in "wisdom, truth, and the perfection of the soul." In adding that "from virtue come wealth and all other good things for human beings," he is telling them the only way to make wealth a genuinely good thing: first, he says, one must become virtuous.[12]

4.2.3 Dependent and Independent Goods

In both passages, from the *Euthydemus* and from the *Apology*, we find Socrates committed to the existence of goods other than virtue, but goods whose goodness depends upon virtue.[13] It is true that Socrates nowhere specifies how virtue transforms other possessions into goods. Nor does he ever say in what way something such as money could benefit the virtuous person. But to see how virtue could turn

---

wrong emphasis on the well-being of their bodies and their material possessions (see *Ap.* 29d7–e3, 41e2–7). To translate "χρήματα" simply as "valuables" is to miss the directness of Socrates' challenge to what his fellow citizens mistakenly believe are the most important goods. Finally, Burnyeat's translation makes Socrates' claim, "from virtue comes χρήματα and all other good things for men" redundant: what other "good things" could there be but "valuable things"?

11. This unlikely implication is sometimes simply *translated* away, as if the passage explicitly stated that wealth and the other things become good through virtue (see, for example, Reeve [1989], 124–25, n.21, following Burnet [1924], 204, note on 30b3). Although this is the sense of the passage, the crucial line actually says that "from virtue come wealth and every other good thing for human beings." (See chapter 1, n.33.)

12. The language of *Apology* 36c4–d1 should be seen as making a compatible point: Socrates tells the jury that he has spent his life trying to persuade all persons not to care for their possessions before they have taken care to make sure that they are the best and most prudent they can be. Socrates' point is not that one should never under any circumstances care about material goods, but rather that one should attach a higher priority to attaining virtue.

13. Thus far we see no reason to disagree with Vlastos's attribution to Socrates of what he terms "the principle of the Sovereignty of Virtue" to characterize the relationship between virtue as an IG and various things that are transformed into DGs by the possession of virtue ([1991], 209–14). Later, however, we will show how we think Vlastos's view fails.

various items into non-moral goods, let us turn again to the *Apology*. At the beginning of his second speech, immediately after his conviction, Socrates considers what "penalty" would be most appropriate for his "crimes." He says the most apt "punishment" would be free meals at the Prutaneion (36d5–7), an honor ordinarily bestowed on Athens' most celebrated heroes. His explanation of the appropriateness of the proposal is revealing: he says that he is poor but needs leisure to exhort his fellow citizens (36e4–5). He repeats the point about his neediness at 36e1. His argument is simple: poverty might interfere with his good work in Athens; since he is such a great civic benefactor, the Athenians would only be giving Socrates his due if they provided him what he needed to continue his mission without impediment.

From the *Euthydemus* passage, we can recognize that Socrates would not call free meals at the Prutaneion an IG. Bestowed upon one with evil designs, such a reward would be an evil, for it would expedite one's evil-doing. But bestowed upon Socrates, free meals would be a good, for it would contribute to his (and Athens') well-being (36d9–e1). Hence, free meals are a DG, good on the basis of the contribution they would make to beneficent activity. Generalizing this, we derive the following: though one may talk about any variety of goods other than virtue, including many or even most of those things commonly called goods, they are all DGs; their goodness depends on their employment in the service of virtue. If one employs one's good looks in such a way as to promote and maintain justice, for example, one's good looks are of value. If instead one uses them to seduce others into evil and injustice, they are evil. If a good reputation is enjoyed by a person of moderation and prudence and assists that person in convincing others to live as he or she does, that reputation is a good thing. But if an evil person enjoys the esteem of others, that esteem is a bad thing. Insofar as a thing serves the ends of virtue, then, it is a good. But only virtue is *always* good, because only virtue is an IG. All other goods are DGs, and thus their value is not secure, for these same things become evils when they serve vice instead of virtue.

So at least sometimes Socrates recognizes the existence of goods other than virtue, but these other goods, he believes, are only DGs whose value can be transformed into evils through the improper or vicious use of them. But does Socrates always allow DGs to be called "good"? If we return to the *Euthydemus* passage cited above, we will see that he does not. Only a few lines after having drawn the conclusion that virtue is the only IG, as opposed to various DGs, Socrates draws another, apparently quite different conclusion from the argument he has just given. This time he says: "of all the other things, none is either good or bad, but of these two, wisdom is good and ignorance bad" (281e3–5).[14] He does not say that the goods other than wisdom are goods, but only dependent ones, or (what is compatible with this) stipulate that they are not goods in themselves, as

---

14. Vlastos ([1984b], 199–201) takes the second conclusion to stand in need of the unexpressed qualification that wisdom is good (*just by itself*) and ignorance is evil (*just by itself*). Again, we see no reason to disagree with Vlastos on this point, although it must be emphasized that sense can be made of Socrates' stating the second conclusion in such different terms only if he wishes to emphasize the very different status of wisdom as an IG and various DGs and, hence, that, strictly speaking, wisdom is the only good.

he did in his first concluding statement (281d8–e1); in the second concluding statement he says they are neither good nor bad, without qualification. This second conclusion should strike us as odd, for Socrates has just finished talking about such things as health and wealth as things that are good when used under the guidance of wisdom. Unless we are to convict Socrates of inconsistency within the space of just a few lines, we must suppose that, in drawing the second conclusion, he is relying on the (suppressed) premise that if a thing is not an IG, it is not *really* a good at all. But the appearance of inconsistency vanishes if we make the quite reasonable assumption that with the second conclusion Socrates is simply emphasizing the difference between an IG and a DG, by claiming that only an IG is really a good.

4.2.4   A Problem in the Gorgias

Keeping in mind the *Euthydemus'* view that only an IG is really a good, let us turn to a well-known passage in the *Gorgias* that might, at first, appear to represent a different way of classifying valuable things for Socrates.

> SOCRATES: Now is there anything which exists that is not good or evil or between the two, neither good nor evil?
>
> POLUS: Necessarily nothing, Socrates.
>
> SOCRATES: Well, do you say that wisdom and health and wealth and all other such things are good, and their opposites evils?
>
> POLUS: I do.
>
> SOCRATES: And by things neither good nor evil, do you mean such things as sometimes partake of the good, and sometimes of the evil, and sometimes of neither, for example, to sit and to walk and to run and to sail, or for example, stones and sticks and other such things? Are these not what you refer to? Or are there other things that you call neither goods nor evils?
>
> POLUS: No, just these. (*Grg.* 467e1–468a4)

Here is it is clear that Socrates is not willing to use the terms "good" and "evil" to refer to the "intermediate things," those things that "sometimes partake of the good and sometimes of the evil." So unless something is *always* good— which is not true of DGs—it is not *really* good, but instead, neither good nor evil. It is important to notice, however, that this is no different from the way Socrates classifies valuable things in the *Euthydemus*. There we saw that although Socrates is willing to refer to DGs as "goods," he makes a point of emphasizing that he regards only an IG, something that is of itself beneficial, as a good in the proper sense. In the *Gorgias* passage, Socrates is pointing out to Polus under what conditions it is rational to want "intermediate things," things that are in themselves neither beneficial not harmful. In both dialogues the point regarding the desirability of such things is the same: it is rational to want the things that are, in themselves, neither good nor evil when and only when they happen to promote what is truly beneficial for us. Accordingly, we find no difference between the two dialogues regarding the Socratic classification of valuable things.

But this passage in the *Gorgias* presents another difficulty for understanding Socrates' classification of valuable things: it appears directly to contradict the view defended in the *Euthydemus* that virtue is the only IG, and hence the only thing that is, for Socrates, good strictly speaking. In the *Gorgias* passage Socrates seems to endorse the view that there are a variety of goods, "wisdom and health and wealth and all other things of that sort." [15]

In the context in which he makes this claim in the *Gorgias,* however, there is no need for Socrates to undertake to examine any of these goods, their dependence upon, or independence of one another. His argument at this point turns on Polus' acceptance of the assumption, made explicit at 477a8–c2, that the soul, the body, and one's possessions, each has its own good condition, together with Polus' acceptance of the claim that the "neutral things" are pursued for the sake of whatever is good. The point of this passage is to gain Polus' assent to the reason that must be given for desiring "neutral things." Goods are those for the sake of which we do everything (468b7–8, c5); neutrals are pursued for the sake of the good, and not for their own sake (468a5–b4, c6); evils are never pursued, if recognized as evils (468c6–7, d5–6). Socrates is not attempting actually to classify any of the particular things listed, for example, health or wealth, as good with any finality. [16]

From the way Socrates in the *Gorgias* characterizes what will count as a good and what as merely a neutral thing, we can conclude that though he is frequently willing to talk as if he recognizes goods other than virtue, when speaking strictly, Socrates does not recognize any goods that are not IGs. Given what he says in the *Euthydemus* and given the unique position enjoyed by virtue in Socratic philosophy as a whole, we may infer that, for Socrates, only virtue counts as an IG. Hence, when Socrates is speaking strictly, only virtue is a good.

4.2.5   Another Problem in the Gorgias

One passage remains, however, that would appear to lend support to the view that there is at least one good other than virtue, if only because it plainly identifies an evil other than vice. At *Gorgias* 512a2–b2, Socrates tells Callicles that one with a chronically diseased body, like one with a chronically diseased soul, is "wretched" (ἄθλιος) and better off not living, since such a person is bound to live badly. No conditions are put on this claim regarding the person who is virtuous but chronically diseased; so this person, too, would be wretched, and have a life not worth living. If chronic disease is an evil sufficient to make one's life not

15. Santas [1979] and Vlastos ([1991], ch. 8), for example, take Socrates to be saying that such goods are components of happiness. As our following argument shows, however, we deny this.

16. At this stage in the *Gorgias* Socrates is relying on the quite common Greek usage of "good." In this sense, a thing is good when it can function well or can be used well. Thus, a knife is "good," for example, when it can cut well. Similarly, the soul is "good" when it can function well as a soul (viz. when it is wise), and the body is "good" when it can function well as a body (viz. when it is healthy). But this non-moral use of good leaves open the moral question of how anything should be used in such a way that it will conduce to happiness. To gain Polus' assent, at this point in the dialogue, Socrates need not attempt to answer the moral question left open.

worth living, as this passage claims, then the evil of disease would appear to be independent of virtue and vice. It might seem to follow, then, that the corresponding good, health, must be an IG.

If this is what the *Gorgias* passage means, it contradicts the *Euthydemus*, which, as we found above, stipulated clearly that health is a DG and not an IG. We believe a resolution is possible. First, in the *Gorgias* as a whole, as we said earlier, no definitive count of the number of goods is ever undertaken; the argument relies upon what Socrates' interlocutors are prepared to accept, namely, that health is indeed a good and that disease is an evil. But, second, Socrates gets Callicles to agree in the end that health is the good of the body and virtue is the good of the soul, and that the latter is an immeasurably greater good than the former, because the soul is "so much more precious than the body" (512a5–6; see 477b5–e6; *Cri.* 47e6–48a3). If the good of the body should come into conflict with the good of the soul, or should in some way contribute to the evil of the soul (e.g., if one's good health enabled one to pursue more actively a life of evil and injustice—see *Euthyd.* 281b4–e1), then health would become, all things considered, an evil. The point here is not simply that health is less important than virtue; rather, it is that health is not *always* good. Hence, health is just another DG, and like other DGs, worth nothing (or it is even an evil) when not employed by virtue.

4.3   Virtue and Sufficiency

4.3.1   *Is Virtue a Sufficient Good?*

We have seen how Socrates often acknowledges that many things can be goods, but that all depend upon virtue for their goodness, and how this turns out to mean, in his view, that only virtue is, in the strict sense, a good. But a thing may be an IG without being an SG; that is, a thing may, of itself, be *conducive* to happiness (as per PE), but not always *suffice* of itself to *ensure* it. This is precisely Aristotle's view of this issue: he accepts PE and the doctrine that virtue is an IG, but claims that virtue alone is not sufficient for happiness. Such terrible misfortunes (as, for example, those suffered by Priam) might befall the virtuous man as to prevent him from achieving the happiness that would otherwise be his (*N.E.* 1100b33–1101a13). So Aristotle, at least, did not think that virtue is an SG. Did Socrates?

Fundamental to the philosophy of the early dialogues is Socrates' conviction that one must always act as virtue requires and avoid the commission of any wrong whatever. In the *Apology*, for example, he explains why he will never abandon his service to the god by telling the jury: "You are not correct . . . if you think that a man who is of any worth ought to take into account the danger of life or death and not consider only this whenever he acts: whether he does just things or unjust and performs the acts of a good or an evil man" (28b5–9; see 28d6–10). The same uncompromising view is repeated in response to Crito's appeal that he escape from prison: "And if we would appear to be doing unjust things then it would be necessary not to consider whether we would die by remaining here and keeping quiet or suffering anything else before we consider injustice'' (48d3–5). He knows all too well that by electing to stay in prison, he will lose everything but his morality. For Socrates, then, whatever could be gained through the doing of injustice could never outweigh the value of acting justly.

4.3.2   Living Well

Socrates justifies his conclusion regarding the supreme value of justice by means of his agreements with Crito that "it is not living but living well that one must consider most important" and that "to live well is the same thing as to live justly" (48b5). Regardless of how Socrates understands the nature of the identity asserted in the second premise, he believes at least that living justly is both necessary and sufficient for living well.

The expression "living well" (εὐ ζῆν), like the expression "doing well" (εὐ πράττειν), is used by Socrates as a synonym for, or is at least biconditionally related to, "happiness" (εὐδαιμονία) (see, e.g., *Rep.* I.354a1–2).[17] Thus, Socrates believes that "living justly and nobly" is both necessary and sufficient for happiness. What is not clear, however, is what he takes "doing well" and "living well" to refer to. On the one hand, he may take the terms to refer to a particular condition of the soul, and whatever activities might be performed under the guidance of that condition (see, e.g., *Ap.* 28b5–9; *Charm.* 160d5–e1; *Rep.* I.335d11–12). In this case, that condition alone would appear to be sufficient for happiness. But it might also mean that some level of achievement in one's activity is required, for which external factors such as opportunity and the powers to accomplish that level of achievement are necessary conditions. Such a level of achievement might at least sometimes require the use of the body, or at least that the body not be an impediment. In this case, the possession of virtue may not always be sufficient for living justly and, hence, for living well, since there may be circumstances that prevent one from attaining the necessary level of achievement in one's activities. Deciding, then, upon whether or not certain standards of achievement must be met for "living well" is crucial to determining whether or not Socrates subscribes to the sufficiency of virtue doctrine.

4.3.3   Good Action

Toward the end of *Republic* I (353d2–354a2), Socrates argues that the soul has a function and that if it is to perform its function well, it must possess its own virtue. Its function is "management, rule, deliberation, and life." The evil soul will perform its function badly, whereas the "good soul will do all such things well." Thus, he concludes that the just soul and the just person live well and "one who lives well is blessed and happy." It is not clear from this passage just what Socrates thinks the soul is to manage and rule over. Nowhere, for example,

---

17. The *Euthydemus* may also be cited here, since the argument shifts from talk of εὐ πράττειν at 278e3, 6, and 279a2 to both εὐ πράττειν and εὐδαιμονία at 280b6, to only εὐδαιμονία from 280b7 through the rest of the argument. Given the role of these terms in the argument, logic requires them to be used as synonyms.

does he specifically exclude the possibility that the soul's function is simply to manage and to rule over itself. If that is what he means, Socrates would have to judge one happy if and only if one is the master of one's soul, apart from any other consequences of such mastery. But in a passage in the *Gorgias* that is almost certainly intended to make the same point as this passage in *Republic* I, Socrates explicitly maintains that one is to be called "blessed and happy" on the basis of his actions, and not merely on the condition of his soul.

> The temperate one is not one to pursue or flee from what is not fitting, but the affairs, and men, and pleasures, and pains he ought to flee and pursue, and to endure remaining where he ought. And so it is most necessary, Callicles, that the temperate person, just as we have reported, being just and brave and pious, is completely good, *and the good person acts well and nobly in what he does, and the one who does well is blessed and happy. But the base person and the one who acts evilly is wretched.* (Grg. 507b5–c5)

According to the *Gorgias,* then, the correct "management and rule" that constitutes the proper functioning of the soul, concerns the appropriate "avoidance and pursuit of things and people." Thus, the good soul is concerned with good action and not merely the maintenance of its own good condition.[18] Moreover, Socrates is attempting to convince Callicles that the temperate person is always better off than the unbridled pleasure-seeker Callicles admires. But, as the passage shows, Socrates drives home his point, not by arguing merely that the soul of the good person is more orderly than that of the intemperate person, but by showing that the good person always *does well.* What qualifies the good person as being "blessed and happy" is the fact that he or she succeeds in his or her actions.[19]

4.3.4 An Adaptive Strategy?

It might be thought that Socrates' view that happiness is achieved through good action need not conflict with the sufficiency of virtue doctrine. When Socrates tells Callicles, "and the good person must do whatever he does well and nobly," he may mean that the good person will always adapt to whatever circumstances arise. When conditions occur that prevent the performance of the actions one

---

18. Burnyeat ([1971], 211, 232) believes that, for Socrates, the well-being of the soul is prior to the performance of virtuous action. From this he appears to infer that the well-being of the soul must be of intrinsic value to Socrates. Irwin points out ([1977], 303, n.71) that this inference is a faulty one: Socrates could think that the well-being of the soul is a logically necessary condition for the performance of virtuous action but of value only because of its contribution to such virtuous activity. Hence, even if it were necessary for virtuous activity, it need not be intrinsically valuable. Its value might nonetheless be instrumental. Our own view does not concern itself with whether or not virtue has intrinsic value (see n.2), but we are committed to the thesis that virtue is at least always preferable to its opposite, but not sufficient in itself to ensure happiness.

19. It might be thought that this passage indicates that Socrates thinks the good person will always do well and, hence, will always be happy. But Socrates need not mean this, nor does he say it. It is true that whatever the good person does will always be done well. But it does not follow from this that the good person will always be able to act. One's actions may be thwarted by conditions over which one has no control.

might otherwise desire to do, the good person simply adjusts his desires accordingly, recognizing that under the circumstances those actions cannot be performed.[20]

A number of passages certainly suggest an adaptive strategy, without which Socrates' morality would itself come into question. For example, when the Thirty ordered him to go out and arrest Leon, Socrates simply went home (32c4–d7). He did not, however, undertake to obstruct the subsequent arrest of Leon (and Leon was indeed brought in and executed). Nor did Socrates, as far as we know, do anything whatever to dissuade his fellow citizens from committing even the most horrendous acts, such as the genocide carried out against the inhabitants of Scione and Melos.[21] Socrates' response to such a charge of indifference would surely be "you know well that if I had tried to engage in political matters, I would have perished long ago and would have benefited neither you nor me" (*Ap*. 31d7–e1).[22] So, it might be thought that the good man always undertakes to do the best thing available to him at the time, all things considered. Had Socrates attempted to prevent the arrest of Leon, or the condemnation of Scione or Melos, he is convinced that he would thereby have diminished or brought to an end the pious mission he daily carried out in Athens, a mission so important that it made him Athens' greatest benefactor (*Ap*. 30a5–7).

But the constraints placed upon the good-souled person by others and by circumstances may be very great, so great as effectively to prevent even the most minimally good action. Would Socrates view a good person living under such extremely inhibiting conditions as happy? We think not. Socrates does believe, of course, that the greatest harm is always harm to the soul. But in arguing for this very point in the *Crito*, he states that "life is not worth living with a diseased and corrupted body" (47e3–5). What is significant is that avoiding a life that is not worth living is also the reason one should avoid having a diseased and corrupted soul (47e6–49a2). Having a diseased and corrupted body, then, must be a sufficiently great impediment to happiness that regardless of how one might try to adjust to it, one's life would not be worth living. As we said earlier, the same point is made with even greater emphasis in the *Gorgias*, at 512a2–b2, where we are told that one with a chronically diseased body, like one with a chronically diseased soul, is "wretched" and better off not living, since such a person is "bound to live badly." Even if Socrates thinks that the good person will attempt to adjust his or her goals and activities to some circumstances, he clearly believes that some things could happen—for example, falling chronically ill with a disabling disease—against which one is powerless to defend oneself, and which would be sufficient to make one's life wretched.[23]

20. This view is defended by Irwin [1986a].

21. Questions about the propriety of Socrates' lack of involvement in Athens' political institutions are raised in Vlastos [1984a], 932.

22. Ibid., Vlastos's translation.

23. It is worth noticing that in Irwin's view [1986a], the virtuous person could never suffer (or at least not suffer for long) from unsatisfied desires. It is thus a consequence of Irwin's view that the maximally virtuous person would not desire to see injustices righted whenever it is highly unlikely that such corrections will ever take place. This strikes us as un-Socratic. After all, Socrates admits that there occur numerous unjust and illegal things that he would not be able to prevent (see *Ap*.

Moreover, Socrates' emphasis in *Republic* I on the proper functioning of the soul indicates that he does not see happiness as something that can always be fostered merely by adjusting to circumstances. On the contrary, the possession of virtue requires that the soul must always aim at actions that improve and never harm people (*Rep.* I.335b2–e6). For Socrates, to improve people is to make them morally better. This is precisely what Socrates tells the jury in the *Apology:* it is a central feature of his divine mission to make people care first about wisdom, truth, and the perfection of the soul (29e1–2). But if "living justly and nobly" and "living well" refer to engaging in various good activities and not merely to the possession of a particular condition of the soul, it is clear that no adjusting to circumstances can ever save the happiness of the good person if circumstances prevent even the minimal involvement in such good actions. This also helps to explain Socrates' obvious concern for the good of the body, health. Having a diseased and corrupted body makes life not worth living precisely because it prevents even the minimum performance of good action required for the happy life.

It is clear from the *Apology* that the improvement of people, the end of good action, can be achieved only (or at least in the main)[24] through the therapeutic effects of philosophical interchange (38a1–8),[25] in which Socrates views himself to be divinely commanded to engage. This is why, after he has been convicted, he rejects a number of counter-penalties on the ground that he knows them to be

31e2–32a3). But nowhere is there the slightest hint that the just person would not desire such injustices to end. Nor is there any hint that Socrates believes that the just person will always have his or her way in "fighting for the just" (*Ap.* 32a1). He or she will do the best he or she can, and will succeed as much as success is possible for one in such circumstances. But one may not always get what one wants. One's failure in such cases, moreover, need not change one's view that what one wanted was what was best, and therefore, to be desired even though presently unobtainable. In short, we do not see Socrates suggesting, as the Stoics do, that one should desire only the way things actually turn out.

Irwin ([1986a], 108–9) concedes that his account is inconsistent with Socrates' various remarks about the ways in which the virtuous person may nonetheless be harmed and come to judge his or her life as miserable and not worth living. He cites Richard Kraut ([1983b], 38–39, n.21) as holding a contrary view. We are in general agreement with the position Kraut sketches. However, Kraut nevertheless fails to distinguish clearly between virtue, considered as the healthy condition of the soul, and virtuous action, saying, for example (what we find unacceptable—see n.25, below), "one can no longer be virtuous if his body is ruined." In our view, harms to the body can prevent virtuous action, but will not alter the virtuous condition of the soul.

24. We have added the qualification because we believe that Socrates might reasonably be supposed to accept that one can also improve others by setting a good example in any of one's affairs, as for example, in one's demeanor on the battlefield.

25. Kraut [1983b] says that virtue "requires such activities as discussion and self-examination." It is an interesting question whether or not Socrates believes that one cannot maintain whatever degree of health in the soul one has already achieved unless one continues always to engage in discussion and self-examination. Would the health of the soul decay or vanish if one was prevented somehow from such activities? If so, it is difficult for us to see any way in which the good man can be assured of freedom from harm, for on this assumption even his soul might suffer harm if he were to be unjustly exiled or imprisoned. Instead, we believe that if one is ever to achieve the virtuous condition of the soul, one must first engage in such activities, and that such activities will be prominent among the natural range of activities to which the already virtuous soul would apply itself (with the proviso given in n.23, above). Kraut's sense of "requires" might appear to involve a constant and continuing need, however, though he also recognizes that "the soul is not corrupted if one is the victim of injustice" ([1983b], 38, with passages cited in his n.18).

evils: imprisonment, imprisonment until a fine is paid, exile, and a cessation of his philosophical activities (37b7–38b1). Imprisonment, even until a fine is raised and paid on his behalf, would all but bring to an end his philosophical examination of others (37c1–2). Exile would be no solution because other cities will be far less likely than Athens to allow him to philosophize (37c4–e2). Plainly, voluntary silence in Athens has the same consequence (37e3–38a5). So when Socrates says he must "talk every day about virtue . . . examining myself and others [for] the unexamined life is not worth living for a human being" (38a1–6), he shows that he requires more than a good soul to make his life worth living; in addition, he needs to examine himself and others. The penalties he considers and rejects in the second speech in the *Apology*, therefore, are evils, for they would hinder the performance of even the minimal level of activity necessary to make Socrates' life worth living. Only if we think of Socrates' conception of happiness in terms of activities, then, can we make sense of his claim that such penalties would be evils. If the relevant condition of one's soul were all that were at stake, no punishments or misfortunes of the sorts Socrates has in mind—not imprisonment, not exile, and not disease—would be evil or harmful, for none of these is a threat to the good condition of Socrates' soul. But Socrates says they would be evils (37b7–8), and so he carefully offers the only counter-penalty that he says will do him no harm (38b2).[26]

4.3.5 Two Important Passages

We are now in a position to understand two passages that provide the strongest apparent evidence for supposing that Socrates accepted the sufficiency of virtue doctrine, for each appears to be an explicit endorsement of it. At *Gorgias* 470e6–7, Socrates says that he does not know if Archelaus, the king of Macedonia, is happy, because he does not know how Archelaus is in terms of education and justice. Polus asks, "Why, is all of happiness in this [education and justice]?" and Socrates responds, "Yes, according to what I say, Polus; for the good and noble man and woman is happy, I say, and an evil and villainous one is wretched" (470e8–11). If the good person is invariably happy, it would appear beyond cavil that virtue is sufficient for happiness.[27]

26. Kraut [1983b] also makes this point, amidst an admirably detailed account of why Socratic principles must not be construed as having the consequence that Socrates would be indifferent to suffering injustice (35–39).

27. In fact, *Grg.* 470e6–7 is entirely ambiguous. On the one hand, we might read "all happiness is in this" (i.e., justice and education) (ἐν τούτῳ ἡ πᾶσα εὐδαιμονία ἐστίν) to mean all happiness consists in justice and education. If this is the proper reading, the lines would provide evidence, at least *prima facie*, for the sufficiency of virtue doctrine. But as Irwin ([1979], note on 470e8) points out, the line may be taken to mean "all happiness *depends upon* justice and education, in which case, Socrates is only asserting (at most) that virtue is necessary for happiness. But Socrates need not mean, moreover, that happiness *requires* that justice have been acquired; he may simply think that happiness "depends on justice" in the sense that no one is happy unless he or she is doing what justice requires. If so, he does not mean to exclude the possibility that someone who leads the examined life and sincerely seeks always to be good, but nonetheless lacks the knowledge necessary for the possession of virtue (and, hence, justice), should be counted as happy. Such a person may not be as happy as the fully virtuous person, for his or her life may have fallen short of the fully virtuous person for reasons

Similarly, in the passage from the *Republic* we have already discussed (353d2–354a2), Socrates begins his concluding argument with Thrasymachus by stipulating that the virtue of a thing is what allows that thing to fulfill its function. At 353e10–11, the specific conclusion Socrates sought to derive from this premise is drawn out: "The just soul and the just person will live well, and the unjust badly." If this conclusion is to be taken literally, virtue does not need enabling conditions; it is sufficient unto itself for its possessor to live well, and hence, happily (354a1–5).[28]

But when Socrates says in these passages that the good person is happy, or that the just soul will live well, we do not have to suppose that he means that goodness and justice are, of themselves, sufficient for happiness, independent of whatever disasters and impediments the person may suffer. Socrates may instead be referring to goodness and justice in persons *as they are under ordinary circumstances,* that is, suffering no substantially impaired capacity for the sort of agency one could, *ceteris paribus,* expect from the good man or woman. If Polus or Thrasymachus had interrupted in either passage with the question, "Do you mean, Socrates, that a virtuous person would live well even if he was systematically prevented from doing his soul's virtuous bidding, due to disease, infirmity, or an injustice done to him?," we should expect a more carefully qualified presentation of Socrates' position. In response to such a question Socrates would have to admit that one cannot judge one's life to be worth living under such conditions, but that the just person would bear such sorrows better than all others. In neither passage, however, is Socrates attempting to distinguish between individuals with healthy souls who are able to engage in virtuous activity and individuals with healthy souls who are for some reason prevented from acting as virtue demands. Hence, we should assume the former to be the sorts of individuals Socrates has in mind when he speaks of "the good and noble man and woman" at *Gorgias* 470e8–11. Happiness, then, is assured for the good and noble man or woman as we would normally conceive of them, able to act on their desires and to fulfill their goals. The only exceptions to the general point that the virtuous are happy are those who

---

we shall give in sec. 4.5.10. In sec. 4.5, we shall argue that Socrates himself is good and, hence, happy, but not virtuous.

28. Vlastos offers an alternative to our account and to the "identity thesis," which holds that virtue is the sole constituent of happiness. In order to make sense of Socrates' recognition of non-moral goods, Vlastos argues that there are degrees of happiness in Socratic philosophy, but that virtue is nevertheless sufficient for happiness. The addition of non-moral goods, under the guidance of virtue, merely enhances the happiness enjoyed by the virtuous, according to Vlastos. But "the difference they can make to our happiness is miniscule" ([1991], 227). Vlastos uses the biblical story of Job to show us a bizarre aspect of the identity thesis, which would not allow Socrates to see that Job was damaged as the result of Satan's bet with God ([1991], 216). We think that Vlastos is right in rejecting the identity thesis, but wrong in attempting to hold on to the sufficiency thesis, for it follows from Vlastos's account that Socrates would have to think that Satan's handiwork manages to diminish Job's happiness *only very slightly,* since what Satan destroys are only "mini-constituents" of happiness, enhancing the happiness brought by Job's virtue only to a minor degree ([1991], 227). But if so, while Job need not be indifferent to his losses, nothing he has lost is a cause for great sorrow either, a consequence that is only *slightly* less paradoxical than the identity thesis that Vlastos rightly rejects. (See also n.30.)

suffer from such severe external impediments that they are unable to act on their moral goodness.[29]

Of course, Socrates makes none of the qualifications we have relied upon in our interpretation of these passages. Nonetheless, they need to be read as we have suggested because of the explicitness of Socrates' remarks about the ruinous effects of disease and incapacity.[30] In each case where he addresses such topics self-consciously, he admits that life is not worth living when one is so bitterly afflicted. It is clear throughout Plato's early dialogues that Socrates frequently expresses his views by taking the more obvious disclaimers and qualifications as assumed. An unqualified reading of these particular passages, which resists the application of views Socrates makes explicit in other passages, must insist that he contradicts himself in the most obvious ways. And such a reading can make no significantly greater claim to textual support than our more charitable interpretation.[31]

29. See *Hip. Mi.* 366b7–c3, where Socrates shows that in making a general point, he ignores counterexamples that would follow from cases of illness or impairment.

30. In a brief footnote, Vlastos ([1991], 218, n.69) attempts to blunt some of the evidence we cite against the sufficiency of virtue for happiness thesis. Vlastos argues that the diseases Socrates recognizes as destructive of happiness must be so devastating as to leave one "incapacitated for the exercise of knowledge and therewith for that of virtue, since Socrates holds that virtue 'is' knowledge." In Vlastos's view, then, only those diseases that somehow would cause the virtuous to lose his or her moral knowledge are sufficient to make life not worth living. Diseases that merely incapacitate the body but do not cause the loss of virtue could never make the virtuous judge his or her life to be not worth living.

But Socrates never draws any such distinction among diseases. Moreover, in both the *Crito* and the *Gorgias* Socrates makes the point that life is not worth living when the body is racked by disease *before* asserting that life is even less worth holding on to when one's soul is unjust. A straightforward reading of what he says about the corrupted conditions of the body and the soul, then, is that each is an evil independently sufficient to make death preferable to life. Recall that in the *Gorgias* Socrates says that disease can make one wretched. According to Vlastos, Socrates can only be referring to diseases which impair the cognitive abilities of the virtuous to the point that he or she could not longer be said to possess moral knowledge. No doubt there are such diseases and the loss of virtue would indeed be a great evil, but the loss of virtue would only be an evil relative the good lost. The mere loss of virtue is not sufficient, of itself, to make one wretched. Wretchedness requires something further, namely, the acquisition of vice. Even if we can imagine a case in which a person is so diseased that he first loses virtue and then actually becomes vicious, it cannot very well be that the disease alone caused him to become vicious. In any case, all Socrates actually says in the *Gorgias* is that one *is* wretched if one possesses "great and incurable diseases throughout the body." Since *moral* expertise provides no protection against morbific disasters, Socrates cannot hold the sufficiency thesis.

31. The same argument and one other would apply in our interpretation of *Euthyd.* 279d4–280b3, where Socrates and Cleinias come to agree that "when wisdom is present, the one in whom it is present is not in need of good fortune" (280b2–3). Contrary to Reeve ([1989], 129–44), we do not believe that this passage should be read as committing Socrates and Cleinias to what we consider to be the absurd view that no misfortune can ever befall the wise person. (1) When Socrates and Cleinias agree that the wise person is not still in need of good fortune, they may be assumed to be making the same sorts of assumptions as we have argued are presumed by the discussions at *Grg.* 470e6–11 and at *Rep.* I.353d2–354a2, namely, that *other things are equal*. The wise person is not omnipotent; whatever one's wisdom, one cannot control all of the things that might happen to one, and some of these things might be quite unlucky. But the wise person, *ceteris paribus*, will always be more fortunate than the unwise person. (2) At *Euthyd.* 281a6–b4 Socrates says "concerning the use of the goods

4.4 Relative and Absolute Good and Evil, Benefit and Harm

4.4.1 A Pair of Passages from the Apology

Two passages from the *Apology* still require attention, for some commentators regard them as compelling evidence that Socrates did accept the sufficiency of virtue for happiness.[32] In the first, Socrates explains why he is undaunted in the face of any penalties that may be inflicted on him for having engaged in the pious pursuit of his mission. "Neither Meletus nor Anytus could harm me—that is not possible—for I do not think it is permitted for a better person to be harmed by a worse" (30c8–d1). In the second, Socrates explains why, having been condemned to death, he can face his death with equanimity: "No evil comes to a good person either in life or in death" (41d1–2). It is not difficult to see why commentators would take these passages to be decisive. Because Socrates is an eudaimonist, he accordingly construes evils in terms of being conducive to unhappiness or wretchedness. This, then, is the harm that always results from evil (see, e.g., *Grg.* 477e3–4; *Meno* 77d2–9). He obviously recognizes that he can be deprived of all of his possessions and put to death. But because he says that none of these things would harm him, it might appear that he cannot believe that any of his possessions, or even life itself, is required for happiness. The goodness of his soul alone would appear to be sufficient.

4.4.2 Some Problems for the Sufficiency Thesis

But in spite of its widespread acceptance, this interpretation is problematical. Immediately after Socrates reveals his confidence, in the second passage, that "no evil comes to a good man in life or in death," he goes on to say: "but this is clear to me, that it was better for me to die and be released from troubles" (41d2–5). His confidence in this regard derives from the fact that his *daimonion* did not oppose him either before or during the trial (41d5–6). Now just how Socrates reaches this conclusion from the mere absence of daimonic interference need not concern us here.[33] What is important is that although he is confident that no harm will come to him at death, he is not confident about just what will happen

we mentioned at first, wealth, health, and good looks, was knowledge the guide and what shows the way regarding the correct use of all such things, or something else? [. . .] So in every possession and action, knowledge provides not only good luck but welfare." His point is that knowledge guarantees the right use of the possessions one already has; it does not guarantee that one will have those possessions in the first place. If so, Socrates does not rule out the possibility that one may have wisdom and yet be savaged by bad luck. (For more on this point, see Brickhouse [1990].) (3) The entire argument here is conditioned by a search for what is good, and one cannot sensibly set out to obtain good fortune, at least much of which would appear to befall one or not regardless of other factors. Socrates argues, however, and Cleinias agrees, that wisdom maximizes one's chances of being truly fortunate, assuming the possession of the equipment needed for right action, and so the pursuit of good fortune would be no other than the pursuit of wisdom. (We owe this point to Michael Ferejohn [1984].)

32. See, e.g., Irwin [1977], 100; Vlastos [1978], 230; Burnyeat [1971], 210; Grote [1875], 243.

33. For Socrates' derivation, see Brickhouse and Smith [1989b], 237–57.

at death. Perhaps, he says earlier, his soul will migrate to Hades, where he will spend his time "examining and questioning the people there" (41b5–6). That, he says, would be "inconceivable happiness" (41c3–4). But at the same time Socrates is aware that death may also be a "dreamless sleep," void of all perception (40c9–d1). Anyone who claims to know which of the two possibilities will actually come to be is guilty of the very sort of pretense of wisdom from which Socrates has for so long sought to free men (29a4–b2). His last words to the jury are noteworthy: "But the time has come to leave. I go to die, and you to live; but which of us goes to a better condition is unclear to everyone except the god" (42a2–5).

At the conclusion of the *Apology* Socrates believes it is better for him to die; but he is not convinced that his is the best lot; some members of the jury, according to his final words at 42a2–5, may enjoy even better. Thus, at the conclusion of the trial, Socrates sees that his life—if he were to continue it—would be so plagued by "troubles" that it is no longer worth living. Yet he also plainly believes himself to be a good man, whose goodness is undiminished by the fact that he has been convicted and condemned to death. When Socrates claims that "no evil can come to a good man," whatever else he means, unless we are to convict him of self-contradiction within the briefest of passages, he cannot mean that moral goodness, by itself, is always sufficient for happiness. Socrates' own moral goodness, for example, is not enough to nullify the "troubles" that now loom so large as to convince him that his life is no longer worth living.

4.4.3 Two Senses of "Harm"

There are two ways in which we might interpret "harm," both of which are used and, we believe, used frequently by Socrates. On the one hand, we might interpret something as harmful to the extent that it impedes or removes some benefit one might otherwise enjoy, or increases some disadvantage one would to some degree suffer anyhow. Let us call this a "relative harm," for harm in this sense may involve no absolutely evil product—the one harmed relatively only enjoys one or more fewer advantages than he or she might otherwise enjoy. He or she might still, all things considered, have an extremely desirable life. Similarly, although the one suffering relative harm might end up being wretched, it is possible that he or she would have been wretched anyhow, only somewhat less so. So relative harms merely move one from the position one would otherwise enjoy or suffer to a somewhat inferior position, all things considered. This conception of harm appears to be what motivates Socrates' discussion of the degrees of wretchedness and evil one finds at various places in the *Gorgias* (e.g., 469b3–c1,[34] 472e4–473e1, 475a2–d4), and, in other places in the same dialogue (e.g., 477a5–479e9), the conception of benefit as the making of someone better, even

---

34. It is noteworthy that at the end of this passage Socrates admits that he would rather not suffer wrong. See also 470a7–8, where to be punished is identified as a bad thing, and 480e6–7, where we must take care not to suffer wrong. Other passages making similar points are cited in Kraut's discussion ([1983b], esp. on 38–39).

where the result is only that they are less wretched than they would have been (473b6–e1). If this, then—the relative conception of harm (and correspondingly, evil)—is what Socrates means to employ when he says "no evil comes to a good person," he contradicts himself in the *Apology*, for it is clear that by the end of the trial both that he regards his life as no longer worth living, all things considered, and that any number of penalties he might have incurred would have caused him, for all his goodness, at least relative harm.

But there is another conception of harm in Socrates' discussions as well, which we might call an "absolute" conception. This conception would appear to be required when Socrates talks about virtue as the only thing that is good in the strict sense, that is, the only thing that is an IG. When he says that virtue is the only thing that is good in this sense, then its opposite, vice, is, in the same restricted sense, the only evil or harm. Certainly Socrates thinks that the only harm that can come to the soul is vice (see, e.g., *Grg.* 477b6–c5, e4–6; *Rep.* I.335c1–4) and Socrates' denial of *akrasia* (see section 3.5, above) ensures that the possession of virtue is an absolute guarantee against vice or vicious activity. An absolute conception of harm, moreover, would be warranted wherever Socrates identifies one with one's soul. That he is sometimes tempted to make this identification is plain from what Socrates says about the afterlife. Though he is uncertain as to what the afterlife is like—or even if there is one—he believes that it is at least possible that death involves a migration to Hades. But surely he believes that what migrates to Hades is only the soul and nothing else. In this conception, no evil or harm can come to a good person, for nothing in one's external circumstances can damage one's soul and whatever goodness it enjoys. So nothing can inflict the worst kind of suffering on the good person, and hence, the good person is indemnified against absolute harm.

It is the absolute conception of evil and harm, then, that we believe Socrates employs when he says that "no evil comes to a good person" and "it is not permitted for a better person to be harmed by a worse." When he says such things, he means that the good person cannot be made vicious. But it might be thought that in our interpretation when Socrates says such things he must be speaking with sheer bravado. Since we maintain that he is claiming that no absolute harm comes to the good soul, Socrates must concede that although neither Meletus nor anyone else could ever harm his soul, unjust treatment could, nevertheless, harm him relatively, indeed, to such a degree as to make his life no longer worth living.

Whatever the oddness of this claim, Socrates *does* come to the conclusion after he has been convicted that it is better for him to die. And he says this with the realization that, for all he knows, death will bring utter extinction. Moreover, in asserting that no harm can come to his soul even if the suffering of injustice can make his life no longer worth living, Socrates is hardly making an empty gesture. There is, in his view, a far worse fate than having one's potential for happiness taken away from one by the evils committed by others. Nowhere in the *Apology* does Socrates explain why the loss of happiness is not the worst thing that can befall a person. But in the *Gorgias*, having stated that he would never want to suffer a wrong (469b12–c1; see also 480e6–7), he goes on to argue that it would be a far greater evil to do wrong (469c1–2, 473a4–5, 474b7–8, 474c4–475e6). But the greatest evil of all, he says, would be to escape having to pay the penalty of wrongdoing and to live for the longest time possible with the greatest of all afflictions, an evil soul (480e5–481b1). So when Socrates warns the jury that they will inflict worse harm on themselves than on him if they follow Meletus and Anytus and convict him (*Ap.* 30c6–8), he is relying on his conviction that it is always worse to do wrong than to suffer it, even if the one who suffers it will, as a result, have a life no longer worth living. Thus, when Socrates immediately goes on to say that a good person can never be harmed by a worse, and later, that no evil comes to a good person in life or in death, he is announcing that no one can make the good person suffer the most wretched of lives, life with a corrupted soul.[35]

4.4.4 Summary and Conclusion

We have argued that Socrates' various remarks about goods, virtue, and happiness are consistent. In order to show why this is the case, however, we have had to rely on a variety of distinctions and interpretations deriving from passages other than the ones in question. Our interpretation of these passages does not rely upon "pure" charity, however. The principles on which we rely are to be found at work in more than one of Plato's early dialogues. Accordingly, we have employed them as they are presented in the text in order to make sense of other Socratic principles and arguments. The conclusion to which our interpretation has driven us is that virtue is not sufficient for happiness; in addition, one must actually pursue the right ends. If one is prevented from engaging in the right activities— for example, from leading the examined life—one can be virtuous, but not happy.

4.5 The Case of Socrates

4.5.1 Was Socrates a Happy Man?

We have argued so far that virtue is not sufficient for happiness. In our earlier work on this topic,[36] however, we agreed that virtue was at least necessary for

35. Socrates would count the corruption of the body through disease or accident as only a relative harm, yet in some instances a harm sufficient to make even the virtuous person judge his or her life no longer worth living. But there is one passage in the *Gorgias* (512a2–b2), noted above in section 4.2.5, where he says that one suffering "from great and incurable diseases" would qualify as "wretched." It would nonetheless be a mistake to infer from this passage that Socrates believes that even the most dreaded diseases could ever bring harm in the absolute sense. The whole thrust of the arguments against Polus and Callicles is to convince them that the worst harm that can come to a person is to be unjust and escape punishment. Though the wretchedness that comes with incurable disease might make the virtuous person see that he or she is better off dead, for Socrates, one will nevertheless always have reason to judge oneself better off than the person who suffers the absolute harm, that harm done to the soul by unpunished injustice.

36. See Brickhouse and Smith [1987b] and [1990c]. It will soon be obvious that we have changed our minds about this, and now reject the thesis that Socrates regarded virtue as necessary for happiness.

happiness. But now an intriguing puzzle presents itself: what do we say about the case of Socrates himself? At the end of the *Apology*, Socrates tells the jury of his confidence that death will be no evil for him, and he exhorts them "to consider this one truth: that no evil comes to a good man in life or in death, nor are the concerns of this person neglected by the gods" (41c9–d2). That Socrates regards himself as a "good man" is an inescapable inference. Yet throughout the early dialogues Socrates seems to believe both that virtue requires moral knowledge (see, e.g., *La*. 194d1–2; *Prt*. 361b1–2) and that he himself lacks that very knowledge (see, e.g., *Ap*. 21b1–d7, *Euthphr*. 5a3–c7; 15c11–16a4; *La*. 186b8–c5; *Grg*. 509c4–7). Were we to accept each of these claims at face value, they are consistent only if Socrates also believes that one can, in some sense, be good without possessing moral virtue itself and, indeed, that he himself is just such a "good man."

What Socrates might have in mind by considering himself a "good man" is not at all clear, for it is by no means obvious in what sense a person could still be good if he or she lacked the moral wisdom necessary for virtue.[37] Moreover, if Socrates thinks virtue is necessary for happiness, as commentators have universally claimed, and Socrates is not virtuous, it would appear that Socrates cannot judge his own life to be happy. But if Socrates believes that even he, who has led an exemplary examined life, has not attained happiness, he must surely think it unlikely that happiness can be within the grasp of other mortals. If so, Socrates' assessment of the human condition is bleak indeed.

Rather than attempt to pursue what Socrates might have had in mind by claiming both to be good and yet to lack virtue, one might simply deny the sincerity of Socrates' disavowal of knowledge and with it the sincerity of any claim that he lacked the virtue he said he was seeking.[38] One advantage of such an answer is that it plainly leaves open the possibility that Socrates was happy. But as our argument in chapter 2 shows, we believe his profession of ignorance was sincere. In this section, then, our task will be to show, first, why Socratic categories of moral assessment require that he view himself as a good person who has nevertheless not attained virtue. We will then show why Socrates—according to his own understanding of the requirements of happiness—was indeed a happy man, by his own reckoning. It follows that virtue is not even necessary for happiness. But we will go on to show why Socrates would nonetheless regard virtue as a thing of inestimably great value.

4.5.2   The Ground of Socrates' Moral Superiority

In a famous passage in the *Apology* (20c4–23c1) Socrates relates that his friend, Chairephon, was once told by a Delphic oracle that no one was wiser than Socrates. He goes on to say that as a result of his attempts to understand what the oracle could have meant, he came to the conclusion that indeed he does possess a

---

37. The tension between Socrates' moral superiority and his repeated disclaimers of moral wisdom is well documented in Vlastos [1971b], 7–8.

38. See, e.g., Gulley [1968], 69; Shero [1927], 109.

kind of human wisdom that that sets him apart from the great mass of his fellow Athenians. Unlike most people, who think they know how best to live when they do not, he is aware that he does not know. In their arrogance, his fellow citizens see no need even to inquire into the nature of virtue. His task, he came to believe, was to carry out the god's wish that he exhort all—especially those who mistakenly think they know—to pursue virtue through philosophical examination.[39] Thus, in spite of the fact that he has not attained virtue himself, Socrates views himself as morally superior not only to those who have actively sought to end his questioning of others, but also to the multitude of Athenians who impiously disregard what the god wants for men.

So when Socrates indicates at the end of the *Apology* that he considers himself to be a "good man," he shows at least that he considers himself to be better than the great majority of his fellow citizens in one crucially important respect. He strives to benefit his fellow citizens by making them recognize that their worldly pursuits will gain them nothing until they rid themselves of their pretense to wisdom and begin in earnest to lead the examined life. Through their utter disregard for philosophical examination, the great majority of Athenians have consistently shown that they care nothing for the attainment of moral wisdom.

Because Socrates is convinced that "the unexamined life is not worth living for a human being" (*Ap.* 38a5–6), it is clear that he must suppose there to be extremely high value in philosophical activity. But even this value is difficult to make out. Despite having lived by this principle for so many years now, Socrates is convinced that he remains ignorant of "anything fine and good" (*Ap.* 21d3–4). And because Socrates sees vice as nothing other than moral ignorance, it might seem puzzling how he could claim to be any better off than those whose vice he has struggled to eradicate through philosophy. After all, he is no less ignorant than they are; his superior wisdom lies solely in his recognition of the ignorance he shares with them. How would Socrates escape the conclusion, then, that despite living a life of exemplary commitment to philosophy, he remains as wretched in his ignorance as those whose disdain for philosophy he deplores?

4.5.3 Socratic Ignorance versus Culpable Ignorance

At *Apology* 22d5–e5 Socrates tells the jury,

> The good craftsmen seemed to me to make same mistake (ἁμάρτημα) as the good poets. Because he performs his craft well, each considered himself to be wisest about the other greatest things. And this error (πλημμέλεια)[40] of theirs obscured their wisdom, so that I asked myself on behalf of the oracle whether I should prefer to be thus as I am, being neither wise with respect to their wisdom nor ignorant with respect to their ignorance (ἀμαθὴς τὴν ἀμαθίαν), or to

---

39. For an account of how sense can be made of Socrates' derivation of his duty to philosophize from the oracle's pronouncement, see Brickhouse and Smith [1989b], sec. 2.5.

40. Burnet ([1924], note on 22d8) suggests rendering πλημμέλεια "want of tact." But the fact that it is meant to parallel ἁμάρτημα indicates that Socrates wishes to connote something far stronger. In thinking they understand the "most important matters" when they do not, the handicraftsmen and the poets are guilty of a very serious failing.

have both things that they have. I then answered myself and the oracle that it
would be better for me to be as I am.

What makes Socrates better than the craftsmen is that he, unlike the craftsmen,
satisfies the Delphic injunction "Know Thyself" (see *Charm.* 164d4–5; *Prt.*
343b3; *Phdr.* 229e5–6; *Phil.* 48c10; *Laws* 11.923a3–5). He is aware, that is, of
his own lack of understanding; the craftsmen (like the politicians and the poets,
to whom Socrates also finds he is superior in wisdom—see *Ap.* 21b9–22c8) do
not recognize their lack, especially in regard to "the greatest things."

Whatever his epistemic limitations are, then, Socrates is not ignorant in precisely the same sense as the craftsmen are.[41] But what exactly is the others' failing, the "mistake" that makes them ignorant in a way Socrates is not? Surely it
cannot be that the politicians, poets, and craftsmen lack the knowledge of virtue,
for Socrates also lacks this. Instead, their "mistake" has to be just that they
suppose they have this knowledge when they do not.

The importance of this false supposition is that those who suffer from it are
likely to harm themselves to even greater degrees by affirming false moral opinions one after the other, and perhaps with ever graver moral consequences, without the benefit of the caution and moderation that self-understanding would provide. But those who, like Socrates, are aware of their own lack of wisdom do not
merely escape these dangers. They may even be able to ascertain a number of
moral propositions whose truth can become a matter of confidence through a diligent pursuit of examination through philosophy.[42]

4.5.4   True Belief versus Knowledge

It is perhaps tempting to think at this point that Socrates' claim that he is good
but not truly virtuous arises from his conviction that over the years he has come
to possess a variety of true beliefs about how best to live, but because he lacks
sufficient justification for their truth, these beliefs do not yet have the epistemic
status of knowledge. On this interpretation, Socrates considers himself a good
person on account of his possession of the relevant true beliefs; he thinks he lacks
virtue, however, because virtue requires knowledge, and he knows that he has not

41. See Hathaway ([1970] 127–42), who finds a distinction between ἀμαθία, which he defines as
"proud ignorance, a defect of character," and ἄγνοια, "intellectual ignorance, the simple absence
of knowledge either of fact or art" ([1970], 134). The difference between Socrates and his fellow
Athenians, in Hathaway's account, is that Socrates suffers only from the latter, and not the former,
sort of ignorance. It is at least some evidence against Hathaway's distinction that Socrates characterizes
his own ignorance as ἀμαθία at *Grg.* 488a3. But even if a terminological distinction cannot be found
to support it, there is nothing impossible in the idea that Socrates could have such a distinction in
mind, for even if both he and Meletus, say, are ignorant in the same sense of the term, there remains
nevertheless an enormous difference in their intellectual and epistemic status.

42. Most recent accounts of the Socratic *elenchos* attempt to show how Socrates can derive epistemologically substantive and constructive results from his examinations of others. No doubt the best
known of such accounts is Gregory Vlastos's treatment of the *elenchos* ([1983a], 27–58). Though we
agree with the arguments Vlastos gives for insisting upon a "constructivist" account of the *elenchos*,
we have a number of misgivings about the specific constructivist interpretation Vlastos offers (for our
own account, see chapter 1).

as yet found the warrants that would transform his true beliefs about how best to live into knowledge.

It is doubtful, however, that Socrates' moral assessment of himself as a good but not virtuous person relies upon the distinction between true belief and knowledge. After all, on some occasions Socrates professes not merely to have true belief but actually to *know* things of moral importance.[43] For example, in the *Apology* (29b6–7) he tells the jury: "I know that it is evil and disgraceful to do injustice and to disobey one's superior, whether god or man." And later, after he has been convicted and is called upon to propose a counter-penalty, Socrates explains why he must reject certain of the possibilities available to him even though any one of them would allow him to escape death:

> Why should I? So that I not suffer the penalty that Meletus proposes, about which I say that I do not know whether it is a good thing or an evil? Shall I choose instead of that something *which I know to be an evil? (Ap.* 37b5–8)

Moreover, although Socrates nowhere actually says that he "knows" that he has been ordained by the god to carry out his "divine mission," it is clear that he is utterly convinced that such is the case. Nowhere in the *Apology* is there the slightest indication that Socrates thinks he only possesses true belief about what the god wishes him to do and that he must somehow find additional warrant for his conviction.[44] Given the strength of his convictions, when Socrates denies that he is truly wise, then, he cannot very well be denying that he is fully justified in holding that certain things are true.

4.5.5 *Knowing That and Knowing Why Something Is True*

As we argued in section 2.2, it is significant that whenever Socrates admits that he is convinced of something he is only claiming that he is confident *that* something is true. Although there are many propositions about whose truth Socrates is utterly confident, it remains no less true, as he explains in the *Gorgias* (508e6–509a10), that he fails to understand *why* such propositions are true; that is, he lacks a theory of what makes true moral propositions true. If when Socrates denies that he is truly wise, he is denying that he has a theory that would explain why moral propositions are true, we can see how Socrates can claim, on the one hand, that he lacks wisdom and, hence, that he has not attained virtue and yet, on the other, that he is utterly confident that many of his moral commitments are correct.[45]

43. Socrates' claims of moral knowledge have not gone unnoticed by Socratic scholars, though how to understand Socrates' claims to knowledge has become a matter of debate. See, for example, Lesher [1987]; Reeve [1989]; Vlastos [1985]; Woodruff [1987] and [1990]. We offer our own account in chapter 2.

44. We cite and discuss other Socratic expressions of knowledge in sec. 2.1.6.

45. Another account of what Socrates means when he denies that he is wise has been advanced by Richard Kraut [1983b]. Kraut recognizes Socrates' occasional claims that, in fact, he does know things of moral significance. So, Kraut argues, "it is best to take the *Apology* to be conceding that Socrates does know something—though not much—about virtue and the good" ([1983b], 273). But, Kraut goes on, "[Socrates'] claim to wisdom is not based on his knowing those few moral truths, but rather

The only sort of wisdom Socrates says that he does possess is a "kind of human wisdom" (20d8–9), which he later says is "worth little or nothing" (23a6–7).[46] In fact, he says that he is "in truth worth nothing with respect to wisdom" (23b3–4). But it does not follow from this that Socrates is not immeasurably better off than those of his fellow citizens who arrogantly think they know what they do not. After all, Socrates suffers from none of the afflictions that would actually make one's life miserable and not worth living (see, e.g., *Cri.* 47e3–49a2 and *Grg.* 512a2–b2). "Those who think they are wise when they are not," however, suffer from the worst of all evils: false belief about how best to live. In their blind ignorance of the fact that they lack even "human wisdom," they see no need to engage in philosophical examination. Thus, in all likelihood, they will live on in their ignorance. The principles by which Socrates has lived his life, by contrast, have been exposed to a form of extensive scrutiny and continuous re-examination that he is convinced has been divinely sanctioned. Thus, not only is he free from the blinding arrogance that afflicts so many of his fellow countrymen, but he is also confident that many of the principles by which he leads his life are true and hence that those actions that derive from his moral principles are good ones.

But even if Socrates is clearly better off than his fellow Athenians, we cannot infer that he is actually happy; he may only be less wretched as a result of his suffering a less wretched form of ignorance. Let us see, then, if there is reason to suppose that he actually is happy.

4.5.6   Doing the Right Things

Socrates is not merely superior to his fellow Athenians because of his greater esteem for philosophy. His regard for philosophy leads him subsequently to act in ways which make him superior to most men. In the *Apology* he tells the jury, for instance, that once he and four others were ordered by the Thirty Tyrants to arrest Leon the Salaminian, but he refused because it was unjust (32c4–d7). Though Socrates does not say so explicitly, he clearly thinks of himself as having done the right thing and, in that respect, thinks of himself as the moral superior of the other four who carried out the wishes of the Thirty. But, of course, Socrates' refusal to participate in the unjust arrest and execution of Leon has nothing to do with the furthering of his philosophical mission in Athens. Rather, its superiority

---

on his knowledge of how little he knows" ([1983b], 273). Socrates' denial of wisdom is categorical, however, a fact which can be explained if one accepts our view that although Socrates may know many things, he lacks an account of how it is that what he knows is true. (See sec. 2.2.)

46. One might argue that because Socrates says that he only possesses a form of "human wisdom" (20d8) and that "the god is really wise" (23a5–6), he thinks any greater wisdom is impossible for humans. But at 20d9–e3 Socrates states that "those about whom he was speaking earlier," namely, the sophists, Gorgias, Prodicus, and Hippias, "may be wise in some wisdom *greater than human*," a sort of wisdom which he emphatically denies having. Now Socrates may well doubt that the likes of Gorgias and Hippias are wise in any way at all. But his denial that he is wise in the way that they claim to be wise shows that the notion of a mortal possessing "wisdom greater than human" is not at all a conceptual oddity. If so, Socrates does not in principle rule out the possibility that a mortal might come to possess a wisdom that is not simply worth "little or nothing" (23a6–7).

derives from the fact that he alone, of those given the order, realized what was most important. And this recognition, it seems, derived directly from Socrates' scrupulous attention to justice—attention philosophy forced him to pay.

So insofar as one leads the philosophical life, one will never act upon a carelessly accepted conception of justice. But it is important to notice that elenctic examination can only show *that* a proposition should be rejected by an interlocutor and its contrary or contradictory accepted. It can never, by itself, provide a complete understanding of the moral principles which show us *why* some propositions ought to be rejected or exactly what it is that makes other propositions worthy of our acceptance. Thus the *elenchos,* by itself, regardless of how regularly one employs it, will never provide a person with wisdom of the sort Socrates says that he lacks. Nor can the most scrupulously careful employment of the *elenchos* provide an absolute guarantee that a false moral conception could never escape one's notice. Such errors would be a good deal less likely to occur, however, and if ever they did, it would not be in virtue of one's having led the philosophical life that they did so. Thus, if happiness derives from good activity (and we argued in 4.3.3 that it does), then Socrates can be assured that he has a greater share of happiness, such as is possible for humans, and thus that he is immeasurably better off than the multitude of Athenians, who needlessly labor under a variety of mistaken moral notions.

Scattered throughout the early dialogues are a variety of principles which Socrates plainly endorses.[47] Socrates' acceptance of these principles appears to have been generated through his practice of philosophy. Thus, by living the philosophical life he has come to recognize a variety of ways in which he could have acted wrongfully; by following his principles he has avoided many evils he might otherwise have committed. And precisely because happiness is assured by good action from the fact that Socrates can make a number of important judgments which guide him to good actions, we can be confident that at least up until the time of his trial, he is to some degree genuinely happy.

One activity especially stands out—his examinations of himself and others. It is precisely this activity, according to Socrates, that has made his life worthwhile. Socrates shows that he regards this activity as necessary for happiness when he says, "the unexamined life is not worth living for a human being" (*Ap.* 38a5–6). He goes on to show that he thinks it is sufficient for happiness when he indicates that so long as he could engage in this activity, Socrates would consider himself

47. E.g., at *Ap* 29b6–7 Socrates says he does "know that it is evil and disgraceful to do injustice and to disobey one's superior, whether god or man." At *Cri.* 49d7–9 he says that he and Crito have long agreed that "it is never just to do what is evil or return evil for evil, or when one suffers evil to repay the evil by giving what is evil in return." They have also agreed, he says, that one "ought to do what he has agreed to do, provided it is just" (49e6–8). At *Gorgias* 479c8–480b6, he makes it plain to young Polus that he thinks it is always best—both just and prudent—that one never do what is unjust, but that if one does act unjustly, justice and prudence require that the wrongdoer go before a judge to be punished. That Socrates holds beliefs such as these and that they are part of or entailments of his conception of virtue has often been noted. Perhaps the best account is to be found in Irwin [1977], ch. 3, esp. 38. Nevertheless, neither Irwin nor anyone else who claims that Socrates has definite moral conceptions but not moral wisdom has accounted for Socrates' apparently complete confidence that he is a good man.

happy: he would count it as an "inconceivable happiness" (*Ap.* 41c3–4) if death offers him the opportunity to pursue his mission with the dead in Hades. In order to understand this claim, we do not need to assume that Socrates would miraculously receive virtue in the afterlife—just engaging in this activity alone is enough for Socrates to judge his condition happy. Accordingly, good activity is sufficient for happiness;[48] virtue itself is not needed. But once the opportunity for good activity has been taken away, as it has been by his conviction, and since he considers all of the possible penalties other than paying a fine to be evils (*Ap.* 37b5–e2), Socrates no longer counts his life as worthwhile, claiming that he will be better off dead, even if death is nothing more than utter extinction (*Ap.* 40c5). The power of the jury to constrain what Socrates can do justly makes clear that no measure of happiness, however small, can be ensured during one's life.

4.5.7   A Problematic Passage

We have argued that because happiness consists in right activity and because one can engage in right activity without possessing virtue, Socrates does not hold the view that virtue is necessary for happiness. But there is one passage, in the *Euthydemus* (281b5–6), which seems to contradict our position. There Socrates poses the obviously rhetorical question: "Does any benefit come from other possessions without intelligence and wisdom?" The apparent implication of the passage is that virtue *is* necessary for happiness, since without virtue, it appears, there can be no goods at all.

In introducing the distinction between moral and non-moral goods in the *Euthydemus,* Socrates is concerned with distinguishing what is an IG from what is a DG. Wisdom is an IG because it is by its nature good; it is always good. Money, on the other hand, is the sort of thing that is sometimes good and sometimes evil. But what makes either of them good is being "used correctly" in action (281a6–b1). Wisdom is always good because, by its nature, it always conduces to good activity. Money lacks this capacity and, hence, needs to be properly directed if it is to be "used correctly." But plainly, on occasion, a non-moral item can be used correctly without being guided by wisdom. Imagine a well-intended, but not fully virtuous person who uses his money to buy wheat to sustain his body for several more hours of philosophical argument to dissuade someone who is thinking about becoming a sophist. Let us suppose that a fully virtuous person would use his money in precisely the same way—to buy the handful of wheat, and so forth. But since there is no difference in the actions in the two cases, in both cases the money became a good because it was "used correctly," though when used in the first case it was not directed by wisdom.

Now those who lack the wisdom to ensure correct usage will sometimes misuse their money, perhaps disastrously. Thus, they have reason not to count their money as a good regarding their lives as a whole. The morally wise person has

---

48. Vlastos ([1991], 232, n.103) claims that our view of the relationship between happiness and good activity is textually groundless. Vlastos provides no reassessment of the passages we have adduced in support of our claim.

no such worry. As long as he or she possesses wisdom, the money cannot but be a good on each occasion and, hence, a good for his or her life as a whole. When Socrates says that there can be no goods without wisdom, he does not mean that nothing could ever be used rightly on any occasion unless the user actually possesses wisdom, for that is patently false. Rather, he means that nothing will *always* be good without wisdom, since false belief about how to live can turn any of those items into great evils.

This, however, may seem to raise an even more difficult problem for our view. If Socrates thinks that happiness consists in good activity and he is happy in spite of the fact that he lacks virtue, why would Socrates have missed anything of value in not having attained virtue? To put the question another way, why wouldn't a life lived by scrupulous adherence to elenctically secured moral principles provide every bit of the happiness found in a life conducted under the governance of moral virtue itself?

4.5.8 What Socrates Cannot Achieve on His Own

By leading the philosophical life, Socrates has become the moral superior of his fellow Athenians. And there is still more to his claim at the end of the *Apology* that he is "a good man." His assessment that he is "good" and his consequent fearlessness in the face of death are, after all, categorical. He goes so far as to claim that he is convinced he has never wronged anyone (*Ap*. 37b2–5). If we are to make sense of the categorical nature of Socrates' assessment of his goodness, we must assume that, as far as he can tell, he has never violated any of the various moral principles he espouses. But if Socrates really lacks moral wisdom, as he claims, it is difficult to see how he could be so confident that he has always acted in a manner consistent with those principles, for the principles he endorses, at least as he articulates them, leave the central moral terms undefined and, thus, their application in specific contexts seems to be left uncertain. In the *Apology*, for instance, he tells the jury: "I show, not by word but by deed that I care nothing whatever about death . . . but it matters everything to me that I do nothing unjust or unholy" (32c8–d3). Nowhere, however, in the *Apology* or in any other early dialogue does he say precisely what he thinks makes something unjust or unholy. Similarly, in the *Crito* he says that "one must never harm or return harm for harm" (49a4–b6) without explicating, in any general way, what counts as something's being harmed.

Socrates no doubt often deliberated about what to do, much as he does, for example, in the *Crito*—by submitting actions to elenctic tests before undertaking them. Whenever he sees that a belief about the permissibility of an action is inconsistent with a belief about a moral principle, Socrates would always choose to reject the belief that the particular action is permissible.

But elenctic testing can carry Socrates only so far in deliberating about whether to engage in a particular course of action or not. First, it is often simply impossible to *foresee* whether an action or its consequences will produce an evil. Moreover, there are innumerable hard cases in which it is simply unclear what one ought to do in order to be consistent with one's moral principles. The press of events, for example, may not afford Socrates the time to engage in elenctic testing sufficient to reach a decisive outcome. Even when he has the time to consider what he ought to do, the most diligent elenctic testing may not yield a compelling answer in difficult cases, since Socrates may simply not have hit upon what it is about performing an act, or not performing the act, that is incompatible with his principles. The fact that he has not discovered the feature of a particular act that would rule it out is no proof that there is no such feature. Thus, his powers of reasoning alone could never warrant his degree of confidence that he is a good man, since it could not by itself warrant the belief that he has never acted wrongly.

4.5.9   A Little Help from the Gods

But according to the *Apology,* Socrates does not have to rely exclusively on the outcome of elenctic testing for moral guidance. He tells the jury that beginning when he was a child he has heard a "voice"—his *daimonion*—which has always "turned him away" (31c7–d4). Later, as part of his explanation that he believes the outcome of the trial will not produce an evil for him, he says: "My accustomed prophetic *daimonion* always came very frequently beforehand and opposed me even in small matters" (40a4–6). It is important to notice that Socrates does not say that there have been times when he engaged in something that was an evil for him and that his *daimonion* failed to turn him away. For all he can say with perfect assurance, such may have been the case, but he is aware of no such instance.

Socrates has been absolutely steadfast in his commitment never to do what he thought would violate one of the principles he thinks he and all persons ought to abide by. Thus, he can say with confidence that he has never consciously done what he believes to be evil. And the great frequency of his daimonic alarms gives him reason to think that he has avoided a host of other evils. Thus, he has considerable evidence that he has scrupulously avoided the commission of many evils and no reason to think that he has ever, even unwittingly, done what he ought not. Moreover, his actions have not merely been non-evil; because he has tirelessly carried out his "mission" in Athens in accordance with the god's command, he has done a great deal of good. Given the evidence, then, he has every reason to think he is "a good man," and none to suggest that he is not.

4.5.10   Why Virtue Is Preferable

If what we have argued thus far is correct, Socrates has reason to count himself as good. But because he cannot offer an account of what makes some things good and others evil, he cannot claim that he has attained the virtue he says he and all other persons ought to seek. We might well wonder, however, why this should make a significant difference to Socrates. After all, in the *Crito* Socrates maintains that "living well and living justly and nobly are the same thing" (48b8–9). But because Socrates has lived well, according to our argument, it is not clear why he would regard himself as having missed anything of value in not having achieved virtue. If what matters for happiness is only *how* one lives, and Socrates has sufficient evidence, based on his strict adherence to his convictions, to judge him self "a good man," he must also regard his own actions as no different from those a virtuous person would have performed in his circumstances. Unless he can show that his actions would differ from those of the virtuous, why would he not think, as the end of his life approaches, that his goodness has accorded him the same benefits that a virtuous person would enjoy?

The answer to this question, we think, may be found in the special and important benefits—in addition to good action—virtue affords. First, although Socrates thinks that it is *how* we live that is of supreme importance, there is no reason to think that he considers "how one lives" to be a function solely of the actions one performs (or omits) taken in isolation from the cognitive and motivational states on which one's actions are based. Were he to think so, Socrates would have to believe that a life led under the guidance of wisdom would be of equal value to one conducted by a series of lucky guesses, felicitous yet systematic mistakes, or consistently bungled attempts at viciousness. The sheer implausibility of any such comparison shows that, for Socrates, understanding why one's actions are correct is a good over and above the correctness of the actions themselves. Since the possession of virtue entails an understanding of why what its possessor does is correct, Socrates would value the life conducted under the guidance of virtue to be superior to his own. This is not to say, of course, that Socrates sees his own activities as resulting from a series of lucky guesses. On the contrary, as we have argued, in each case he can give a reason for his thinking *that* what he does is good and not evil. Thus, in that respect, he is better off than one who happens to do the right thing without believing that it is right. But because he lacks moral wisdom, he is unable to provide an explanation—in terms of what virtue is—of how his actions are good. To that extent, his life is clearly deficient.

There is yet another reason why Socrates would, in spite of his recognition of his own goodness, continue to seek moral virtue. If what we have said about Socrates' *daimonion* is correct, at least by the end of his life, he has sufficient experience with its warnings to be confident that if it has "turned him away" from doing something, he can infer that what he had intended to do would have, in some way, produced an evil, and hence that desisting from it would prevent an evil. But in spite of the enormous benefit afforded him by the daimonic alarms that have warned him away from the commission of evils, his *daimonion* would nevertheless not allow him to draw authoritative inferences regarding what course of action would express moral virtue.[49] It is safe to assume that Socrates would recognize three sorts of actions: virtuous actions, that is, the sorts of actions virtuous people would perform as expressions of their virtue; vicious actions, the sorts of actions vicious people would perform as expressions of their vice; and actions that are neither virtuous nor vicious. In this account, non-virtuous people could perform virtuous actions by performing the sorts of actions virtuous people would perform under relevantly similar circumstances. But they would not likely always do so. To the extent that Socrates falls short of this standard in his own life, he

---

49. For a more detailed account of the epistemic limitations of Socrates' daimonic alarms, see Brickhouse and Smith [1989b], 237–57.

would regard himself as not as happy as one who always did the very best things he or she could do. Moreover, moral wisdom would endow its possessor with the ability to recognize instances of all three sorts of actions. In desisting from actions from which his *daimonion* turned him away, Socrates can only infer that what he has done is not vicious; he cannot be sure he has acted as a virtuous person would act. To distinguish authoritatively the virtuous from the merely non-vicious he would need to know what virtue is, and to acquire that knowledge his only aid is his capacity to reason.

Even when Socrates is confident that some particular course of action would express virtue, unlike the possessor of moral wisdom, he may not know *how* to bring it about in the most effective manner. He is absolutely confident, for example, that virtue is the most precious of all goods and that the god wishes human beings to pursue virtue in preference to any worldly ends. Because Socrates lacks moral wisdom, however, he does not know how best to achieve that goal. He can only be absolutely steadfast in working his *elenchos* on all who claim to know when they do not. But because he does not know, he cannot, for example, say exactly what laws should be changed in order to facilitate the production of virtue. Thus, he has reason to prize an ability which the virtuous person would possess. Once again, because he has scrupulously avoided evil, he can be confident that he will not suffer the misery of a life of ignorance. But with all its goodness, Socrates' life falls tragically short in its mastery of virtue. Still, in spite of his failure to attain virtue, at the time of his death Socrates regarded himself as better off for having spent his life in its pursuit.

Finally, though virtue is not sufficient for happiness, it does provide its possessor the ability to transform all potential (dependent) goods into actual goods. It cannot by itself ensure happiness, for catastrophes can befall even the virtuous person, so as to prevent him or her from being able to make this transformation. But given the opportunity, the virtuous person will be able to turn even the most ordinary things of life into good things. This is why, as Socrates says to his jurors in the *Apology*, he exhorts everyone to pursue virtue above anything else, for it is only through virtue that wealth and all other dependent goods become dependably good for human beings (*Ap.* 30b2–4). Socrates does not have this power, despite his having led a good and happy life; accordingly, his life has not been—could not be—as happy as it would have been, all other things being equal, had he managed to become truly virtuous.

4.5.11   Summary and Conclusion

A summary of the positions we have attributed to Socrates may be helpful. We shall present this summary in terms of each item under discussion—goods, virtue, and happiness.

Goods

1. (PE) (The Principle of Eudaimonism)—A thing is good only insofar as it is conducive to happiness. A thing is evil only insofar as it is conducive to wretchedness.
2. A thing is good in itself (or an independent good—IG) if and only if it is

a good, and its being a good is in virtue of nothing other than itself. A thing is evil in itself (or an independent evil—IE) if and only if it is an evil, and its being an evil is in virtue of nothing other than itself. IGs can never be evils, and IEs can never be goods.

3. A thing is a dependent good (DG) if and only if it is a good, and its being a good is in virtue of its contribution to or employment by some other good. A thing is a dependent evil (DE) if and only if it is an evil, and its being an evil is in virtue of its contribution to or employment by some evil other than itself. DGs can be evils when they contribute to or are employed by evils; DEs can be goods when they contribute to or are employed by goods.

4. Though it is occasionally useful to talk about DGs as goods, since only IGs are always good, they are the only real goods. Similarly, since only IEs are always evil, they are the only real evils.

5. There are different goods and different evils unique to different things, viz., health is good, disease evil, for the body; virtue is good, vice evil, for the soul. But the greatest good of all—so great as to outweigh any consideration of any other goods, should they come into conflict so that one had to choose between them in one's life—is good action, especially activity that is unimpeded by anything else, and guided by virtue. The greatest evil of all—so great as to outweigh any consideration of any other evils, were they to come into conflict so that one had to choose between them in one's life—is evil action, especially action that is unimpeded by anything else and guided by vice.

6. A relative good is one that moves one's condition more towards the extreme of happiness from where it would otherwise be. A relative evil is one that moves one's condition more towards the extreme of wretchedness that it would otherwise be. One can receive a relative good and still be wretched, or a relative evil and still be happy.

7. An absolute good is one that makes its possessor happy. An absolute evil is one that makes its possessor wretched.

8. The only absolute good is good activity, and the best absolute good is unimpeded activity guided by virtue. The only absolute evils are vice and evil activity, and the worst absolute evil is unimpeded activity guided by vice.

Virtue

9. The virtuous condition of the soul is neither necessary nor sufficient for happiness. Vice is sufficient but not necessary for wretchedness.

10. Only good action, and especially unimpeded activity guided by virtue, will enable us to live a happy life. Such activity is both necessary and sufficient for happiness. And the happiest life is ensured by living without impediment a life that is guided by virtue.

Happiness

11. To be happy is the same as to live well or to do well. To be wretched is the same as to live ill or to do ill. To live well is to engage in good activity. To live ill is to engage in evil activity.

12. Though nothing can make the good person suffer the most extreme (abso-

lute) wretchedness, circumstances can make his or her life no longer worth living, that is, circumstances can make him or her capable no longer of living or doing well, or being happy.

Item number 12 explains the lack of symmetry one finds in items 8 and 9, for one may not live well despite one's good or virtuous soul, but one will never fail to live ill with a vicious soul. In this asymmetry, we find Socrates' own version of the Greek proverb "χαλαπὰ τὰ καλά" (good things are difficult—*Hip. Ma.* 304e8; *Cra.* 384b1); for evil is always easy to obtain (see *Ap.* 39a6–b1), but moral goodness must have a friendly environment to achieve its goals.

5

Socratic Politics

5.1 "The True Political Craft"

5.1.1 Public and Private Politics

At *Apology* 31c4–32a3, Socrates explains to his jurors why, despite his lifelong commitment to the moral improvement of his fellow citizens, he has not made it his business to act as a "public man" (δημοσιεύειν: *Ap*. 32a3). No doubt the Athenians regarded this as a serious issue; the very idea that one could lead a worthy life as a "private man" might well strike them as implausible or perhaps even dangerous. As Thucydides' Pericles says of the Athenians,

> We alone do not regard a man who takes no part in political life as one who minds his own business; we regard him as having no business here at all. (Thuc. 2.40.2, trans. C. M. Reed)

Socrates' explanation is that his *daimonion* opposed his engaging in political activities (*Ap*. 31d5). As we shall argue in the next chapter (see section 6.3), there can be no question that at least once, and perhaps on several occasions, Socrates intended to do the very thing his *daimonion* opposed. So even Socrates, prior to his *daimonion*'s opposition, shared his fellow Athenians' judgment that at least sometimes the best way to pursue moral reform is through aggressive involvement in Athens' political institutions, such as the Assembly. But given his *daimonion*'s opposition, Socrates became convinced that—aside from the performance of his required duties as a citizen—he must desist from such action. The opposition from his *daimonion* must have struck Socrates as a puzzle: "If I am supposed to neglect my own affairs and always act in my fellow Athenians' interests, exhorting them to care for nothing more than virtue" (see *Ap*. 31b1–5), "as I believe the god has commanded me to do, why should I be prevented from taking this mission to the place it would appear I could do the most good—for example, to the Assembly of the people, where the state's most important decisions are made?" The answer, he comes to think, must be that if he had taken his exhortations to the Assembly or other public institutions, he would not have been tolerated for very long:

> I think this opposition [sc. the *daimonion*'s] is a completely good thing; for you know well that if I had tried to engage in political matters, I would have perished long ago and would have benefited neither you nor me. (*Ap*. 31d6–e1)

It is tempting to conclude from such words that Socrates had nothing whatever to do with politics or political issues.[1] That we should be suspicious of such a sweeping conclusion, however, is evident from another often-quoted text: in the *Gorgias,* Socrates says

> I think that I am among the few—if not to say the only one—of the Athenians
> who attempts to practice what is truly the political craft, and the only one now to
> engage in political activity. (*Grg.* 521d6–8)

So when Socrates says at his trial that he has not been a "public man" and that his *daimonion* has prevented him from engaging in political activity, we must understand him as saying something that is consistent with his being alone—or nearly alone—among Athenians in attempting to practice "the true political craft." It would be worth our while, then, to see what the distinction is between "the true political craft," in which Socrates does attempt to engage, and the public life, in which Socrates has been prohibited from engaging.

5.1.2 Politics and Rhetoric

At *Gorgias* 464b2–465e1, Socrates distinguishes between the genuine craft of politics and various forms of what he terms "flattery," which merely mimic politics. Just as the proper care of the body has two branches, according to Socrates— medicine and physical fitness—so does the proper care of the soul have two branches—the judicial craft and the legislative craft. Physical fitness and the legislative craft are each concerned with prophylactic care; medicine and the judicial craft are corrective. Later, we discover that Socrates regards the prophylactic branches to be superior to the corrective (*Grg.* 520b2–3), no doubt because they prevent evil from occurring, rather than merely correcting evil that has already occurred.

Each branch, according to Socrates, also has an imitator: cookery imitates medicine; self-adornment (presumably, something like fashion or cosmetology) imitates the physical fitness craft; rhetoric imitates the judicial craft; sophistry imitates the legislative craft (*Grg.* 465c1–3). Just as the prophylactic crafts are superior to the corrective ones, so the imitators of prophylaxis are superior to the imitators of correction (*Grg.* 520b2–3). Moreover, because Socrates regards the soul and its care as much more precious than the body and its care (see *Ap.* 30a7–b1; *Cri.* 47e7–48a4), it follows that he would regard the branches of genuine politics as much more noble than the crafts of medicine or physical fitness.

Given his contemporaries' conception of politics, Socrates' own analysis, as it is found in the *Gorgias,* is extraordinary. For people like Callicles, to engage in politics is to practice the rhetorical (or oratorical)[2] life. That is, the political man

---

1. Those who have drawn this inference no doubt had (Ps.-)Plato's letters in mind, in which the author reports a withdrawal from the official activities of the state. But plainly, Plato was not apolitical in the sense of having no interest in political thought. See [*Epist.* 5] 322a4–c1; [*Epist.* 7] 324b8–326b4. For other discussions of Socrates' political views, see Kraut [1983b], 194–244; and Reeve [1989], 155–60.

2. See Irwin [1977], 116–17; Irwin [1979], 8–9; and Dodds [1959], note on 480a1–481b5, 257.

is none other than the "public man," the demagogue who distinguishes himself as a leader in the Assembly, the courts of law, and other political arenas, by making great speeches that move the people (see, for example, *Grg.* 500c4–7). For Socrates, the criterion by which we distinguish the genuine practitioner of the political craft is completely different: does he or does he not always attempt to act "with a view to what is best, aiming to make the citizens as good as possible" (502e2–5)?

5.1.3   Why the Political Craft Can Be Practiced Only by a "Private Man"

It follows from Socrates' conception that one can be a genuine practitioner of the political craft without ever making a speech in a public gathering—without ever so much as setting foot in the Assembly or in a court of law. In other words, one can live as a "private man," and yet be a genuine political craftsman—so long as one always acts in such a way as to make those upon whom one acts as good as possible. Conversely, one can live as a "public man," and yet be no more than an imitator of the genuinely political man.

But Socrates' view is even more radically paradoxical than this, for he does not just regard the private life as *compatible* with genuine political craftsmanship; for all practical purposes he regards it as *required* for such craftsmanship. Conversely, Socrates does not just think that the public man often fails to practice the political craft in democratic settings; he thinks that the public man *is very likely doomed to such a failure.* The reason for this is Socrates' conviction that (with very few exceptions) persuasion in public speaking can be achieved only through flattery (κολακευτική—*Grg.* 464c5), which aims only at gratifying its audience, but never at achieving what is actually good. This is why even that great admirer of orators, Callicles, is at a loss to think of one orator, past or present, who can honestly be said to have improved the citizenry (*Grg.* 503b5–d4, 515c4–517a6). Socrates is convinced that a genuine political craftsman would have no more chance in a court of law, were he opposed by a rhetorical flatterer, than would a physician pleading his case to a jury of children on a charge prosecuted by a cook (see *Grg.* 521e3–522b2). So it is that

> no one will save himself who genuinely opposes you or any other populace and prevents many unjust and illegal things from happening in the state. Rather, it is necessary, if one is really going to fight for what's right, to act as a private man and not as a public man. (*Ap.* 31e2–32a3)

Although Socrates seems to think that anyone who tries to improve the city through public institutions is doomed to failure, he is not committed to the view that political power inevitably corrupts its possessor, for Socrates himself allows that there was at least one man who held power in the world of Realpolitik and was nonetheless a good man: Aristeides, son of Lysimachus (*Grg.* 526b1–3). In allowing some vague hope that virtue and public life might be compatible, therefore, if only the public man first becomes truly virtuous (see *Grg.* 527d1–5), Socrates does not contradict himself.

5.1.4   Political Discourse

The fact that a "good man" once actually led a "public" life, however, is irrelevant to what Socrates perceives as the conditions he faces in Athens. In the world in which Socrates finds himself—where he is the wisest of men precisely because he alone recognizes his own profound lack of wisdom (*Ap.* 23b2–4)—there not only appears to be a dearth of persons capable of practicing the political craft in public fora, but there is also no evident form of discourse by which the political craft could be pursued in such fora. In the *Gorgias,* Socrates recognizes but two forms of discourse, that of rhetoric, by which one makes speeches to masses of people, and that of dialectic (or discussion—διαλέγεσθαι), in which one asks or answers questions of another (*Grg.* 448d9–10, 471d3–5). Rhetorical discourse, in Socrates' view, is well suited for those who plead their cases in the law courts, trying only to convince the greatest number of jurors to vote for one's own side of the case. This is the form of discourse which Polus and Socrates' other interlocutors in the *Gorgias* seem to prize. The problem is that the rhetorical form of discourse is "without value with regard to the truth" (*Grg.* 471e7–472a1). Socrates prefers dialectic, which *is* suited to getting at the truth, but which allows him to persuade only a single person at a time—the very one with whom he speaks (see esp. *Grg.* 471e2–472c4). Socrates says,

> Do not command me now to put the vote to those who are present, but if you do not have a better refutation than these, as I said just now, let me lead the way and try the refutation that I think is needed. For I know how to produce one witness for what I am saying, and that is the very one with whom I am having the argument; leave the many out of it. I know how to get the vote of the one; I do not have to bother with the many. (*Grg.* 474a2–b1)

The same contrast is evident in the conclusion of Socrates' argument with Polus: whereas Polus, with his rhetorical style, can command the assent of everyone except the one man with whom he speaks (Socrates), Socrates gains the agreement of Polus himself without once appealing to what "the many" believe (*Grg.* 475e8–476a2).

This pair of alternatives, rhetoric and dialectic, is never plainly stated, in the *Gorgias* or anywhere else, to exhaust the field. However, nowhere in the early dialogues is another form of discourse identified by which a speaker can accomplish both of the goals of the other two forms of discourse: persuading "the many" and stating the truth. So it looks as if one who was seriously interested in practicing the authentic political craft would be forced to employ a form of discourse unsuited to the life of the demagogue. For this reason too, then, "it is necessary, if one is really going to fight for what's right, to act as a private man and not as a public man" (*Ap.* 32a1–3).

5.1.5   Acting as a "Private Man" versus Acting "in Private"

When Socrates says that he has acted as a "private man and not as public man," we must not suppose that he did his business out of the public eye. To the contrary, as he says in the *Apology*, he has performed his philosophic mission right out in the open for any to observe, speaking in Athens' many public places with famous politicians, poets, and craftsmen (21b9–22e5), citizens and foreigners (23b5–6, 30a3–4), young and old (30a2–3, 30a8). Although he has eschewed the activities that constitute what his fellow Athenians would call a "public life" (see 36b6–c4), Socrates considers himself a "gift" to Athens from the god, a gadfly who stings the body politic into concern for virtue and the proper care of the soul (30d7–31b5). So Socrates' mission is public both in venue and in purpose. It is practiced "as a private man" only in the sense that the conversations that constitute Socrates' mission do not take place within Athens' legal institutions, but rather in the marketplace, the gymnasium, and other public places, as well as private homes and wherever else Socrates can find dialectical partners to engage in discussion with him.

It does not follow from the fact that Socrates lived as a "private man" that he did not or could not discuss matters of profound political consequence. What his *daimonion* opposed was Socrates' decision to engage in those activities generally regarded as political: haranguing the Assembly, bringing legal suits against wrong-doers, and so on. He has been free all along to discuss any issues—even the very issues his fellow citizens were debating hotly in the Assembly—in private dialectical conversations. So we are now in a position to understand why Socrates would have regarded himself as "among the few—if not the only one—of the Athenians who attempts to practice the true political craft, and the only one right now to engage in political activity" (*Grg.* 521d6–8) and also as one who has not pursued what were commonly recognized as political roles. Let us now see what issues of "profound political consequence" we can find addressed in Socratic philosophy, and attempt to determine precisely what Socrates had to say about them.

5.2 The Socratic Doctrine of "Persuade or Obey"

5.2.1 A Problem of Interpretation

> . . . in war and in court and everywhere one must do what the city and country commands, or you must persuade it as to what is naturally just. (*Cri.* 51b8–c1)

In this passage and others like it in the *Crito*, Plato's Socrates expresses what has come to be known as the "persuade or obey" doctrine. A straightforward reading of the passage suggests that there are only two proper courses of action a citizen may follow in response to a command by the state: either obey the command or persuade the state to rescind its command. But scholars have resisted this reading and proposed a variety of other ways to construe what Socrates says about the citizen's obligation to obey the law.[3]

One reason for scholars' reluctance to accept the *Crito*'s doctrine at face value is that it appears to conflict with various other things Socrates says in the early dialogues, especially Socrates' famous absolute prohibition of injustice (see, e.g.,

---

3. A list of the various major interpretations may be found in the bibliography of Kraut [1983b]. Kraut also discusses a number of different interpretations in [1983b], ch. 3.

Cri. 49d5–9). Surely the state could command an injustice which, it is argued, Socrates' interest in justice would require him to disobey.

Nearly everyone[4] has also agreed that a specific case of the relevant sort of conflict is identified by Socrates himself: Socrates seems all too willing to disobey legal authority when he tells his jurors in the *Apology* that he would disobey them if they required him to give up philosophizing:

> If you should say to me, "Socrates, we will not now be persuaded by Anytus, but will let you go on this condition: you will not any longer spend your time in this investigation or philosophizing, and if you are found doing this again you shall be put to death." If you should let me go on this condition, I should tell you, "Men of Athens, I hold you in high regard and I love you, but I will obey the god more than you, and just as long as I breathe and am able, I will never cease from philosophizing or from exhorting you and from declaring my views to any of you I should ever happen upon." (*Ap.* 29c5–d6)

We could not effectively review and specifically refute each of the many interpretations that have been put forward on this issue—there have been too many of them. Instead, we propose to look closely at the relevant texts and their contexts, allowing them to motivate an interpretation unlike any we have found in the vast literature on this topic. Let us first consider carefully what Socrates says in the *Crito*.

5.2.2　Civil Disobedience in the Crito?

A number of scholars have tried to show that the arguments of the *Crito* can be understood as leaving Socrates room to accept certain forms of disobedience to the law.[5] We think this is a mistake. The problem with this view, we think, can be found in the way Socrates characterizes the authority of the state over its citizens.

Though he has urged Socrates to violate the law, Crito is no anarchist. His concern is only that in this case civic authority is in conflict with Socrates' (and others') welfare, through no fault of Socrates. So Socrates does not need to argue *that* the state has authority; he must instead try to convince Crito about the *extent* of its authority.

At 50e3–51c3, Socrates compares the authority of the state over the citizen to two other recognizable forms of authority, that of parent over offspring and master over slave. These two forms are hardly equivalent: parents do not *own* their offspring; parents do not use children for their own purposes; children are reared and nurtured and trained to become citizens in their own right. So the relation of master to slave is not the same as that of parent to child.[6] But Socrates does not

---

4. To our knowledge, we are the only ones who have ever denied the relevance of the following passage to the issue of Socrates' attitude toward legal obligation. See Brickhouse and Smith [1984c] and [1989b], 137–53.

5. See, for example, Woozley [1979]; see also Woozley [1971], 306–8; Vlastos [1974]; Kraut [1983b]; Reeve [1989], 115–21; Santas [1979], ch. 2.

6. For the comparison Socrates makes, however, it must be that there is something common to the two relationships, and it is clear that what is common is that each is a strongly authoritarian relation-

insist that these forms of authority are alike in every respect. He requires only that each is a recognizable relationship of an authority to an inferior with respect to that authority.

In comparing the master-slave and parent-child relationships to that of state and citizen, Socrates tells us nothing about the former pairs. They are the models—assumed by the argument to be well understood—by which the problematic pair of state-citizen is to be made clear. This requires Socrates to construe the model relationships (at least for the purposes of this argument) in a conventional way; otherwise neither Crito nor Plato's readers will comprehend the comparison to them.

Now given this understanding of the model relationships, Socrates' point is simple: the authority we should recognize in the state's relationship to the citizen is *even more complete and one-sided* than what we conventionally accept in the models:

> . . . could you say, first, that you are not our offspring and slave, both you yourself and your ancestors? And if this is the case, do you think justice between you and us arises from equality, so that whatever we try to do to you, do you think it is just for you to do the same in return to us? Between you and your father there was no equality arising from justice, or your master if you happen to have one [. . .] or are you so wise that it escapes you that your country is more estimable, more worthy of respect, more holy, and held in higher regard by the gods and by men of intelligence than your mother and your father and all of your ancestors. . . . (*Cri.* 50e3–8, 51a7–b2)

It is plain that conventional wisdom would not permit a minor child to disobey his or her parent, or a slave to disobey his or her master. If there can be moral grounds within Socratic philosophy for a citizen to disobey the state, then, they are certainly not evident at *Crito* 50e3–51b2.

5.2.3   Is There an Apology/Crito Problem?

At *Apology* 28d10 and following, Socrates compares his mission in Athens to the military posts to which he was stationed at Potidaia, Amphipolis, and Delion. "I would have done a terrible thing," he says, "if I remained where [the commanders whom you chose to command me] stationed me, like anyone else, and risked death, but when the god stationed me [. . .] I deserted my post through fear of death or anything else whatever" (28d10–29a1). Socrates points out to his jurors that the fear of death is really "the basest sort of ignorance" (29b1–2), for no one really knows if death is bad or good (29a6–b1). At 29b2–7, Socrates concludes:

---

ship. Indeed, it seems that Socrates has chosen these two relationships precisely because they were the most authoritarian relationships he could think of, excluding that of state to citizen, which is the relationship under dispute. So we must not suppose, contrary to what Kraut claims ([1983b], 94–105), that the "offspring" Socrates has in mind are only adult or even nearly adult "offspring." Rather, the "offspring" are intended to be understood as young children. Otherwise, the implied likeness between a child and a slave would be absurd.

In this also, perhaps I differ from many people, and if I were to say that I am wiser, it would be in this: that not knowing sufficiently about what's in Hades, I don't think I know. But I do know that it is evil and disgraceful to do injustice and to disobey one's superior, whether god or man. (*Ap.* 29b2–7)

Though there have been a number of ingenious efforts to interpret Socrates' words here as identifying only his *moral* superiors,[7] it is clear in context that included in the class of "human" superiors would be the likes of his commanders at Potidaia, Amphipolis, and Delion, whose authority over him was legal and military. Given Socrates' negative appraisal of his fellow humans' moral wisdom, it seems most unlikely that he would count his former military commanders as his *moral* superiors, or indeed, that the class of Socrates' moral superiors would have any members.[8] The upshot of Socrates' remarks here in the *Apology*, then, reflects the same view we find in the parent-child, master-slave, and citizen-state comparisons of the *Crito:* Socrates, it seems, believes it is never right to disobey the legitimate commands of civil authority. Perhaps even more remarkable than this is the fact that Socrates' notorious profession of ignorance seems not to apply in this case—for all he does not know, Socrates says he *knows* this.[9]

But Socrates is also the one who argues repeatedly that one ought never to do an evil or injustice, even in return for evil or injustice done to one.[10] Is it not evident that the two principles—never do evil and never disobey civil authority—could be made to compete? Is it not obvious that one could be commanded by civil authority to do an injustice or other evil?

Most scholars have supposed that precisely such a command is contemplated by Socrates in his famous hypothetical vow to disobey the jury in the *Apology* (29c5–d6). There Socrates imagines the jury letting him go on the condition that he give up philosophy, to which he says his response would be to disobey. But his vow in the *Apology* can be construed as pertinent to the arguments of the *Crito* only if there is some plausible way to understand his vow as committing him (even hypothetically) under some specifiable circumstance or other to disobeying a valid command of an authentic civil authority.

In fact, we have argued at length elsewhere that Socrates' words at *Apology* 29c5–d6 in no way commit him to civil disobedience.[11] Socrates makes his vow as he stands before an Athenian jury, indicted for impiety and under threat—as a specific part of the indictment itself—of execution. His trial is an ἀγὼν τιμη----τός,[12] the trial procedure in which the penalty for committing the crime in ques-

---

7. See, e.g., Kraut [1983b], 23, n.36.

8. Moreover, unless one understands the phrase to refer to one's moral superiors *only when their commands reflect such moral superiority,* it is not at all clear that Socrates would accept the claim. After all, one's moral superiors need not always be right—and inferiors need not always be wrong—when their points of view conflict. But if this were supposed to provide the meaning of Socrates' phrase, it reduces to the triviality that one ought always to do what is right.

9. For discussions of this issue, see Vlastos [1985]; Lesher [1987]; Brickhouse and Smith [1989b], secs. 2.6 and 3.2, and ch. 2, this volume.

10. See, e.g., *Cri.* 49d5–9.

11. See Brickhouse and Smith [1989b], sec. 3.3.

12. See MacDowell [1978], 253; Harrison [1971], vol. 2, 80–82; Lipsius [1905–1915], 248–62.

tion is not prescribed in advance by the law. So the jury must first decide whether the defendant is guilty or innocent. Then, if they find him guilty, thcy will be asked to decide between the prosecution's penalty, which must be specified in advance of the trial in the indictment, and whatever counter-penalty the now-convicted defendant might propose. The prosecutor may not change his proposed penalty after he has submitted the indictment, nor may the jury assign any penalty other than one of those proposed by the litigants themselves.

Socrates makes his vow not to comply before he has been convicted (and hence before he has offered his counter-penalty), but after the penalty proposed by the prosecution has been stated. At *Apology* 29c5–d6, he imagines the men sitting in the jurors' seats (whom he fails throughout his defense speech to address by the title "jurors")[13] offering to let him go free on the condition that he give up his philosophical mission. If he is caught philosophizing again, however, he shall be put to death. Socrates says he will obey the god rather than the "men of Athens" to whom he speaks. But what precisely does Socrates have in mind here? Is he imagining that they agreed to find him innocent on the condition that he promise to abandon his mission? If so, we needn't worry that his disobeying their "order" would cause conflict with what he says in the *Crito*. Juries were neither legally nor even practically empowered to make such conditional acquittals (they did not even have a formal opportunity to discuss the case among themselves, much less to negotiate conditions with the litigants).[14] So if Socrates were freed and then disobeyed the condition his jurors offered him, he would not be guilty of disobeying any valid command of an authentic legal authority. Neither would he be violating a just agreement, for as Socrates clearly says, he would never agree to such a condition, precisely because he thinks it would be wrong to do so.

Perhaps instead we should imagine that Socrates' jury is threatening to find him guilty and then assign quitting philosophy as his penalty. This could be the case, however, only if Socrates himself offers abandoning philosophy as his counter-penalty, which he obviously would never do (see *Ap*. 37e3–38a6). Recall that the penalty proposed by the prosecution is already fixed and cannot be changed. Since the jury can only choose between the penalties proposed by the litigants themselves, the jury could not legally assign the abandonment of philosophy as Socrates' penalty. If somehow they did so, Socrates would be under no legal obligation to obey the jury's command.[15]

13. See Brickhouse and Smith [1989b], 210–12. We do not think there is any special significance in Socrates' form of address, though the fact that he does not address the jurors by their legal title, δικασταί, certainly leaves open the possibility that what Socrates says to them does not always take their legal role into account. In saying, as he does at *Apology* 29c5–d6, that he would disobey these "men of Athens," then, we are not required to assume that he is addressing them strictly as jurors.

14. See MacDowell [1978], 251–52.

15. Yet another possibility has been proposed by Spiro Panagiotou [1987]. According to Panagiotou, the situation Socrates has in mind is that he would be found guilty, condemned to death, but then pardoned on the condition that he give up his mission. We do not find this convincing. First, the jury was not empowered to suspend sentences or to grant pardons; these functions could be performed only by the Assembly, as Panagiotou himself notes ([1987], 40; 41–42, n.7). Moreover, the legal procedure by which a pardon might be granted would have to be initiated by the convict himself, and any condition according to which the pardon would be granted would have to be explicitly accepted in

The simple fact is that what Socrates says at *Apology* 29c5-d6 does not create conflict with the most straightforward reading of the "persuade or obey" doctrine he articulates in the *Crito*. In saying this, however, we are not claiming that Socrates is making a legal point in response to his jurors in this passage. Socrates is not saying that he would disobey the jurors *because* they would have no legal authority to command him in the relevant way. Rather, we are claiming only that in saying he would disobey them, the legal context is such that his disobedience to the jury involves no direct or implied violation of the law or legal authority. To put it another way, law and legal authority have *nothing whatever* to do with this passage, either in its assumptions or in its implications.

Socrates does not have to assume that the "men of Athens" to whom he speaks at *Apology* 29c5–d6 have the legal authority to make such a command;[16] they do not, and we may suppose that Socrates knows perfectly well that they do not. Nor does Socrates have to assume that these "men of Athens" are so confused about Athens' laws as foolishly to presume they have that authority. Socrates imagines only that these "men of Athens" have the power to kill him if he should disobey their order, not that they have the legal authority to do so. Accordingly, the legal status of the "men of Athens" whom Socrates imagines ordering him to cease philosophizing—and the legal status of this order—are never specified. And Socrates' answer is appropriate: he does not lecture them as to the legal impropriety of their command, for they need not be mistakenly assuming any specifically legal authority when they contemplate such a command. Because what is morally appropriate and not what is lawful is the explicit issue here, Socrates' reply to the jurors' hypothetical command is not an evasion. Instead, Socrates confronts the Athenians directly: he says he would obey the god rather than them, and so would prefer to die than to give up philosophizing, were these his only choices.

5.2.4 Reinventing the "Problem"

At this point, one might concede that our understanding of the legal circumstances is correct but nevertheless dismiss the significance of those circumstances by insisting that whether or not the particular command Socrates hypothesizes the jury issuing could be legally made, surely *some command proscribing philosophizing could be made by an appropriate legal authority*. Perhaps such a command would be legally binding if it were passed by the Assembly.[17] One might suppose that Socrates would disobey such an order. Hence, we are back to the original question: is there not an inconsistency in Socrates' principles?

---

advance by the convict. Plainly, Socrates would not propose quitting philosophy as a condition for his pardon. "Refusing" to accept such a condition would hardly constitute legal disobedience.

16. Contrast the view of Reeve, who claims that Socrates' hypothetical vow to disobey the jury can only be understood as conceding "even *per impossibile*" the legal authority of the jurors to make the command that Socrates says he would disobey ([1989], 116). We find it quite implausible for Reeve to claim that Socrates would require the jurors to assume an impossibility in order to make his point. A detailed criticism of Reeve's view may be found in Smith [1992].

17. This is precisely the line taken by Richard Kraut. [1983b], 13–17.

We believe that the supposition behind this concern cannot be supported under Socrates' understanding of Athenian law. For Socrates, in order for a command of the Assembly to be binding, it is not enough that the majority of Athenian citizens agree to it; as Socrates clearly says about the mass trial of the Arginousai generals (*Ap.* 32b1–c3), general agreement about something—even where enforced by irresistible power—does not make what is agreed upon legal. Before Socrates would find himself in the awkward position of having to choose between his duty to philosophize and his duty to the state, any command to cease philosophizing would have to be genuinely legal. But since Socrates believes that he has a pious duty to philosophize, any law proscribing philosophy passed by the city of Athens would—in Socrates' eyes, at least—be in direct conflict with the *already established* law proscribing impiety.[18] So even if the *Athenians* saw no direct conflict between a ''law'' prohibiting the practice of philosophy and the law proscribing impiety, *Socrates* would.

Now what would Socrates make of such a case? It seems he would have but four choices: (1) he could treat each of the conflicting laws as equally valid and obey whichever one he felt like obeying at a given time; (2) he could treat each law as equally invalid and behave however he chose to, on grounds other than obedience to law; (3) he could regard the new law as invalidating the prior law; or (4) he could regard the new law as invalidated by the prior law. That Socrates would make the first choice (namely, that both laws were equally valid) seems unlikely, since it involves maintaining an inconsistent position regarding the pair of the candidates. Even if he did regard both laws as equally valid, it seems reasonable to suppose that the law he would inevitably obey would be the law he took to require him to philosophize, namely, the law proscribing impiety. We could expect the same behavior from Socrates if he made choice (2), according to which neither conflicting law would be regarded as valid; for Socrates thinks he has good reasons to philosophize independent of what he construes the law to require on this issue.

So let us imagine for the moment that the Athenian Assembly actually did pass a new decree proscribing philosophy. On either option (1) or (2) Socrates might simply consider himself free to ignore the new decree, convinced as he would be that it conflicted with the law forbidding impiety.[19] If so, he might be arrested, tried, convicted, and condemned to death—just as he was for practicing his mission under the current laws. So long as his arrest, trial, conviction, and execution are performed according to due process, Socrates would have no more moral ground for resisting than he finds he has during his discussion with Crito in the Prison of the Eleven. He might well argue at his trial that he could not be held responsible for breaking the law on the ground that the relevant laws conflicted. But convincing the jury might be just as impossible as it was at his historical trial.

What about choices (3) and (4)? We can think of at least one good ground for thinking that of these two options, Socrates would select (4) and not (3); that is,

---

18. See Brickhouse and Smith [1989b], sec. 3.3.6.
19. We argue for this option in Brickhouse and Smith [1989b], sec. 3.3.4.

he would regard the prior law as having precedence. The Athenian legal system, through a procedure called a γραφὴ παρανόμων/*graphē paranomōn,* allowed a citizen to challenge a newly proposed law on the ground that it violated a prior law. If the suit were successful, the new law would be struck from the books and a fine would be assessed against its sponsor in the Assembly.[20] This shows that when conflict arose between laws, the principles of Athenian law gave precedence to the prior law. Now we have no reason to think that Socrates would not have accepted this tenet of Athenian law, and we have good reason for thinking that Socrates generally accepted the tenets of Athenian law. Hence, were a case to arise in which Socrates would feel the need to decide which one of the conflicting laws was legitimate, we would expect him to treat the prior law as the valid law. Accordingly, in the situation we have been considering, Socrates would see the new law as illegal precisely because what it required would be against the prior law proscribing impiety. If he disobeyed the new "law," on this hypothesis, he would disobey no *valid* law.

One might suppose that instead of simply refusing to obey the new law, Socrates would think he needed to swear out a *graphē paranomōn* against the new law. It is easy enough to imagine that the effect of his doing so might be that the Athenians would be unmoved by Socrates' argument, and vote to uphold the new decree. Socrates, however, might well remain convinced that the new "law" is illegal. But having tested the new law by a legally correct procedure, Socrates would no longer have any legal means of resisting the new law. That is, he would now have attempted, but failed, to persuade. According to our reading of the "persuade or obey" doctrine, Socrates would now have to obey the new law or leave Athens, as he says the Laws have always permitted him to do if he were no longer satisfied with them (*Cri.* 52a8–d7).

Precisely because Socrates never imagines a case such as this, one can only speculate as to what his decision would be. On the one hand, he could surely no longer be satisfied with the laws of Athens, as he is said to be in the *Crito,* in which case leaving Athens would certainly hold more appeal than it did without such a new law. On the other hand, unless we know more about exactly what was and was not prohibited by the new law, we cannot be certain that Socrates could not continue to call the new law into question in the hopes that it might soon be rescinded. He may not willingly violate the new law, of course, but it is not clear precisely what the new law is supposed to prohibit. Plainly, any legislative decree prohibiting calling laws into question would itself be of questionable legality, and in any case it is most unlikely that such a law would ever pass the Assembly. So even if the Assembly were to prohibit the practice of philosophy, there would nevertheless be a number of legally permissible tacks Socrates could take to pursue the nullification of the command. Perhaps he would see his mission as requiring that he attempt to get the law nullified.[21] As he deliberated about what he should do in such a circumstance, his *daimonion* might come into play: even if he

---

20. See MacDowell [1978], 50–52. We discuss this in Brickhouse and Smith [1989b], 151.

21. See Xenophon's account in *Mem.* 1.2.31–37, in which Socrates confronts a law against teaching "the art of words."

thought he had good reason to make one decision, it might well be that a daimonic alarm would compel him to reverse himself.[22] But unless he would be prepared to change the position he announces in the *Crito*, one avenue would not be open to him in our view: even though he has *(ex hypothesi)* made a sincere attempt to persuade the state to rescind the new law, he may not now disobey it, any more than a minor child may disobey his parent or a slave may disobey his master.

5.2.5 Socrates and Political Activity Again

In order to get this far in our speculation about Socrates' response to a legal ban on philosophy, however, we have had to make a number of great leaps away from the texts. In fact, we believe that at least one of the suppositions that got us this far is not true to Socrates' character. Socrates, let us recall, is the man whose *daimonion* has prevented him from aggressively pursuing institutional politics, that is, from attempting to play any role in Athens' recognized political arenas other than those for which he is conscripted or selected by lottery (as, for example, when he ends up a Prutanis during the aftermath of the Arginousai affair). He might well see some new decree (for example, one prohibiting philosophy) as conflicting with a prior law; but what action would he feel required to take? In the past, he has taken no legal action when he saw Athens go wrong, which he suggests has happened often when he tells his jurors: "no one will save himself who genuinely opposes you or any other populace and prevents many unjust *and illegal* things from happening in the state" (*Apology* 31e2–4).

With these words, which we discussed at length in section 5.1, Socrates explains his life as "a private, not a public man" (*Ap.* 32a2–3). We may infer that Socrates does not believe he must take formal steps in opposing what he sees as "many unjust and illegal things" that occur in the state. The mere fact, then, that Socrates would see the prohibition of philosophy as illegal, therefore, would not be sufficient inducement for him to play what is to him the unfamiliar role of "public man" by opposing the new decree with a *graphē paranomōn*.

It might be argued, however, that a decree prohibiting philosophy would be

---

22. See *Ap.* 31c8–d1, 40a4–6, c2–3, 41d6; *Euthphr.* 3b5–7; *Euthyd.* 272e4; *Rep.* VI.496c4; *Phdr.* 242b8–9; and *[Theages]* 128d2–131a7 (see also *[Alc.* I] 105d5–106a1). For a discussion of the workings of the *daimonion,* see Brickhouse and Smith [1989b], sec. 5.5. Gregory Vlastos argues (in [1989a], revised in [1991], ch. 6) that Socrates would always follow his own reasoning, even where divination was involved. Accordingly, Vlastos seems to think that Socrates always provides a convenient interpretation of the *daimonion*'s alarms. On the contrary, we think that if a daimonic monition opposed Socrates (for example, if he was about to go address the Assembly because he thought it would be best for him to argue against some law they were likely to pass—see *Ap.* 31c8–d1), he would always modify his own reasonings according to his daimonic promptings; by its very nature, the *daimonion* often shows Socrates that the ways he intends to act, and hence in some way or ways the reasons he may have for acting as he intends, are incorrect. The texts provide no grounds for doubting that Socrates would always follow the *daimonion*'s promptings no matter what course of action or pattern of reasoning it opposed. This does not mean that Socrates became unreasonable; it means rather that he would re-evaluate and adjust his reason to what he considered the indisputable fact, revealed by the *daimonion,* that he had been about to act in some improper or wrongful way. We provide additional arguments against Vlastos's position in sec. 6.3.

different from the "many . . . illegal things" Socrates has ignored in the past. The other illegalities, one might suppose, have never directly obligated *Socrates* to take any particular action. But a law prohibiting philosophy would have direct consequence on the way Socrates lives his life. Now, in fact, the text neither explicitly says nor implies that the injustices and illegalities Socrates ignored in the past were restricted to acts to be undertaken by others. Thus, any attempt to show that Socrates would regard a prohibition of philosophy as importantly different from the many illegalities he has ignored in the past simply has no textual basis.

But the texts also tell us what Socrates would do in a situation where he is directly given a command to act in a way he does not find acceptable: when the Thirty ordered him to go out and arrest Leon of Salamis, Socrates did not protest their order or create a disturbance—he simply went home (*Ap.* 32c4–d7). His behavior has been taken by some[23] as showing that Socrates would never obey even a legal command to do what Socrates conceived as an injustice. Such a conclusion involves a very dubious argument from silence: by Socrates' not explicitly stipulating to his jurors that the Thirty's order was illegal—as he had in the case of the trial of the Arginousai generals under the democracy—he shows either that he construed the Thirty's order as legal or that its legal status had no effect on his deliberations. We have disputed this at length elsewhere.[24] Without repeating our arguments again here, it is worth noting that nothing requires Socrates to preach to the choir; let us recall to whom he is speaking on this matter. He must insist on the illegality of the trial of the generals precisely because many of those on the jury might have initially supposed the decision to try the generals *en bloc* was a legal one. But no one on the democratic jury would need Socrates to emphasize the supposed illegality of anything having to do with the Thirty. (The obvious partisan identification of the jurors is indicated at *Ap.* 20e8–21a2.) Accordingly, Socrates' silence on this point hardly cries out for attention, and the inference from it is insecure even for an argument from silence. Moreover, we need not think that Socrates' disobedience of the Thirty had anything to do with his conception of legal authority; rather, he was free to do what he personally thought was just precisely because there was no legal impediment to his making up his own mind.

If we are right about this case, therefore, we may suppose that Socrates' reaction to what he considered to be illegal decrees would be the same whether or not they included his own actions within their scope: he would simply ignore them and continue his mission as a private person. In failing to obey the decrees he was convinced were illegal, moreover, he would in no way force upon us a reassessment of his arguments in the *Crito*. Plainly, the same goes for cases where the relevant laws conflict, for, as we said elsewhere, "when two laws contradict one another, even the most steadfast adherent to civil authority cannot find a way to comply with both."[25] Scholars have insisted that the texts provide an answer to

23. See Colson [1985];, Kraut [1983b], 17–24. See also our reply to Colson's argument in Brickhouse and Smith [1989b], 185–93.
24. See Brickhouse and Smith [1989b], sec. 4.3.5.
25. See Brickhouse and Smith [1989b], 152.

the question: What would Socrates do if a legal ban were to be placed on philosophy? But the fact is, the texts do not answer this question. They do not even begin to put Socrates in the position of having to ask it. The entire issue, we believe, is an artifact of scholarly speculation.

5.2.6 Just Obedience versus Obedience to Just Laws

We do not need to try to reconcile the *Crito*'s doctrines with a legal ban on philosophy, then, for Socrates would not believe there could be a legal ban on philosophy without radically changing the laws to which Socrates refers in the *Crito*.[26] But it is not unfair to ask what Socrates would do about a law which does not conflict with any prior law, but which Socrates would conceive as commanding an injustice. It is tempting to imagine that the Laws who speak to Socrates in the *Crito* are not the actual positive laws of Athens—flaws and all—but rather an idealized version, purified of any injustice.[27] The problem with this account is that the Laws who lecture Socrates in the *Crito* are plainly capable of making an error of judgment regarding justice; otherwise the "persuade" disjunct of the "persuade or obey" doctrine would be no more than rhetorical window dressing. Because the citizen might well recognize a moral error in the Laws, the Laws do not simply command obedience—the citizen is invited to persuade them when they err. But the Laws do not guarantee that they will change even if a citizen presents them with a morally compelling reason for doing so. So what would Socrates do if an unjust law were enacted and all legal challenges to it were turned back?

It is, perhaps, revealing that in Xenophon's account, Socrates simply identifies the just and the lawful (*Memorabilia* 4.4.12–25; see also *Cyropaedia* 1.3.17). One might be tempted to infer from such evidence that Socrates supposed simply that there could be no unjust laws, and hence that any "law" that was unjust would in fact be no law at all. But this is artificial. First, as we have just seen, the Laws Socrates personifies in the *Crito* are plainly capable of making mistakes with respect to justice. Second, even Xenophon's Socrates recognizes that the laws might change (*Mem.* 4.4.14), and so insists that the issue is not the justice of the laws themselves (for if a law is revoked, either the law or its revocation must be just—not both), but rather the justice of *obedience* to the laws. According to Xenophon's Socrates, it is always just to obey the law—both the law before it is revised, and the law after it is revised (*Mem.* 4.4.15–16).[28] It is also plain that

26. See Brickhouse and Smith [1989b], 152–53, for a discussion of how much distortion is required to generate the kind of case scholars have imagined.

27. See, for example, Woodruff [1982], note on *Hip. Ma.* 284d6–7, 41; and Colson [1989].

28. The same equation of just with lawful can be found articulated by Aristotle at *EN* 5.1129a32–34. We take such evidence to show that the view we are attributing to Socrates is one that would be familiar to the Greeks. See also Soph. *Philoctetes* 50–53, 1144 (see Blundell [1987], 311–12, for a commentary on this passage); Lys. 12.28; Dover [1974], 147f., 155. Even in the late dialogue, the *Politicus*, Plato advocates complete obedience to existing laws (see 300e11–301a4). The identification of obedience to the law and justice is represented by Thrasymachus (*Rep.* I.338e3–6, 339b7–9, 339c10–12) and Glaucon (*Rep.* II.359a3–4) as the common opinion of justice. The mutability of Athenian law was a frequent source of humor in Aristophanic comedy—see Ar. *Hipp.* 267f.; *Eccl.* 577ff., 586f., 797f.

Plato's Socrates does not approve of *all* the laws he feels constrained to obey (see *Ap.* 37a7–b2).

But does it make sense to distinguish between the justice of *obeying* the laws and the justice of the *laws themselves?* To see that it does, let us return to the models Socrates offers for the relationship of citizen to state in the *Crito.* Suppose a master were to order his slave to commit what even the slave is convinced (let us imagine rightly) is an immoral act. Perhaps the slave would protest the command. But suppose the master is adamant and will not rescind the command. If we are right, Socrates' view—both in Xenophon and in Plato—would be that moral duty requires the slave to obey the master. *Ex hypothesi,* the act in question is unjust; but whose injustice is it?

A case can be made that the slave is actually guilty of wrongdoing only if the slave is regarded as an independent moral agent. But to the Greeks of antiquity the slave plainly is not independent of his master, morally or legally. What is important is not merely that the slave was coerced (we can well imagine there being some implication of threat to the slave if he should disobey the master's command), but rather that the slave's actions are performed under the master's authority. If there is blame to be assessed, it must apply solely to the master. That this *is* the conventional understanding of such a case is clear from Athenian law, which held the masters responsible for what slaves did under their masters' orders.[29] The case is plainly similar if we imagine a minor child acting under orders from his or her parent.[30] The responsible agent in such cases is not the child or the slave, but rather the parent or the master. Where such authority is involved, the superior alone is culpable.

It is surely sensible, then, to understand Athenian conventions as holding that minor children and slaves were supposed always to obey their parents and masters respectively. Moreover, in obeying their parents or masters, neither children nor slaves ever do wrong—even when what they are commanded to do *is* wrong—for when they are under the commands of their superiors, *they* are not responsible for the wrong they do. The same transference of responsibility would apply, we may obviously assume, in assigning credit for any good done by a child or slave under orders: the child or slave might rightly be praised for obedience; but credit for any good done would go solely to the parent or master who commanded that the good-producing action be done.

Socrates explicitly conceives of the authority of parent over minor child and of master over slave as similar in the relevant way to that between state and citizen. Accordingly, the citizen may have exceptionless duties to obey legal authority and never to do wrong, and these duties may be seen to be perfectly consistent. Unjust laws may be passed; but in obeying them, the citizen does not act unjustly.

Scholars who have attempted to provide exceptions to Socrates' doctrine of legal obedience have done so mainly because they saw an inevitable conflict between such a doctrine and Socrates' famous prohibition against injustice. We are

---

29. See MacDowell [1978], 81. We are indebted to Charles Young for calling this to our attention.
30. See MacDowell [1978], 84.

now in a position to see why there need be no such conflict. In our view, Socrates can consistently require that the citizen never act unjustly and that the citizen never disobey the law even when the law itself is unjust and even where the citizen's actions in accordance with the law will produce injustice. The reason for this is that the responsible agent of injustice in such cases is the state, and not the citizen acting as the state's "offspring" or "slave."

5.2.7　The Moral Consequences of Socrates' View

One might detect in the view we have attributed to Socrates a precursor to those who, accused of war crimes, attempt to appeal to the fact that they were "only following orders." This consequence is to some degree mitigated by the way Socrates conditions the doctrine for which he argues in the *Crito*. In fact, anyone reading the *Crito* will notice that Socrates' arguments are explicitly subjected to a number of provisions, and we are in no position to guess what Socrates would say if one or more of these provisions were removed. The "Laws" to which Socrates says he owes obedience are the laws of Athens, the laws by which his parents married and under which Socrates himself was raised and nurtured. They are laws with which he has made a just agreement, and with which he has been manifestly satisfied, which all along had allowed him to leave Athens with his possessions, and to which (by undergoing the process of δοκιμασία)[31] he has sworn allegiance. Socrates' political doctrine, such as it is, is never generalized to other people, living under other legal systems, in other states. Attempts to discern what he would say about such things seem hopelessly speculative.

Nothing significant follows from the fact that Socrates did not leave Athens when the notorious Thirty were installed in power. It surely does not follow that he regarded the reign of the Thirty as legitimate. Even if he had initially been willing to consider the new government's legitimacy, it does not follow that he saw any of their subsequent excesses as permitted by the principles of their original constitution.[32] The Tyrants held power for only eight months; Socrates hardly had time to show that he was satisfied with their government (cp. *Cri.* 51d1–e4, 52b1–c3). In fact, he did not even last that long before coming into dangerous conflict with those in power (see *Ap.* 32c4–d7).

Far more troubling is Socrates' commitment to political passivity; he views engagement in the political affairs of his *polis* to be a sure route to an early demise (*Ap.* 31e2–4). It is for this reason, then, that he does not attempt to persuade his state to refrain from committing genocide on Scione and Melos,[33] or from any of the other "many unjust and illegal things" (*Ap.* 31e4) he sees happening. It would be comforting if we could suppose that the Athens to which Socrates explicitly claims to owe absolute obedience was a just and merciful place. But it was not always so, and Socrates knew all too well that it was not.

---

31. See Kraut [1983b], 154–58.
32. See Brickhouse and Smith [1989b], 186–92.
33. See Thuc. 5.32, 5.116.

5.2.8   Was Socrates an Authoritarian?

If our interpretation of the relevant passages in the *Apology* and the *Crito* is correct, Socrates' remarks about the duty of the citizen to obey the law are consistent with his other doctrines. But some may object that our interpretation comes only at a very high cost, since in our view Socrates thinks the citizen who fails to persuade the State to rescind a legal command must fully abandon his autonomy to the authority of the State. According to our reading of the *Crito*, Socrates makes no allowance for the justified disobedience of a citizen who, unable to persuade the State to withdraw its command, is nevertheless convinced that the command is unjust. Where the citizen fails to persuade, he must obey, regardless of how odious the State's command. Some might suppose this leaves Socrates with an unacceptably authoritarian view.

It is important to keep in mind that there is no reason to think that Socrates was ever asked to carry out a legal order to engage in any of the many evils the city of Athens committed. Nor is there any reason to think that Socrates ever actively supported the commission of any of those evils. By removing himself from the arena of organized politics, he effectively takes himself out of the ranks of those in authority who promoted immoral policies. And if those policies ever required Socrates' own personal involvement in their implementation, the fact that he merely followed orders is pertinent, for surely the defense that "I was only following orders" has some validity, provided that the person carrying out those orders occupies an inferior position in an institutional hierarchy issuing the orders, and did not in any way amplify the evil created by the carrying out of those orders. If we add that the inferior actually in some way opposed the order he carried out, his defense becomes even stronger.

Just how authoritarian, if at all, is Socrates' view? Plainly, he would be an authoritarian if his view would prohibit any dissent or criticism of legal commands by those subject to them. But this is *not* Socrates' position. Socrates, by contrast, says that the Laws actually invite criticism and recognize their fallibility (51e7–52a3). Moreover, the Laws never claim that when a citizen fails to persuade them to rescind a command, that failure is evidence of the rightness of what they have ordered. Even in rejecting attempts to persuade, the Laws make no claim of infallibility.[34]

The Laws, instead, are more like a modest umpire or referee in a sports contest who recognizes his own fallibility as well as that of the players and who also welcomes attempts by players to persuade him whenever they believe that he has erred in a call. But regardless of how open an umpire or referee is to protests and to reconsidering his calls when they are protested, in the end the game cannot proceed if any player is free not to count the umpire's or referee's ultimate decisions as authoritative. When no one is empowered to make authoritative calls in a sports contest, the problem is not that the nature of the game is altered; the

---

34. See also *Rep*. I.339c1–6, and perhaps *Ap*. 37a7–b1. Socrates is plainly not committed to the view that the laws are inerrant. Katsutochi Uchiyama first pointed out to us that our view of Socrates did not make him an authoritarian.

problem is that the game simply cannot be played. Similarly, we think that Socrates recognizes that, despite the fallibility of the Laws, the city simply cannot survive if there is no source of authoritative decision making which can conflict with and even override the opinions of individual citizens. It is precisely for this reason that the Laws think they must upbraid Socrates for contemplating escape:

> Do you think it is possible for that city to exist and not to be overthrown in which the sentences arrived at have no force but become invalid and are overturned by private persons? (*Cri.* 50b2–5)

Socrates' point is that the State itself can survive only if its commands are regarded as ultimately authoritative. This does not mean that Socrates thinks that dissent is never appropriate, or that ineffective dissent could never be morally correct. Moreover, Socrates' view leaves open the question of whether a particular State such as Athens ought to survive, just as the reason why the umpire's calls must be obeyed leaves open the question of whether the game of baseball (or any particular game of baseball) should continue to be played. We can imagine umpiring becoming so bad that, while the game can still be played, it is not worth playing any longer. So, similarly, although Socrates seems satisfied with the Laws he imagines in the *Crito* (50c9–e1), we can imagine a State whose commands are so corrupt that the State is not worth preserving. Perhaps a State in which philosophy was forbidden by law would qualify as not worth surviving in Socrates' eyes. But that, as we noted above, is a very different situation from the one Socrates actually faces in the *Crito*.

Scholars have assumed that either we must understand the "persuade or obey" doctrine as leaving open the possibility of justified disobedience or we must convict Socrates of authoritarianism and self-contradiction. We can see now why these are not the only options. In this section, we have defended the consistency of Socrates' position, and also sought to show that, despite the strength of his parent-child and master-slave models, Socrates does not endorse blind obedience or authoritarianism. Perhaps Socrates erred in recognizing no justified disobedience. But even if so, we hope we have shown that scholars need not be so eager to avoid the most straightforward understanding of Socrates' arguments. The position he articulates in the *Crito* is not only consistent with what he says in the *Apology* and elsewhere; it is also not so implausible that we should feel charitably compelled to revise it through creative interpretation.

5.3 Socrates and Political Theory

5.3.1 Athenian Politics

In the last years of the fifth century B.C., what had been a long-standing tension became bitter and violent. On the one side were the oligarchs, rich landowning aristocrats, who regarded themselves as superior to the δῆμος, or common people, and hence, constantly sought ways to disenfranchise the common people. On the other side were the democrats, whose most revered leaders were also from among the wealthiest economic class in the state, but whose political ideology was more inclusive: all adult male citizens, according to the democrats, had an equal right to participate in governing the state.[35]

The government of Athens in Socrates' time was a constitutional democracy whose principal governing body was the popular Assembly, which paid up to (but not beyond) its quorum of 6,000 citizens to attend.[36] Payment was on a first-come, first-served basis; the constitution recognized no special privileges for the wealthy, the famous, or the well-born, though in practice no doubt each faction protected its favorites. All decisions made in the Assembly were made by a simple majority of those present. The Council of Five Hundred, a smaller body, did little more than set the agenda for the Assembly. Moreover, those who served on the Council were selected by lot—fifty men from each of the ten official tribes.[37] The presidency of the Council rotated regularly from tribe to tribe, and one man could serve on the Council only twice in his lifetime.[38]

One other extremely important element in Athens' government was the jury-court system. Jurors volunteered for duty, and 6,000 of these volunteers were selected by lot for service for one year.[39] Specific juries would be assigned to each case by lot; those that were actually assigned to a case were paid for their service.[40] To prevent tampering, juries were made large (no fewer than 200 jurors were assigned to any trial; sometimes, as many as 1,000 or even more might be assigned),[41] though by the beginning of the fourth century various changes were made precisely because the old system did not always achieve even the minimal requirements of procedural justice.[42] One problem seemed to be that litigants could find out which juries would be working which cases in advance of the actual litigation.[43] Even the most important cases were decided in a single day; as many as four minor cases might be decided in one day.[44] In most cases, the trial was initiated by a private citizen (and not a magistrate),[45] and the litigants spoke for themselves; there were no professional prosecutors or defense lawyers, though speeches might be written by professionals for presentation by the litigants.[46]

The effect of this form of government was that every adult male citizen could expect to have a substantial role in both legislation and litigation. But twice in

---

35. Strauss actually counts "a minimum of six leading factions" within the political spectrum in Athens in the postwar years ([1987], 104). These factions and their members would no doubt differ in the ways they regarded issues of importance to the oligarchic-democratic split, which makes an easy identification of a policy along this division somewhat more tricky than it would be if there had been only two parties. The characterizations that follow, therefore, are intended only as rough sketches, to help identify the scholarly issue regarding Socrates' own sympathies rather than to offer a precise picture of Athens' politics at the time in question.

36. Sinclair [1988], 67.

37. Roberts [1984], 53.

38. Jones [1969], 105–6.

39. MacDowell [1978], 34.

40. Ibid.

41. Ibid., 35–40.

42. Ibid., 36, 38.

43. Ibid., 38.

44. Ibid., 249.

45. Ibid., 237.

46. Ibid., 250.

one decade at the end of the fifth century, this government was overthrown by the oligarchic faction. In 411, a group of 400 oligarchs took power for nearly a year, until the democracy was restored and the oligarchs themselves were exiled. After Athens lost the war with Sparta (in 404), one of the conditions of the peace agreement was that these exiles be permitted to return to Athens. Within a year—and with the help of threats from the Spartan general, Lysander—thirty of these men were installed in power during one of the bloodiest periods in Athens' history. Like the earlier one, this oligarchy did not last long; the democrats regained power only eight months later after a civil war.

5.3.2   Socrates versus Democracy

Socrates lived the last years of his life in this atmosphere of violent partisan politics and disastrous foreign and civil wars. It is natural for us to wonder with which side Socrates sympathized.

Many scholars have concluded that, to one degree or another, Socrates must be counted among those loyal to the oligarchic faction.[47] Two general sorts of reasons are given for this conclusion: (1) careful scrutiny of the various ancient testimony reveals a variety of powerfully anti-democratic points of view within various statements Socrates explicitly makes, or implied by them; and (2) prosopographical study of Socrates' associates shows a clear majority to be from among Athens' oligarchic faction—indeed, some of the most violent and dangerous of these men may be counted among Socrates' closest associates. We wish to dispute scholars' understandings of both sorts of evidence. Let us look first at the philosophical views Socrates expresses, and try to see what political philosophy they represent. Then we will turn to his relationships with others.

Before we are in a position to assess Socrates' own ideological commitments regarding democracy, we must first identify which texts will—and which texts will not—count as appropriate evidence. Because we have elected in this book to focus on Plato's early dialogues and the Socrates whose views are represented therein, however, we have already decided this issue. On the question of Socrates' political sympathies, this selection of texts is critical, for if we are right, there can be no reconciling the Socrates who speaks in Plato's early dialogues with the one we find in Plato's middle period works or the one we find in the works of Xenophon. Plato's middle period Socrates and Xenophon's Socrates are simply hostile to democracy.[48] Because our focus is the Socrates of Plato's early dialogues, however, we shall adhere to the principle we have followed thus far: when other ancient sources conflict with views attributed to Socrates in Plato's early dialogues, we shall accept the version found in the early dialogues. Our question, then, is this: What is Socrates' attitude toward democracy in Plato's early dialogues?

47. These include Stone [1988a], 117–39; Grote [1888], vol. 7, 144–46; Guthrie [1971], 61–64; Vlastos [1983c], 495–516; A. E. Taylor [1933], 103.
48. See, for example, *Mem.* 2.6.26, 3.1.4, 3.7.5–9, and 3.9.10.

5.3.3 A Look at the Texts

Scholars who have concluded that the Platonic Socrates sympathized with the oligarchs have pointed to a number of passages that seem plainly to express views inconsistent with the political ideology of Athenian democrats.

5.3.3.1 The Importance of Experts

• *Ap.* 24e4–25c1: Meletus claims that all men make the young better (except, of course, Socrates), whereas Socrates argues that it is much more likely that those capable of making the young better are but one or a few, whereas most people would make them worse. Socrates makes this argument by comparing the treatment of the youth to the training of horses.

• *Cri.* 47a2–48c6: Socrates says that in regard to questions of "right and wrong, shameful and noble, good and bad" (47d9–10), one should disregard the words of the many, who have no special training and heed instead only the one who knows (47c1–2).

• *La.* 184c9–e9: Laches and Nicias disagree on whether Lysimachus should train his sons in heavy-armed fighting. Socrates is asked to cast the deciding vote, but demurs, saying that one should pay no heed to the majority but instead ask the one who knows, and ignore the others. If no one can be found who is an expert on the subject, one should go on looking for one who is.

Each of these passages reveals Socrates' commitment to the view that nothing—not even a huge majority—can outweigh or override the single opinion of an authentic expert. Plainly, Socrates assumes that moral expertise will not be found in the greater masses of people, but rather only in one or a few people, if any have it at all. Contrary to popular democratic ideology, Socrates regards the teaching of virtue to be no different from the teaching of any other expertise—such teaching is the sole province of the expert.

5.3.3.2 The Democratic Ideology

• *Prt.* 319a8–328d2: Socrates claims that he regards civic virtue as unteachable. Protagoras responds with a great myth according to which everyone is innately capable of instructing others in civic virtue to some degree, though some are more capable than others. This, he explains, is why everyone's opinion is worth something in questions of what is just and lawful (327b2–4).

• *Meno* 92d7–94e2: Anytus, later one of Meletus' supporters in the accusation of Socrates, argues that people learn virtue from their elders, and that most people teach it to their children. Socrates angers Anytus by responding that none of the great Athenian leaders has managed to teach virtue to his children, and concludes that it must not be teachable.

Socrates' view is clearly in contrast to Protagoras' compelling expression of democratic ideology in his great myth, according to which everyone has some expertise in judging civic issues and so no one's opinion should be overlooked. Socrates makes no secret of the fact that he does not accept Protagoras' theory. The above two passages also show that Socrates did not regard virtue as teachable in the way Athenian democratic ideology insisted it was. Protagoras (in the *Prota-*

goras) and Anytus (in the *Meno*) voice the popular democratic opinion that everyone (or nearly everyone) taught virtue to the young. (Socrates' accuser, Meletus, expresses the same view in the passage from the *Apology* cited above in 5.3.3.1.) In the *Protagoras* and *Meno*, Socrates insists that virtue cannot be taught at all, precisely because there are no experts in virtue.

5.3.3.3 The Many Failings of the Many

• *Ap*. 31e1–32a3: In this passage, Socrates says that he thinks that no one "who genuinely opposes you or any other populace and prevents many injust and illegal things from happening in the state" will survive for long.

• *Cri*. 48c2–6: Socrates regards "the many" as valuing any number of things that are morally irrelevant, and characterizes them as those "who carelessly put people to death and bring them back to life again, if they could, without thinking."

• *Cri*. 49c10–d5: Socrates says that one ought never to return wrong for wrong nor do evil to any person, but also says that "there are few who believe these things, or ever will. So those who do and those who do not have no common counsel, but must necessarily despise one another, in view of their respective views" (49d2–5).

• *Grg*. 471e2–472d1: Socrates introduces the two modes of refutation—the rhetorical and the dialectical (discussed in section 5.1.4)—and identifies the rhetorical as capable of producing the greater number of witnesses at any given time, but "worth nothing with regard to the truth" (471e7–472a1). Socrates also allows that on the point under dispute, Polus will find "nearly all, Athenians and foreigners, are in agreement with what you say, if you want to bring forward witnesses against me, testifying that I do not speak the truth" (472a2–5).

These passages show that Socrates regards "the many" as committed to a number of immoral and unjust points of view. These passages show that Socrates thought there was bitter opposition between "the many," on the one hand, and, on the other, "the few" who accept the truth and stand for justice and law. We find the antagonism between "the many" and "the few" is likely to lead to the death of "the few" good men. So democracy—the government by "the many"—is certain to be dangerous to "the few" good men whose points of view are in opposition to the immoralities "the many" accept. This is not a temporary problem: Socrates obviously thinks it is unlikely that "the many" will ever be brought to accept the correct moral view.

5.3.3.4 Famous Democrats

• *Gorgias* 472a5–b3: In his dispute with Polus, Socrates names a few famous men on whom Polus could count to give such false witness, including Nicias and his brothers, Aristocrates, and the whole house of Pericles.

• *Meno* 92d7–94e2: In the same passage in which he confronts Anytus, Socrates explicitly mentions Themistocles, Aristeides, Pericles, and Thucydides (son of Melesias), as having failed to teach their sons to be virtuous.

• *Grg*. 515c4–517a6: Socrates argues that the most distinguished politicians of

Athens' past—Pericles, Cimon, Miltiades, and Themistocles—all made the citizens wilder and less controlled.

Socrates regards the most famous and influential men of the democratic faction with disdain. All three passages mention Pericles, perhaps the most beloved leader of the democrats; but others are mentioned as well. We learn how seriously the Athenians regard failing to take proper care of their children from Crito's appeal to Socrates on behalf of Socrates' children: "Either one ought not to have children, or be willing to suffer hardship for them, bring them up, and educate them" (*Crito* 45d4–5). Because Socrates regards the understanding of virtue as a matter of such importance that it is "most honorable to have it and most disgraceful to lack it" (*Grg.* 472c7–8), the great Athenians' inability or neglect as regards their sons' educations would qualify as a terrible embarrassment, or worse. No wonder Anytus, an influential democrat, was offended.

The evidence we have surveyed supports the following conclusion regarding Socrates' politics: Socrates not only rejects any number of features of Athenian democratic ideology, he regards "the many" as morally corrupt and as dangerously hostile to genuine morality and to "the few" good men who would seek to promote genuine morality. Socrates also repeatedly used Athens' greatest and most beloved democratic leaders as examples of moral, political, and pedagogical inadequacy. Such views might well have tarred Socrates as a subversive in the eyes of the radical democrats.

5.3.4 Socrates versus Oligarchy

With the possible exception of Socrates, whose position we are now trying to understand, those who rejected democracy in ancient Athens typically supported oligarchy; democracy and oligarchy were generally perceived as the only two realistic options for Athens' government. Scholars have no doubt relied on this fact in noting the sort of textual evidence we have discussed above and going directly from that evidence to the conclusion that Socrates was an oligarchic ideologue, involved "in a conspiracy against the democratic constitution of Athens"[49] and seeking "the replacement of the . . . democracy by the rule of an aristocratic-oligarchic elite."[50]

But it is worth noting that Socrates' frequent attacks on specific democrats and on democratic ideology are never balanced in Plato's early dialogues by praise for specific oligarchs or by endorsements of specific aspects of oligarchic ideology. We find no calls, for example, for a return to "the ancestral constitution";[51] there are also no celebrations of the virtue or wisdom of specific members of the oligarchic faction (in contrast to Socrates' many denigrations of democratic leaders), no claims to the effect that oligarchs were able to give their sons the education that Pericles could not give his sons. No specific "few" are ever identified who could

---

49. Winspear and Silverberg [1960], 84.

50. Wood and Wood [1978], 97.

51. For an excellent discussion of the anti-democratic sentiment behind this phrase during the oligarchic upheavals during the latter part of the fifth century, see Andrewes [1974], 212–13.

rule the state in such a way as to avoid the "many injustices and illegalities" that happen in the democratic state. Instead, we find Socrates expressing any number of opinions a doctrinaire oligarch would never express. Let us now turn to these.

5.3.4.1 Praise and Blame for Other Famous Politicians

• *Grg.* 526a2–b3: Socrates says that there have been a few very powerful leaders who have nevertheless been good men and thus deserve special praise—"for it is hard, O Callicles, and deserving of much great praise when one who has great power to do injustice lives a just life" (526a3–5). Though there have been few such people, Socrates identifies one of them as Aristeides, son of Lysimachus. (See also *Meno* 94a1.)

• *Meno* 92d7–94e2: In this passage, cited above in 5.3.3.4, Socrates singles out a number of famous Athenians who were unable to teach their sons virtue. Aristeides and Themistocles are mentioned; so are Pericles and Thucydides.

• *Grg.* 515c4–517a6: In this passage, also cited above in 5.3.3.4, Socrates notes that a number of famous Athenians made the citizens wilder and less controlled after they came to power. Pericles, Cimon, Miltiades, and Themistocles are named as examples.

In the first passage, Socrates offers what appears to be the highest praise we ever find him offering to any man—to Aristeides, a man who, according to Socrates, remained good even though he held great power in the state. Aristeides was one of the early leaders of the democratic faction, in no way associated with the later oligarchic movement.[52] Socrates offers such praise despite the fact that Aristeides is also included in the group of men who were not able to educate their sons in virtue, and despite the fact that Aristeides was once ostracized.[53] Socrates' admiration for Aristeides, then, must have to do with Aristeides' private moral character—and not his political or pedagogical expertise—but nonetheless, praise of Aristeides is not at all what one would expect from an oligarchic sympathizer.

We might expect, instead, praise of Cimon, whose hostility to the development of the democracy was well known,[54] and of his father, Miltiades. But the passage from *Gorgias* 515c4–517a6 shows that Cimon and Miltiades were no better statesmen, in Socrates' view, than was the man whom the oligarchs would hate above all others, Pericles.[55] And the *Meno* passage shows that even Thucydides, Pericles' bitter political rival within the democratic party in Athens,[56] comes in for precisely the same criticism.

As these passages show, Socrates shows equal disrespect for political rivals from both political factions, and even for rivals who share affinities for the democratic or oligarchic points of view. Aristeides is singled out for praise, as we have seen. But his greatest rival, Themistocles, is identified as "among the best men of earlier times" (*Meno* 93e11) in spite of the fact that he is said to have been

---

52. See Bury [1962], 249, who calls Aristeides one of the "three most prominent" of "the progressive democratic statesmen" of the time.

53. Ibid.

54. Ibid., 328.

55. For the political rivalry between Cimon and Pericles, see ibid. 329.

56. Ibid., 349.

unable to train his sons to be virtuous. Elsewhere Socrates indifferently identifies men of such disparate political sympathies as "Pericles and Cimon and Miltiades and Themistocles" (*Grg.* 515d1) as all equally incapable of making the Athenians better. Indeed, Socrates suggests that they have all made the Athenians worse.

The remarkable thing about such passages is that they are so often cited as evidence for Socrates' hostility to democrats and the democracy, while their equal treatment of oligarchs goes unmentioned. In context, moreover, Socrates' point in using such examples is not to single out those whom he regards as the most notorious moral failures, but rather to identify Athens' most notable citizens and leaders on either side of the political spectrum. Socrates' use of such figures seems to be for emphasis: his identification of a number of famous men who surely would have taught it to their sons if such a thing were possible is evidence for his claim in the *Meno* passage that virtue cannot be taught. If anything, Socrates is complimenting such men for being the most likely to have virtue to teach, if only teaching virtue were possible. His remarks do not betray a political agenda or a partisan bias. Similarly, at *Gorgias* 515c4–517a6, his point is to show that none of the most accomplished leaders of Athens had ever really succeeded in practicing what Socrates regards as the "true art of politics." The criticism is made by using a carefully bipartisan selection of what Socrates regards as failed leaders. If such passages may be counted, as they almost universally are, as evidence for Socrates' disdain for democracy and its most revered leaders, they must count no less for his disdain for oligarchy and its most famous leaders.

But these passages all concern statesmen of former days. What does Socrates think of more recent leaders? At *Gorgias* 503a5–b5, Socrates confesses that he knows of no man who made the Athenians better by his oratory in the state. Callicles concedes the point as regards contemporary orators, but goes on to insist that men from earlier times like Themistocles, Cimon, Miltiades, and Pericles had indeed improved the body of citizens.[57] It follows obviously from this that Socrates has no more regard for any of the political leaders of the end of the fifth century than he has for those of former times.

5.3.4.2 Breaking Laws

• *Cri.* 51b3–c3: In this and other passages from the *Crito* (discussed above in section 5.2), Socrates articulates his doctrine of "persuade or obey." According to Socrates, the citizen must treat the state with more reverence and respect than he treats his father or, if he is a slave, his master. Socrates concludes that it is *impious* to use violence against the state—even more than it is to use violence against one's parents.

• *Ap.* 32a9–e1: Socrates describes two of his most dangerous clashes with government. When the democracy was in power, a mob wanted to try the generals of the battle off the Arginousai islands *en bloc*, for failing to remain and gather up

---

57. Callicles' own selection of great leaders is also bi-partisan. But just as we should not be surprised to see Socrates' indifference to party politics, Callicles' own is not puzzling. Callicles does not hold a political ideology; rather, he seeks involvement in public affairs to promote his own private interests. Accordingly, he would approve of anyone who held political power, no matter what faction the powerful person represented.

those who had been killed.[58] In his role as *prutanis*, Socrates opposed this decision, because, as he says, it was unjust and illegal. Socrates goes on to recall that
when the Thirty were in power, they sent for him to go out and bring in Leon of
Salamis to be put to death. Socrates did not obey, but simply went home. Socrates
characterizes the Thirty's action as an example of their "wanting to infect as many
others with their guilt as they could" (βουλόμενοι ὡς πλείστους ἀναπλῆσαι
αἰτιῶν—32c7–8). He considers his own response to show that he is the sort of
man who would refuse to do anything unjust or impious (32d2–3).

No one has ever doubted that the "Laws" Socrates refers to in the *Crito* are
the democratic laws currently in effect in Athens, even if, as some have argued,
they are these laws in a somewhat purified or clarified sense.[59] It follows that any
Athenian who violated the laws of Athens, according to Socrates in the above
Crito passage, commits impiety and injustice. Moreover, we see from the *Apology*
passage that Socrates was willing to risk everything against those of the democratic faction who acted contrary to these laws, and describing the acts of the
Thirty, who overthrew these laws, with obvious and unmixed hostility. This is
not at all the tone we would expect from a man who sympathizes with those who
seek "the replacement of . . . democracy by the rule of an aristocratic-oligarchic
elite," as some have said.[60] Rather, it would appear that Socrates is inclined to
obey completely (see section 5.2), and to defend and protect—even to revere—
the democratic laws of Athens as if they were his parents and masters.

Further evidence for this conclusion comes from another passage in the *Crito*,
where Socrates makes no objection to the Laws' characterization of him as completely satisfied with them and as having shown no interest in other cities or
other laws

• *Cri.* 52b1–c3: Socrates, speaking for the personified Laws of Athens, claims
that he has shown himself to be satisfied with the Laws and the city of Athens,
by never leaving the city even though he was always free to go (except on military
duty), and by having children in Athens, showing that it pleased him. The Laws
claim that Socrates "had no desire to know other cities or other laws, but [was]
contented with us and our city" (52b7–c1). At 52d6–7, Socrates and Crito are
forced to agree that what the Laws have said is true.

No oligarch could honestly speak this way. Moreover, there is no evidence,
from Plato or any other source, that Socrates ever took part in any of the activities
designed by the oligarchs to help topple the democratic state.

5.3.4.3 *Socrates on Common Crafts and Craftsmen*

• *Grg.* 489e2–491e1: Callicles holds that the truly superior person is none other
than the powerful person, and means by this the one most able to take more than
his share. Callicles claims that such a person deserves the greatest share he can
take. Socrates compares this to the absurdity that the best weaver deserves the

58. See Brickhouse and Smith [1989b], 174–79.
59. See, for example, Woodruff [1982], note on *Hip. Ma.* 284d6–7, 41; and Colson [1989]. For
the reasons we have stated in sec. 5.2.6, we are convinced that the Laws for whom Socrates speaks
are none other than the unmodified statutes of Athens.
60. Wood and Wood [1978], 97.

largest cloak, or the best shoemaker deserves the biggest shoes. Callicles responds
that Socrates can never stop talking about cobblers and fullers, cooks and physicians, and denies that the subject of superiority has anything to do with such
people. Instead, Callicles has the man powerful in public affairs in mind.

• *Ap.* 21b1–22e5: In his attempt to discern the meaning of the oracle to Chairephon, Socrates goes to those who have a reputation for wisdom and first discovers
that the "public men" knew nothing that was fine and good, but thought they did;
indeed, "those with the greatest reputation seemed to me to be nearly the most
deficient . . . and others who were held as more base seemed to be superior as
regards intelligence" (22a3–6). The poets and prophets, too, knew nothing of
value; their poetry and prophecy was the result of divine inspiration, not wisdom.
Finally, Socrates went to the craftsmen, who did indeed "know many fine things"
(or have much fine knowledge—πολλὰ καὶ καλὰ ἐπισταμένους [22d2]), but
who wrongly supposed that because they were able to practice their crafts well,
they were also wise about "the most important things" (22d7), which was not
true. Socrates thus concludes that even though he does not have the wisdom the
craftsmen have (knowledge of their crafts), because he also lacks their folly (about
"the most important things"), he is wiser than they are.

One feature of the oligarchic ideology was the view, expressed very plainly
by a number of our best sources on the historical Socrates,[61] that manual labor
stunts one's ability to deliberate effectively about moral or political issues. Yet
we find no trace of this bias expressed by the Socrates of Plato's early dialogues.
On the contrary, Socrates actually appears to look with a certain degree of approval on the craftsmen. Callicles regards them, it is clear in the *Gorgias*, as
beneath notice; he is interested only in the great and powerful men. Socrates, on
the contrary, regards the very men whom Callicles reveres and admires as "nearly
the most deficient" (*Ap.* 22a3–4) in wisdom, whereas the craftsmen do genuinely
"know many fine things" (*Ap.* 22d2). The craftsmen, of course, are still less
wise than Socrates because they think their craft-knowledge makes them wise in
ways they are not. But unlike the great politicians, at least they have some worthy
knowledge—knowledge of their crafts. The great politicians have none at all.

In Socrates' notorious use of craftsmen and the crafts they practice as models
for the philosophical and political knowledge he seeks, there is no trace of the
oligarchic doctrine that manual labor is morally corrosive. Socrates lends no support whatever to those who would insist that for a man to be good, he must be a
man of leisure. Moreover, Socrates himself must not be mistaken for a man of
leisure, if leisure requires any significant wealth. Although he practices no craft,
he toils ceaselessly in his philosophic mission, and is "in great poverty due to
[his] service to the god" (*Ap.* 23b9–c1). This is no model of an oligarch's life.
Socratic philosophy never equates wealth and leisure with moral nobility.

5.3.5   A State without Politicians?

The evidence we have surveyed in the last two sections shows that Socrates could
not be counted as a partisan democrat or as an oligarch; he was, then, not a man

61. See, for example, Pl. *Rep.* VI.495d4–e2, *Laws* 919c3–d2; Xen. *Oec.* 4.2–3; Arist. *Pol.*
1328b39–1329a2, 1337b5–15.

of factional affiliations. Because he also respected the ultimate authority of civil law, moreover (see section 5.2), he was anything but an anarchist. It is plain enough that Socrates would regard a government by moral experts to be the ideal. But he was also convinced that no moral expert could be found. How, then, *should* decisions be made in the state? Did Socrates think that all or most of the choices "public men" made on behalf of the state were *moral* choices, and, hence, choices for which no expert could be found? And did Socrates believe that there were choices that had to be made one way or the other in the state, for which no experts could be found?

In fact, a number of texts very strongly suggest that Socrates believed that most of the choices a city makes ought not be decided by ideology or partisan politics. For many questions, we should neither take a vote or pick lots, as the democrats would do, nor look to the wealthy land owners and patrician families, as the oligarchs would do. Instead, wherever experts were available, all of the relevant decisions should be left to them.

> When the city has an assembly to choose physicians, or shipbuilders, or any other group of craftsmen, the orator will not give advice, will he? For it is plain that it is necessary to choose the most skilled person in each case. And in regard to building walls, or the equipment of harbors or dockyards, we call on none but the architects. And in choosing generals, or in regard to arranging soldiers for battle against the enemy, or on an occupation force to be left behind, the generals give advice, but the orators do not. (*Grg.* 455b2–c2)

This passage leaves little doubt about how Socrates thinks these issues should be decided (see also *Grg.* 503d5–504a6, 512b3–d6, 514a5–e10). It follows that the State has little need for the advice of Gorgias and the other rhetoricians.

But if not, then, by the rhetoricians, who *should* be the ones to make decisions in the state? Remarkably, it seems that Socrates thinks that all decisions about carrying out a goal must be made by those craftsmen who have that goal as the object of their craft; everyone else should keep out of it. Thus if the goal is to erect a public building, the city architect alone should decide how it is to be constructed. The sort of political structure Socrates favors—if it can be called a structure at all—is in a way oligarchic and in a way democratic. It is oligarchic insofar as each distinct decision will not involve "all the people" or even "the many"; instead, each decision will be made by "the few" qualified craftsmen, including the decision as to who the qualified craftsmen are (see *Grg.* 455b7–8). All others should not meddle in such decisions, but should mind their own business. But because each decision would require a different "few," a great many people, from all walks of life, will be called upon to make decisions for the state.

Socrates never tells us anything more about how such a system could be made to work, but it is clear that such a system could be put into place within a variety of constitutional schemes. There would no doubt still have to be managers to oversee the process and, given limited resources, to decide which projects to promote and which to delay. In all such administrative matters, important evaluations would still need to be made, and the fact is that Socrates does not tell us how or by what structure he thinks such decisions would best be made. It is clear, however, that Socrates sees no use for what the Athenians and the rhetoricians mean by "the public man," for Socrates regards this person as having nothing to offer the state at all.

It is tempting to see in Socrates' remarks in the *Gorgias* about the proper role of craftsmen in the state a forecast of Plato's "one person, one job" principle on which the ideal state depicted in the *Republic* is based (see, for example, *Rep.* IV.433d7–434c7). Indeed, what is often regarded as the greatest novelty introduced in the *Republic* is that Plato seems to have come to believe that master statecraftsmen could come into existence—the philosopher-kings—who could then rule the state in the way Plato's Socrates of the early period all along said they should, if only they existed. So the real difference seems only to be that Plato thinks it is possible to establish what Socrates thought unlikely. No doubt, this difference derives from Plato's "discovery" of a new method of inquiry, which replaces the *elenchos* in the middle period. From this new method Plato thinks genuine wisdom could be produced.[62]

So instead of Plato's philosopher-kings, we find no one at all as the captains of Socrates' ship of state. Most of what would ordinarily be called political decisions, we find, should be made by non-politicians. No one is qualified to make the remainder of the decisions that would presumably need to be made, but Socrates does not doubt that they will be made anyhow—by proud and dangerous incompetents. This is why, no matter where he might find himself, the good man should not try to live as a "public man," for it is among "public men" that he will most surely find the most arrogant and ignorant—and, hence, the most dangerous—of men.

5.4 Socrates' Personal Associates and the Trial

5.4.1 Birds of a Feather?

Earlier (5.3.2), we said that two sorts of evidence had been cited for supposing that Socrates was an enemy of democracy—his philosophical opinions about Athens' "public men" and the ideals they stood for, on the one hand, and the political affiliations of his own friends and associates, on the other. We have now looked at the first sort of evidence: the opinions he actually expressed as well as their implications. We found that Socrates was no more an enemy of democracy than he was of oligarchy. Having completed our review of his views of Athens' public men and on political philosophy, we can now turn to the claim that Socrates' political ideals are betrayed by his associations with other people, whose political views and activities are not in doubt.

In fact, we think there is little or nothing to recommend the value of such evidence. "Guilt by association" is obviously not a secure method by which to decide such matters, especially when, as in this case, no corroboration of the guilty verdict can be found in anything said or done by the one being judged. Moreover, we are not only unimpressed by the evidence usually cited regarding

---

62. For a discussion of this transformation in Plato's thought, see Vlastos [1988].

Socrates' associates; we also think that in Socrates' case, there are special reasons for resisting such evidence.

We should begin by reminding ourselves that Socrates saw himself as Athens' gadfly, working his philosophical mission in the public places of Athens. As he tells his jurors, he will talk to anyone, "young and old" (*Ap.* 30a2–4, 30a8), "foreigner and citizen" (*Ap.* 30a3–4), "rich and poor" (*Ap.* 33b1–2). He does not carry out his mission by talking only to the members of one political faction; nor is it his mission to discuss factional ideologies or to promote oligarchy. Instead, his mission is to tell the Athenians

> not to care for your bodies or for wealth more than for the perfection of your souls, or even so much; and I tell you that virtue does not come from wealth, but from virtue comes wealth and all other good things for human beings both in private and in public. (*Ap.* 30a8–b4)[63]

This message is not masking some political agenda: it applies to all Athenians, no matter what their political affiliation.

It may nonetheless turn out that Socrates is somewhat more effective at targeting the wealthier and more powerful Athenians in the actual practice of his mission (about which we shall have more to say in section 5.4.3). But this is not to say that he shunned the democratically inclined craftsmen. Let us recall that when he first heard the oracle given to Chairephon, Socrates spoke to the craftsmen (*Ap.* 22c9–e5), individuals who did not have the leisure to follow him every day and engage in elenctic arguments. It is the fact that the practice of philosophy requires free time, and not shared political sympathies, that explains why Socrates' most visible following included "the young men who have the most leisure, the sons of the richest men" (*Ap.* 23c2–3). The attraction Socrates apparently had for certain "wealthy, young men," then, need have nothing whatever to do with shared political sympathies.

5.4.2   Socrates' Associates

When scholars indict Socrates on the evidence provided by the affiliations and careers of his associates, usually men like Critias, Charmides, and Alcibiades top their lists. Critias, the leader of the notorious Thirty Tyrants, appears in Plato's *Protagoras* (316a5, 336d6, 337a2) and is one of the principal interlocutors in the *Charmides* and the late dialogues, the *Timaeus* and the *Critias*. Though we may legitimately doubt the historical value of these later dialogues, Plato plainly depicts Critias in the *Charmides,* an early dialogue, as having been acquainted with Socrates for quite some time (see 156a7–8). Socrates is shown to be attracted to the young Charmides—later also one of the Thirty—in Plato's *Charmides* (155c7–e2) and *Symposium* (222a8–b4). Closest of all was Socrates' tie to Alcibiades: that the two were lovers in some sense or another[64] is clear from many

---

63. See ch. 1, n.33, above.

64. We learn from the *Symposium* (217a2–219d2) that Alcibiades was terribly frustrated by the chastity of the relationship, which Socrates seems to have maintained as a primarily (if not completely) intellectual one. See also *Prt.* 309a1–d2, where Socrates' attraction to Alcibiades is completely eclipsed by the opportunity to have a searching conversation with Protagoras.

texts (*Prt.* 309a1–b2; *Grg.* 481d1–4; *Symp.* 213c6–d6, 214c8–d4, 216e7–219e5, 222c1–d3; see also *Prt.* 316a4–5). But these were not the only evil men among Socrates' associates: unsavory characters populate many of Plato's dialogues.[65] From the fact that a man frequently speaks with criminals of various stripes, however, we cannot draw the inference that the man himself is a criminal or a traitor. Obviously, everything depends upon why the person is associating with such bad people.

We have already established, in section 5.3, that as far as we can tell from the evidence of Plato's early dialogues, Socrates was not conspiring with these men to commit similar acts of crime or treason. In fact, as we have argued, Plato's Socrates would eschew both treason and crime as violence to the state he regarded as his parent and master (see *Cri.* 50e1–51c3, and section 5.2, above). Moreover, the evidence we reviewed also showed that Socrates could not even be counted as agreeing with the ideals of such men.

It is also seldom noted in this connection[66] that Chairephon must be counted among the associates of Socrates. It was to Chairephon that the Pythia at Delphi gave the famous oracle about Socrates' wisdom (*Ap.* 20e8–21a8). Indeed, Chairephon is the only historical person directly associated with Socrates in Aristophanes' *Clouds* (104, 144–47, 156, 1499, 1505) and *Birds* (see esp. 1296, 1554–64), a man whom Socrates identifies as having been a friend (or associate—ἑταῖρος) since their youths (*Ap.* 20e8–21a1).[67] But their friendship is significant because Chairephon went into exile during the reign of the Thirty and returned with the democrats, making his political affiliations perfectly clear (see Socrates' attribution at *Ap.* 20e8–21a2).

According to Plato's *Laches,* Socrates was also on friendly terms with the Athenian generals Nicias[68] and Laches, whose military careers both ended in disaster,[69] but neither of whom was involved in either of the oligarchic coups (of 411 and 404). Of course, this fact alone hardly tells us anything about their politi-

65. Mogens Herman Hansen counts "about a half" of those who talk with Socrates in Plato's dialogues as "criminals and traitors." These quotations are from a letter from Hansen to N. Smith dated February 2, 1987, in which Hansen refers to his argument for this conclusion in his article ([1980], see esp. 73–76 and nn.81–91). Since neither of the authors of this book reads Danish, we would not have been able to cite Hansen's work here without his generous assistance. As will become obvious, however, we do not agree with the conclusions Hansen draws from this evidence.

66. In making this comment, we do not have in mind Hansen, who does recognize Socrates' friendship with Chairephon ([1980], 74). For an example of the sort of oversight we are criticizing here, see Chroust, who writes 34 pages ([1957], 164–97) on what he calls "the political aspects of the Socratic problem" without once mentioning Socrates' longtime friendship with Chairephon.

67. Socrates' description of Chairephon as an "ἑταῖρος" may itself have political significance. Athens' ἑταιρεῖαι were recognized as having strong political roles—they were, according to Thucydides, "associations for the management of lawsuits and elections" (8.73.3). Socrates' identification of Chairephon as an "ἑταῖρος," therefore, would perhaps be surprising if Socrates could be counted among the oligarchic faction; instead, it could actually suggest a democratic affiliation. On the political role of the ἑταιρεῖαι, see Strauss [1987], 20.

68. Socrates also identifies Nicias, at *Grg.* 472a5–6, as one who would be willing to give false testimony on Polus' behalf. This would appear to be some evidence against a very close relationship between Socrates and the general; it certainly distances Socrates from what he takes to be Nicias' moral views.

69. For summaries, see Bury [1962], 453–63 (Nicias) and 448 (Laches).

cal leanings, since both were dead by the time of the first of these oligarchic upheavals. J. K. Davies speaks of a "family taint of oligarchic sympathies" regarding Nicias' grandson by the same name,[70] but he also notes that Nicias' brother, Eucrates,[71] and Nicias' son, Niceratos,[72] were both murdered by the Thirty. In fact, Davies says Nicias' own "relationship with the old aristocracy is tenuous."[73] There is, moreover, no oligarchic "taint" on Laches at all.

Socrates also seems to be on good terms with a certain Callias, son of Hipponikos, at whose house most of the dialogue of the *Protagoras* takes place (*Prt.* 311a1–2; see also *Ap.* 20a5).[74] Again, although Callias would not be the sort of man whose friendship one would point to with pride,[75] his political associations, such as they were, seem to have been with the democrats against the oligarchs.[76]

If we look at all of Socrates' associates, then, contrary to what is often assumed, we do not find a tight clique of oligarchic revolutionaries. And though most are wealthy men, many have ties to the democracy. But even if we look just at those among Socrates' associates whom scholars usually cite—Critias, Charmides, and Alcibiades—we will not find clear evidence of an oligarchic faction, for though Critias and Charmides were among the Thirty, Alcibiades, who died before the second coup, fought *against* the four hundred and helped to return Athens to democracy after the first coup.[77]

Moreover, when Charmides is present among Socrates' associates, he is depicted as a youth for whom Socrates feels a strong physical attraction (see esp. *Charm.* 154d1–5, 155c7–e2), but about whose moral character Socrates is agnostic (*Charm.* 154d7–e1, 175e6–176a5). We are told that Charmides was to continue to learn from Socrates (*Charm.* 176a5–d5), but we find no trace of evidence for supposing that their relationship continued to be close once Charmides became an adult. We know of at least two lessons Charmides did not learn from Socrates: Charmides decided to become a "public" man, in conspiring with Critias and the other members of the Thirty. And in conspiring with the Thirty, Charmides did violence to the laws of Athens. In this, as we have seen, he could not have been following Socrates, who condemned such things.[78]

70. Davies [1971], 406.
71. Ibid., 404; see Lys. 18.5; Suda *A* 3069.
72. Davies [1971], 405; see Lys. 18.6, 19.47; Plut. *Mor.* 998b.
73. Davies [1971], 404.
74. Ibid., #7826, 254–70.
75. Davies refers to Callias' "urbane extravagance and aristocratic fecklessness" (ibid., 261).
76. See Strauss [1987], 102, who makes this inference from what Callias' oligarchic opponent, Andocides, does and does not say at Andocides' trial (see Andoc. *Myst.* 117 ff.).
77. Thucydides tells us that Alcibiades initially supported the abolition of the democracy in the hopes that he might be restored at Athens if the democracy under which he had been sentenced to death in absentia were removed. But later, it is plain that Alcibiades worked with the enemies of the four hundred to restore the democratic government, and was restored as his reward. See Thuc. 8.45–97. Given the use to which Socrates' association with Alcibiades has been put, it is remarkable that one of the principal texts cited in support of the claim that this association put a political taint on Socrates—Xenophon's *Memorabilia* (1.2.12)—distinguishes the activities of Critias under the oligarchy from the "hubris and violence" of Alcibiades under the democracy.
78. Xenophon's claim that it was Socrates who persuaded Charmides to go into politics (*Mem.* 3.7.1), which is repeated by Diogenes Laertius (2.29), simply cannot be squared with the Platonic

Even if we accept that at one time Socrates and Critias had been close,[79] there is also ample evidence for great strain in Socrates' relationship with Critias by the time the latter had become the leader of the Thirty. In Plato, we learn that the Thirty hoped to implicate Socrates in their evils by ordering him to go out and arrest Leon of Salamis (*Ap.* 32c4–e1). Socrates disobeyed and simply went home, which he says put him in great danger (*Ap.* 32d7–8). In this passage it is clear that Socrates has nothing good to say about the Thirty, which is what we would expect from someone who regarded violence against the established constitution of Athens as an even greater impiety than violence against one's parents (*Cri.* 51c2–3). This and other stories of friction between Socrates and the Thirty may be found in a number of ancient texts by various authors.[80]

Looking closely at the many and various associates of Socrates in Plato's early dialogues, then, we find little support for the view that Socrates was sympathetic to oligarchic rule or committed to the overthrow of the Athenian democracy. Socrates was, at least at some time, on friendly terms with some of those who were oligarchic extremists and revolutionaries. But he was also on good terms with many other men whose political commitments were directly opposed to those of the oligarchs. Unless we ignore many of Socrates' associates, then, including some of his closest friends (such as Chairephon), we will find no political ideology that is common to all of Socrates' associates.

5.4.3 Why Socrates Sought Association with Such Bad Men

We have argued that Socrates' associations cannot support the view that Socrates was a dangerous oligarchic revolutionary. But there is something about Socrates' associates that may well suggest something wrong. Plato does, in fact, make an astonishingly large number of Socrates' interlocutors "traitors and criminals."[81] If we add "notorious failures" (such as Nicias) to this characterization, we will find blameless men represented only very rarely among those with whom Plato's Socrates speaks. Perhaps scholars have sensed this taint, and sought to explain it in political terms. If it is not the sign of some political association, then, why does Plato so persistently put Socrates in the company of such bad men?

Let us return to Socrates' own characterization of the mission he believes the god commanded him to pursue in Athens. Socrates says that when he first heard about the oracle given to Chairephon, he was astonished because he could not believe that what it appeared to be saying could be true—surely there must be someone wiser than he (*Ap.* 21b3–9). His first response, in attempting to discover

---

Socrates' proscription of such activities. It is not our purpose here to argue for the greater historical reliability of the Platonic portrait.

79. Vatai suggests that Socrates and Critias had been lovers ([1984], 65), but cites no text to support this claim.

80. Regarding the Thirty's order to arrest Leon, see also [*Epist.* 7] 324d8–325a3, 325c1–5; Xen. *Mem.* 4.4.3. Other sorts of conflicts are reported in Xen. *Mem.* 1.2.29–38; Diod. 14.5.1–3. Because these other incidents are not discussed in Plato, they do not concern us here. We do discuss them, however, in Brickhouse and Smith [1989b], 181–84.

81. The phrase is Hansen's. See n.65, above.

the meaning of the oracle, was to seek out those with the greatest reputation for wisdom and to examine them so as to find out how to solve the oracle's riddle. Socrates' first targets were the "public men," those with the greatest authority and influence in the state. He tells of the first such encounter as follows:

> So examining this one—I don't need to call him by name, but he was a politician . . . and in discussing with him, it seemed to me that this man was thought to be wise by many other people, and most of all by himself, but was not. And then I tried to show him that he thought he was wise, but was not. From that time, I have been hated by him and many of those present. (*Ap.* 21c3–d1)

Socrates says he then went to another such man—one even more highly regarded for wisdom than the first—and got the same results he had achieved the first time (*Ap.* 21d7–e2). After a number of such trials, Socrates concludes that "those with the greatest reputation seemed to me nearly the most deficient . . . and those others who were held to be baser seemed to be superior men as regards intelligence" (*Ap.* 22a3–6). From these surprising results, Socrates moves on to examine the poets and the craftsmen, with similar consequences.

At the end of his research, Socrates comes to the conclusion that he really is the wisest of men, for according to his understanding of the oracle he alone recognizes how impoverished he is with regard to wisdom. His mission on behalf of the god, then, becomes (among other things) a mission to seek out those who are the most in need of enlightenment, the high and powerful men whose reputations for wisdom—and whose authority in convincing others to do their bidding—were the greatest. As Socrates says, those with lesser reputations were not as much in need of Socratic humiliation (*Ap.* 22a5–6), although none are as wisely humble as Socrates himself.

The result is that Socrates seeks out those who think they are wise about the most important things when they are not. Those most self-satisfied with their own wisdom are those most likely to make mistakes regarding the most important things in their lives. Such men are especially likely to go wrong in particularly catastrophic ways. And because one's reputation among other men tends to support one's own self-image, those most prone to catastrophe, in Socrates' view, would be those who not only are self-satisfied, but whose smug self-image is buttressed by the admiration and supporting esteem of others. Such men are likely to be the very worst men in any society; and Socrates regards associating with and examining such men—attempting to show them that they are not wise—as crucial to his mission. So if we were to "read the indictment" of this criticism of Socrates as if it were a legal indictment (see *Ap.* 19b3–4), we would read that "Socrates does wrong by associating most closely with the most evil of men." To such a charge, we should suppose, Socrates would eagerly admit his guilt: he has aggressively pursued such associations, which we see documented in Plato's depictions of Socratic conversations, precisely because such men more than any others are in need of being stung by Socrates, the gadfly.

Moreover, when we do see Socrates conversing with such men, we do not find him either cozying up to their most egregious moral or political commitments, or offering to them further grist for their most arrant aspirations and values. Perhaps one of these men depicts Socrates' real goals most vividly; Nicias warns Laches about speaking with Socrates:

> You do not seem to me to know that whoever is closest to Socrates and draws near into a discussion with him, if he would but begin to discuss something else, will necessarily not stop being led around by him in the discussion until he falls into giving an account of himself—of the way he is living now and of the way he has lived in the past. (*La.* 187e6–188a2)

Socrates, let us recall, *refutes* the people he speaks with; he shows them that they do not know what they supposed they knew. Because his entire approach in discussion is adversarial and *ad hominem,* therefore, we should understand that Socrates' interlocutors do not stand for points of view Socrates agrees with. If anything, therefore, the positions for which his interlocutors are best known are those most likely to be targeted and refuted by Socrates. In this peculiar way, then, the characters of Socrates' associates tell us more about what Socrates is *not*—what he *does not believe* and *does not stand for*—than they do about anything he is, believes, or stands for. No doubt Socrates would know of such men, and seek them out, precisely on the basis of their most notorious or extreme points of view. And no doubt Plato would select such interlocutors in portraying Socrates at work—in inventing "Socratic conversations" (as he almost certainly did)—precisely because the most notorious men would provide especially good and fitting moral contrasts to Socrates himself.

A final reason for Socrates' seeking out the worst of men might be seen in Socrates' own search for the truth. As we said in section 1.3.3, Socrates is convinced that he can discover important moral truths by challenging a variety of people whose beliefs differ, and by determining which beliefs, upon reflection, they regard as true. Over time, as he practices the *elenchos* on a wide variety of persons, Socrates comes to have increasing confidence that the positions to which people are driven as a result of elenctic examination are genuine moral truths. Accordingly, some of the most valuable interlocutors for Socrates' search are those whom we should rightly regard as the most thoroughly corrupt, those most disdainful of commonly accepted moral points of view. Such people are particularly useful for Socrates' searches because if he can show that even these people turn out to accept some Socratic moral proposition, on examination, the proposition is given especially revealing support; others might simply agree to the principle out of a sense of shame (see, for example, *Grg.* 482d2–e2). Accordingly, Socrates is delighted when the most shameless of those present (in the *Gorgias*)— Callicles—becomes engaged in the discussion:

> Soc.: If I happened to have a soul made of gold, O Callicles, don't you think I should be delighted to find one of those stones with which they test gold, the best one, which—if I were about to bring my soul to it and it agreed with me that my soul had been well taken care of—would give me complete assurance that I am in good condition and in no need of other test?
>
> Call.: Why do you ask this question, O Socrates?
>
> Soc.: I will tell you: I am thinking in coming upon you I have come upon such a godsend.

CALL.: How so?

SOC.: I know well that whenever you agree with me about anything that my soul believes, this must indeed be the truth itself. (*Grg.* 486d2–487a1)

It is fair to conclude that Socrates had nothing in common with evil men with whom is he is often associated. In fact, quite the reverse is true. We are on safer ground in concluding that the persons he sought out served as so many philosophers' stones: proud, powerful, and shameless men by whom Socrates could test the metal (and the mettle) of his soul. Such associations help to define Socrates by contrast to them; no doubt this is why Plato chose to portray the conversations he did. Whether or not most of these conversations ever took place, the cast of characters, it seems, was just what Socrates himself would have prescribed.

5.4.4 Socrates' Trial

We cannot leave this subject until we look briefly at the evidence provided by Socrates' trial. Virtually every scholar who has written about the trial of Socrates has agreed that the real motivation behind the prosecution was political,[82] a claim we have disputed in detail elsewhere.[83] The evidence we have discussed in this chapter, however, should be enough to call such a claim into question. (In the next chapter, we shall attempt to show just how religion was the real issue at Socrates' trial.) We have shown that neither Socrates' own views nor his associations support the view that he was a political threat to Athens. This is, however, unfortunately quite compatible with his having been *seen* as such a threat.[84] Certainly, the very same doctrines and associations have led a number of scholars to endorse the same prejudices. Let us look, then, at the trial itself, to see to what degree politics played a part.

Although there is some ancient support for supposing there to have been a political motivation in the prosecution of Socrates, it is striking that we find absolutely none of this evidence in what are almost certainly our most important sources on the trial—Plato's *Apology* and Xenophon's *Apology*. Xenophon does later (in *Mem.* 1.2.9–64) discuss the political motives of "the accuser." Like

---

82. See, for examples, Barker [1951], 93–94; Bonfante and Raditsa [1978]; Burnet [1924], note on 18b3; Bury [1926]; Chroust [1957], 26, 164–97; Hansen [1980]; Lofberg [1928], 602; MacDowell [1978], 202; Montuori [1981], 167–68, 177–86; Roberts [1984], 243–46; Seeskin [1987], 75–76; Stone [1988a]; Vlastos [1983c]; and especially Winspear and Silverberg [1960], esp. 64–85. Zeller ([1963], 217) and Guthrie ([1971], 62–63) take the more cautious view that the trial was only partly the product of a political motive. Perhaps I. F. Stone, in his recent book on the trial, puts this point of view most succinctly. Stone proclaims that "it was the political, not the philosophical or theological, views of Socrates which finally got him into trouble. The discussion of his religious views diverts attention from the real issues" ([1988a], 138–39). In Brickhouse and Smith [1989b], 69–87, we argue against these scholars. A few other scholars have also questioned the relevance of politics at Socrates' trial; see, for example, Cohen [1988]; Finley [1968], ch. 5; Hackforth [1933], 73–79; and Irwin [1989], who advances a view in many ways similar to ours on this topic.

83. See n.82.

84. So Vlastos [1983c], for example, argues that Socrates did not deserve to be condemned as a "crypto-oligarch," but remains convinced that such a prejudice fueled the prosecution.

most other scholars, however, we take "the accuser" to refer not to any of Socrates' actual prosecutors, but, rather, to Polycrates the sophist, who published an accusation of Socrates a number of years after the actual trial.[85] Why, then, would the political motive be nowhere in evidence in Plato's and Xenophon's accounts of the trial itself?

Scholars have imagined a wide variety of reasons why Xenophon and Plato would suppress the political issue, but their accounts, for obvious reasons, are derived with little support from the texts. Moreover, scholars often claim that Socrates' actual prosecutors could not mention the pertinent political issues aloud in court, supposing that such talk would have been outlawed by the Amnesty of 403/2.[86] Accordingly, Socrates himself would be free to pass over them in silence at his trial. But there are a number of flaws in this reasoning. (a) In fact, the Amnesty would not have ruled out open discussion of Socrates' political activities or those of his associates. It ruled out only the possibility of prosecution for crimes committed prior to, or during, the rule of the Thirty, or for the violation of laws that had been nullified by the Amnesty itself.[87] Insofar as the prosecutors might have supposed that Socrates' political activities or associations—before, during, or after the rule of the Thirty—could be used in a prosecution for crimes still being perpetrated after the restoration of the democracy—for example, seditious oligarchic agitation—they were free to speak openly and in detail about them. (b) The Socrates who speaks to us in Plato's *Apology*, at least, not only claims to be eager to discuss any issue that has led to prejudice against him (see *Ap.* 18a7–19a7), but actually does spend a substantial amount of time, in giving his defense, discussing such issues. If there had been such slanders in the air by the time of the trial, he had, as we have seen, ample ammunition with which to rebut any slanders about his political affiliations or associates. Because he was so willing to combat other slanders he regarded as dangerous to him, his utter lack of attention to the political issues scholars have discussed at such length strongly suggests that Socrates did not see these political issues as any threat at his trial. If he had—certainly if the prosecution had made them an issue, which, as we have said, they could have done—he would have had to make some clear reply.

85. For a detailed reconstruction of Polycrates' accusations, see Chroust [1957], 69–100. In addition to Xenophon's *Mem.*, the ancient sources include Aisch. Rhet. 1.173; Isoc. *Bus.* 5; D.L. 2.38–9; Libanius, *Ap.* The only scholar we know of who rejects the identification of Xenophon's "accuser" with Polycrates is Hansen ([1980], 59–64). At least some support for the established view, which we follow, may be found in the fact that when Xenophon mentions the one or ones who actually did prosecute Socrates, he does not refer to "ὁ κατήγορος" ("the accuser"—1.2.12, 26, 49, 51, 56, 58), whom he identifies in all of the passages in which political issues are raised, but rather to "οἱ γραψάμενοι" (1.1.1) or "ὁ γραψάμενος" (1.2.64)—"the one(s) who wrote the indictment." This would appear to distinguish those who would qualify as "γραψάμενοι," namely, Meletus, Anytus, or Lycon, from Xenophon's "κατήγορος," namely, Polycrates. We argue in Brickhouse and Smith ([1989b], 84–85) that Polycrates was in all likelihood the primary source of all of the ancient evidence for there having been a political motive behind the prosecution of Socrates. Later writers simply echoed or responded to Polycrates' accusations.

86. See, for example, Allen [1975], 12; Burnet [1924], 101; Bury [1940], 393; Davies [1971], 187; Navia [1985], 14 and 39, n.20; Roberts [1984], 245.

87. See our discussion in Brickhouse and Smith [1989b], 32 n.113, and 74; see also Loening [1981], esp. vii.

Finally, (c) we find it particularly revealing that the actual indictment against Socrates was religious. Those who find a political motive lurking behind the prosecution simply cannot explain why Meletus and his supporters would choose such an unrelated indictment. It is certainly not as if the Amnesty or any other enactment prohibited trials on charges of sedition or other actions against the government. Given the sorts of people and activities scholars have imagined Socrates to have promoted, why would the prosecutors not have indicted him on subversion?[88] In 399 B.C., within months of Socrates' own trial, Andocides quotes from a law that seems made to order:

> If anyone subverts the democracy at Athens, or holds office when the democracy has been subverted, he shall be an enemy of the Athenians and shall be killed with impunity, and his property shall be confiscated and one-tenth of it shall belong to the Goddess; and he who kills or helps to plan the killing of such a man shall be pure and free from guilt. All Athenians shall swear over unblemished sacrifices by tribes and by demes to kill such a man. The oath shall be as follows: "I shall kill, by word and deed, by vote and by my own hand, if I can, anyone who subverts the democracy at Athens, and anyone who, when the democracy has been subverted, holds any office thereafter. . . . " (Andoc. *Myst.* 96–7; trans. MacDowell, 175)

Given the availability of a more suitable charge, if the motivation for the prosecution had been political, it seems that the trial was, after all, a religious one. One advantage of this view is that we do not now need to see Socrates as dithering or slickly avoiding the real issues when he presents his defense in Plato's *Apology*. Instead, his focus is on the genuine concerns his prosecutors represented in their indictment, and about which his "first accusers" have slandered him for so many years: does Socrates or does he not believe in the gods of the state, and if so, how and why he has gotten his reputation as a dangerous atheist? From those, then, who would claim that Socrates' "discussion of his religious views diverts attention from the real issues,"[89] we must beg to differ; it is the scholars themselves who have diverted attention from the real issues.

88. See MacDowell [1978], 175–91, for a review of such laws.
89. See Stone [1988a], 139.

6

Socratic Religion

6.1 Socratic Piety

6.1.1 The Puzzles of Socratic Religion

Socrates was tried, convicted, and condemned to death on the charge that he was impious. The three specifications of this charge were that he did not believe in the gods the state believed in, he invented new divinities, and he corrupted the youth.[1] Until recently, scholars have typically regarded these charges as masking the real motivations behind the prosecution, motivations of a political—and not a religious—nature. As we saw in chapter 5, few have felt any need to look carefully at the charges themselves and ask what could have motivated the prosecution to suppose that Socrates was guilty of religious offenses; for few have been convinced that anyone really believed that Socrates *was* guilty of religious offenses.

No doubt scholars have not taken the charges seriously because, on the one hand, a number of ancient authorities specifically say that the motivation for the trial was political, and, on the other, the ancient authorities provide little reason for supposing that Socrates could be regarded as posing a threat to whatever passed as Athenian religious orthodoxy. But, as we showed in chapter 5, the political interpretation of the trial ultimately fails to make sense of all that we know about Socrates, the trial, the relevant Athenian laws, and even the ancient sources themselves. In fact, the two most proximate sources on the trial, Plato and Xenophon, certainly treat the charge of irreligion as if it had been a serious issue to Socrates' prosecutors.

In Plato's *Apology*, Socrates characterizes the most dangerous prejudices against him as deriving from what he calls "the first accusations," which were used to slander him long before Meletus wrote the actual indictment (*Ap.* 18a7–c1). According to these accusations,

> There is a Socrates, a wise man, a thinker about the things in the heavens, and who has inquired into the things under the earth and who makes the weaker argument the stronger. (*Ap.* 18b6–c1)

---

1. Plato states the formal charges against Socrates at *Ap.* 24b8–c1. A similar statement of the charges is given by Xenophon at *Mem.* 1.1.1. Xenophon's version is repeated almost word for word by Diogenes Laertius at 2.40. For a discussion of what the charges mean, see Brickhouse and Smith [1989b], 30–37.

These accusations are repeated, with the addition that he teaches others to do the same things, at *Apology* 19b4–c1. Plato's Socrates says that Meletus relied on these accusations in bringing the actual formal charge of impiety against Socrates (*Ap.* 19b1–2). These accusations are especially dangerous, Socrates claims, because "people who hear [such accusations] think that those who investigate these things also do not believe in the gods" (*Ap.* 18c2–3). Plato's Socrates responds to these accusations by claiming that they least of all fit him. Their source, he says, is a vicious distortion of his philosophical activities, which amount to no less than a religious mission assigned him by the god of Delphi (see *Ap.* 20e6–23c1). He concludes his defense with a distinctly religious plea:

> Clearly if I would persuade you and force you to break your oaths, I would teach you to not to believe there are gods, and in making my defense I should really accuse myself of not believing in the gods. But that is not at all the way it is. I do believe in them, O men of Athens, more than my accusers do, and I leave it to you and to the god to judge regarding me, and decide what will be best for me and for you. (*Ap.* 35d2–8)

Xenophon similarly acknowledges the specifically religious nature of the charges by devoting the first chapter of his *Memorabilia* to an argument that Socrates—of all people—was entirely innocent of impiety. Like Plato, Xenophon carefully distances Socrates from the sorts of naturalistic inquiry that seem to have been commonly associated with atheism[2] (*Mem.* 1.1.11–15). Xenophon concludes his defense of Socrates on this issue by saying,

> I am amazed, therefore, how the Athenians could have been persuaded that Socrates was not temperate regarding the gods, when he never did anything impious against the gods, neither by word nor deed, but what he said and did regarding them were always the words and deeds of one who deserves to be recognized as a most pious man. (*Mem.* 1.1.20)

If we can believe Plato's and Xenophon's depictions at all, it seems a great mystery how Meletus and his supporters could have been persuaded to accuse such a pious old man. Equally mysterious is how the Athenian jurors could have been convinced that he deserved to be convicted and condemned to death. This, then, is one of the great puzzles regarding Socratic religion. We shall attempt to solve this problem in the second section of this chapter.

Another puzzle is even simpler to state. On the one hand, we find Socrates characterizing himself as having had "since childhood" (*Ap.* 31d2–3) a "divine sign" (*Ap.* 40c2–3, 41d6; *Euthyd.* 272e4; *Rep.* VI.496c4; *Phdr.* 242b8–9) or "voice" (*Ap.* 31d3; *Phdr.* 242c2), a "something divine" (*Ap.* 31c8–d1, 40a4; *Euthphr.* 3b5–7; *Phdr.* 242b8-9) which would always oppose him when he was about to do something wrong (*Ap.* 40a4-6, 40c1–3).[3] On the other hand, we find

---

2. This association is reflected clearly in Aristophanes' depiction of Socrates in the *Clouds*. See, for example, lines 366, 379, 247, 424.

3. Xenophon's account of Socrates' *daimonion* is somewhat different from Plato's. According to Xenophon, Socrates' *daimonion* dispenses the advice *to do* things, and hence does not simply "turn Socrates away." (See, for example, Xenophon, *Mem.* 1.1.4, 4.3.12, 4.8.1; *Ap.* 12.) Other ancient

Socrates telling Crito, "I am—not just now, but always—the sort of man who is persuaded by nothing but the reason (λόγος/*logos*) that seems best to me when I reason about it" (*Cri.* 46b4–6). How can a man claim to be such a complete rationalist when he also claims to follow signs and voices? We shall take this problem up in the third section of this chapter.

We shall consider a related problem in the fourth section: how can the same Socrates, who embodies the life of reason, calling upon all to lead "the examined life" (*Ap.* 38a5–6), also refer to his trust in "oracles and dreams and in every way in which any other divinity has ever commanded a human being to do anything whatsoever" (*Ap.* 33c4–7)? In this section we shall also consider Socrates' conception of the relationship between rationality and divination, and the epistemological status of the prophecies of seers.

In the fifth and final section, we shall consider Socrates' conception of death and the afterlife, paying special attention to his vigorous disavowal of knowledge on the topic, on the one hand, together with his apparently confident judgment that some fates are worse than death. One surprising result of our interpretation will be that Socrates believes that, in some way or other, everyone will be better off in death.

6.1.2 Socrates and Piety

Before we turn to Socrates' conception of—and responses to—the gods, his *daimonion*, other forms of divination, and the afterlife, let us first return briefly to his conception of piety. In sections 2.5.2–2.5.4, we showed why we thought Socrates would regard piety as something like the knowledge of how to give aid to the gods in promoting wisdom in other human beings. As successful as this definition might be in surviving elenctic tests, however, it is unlikely that Socrates would consider himself to be in a position to express plainly and completely what piety is, for he proclaims nothing more often than his own ignorance.[4] It is also clear that Socrates is not a pious man—that is, he lacks the virtue of piety—for no one can be pious without being wise. But it is equally plain, from his defense in the *Apology*, that he regards himself as innocent of the charge of impiety on the ground that the very actions for which he has been brought to trial were performed in obedience to the god (*Ap.* 28e4–6, 29d3–4, 37e6), or to the Delphic oracle (*Ap.* 22a7–8, 22e1, 29a3). Socrates says the god commanded him to do what he has done (*Ap.* 30a5, 33c4–7), and so his examinations of others constitute a mission or service he performs for the god (*Ap.* 21e5, 22a4, 23c1, 30a6–7). Accordingly, he describes himself as the god's "gift" to Athens (*Ap.* 30d7–e1, 31a8). It seems clear that Socrates thinks he has acted piously in pursuing his mission in Athens. He has spent his life in giving aid to the gods by promoting

references to Socrates' *daimonion* may be found in Plutarch, *Mor. de gen.* 580C–582C, 588C–E, 589F, 590A.

4. *Ap.* 20c1–3, 21d2–7, 23b2–4; *Charm.* 165b4–c2, 166c7–d6; *Euthphr.* 5a7–c5, 15c12, 15e5–16a4; *La.* 186b8–c5, 186d8–e3; 200e2–5; *Lysis* 212a4–7, 223b4–8; *Hip. Ma.* 286c8–e2, 304d4–e5; *Grg.* 509a4–7; *Meno* 71a1–7, 80d1–4; *Rep.* I.337e4–5.

wisdom in other human beings, even though his actions were guided by no special expertise.

In the preceding chapters, we identified a number of things that Socrates could reasonably regard as the benefits his fellow Athenians derive from his practice of his mission. In 4.5, we argued that it is possible for one to be a good person without being fully wise and (hence) virtuous, and that Socrates regarded himself as just such a person. His commitment to the examined life, more than anything else, is what we believe he would credit as having made him a good person. The "all-glorious benefit" of Socrates' mission, then, would be that it has the power to make people good, precisely by promoting wisdom—if only the "human wisdom" that they are ignorant of the "greatest things." But even this sort of wisdom is a great benefit. As we suggested in sections 1.3.1–2, and 3.1, Socrates' mission allows people to come to see that they are deeply confused about many of their most basic conceptions of value, and that their confusions lead them to do things contrary to what they themselves would think they should do, if only they reflected about it. We argued in sections 1.3.3 and 3.2 that Socrates is also convinced that the *elenchos* can bring to light generally applicable moral truths that in fact everyone really believes. And because we all desire what is really good for us and invariably do what we think is best for us (see 3.5), it is crucial for us to be able to discern good from evil. Even if we cannot reasonably think we will ever become master moral craftsmen, we can certainly become better judges, and thus more often achieve what we really desire. So although Socrates has nothing perfect to offer his fellow Athenians as an "all-glorious benefit" of his pious mission, he nonetheless gives them something of great value, which they could not improve upon by any other means except, perhaps, divine dispensation. This, then, is why Socrates would regard himself as a good man with regard to piety, even though he lacks the virtue itself. In the remainder of this chapter, we will discuss Socrates' other religious beliefs.

6.2 Socratic Theology

6.2.1 *Omniscience and Omnibenevolence*

The most fundamental tenet of Socratic theology is that the gods are truly wise (*Ap.* 23a5–6; see also Xen. *Mem.* 1.1.19). Because the possession of wisdom guarantees also the possession of virtue, for Socrates,[5] it follows that the gods are completely virtuous. Thus, Socrates thinks we can be assured that the gods are completely good.[6] Socrates proclaims that humans get nothing good that does not

5. This follows because of the unity of the virtues. Commentators disagree about just what Socrates is committed to with the unity of the virtues thesis. Vlastos ([1978] and [1991], ch. 8) denies that Socrates thinks that "courage," "wisdom," "temperance," "justice," and "piety" all name the same thing. The contrary view is defended by Penner [1973] and [1992]; Irwin [1977], 86–90; and C.C.W. Taylor [1976], 103–8. Although Kraut thinks that virtue terms name the same thing, he denies that they have the same scope (see Kraut [1983b], n.28, 261). We describe and defend our own view of the unity of the virtues in 2.5.5–6.

6. See Vlastos ([1989a], revised as [1991], ch. 6; in the remainder of this discussion, we will refer only to the more recent [revised] version, unless otherwise specifically noted). Vlastos claims that

come from the gods (*Euthphr.* 15a1–2), including—at least according to a literal reading of the conclusion of the *Meno*[7]—virtue itself (*Meno* 99b11–100b6).

This line of reasoning also explains why Socrates finds myths portraying the gods as fighting with one another hard to believe (*Euthphr.* 6a6–8), for the only sorts of disagreements that could make gods or men become enemies are disagreements about the just and the unjust, the fine and the foul, good and evil (*Euthphr.* 7b2–d10). If the gods truly are omniscient about good and evil, however, they should not disagree, and, hence, should never fight. Moreover, the gods would never, in Socrates' view, do anything evil or harmful. This, too, follows from their moral omniscience, for, as we discussed in chapter 3, Socrates is convinced that one cannot know the good and fail to do it, or, conversely, know the evil and do it.

Plainly, then, we have no reason, according to Socratic theology, to fear that we shall be visited with any evil from the gods; for everything they do is good. This theology is summed up in Book II of Plato's *Republic*:[8]

"Is not the god truly good and must one say so?"

"Of course."

"Moreover, nothing good is harmful, is it?"

"It does not seem so to me."

"Well, then, does that which is not harmful do harm?"

"Nor that."

"Does that which does no harm do evil?"

"Not that either."

"And that which does not do evil would also not be the cause of any evil."

"How could it be?"

"And what about this? Is the good beneficial?"

"Yes."

"And therefore the cause of doing well?"

"Yes."

Socrates' ascription of beneficence to the gods does not simply follow from his view that they are perfectly wise. Vlastos argues, "To allow one's gods infinitely potent intellect is not of itself to endow them with flawlessly good will" ([1991], 163–64). But one of the most notorious features of Socratic philosophy is the tenet that one cannot know the good and fail to do it (see our discussion of this in 3.5). Given this thesis, it *does* follow, in Socratic philosophy, that omniscience entails omnibenevolence.

7. Some may not accept our employment of this part of the *Meno* to aid our understanding of the philosophy of Plato's early period Socrates, on the ground that traces of a number of middle period doctrines may already be found in that dialogue. We agree that caution is required in general. However, we also regard the specific claim we are considering here consistent with, and one possible extension of, the claim made at *Euthyphro* 15a1–2.

8. Although we do not regard this part of the *Republic* as among the early dialogues with which we are specifically concerned in this book, we find the doctrine Plato's Socrates articulates in this passage entirely consistent with what Plato's Socrates says about the gods in the early period dialogues.

"The good is therefore not the cause of all things, but of those that are well it is the cause; it is blameless for evil things."

"Completely true," he said.

"Neither, therefore," I said, "would the god be the cause of all things, as the many say, since he is good; but he is the cause of few things for human beings, for many things he is blameless. For there are many fewer good things for us than evil; and for the good things we must assume that the cause is nothing other than the god, but for the evil things we must search for another cause, but not the god." (*Rep.* II.379b1–c7)

In the *Republic,* Plato's Socrates goes on to say that this is why many of the traditional myths must be rejected within the ideal state, namely, all of those which portray the gods as sources of evil. The early period Socrates does not advocate the abolition of such myths; the most he ever says about them is that he finds them hard to believe (*Euthphr.* 6a6–8).

6.2.2   Socrates and "The Gods the State Recognizes"

Could Socrates' attitude towards such myths have been what landed him in court? The first two specifications of the legal charge against Socrates were that he "did not believe in the gods the state believes in" and that he "invented new divinities."[9] The proper interpretation of these accusations has long been a matter of scholarly debate,[10] but most scholars have claimed that these charges hide the real concern of the prosecutors, which, in their view, was political rather than religious.[11] Because this view falls apart, as we argued in chapter 5, it seems reasonable to look for a genuinely religious motive behind the plainly religious accusations.

Recently, a few scholars[12] have argued for what they regard as the genuinely religious motivation behind Socrates' prosecution, a motivation which they argue was derived from Socrates' moralistic conception of the gods, a conception owing in part to philosophical developments beginning much earlier in Ionia. The "nature-philosophers," as they were called, had already begun to erode traditional Greek religious beliefs by attempting to provide naturalistic explanations for phenomena traditionally explained in terms of divine agency. This tradition, which may have begun with Thales the Milesian,[13] is burlesqued in Aristophanes' *Clouds,* in which Socrates appears as the head-master at a "Think-Shop" at which such inquiries were characteristic. Of course, Socrates did not engage in precisely

---

9. See n.1, above.

10. For a summary of the various positions, see Brickhouse and Smith [1989b], 30–36.

11. See ch. 5, n.81, for references.

12. See Connor [1991]; McPherran [1990] and [1991b]; Vlastos [1991] chapter 6.

13. Vlastos says that Thales' younger associate, Anaximander of Miletus, was "the true founder of Ionian *physiologia*" (Vlastos [1991], 159, n.13), but gives no reason for not considering Thales. Thales' pair of primary principles—that "everything is full of gods" (Arist. *De An.* A5, 411a7–9), and that the first principle of all things is water (see Arist. *Met.* A3, 983b20–27)—certainly tempt one to think that a rational and naturalistic restructuring of divinity had already begun in his philosophy. There is too little evidence to make any conclusive judgment on this matter, however.

these sorts of innovations, but might it not be that Socrates' conceptions of the gods as perfectly moral beings was a similarly revisionary move, designed to rationalize Greek religion no less than did the speculations of the nature-philosophers?[14] Because what Socrates did was so plainly revisionary, we are told, to suppose Aristophanes' assimilation of Socrates to these other revisionaries is not surprising. It is also not surprising that Socrates is eventually brought up on religious charges and convicted.

One product of Socrates' revisions, we are told, is that he ends up actually being guilty of the charges—he disbelieves in "the gods of the state," and "invents new gods," gods of a thoroughly moral nature. As Vlastos has put it,

> What would be left of her [Aphrodite] and of the other Olympians if they were required to observe the stringent norms of Socratic virtue which require every moral agent, human or divine, to act only to cause good to others, never evil, regardless of provocation? Required to meet these austere standards, the city's gods would have become unrecognizable. Their ethical transformation would be tantamount to the destruction of the old gods, the creation of new ones—which is precisely what Socrates takes to be the sum and substance of the accusation at his trial.[15]

6.2.3 How Revolutionary Were Socrates' Views?

Because Socrates believes in completely wise gods and because he thinks the highest form of wisdom is practical, he believes the gods are thoroughly moral. Of course, contrasting accounts to this can be—but are certainly not always— found in Greek literature. There is no single, coherent conception of the gods to be found in Greek myths. In poets as diverse as Homer and Hesiod, or Aeschylus and Euripides, the gods are presented as having very different and often conflicting attitudes and motives in acting as they do towards each other and towards mortals, good and evil.

Socrates' understanding of the gods, then, is different from those mythical and literary conceptions which portray the gods as beings who often did visit mortals with disaster. But just how different was Socrates' conception from those of his contemporaries? The fact is that the ancient sources themselves never suggest that any of Socrates' contemporaries showed any particular concern over his moralizing conception of the gods.

With the exception of Aristophanes, all of the ancient characterizations of Socrates' public or private practice of customary religious rituals make Socrates look unremarkable and ordinary. Xenophon's Socrates, it seems, never misses a chance to perform a sacrifice, and Plato's, too, can occasionally be found offering a sacrifice (*Phd.* 118a7–8; *Symp.* 176a1–4), or a hymn to the gods (*Phd.* 61b2–3; *Symp.* 176a1–4), and claiming to have the standard collection of ritual objects (*Euthyd.* 302b4–d5)—not, we may assume, simply for window dressing. Not

---

14. See Vlastos [1991], 162; McPherran [1991b].
15. Vlastos [1991], 166. See also Connor [1991], 56.

once is there any suggestion that Socrates thought standard religious practices to be empty gestures or in need of revision.

Of course, Plato and Xenophon were apologists, but even if we turn to Socrates' most vehement critics, we find no trace of evidence that they considered Socrates' moralized conception to be in any way criminal. In the *Clouds,* for example, Socrates is not depicted as having changed the Athenian traditional gods in some moralistic way. Instead, Aristophanes assimilates Socrates to the Ionian scientific revolution, whose threat to religion is atheism. So, too, in Plato's *Apology,* we find both the "first" and the "later" accusations explicitly tied to Socrates' alleged role in scientific inquiry, and thus atheism ("first accusers": 18a7–19d7; "later accusers": 26d1–e2). Nothing *whatever* can be found that suggests that his accusers took Socrates' belief in the goodness of the gods to be grounds for the legal action they brought against him, and no trace of Socrates' moralizing of the gods can be found in his characterization of the prejudices of his "first accusers." If even Socrates' accusers could not manage explicitly to find fault with his alleged moral innovations to religion, it is hard to believe such innovations actually troubled anyone else. To these accusers, we might add "the accuser" (no doubt, Polycrates)[16] to whom Xenophon responds in *Memorabilia* 1.2. Xenophon's "accuser" finds many faults with Socrates, but religious innovation is not one of them.

Even Euthyphro, a man who is fanatically devoted to a literal understanding of certain amoral traditional myths, seems unperturbed by Socrates' explicit skepticism about Euthyphro's conception. When Euthyphro cites myths attributing savage acts to Zeus, Socrates suggests that perhaps the reason he is being prosecuted is that he finds such stories about the gods hard to believe (6a6–8). Euthyphro is eager to tell Socrates a number of other "amazing things" about the gods (6b5–6, 6c5–7), but seems nonplused at Socrates' reluctance to believe in morally repugnant myths. In fact, Euthyphro seems to concede Socrates' point that such myths are hard to believe (though Euthyphro does enthusiastically believe them) by suggesting that he can tell Socrates some myths that are *"even more amazing"* (6b5), as if the myths Socrates finds hard to accept are amazing enough in themselves. When Euthyphro does speculate about the grounds for Socrates' prosecution, he unhesitatingly locates the innovation in question not in Socrates' moralistic conception, but rather in Socrates' claim to have a private divine sign (3b5–7). On this point, the ancient authorities speak in one voice: Plato and Xenophon both clearly identify the charge of innovation as motivated not by Socrates' ethical transformation of the gods, but rather by his claim to have a private "divine sign"—his *daimonion* (Pl. *Ap.* 31c7–d4; Xen. *Ap.* 12). Where the ancients agree, we see no reason not to believe them.

The upshot of our remarks so far, then, is this: there is no ancient evidence for supposing that his contemporaries were troubled by Socrates' alleged ethical transformation of the gods, however revolutionary that transformation may seem to us. We are inclined to take this as evidence against the view that Socrates' moral transformation of the gods was the ground for his prosecution.

---

16. This identification is defended in Brickhouse and Smith [1989b], 71–72, 84.

6.2.4 What Socrates Himself Says

Those who allege that Socrates' conception of the gods is so revolutionary as to make him stand outside the law must argue that in the *Apology* Socrates carefully avoids the actual formal charge—that he disbelieves in "the gods of the state"— by getting Meletus to construe the charge as one of atheism. This conception of the charge allows Socrates to refute the claim that he is an atheist without actually affirming his belief in the gods *of the state*.[17] The reason for this, we are told, is that Socrates does *not* believe in the gods of the state, for Socrates is aware of having transformed them beyond recognition.[18]

Before we accept such an implication, we would do well to stop and consider the consequences of this view regarding Socrates' behavior at his trial. For example, it follows that Socrates knows full well that he is guilty of (at least one of) the specifications of the formal charge, but because his nominal accuser, Meletus (and perhaps Meletus' supporting speakers, Anytus and Lycon, as well) have stupidly interpreted their own charge in such a way as to leave the *real* problem unstated, Socrates prudently leaves it unstated as well. Socrates does not express innocence of the *real* accusation against him because he does not have to, once it has been more conveniently interpreted for him by Meletus. Of course, the jury must now be distracted from making the connection that Meletus and his fellow accusers have bungled. Is this why we should suppose that Socrates professes his belief in gods so emphatically, then? Does he hope by this sly exchange of the generic term "gods" for "gods of the state" to confuse the jury into supposing that he has refuted the accusations against him when in fact he has not?

This plainly is not the way Socrates behaves at his trial; he openly and repeatedly admits before the jury to holding a number of moralizing beliefs about the gods (21b6–7: it is not the part [οὐ θέμις] of the god to lie; 23a5–6: the god is really wise; 30c8–d1: it is not the way things are [οὐ θεμιτόν] that a better man be injured by a worse; 30e1–31c3: the god sends Socrates to Athens because the god cares for humans; and so on). So Socrates has hardly hidden his guilt of disbelieving in the gods of the state—if such moralizing beliefs do indeed make him guilty—and it is not as if he would make it difficult for anyone to prove that guilt. Yet at the end of his defense speech, Socrates is amazed to discover how near he came to winning acquittal. The closeness of the vote cannot be because Socrates repeatedly offended the religious sentiments of his jurors.

The view we have been considering, that Socrates' conception of the gods made him guilty of the formal charges, has at least two other very troubling consequences: (a) if Socrates' alleged moralizing innovations had actually been a serious issue in his prosecution, trial, or conviction, Plato's Socrates would be a liar. Moreover, (b) if Socrates' moralized conception of the gods had been the real issue at his trial, the prosecution itself has avoided bringing the *real* issue to light, and has failed to do so for no apparent reason and despite ample opportunities to do so. Let us review each of these points in order.

---

17. Vlastos makes the following point about Socrates: "that he believes in the gods is clear enough; that he believes in the gods *of the state* he never says" ([1991], 166, n.41, his emphasis).

18. See above n.17. McPherran [1990] also accepts this point.

From 20c4 to 24b2 in Plato's *Apology,* Socrates imagines someone asking him how the prejudices which have led to his appearance in court came into being, if, as he has already claimed, he is not a nature-philosopher and/or a sophist. He responds by telling the notorious story of the oracle to Chairephon, and of his attempt to understand it,[19] through which he comes to conceive of his elenctic activities as a religious mission.[20] He concludes that his activities in examining others for wisdom are what aroused the terrible enmity he now faces. Because the young men like to imitate him, people say that Socrates corrupts the youth (*Ap.* 23c2–d2). But this slander is not the result of Socrates' skepticism about the capacity of the gods to do evil or injustice; rather, it is the invention of those who wish to hide their shame in having been shown to be ignorant:

> And whenever someone would ask [those who promote the prejudice against Socrates] "by doing or teaching what [does Socrates corrupt the youth]?" they have nothing to say, but do not know, and yet lest they not seem confused, they say those things that are convenient against all philosophers, "the things in the air and under the earth," and "they do not believe in the gods," and "they make the weaker argument the stronger." For I think they would not want to say the truth, that it is being made very clear that while pretending to know, they know nothing. Therefore, inasmuch as they are lovers of honor, and vehement, and many, and speak eagerly and persuasively about me, they have filled your ears for a long time with vehement slanders. (*Ap.* 23d2–e3)

Socrates goes on to say that it is from among these people that Meletus, Anytus, and Lycon have arisen. He concludes his account of the origin of the prejudices against him with the following words:

> That is the truth, O men of Athens, and I speak without hiding anything from you, great or small, or holding anything back. But I know pretty well that I am making myself hated by these things; this is proof that I say the truth and that this is the slander against me, and these are its causes. (*Ap.* 24a6–b1)

If one of the "real" charges against Socrates is that he believes in thoroughly moral gods, as the view we have been considering claims, then in saying these words Socrates is just lying to the jurors; for according to the view we have been considering, the slanders against Socrates must be traced back not simply to his elenctic examinations, but rather—at least in some way "great or small"—to his skepticism about gods who would do evil and injustice. It is one thing for one to say that Socrates has conveniently neglected a dangerous issue; surely it is another to find that he specifically addresses that issue—the *real* source of the prejudice

---

19. Some have argued that even here Socrates betrays a kind of impious skeptical disrespect for the god. So Burnet claims that Socrates "tries to prove the god a liar" ([1924], note on 21b8), and Nehamas speaks of "Socrates' effort to prove the oracle wrong" ([1986], 306) and says that Socrates "tests the oracle's wisdom as rigorously as he tests the wisdom of those by means of whom he tests the oracle itself" ([1986], 305). What such scholars miss is that Socrates begins his inquiry into the meaning of the oracle with the conviction that although the god can speak in riddles (*Ap.* 21b3–7), it is not within the god's nature to lie (*Ap.* 21b6–7).

20. For discussion and explication of the process by which this transformation takes place, see Brickhouse and Smith [1989b], sec. 2.5.

against him—and flagrantly *lies* about it in order to deceive his jurors. Moreover, if Socrates is lying here, he is also lying when he repeatedly vows to his jurors that they will hear nothing but the truth from him (e.g., at *Ap.* 18a5–6, 20d5–6, 22b5–6, 28a6, 28d6, 32a8, 33c1–2). Socrates, it seems, turns out to be precisely the sort of slick and deceptive speaker the prosecution has made him out to be (see *Ap.* 17a4–b8).

Moreover, Meletus, Anytus, and Lycon turn out to be inexplicably incompetent prosecutors. For one thing, it is difficult to believe that Socrates could have told the story of how the prejudices against him had arisen if these men had already made the case that Socrates' rejection of the common belief in immoral gods threatened civic cult. When Socrates interrogates Meletus at the trial, Meletus has a number of opportunities to make this accusation. Yet if we were to accept the view that Socrates' moralized conception of the gods is one of the real issues behind Meletus' prosecution, Meletus consistently and incredibly bungles each opportunity to show the jury that Socrates' conception is criminal. At 26a8–b7, for example, Meletus makes clear that he thinks Socrates corrupted the youth by means of his teachings about the gods. Socrates then seeks clarification from Meletus as to precisely what Meletus thinks these teachings are:

> With regard to these gods themselves, O Meletus, whom the argument is now about, speak more clearly both to me and to these men. For I cannot understand whether you say that I teach and believe that there are some gods, and thus that I believe there are gods and am not a complete atheist and a wrong-doer in that way, and yet that these gods are not the gods of the state, but others, and this is what you accuse me of—believing in others; or do you say that I do not believe there are gods at all and teach this to others? (*Ap.* 26b8–c6)

If the *real* issue were Socrates' moral transformation of the gods, it is hard to imagine why Meletus would unhesitatingly answer as he does: "That is what I say, that you do not believe there are gods at all" (*Ap.* 26c7). Why would Meletus not instead answer that, however Socrates might claim to believe in gods, according to Socrates' teaching the gods would never do evil and, hence, much or all of Athenian cult religion was a sham? Surely, if such moralistic teaching were such an obvious threat to Athens' customary religion, even someone as dim as Meletus could see how to make the threat clear: Socrates' theology is impious precisely because it would destroy Athens' religion.

Moreover, even if we suppose that Meletus was so foolish that he could not make the obvious connection, we know that Anytus was an accomplished and canny politician; surely *he* could see that Meletus was bungling their case, and could now call out his suggestions for the right answers to Socrates' questions. Even if we are to imagine (without benefit of ancient evidence) that Meletus' supporting speakers are under a gag-order during this interrogation, surely the jurors themselves are not.[21] If Socrates' skepticism about the immorality of the gods was so notorious, why do they not call out their suggestions and accusations

---

21. It was not uncommon for jurors to create a disturbance during trials. In Plato's account of the trial, Socrates repeatedly pleads with the jury not to do so—see *Ap.* 17d1, 20e4, 21a5, 27b1, 27b5, 30c2, 30c3. For a discussion of such disturbances, see Bers [1985].

at this moment? We do not know that they did not, but if they did, it is remarkably foolish of Socrates not to have acknowledged that his attempt to avoid the "real" issue had failed. If the jurors ever did cry out their recognition of Meletus' error, surely Socrates would have had to address the issue of how his moral religion fit civic cult, after all. Instead, he continues his interrogation of Meletus on different points, and then turns to other issues in the last part of his speech, which stretches on for another eight Stephanus pages after Socrates is done with Meletus (28a2–35d8).

So we suggest that the best interpretation of the charges, the prejudices that led to them, and to Socrates' being convicted, is precisely what Plato's Socrates says in the *Apology*. Neither Socrates nor his accusers acknowledge the purported significance of the distinction between the expressions "the gods of the state" and "the gods" either because no one present sees the distinction, or because no one present sees it as pertinent to this case. Accordingly, when Socrates does make it clear that he believes in the gods, he is responding to Meletus' charge that Socrates is an atheist, which is the only conception of the charge anyone supposed was relevant to the trial. Only this account makes sense of what we know about the trial.

6.2.5 A Final Issue Considered

What, then, should we think about what Socrates says in the *Euthyphro*, when he wonders aloud if perhaps he has been brought up on this religious charge because he finds myths about the immorality of the gods hard to believe? It appears that Socrates is at least aware that his own views do not entirely cohere with those of (at least some of) his contemporaries. They certainly do not cohere on this point with those of Euthyphro, for example. Let us not forget, however, that his hypothesis about the motives of his prosecutors is offered as a step in Socrates' bid to engage Euthyphro in elenctic argument. Plainly, not all such "bait" must be taken as reflecting a serious Socratic conviction.

But even if Socrates had been convinced, as he stood with Euthyphro before the King-Archon's office, that his skepticism about the traditional myths of divine immorality led to his indictment, if Plato's account in the *Apology* is at all correct, by the time his trial actually began, either Socrates had become convinced that such skepticism was irrelevant to the charges he faced or he had become devious. The fact is that not once at his trial does Socrates mention his difficulty in believing immoral myths. Of course, as he stood before the King-Archon's office with Euthyphro, Socrates did not yet know the exact grounds for the charges against him, so his opinion about the real motive behind the trial at that point was purely speculative. In any case, by the time he spoke before the jury, he knew well what his accusers had to say, and he knew well what prejudices they had sought to employ in their prosecution. Thus, at that time, he knew exactly what the grounds of the actual prosecution were. Given Socrates' own characterization of the "first accusations," it appears (again) that the problem is that he has been assimilated to the nature-philosophers. This has nothing to do with his skepticism about myths regarding the immorality of the gods. And given the testimony of

Meletus, it appears that the charge of disbelief in the gods of the state really was intended to make the connection between the science Socrates is depicted as pursuing and atheism. So either Socrates' speculation in the *Euthyphro* turned out to be off the point, or someone—Plato, we must suppose—is willfully misrepresenting how the issue was actually presented to the jury.[22]

6.2.6   Concluding Remarks

The upshot of our argument is that we also find no evidence for believing that Socrates or any of his peers—friend or foe—saw any threat in Socrates' conviction that the gods were thoroughly moral beings. Moreover, we cannot find any evidence that whatever tension may have existed between Socrates' conception of the gods as moral beings and established religion in Athens actually motivated any of the accusations against him. The only religious tension we do find alleged in the accusations is between Socratic philosophy and theism, a tension Socrates eagerly and, all things considered, quite effectively disputes as based upon a slanderous distortion of what he does in his philosophizing.

The idea that Socrates might not be dangerously critical of his culture's religious attitudes—and especially the idea that he might genuinely believe in dreams and oracles and signs and voices, as we shall argue later in this chapter—is very troubling to some scholars precisely because Socrates has for centuries been held up as the hero of reason. Professional philosophers routinely hold him up as a model of the sort of thinker they try to encourage their students to become—free to question anything, constrained by nothing but reason itself. So Socrates has become the perfect philosophical martyr: he gave up everything else to live the life of philosophical reason, despite all its dangers, and the mob killed him for it. The problem with the ordinary representation of this view is that it is based upon a very anachronistic conception of what "the life of philosophical reason" is taken to be.

Unlike contemporary philosophers, Socrates saw no need to investigate religious beliefs per se. As Aristotle tells us, Socrates confined his philosophical attentions to ethics (*Metaph.* A, 987b1–4), and so it should not be surprising to us that Socrates seems to have attended to theological issues only insofar as they related to ethical concerns. In fact, Plato himself characterizes Socrates as one who cannot possibly live up to our own image of the religiously critical contemporary philosopher. Socrates' lack of interest in questioning religion in general is starkly evident in his response to Phaedrus' expressions of skepticism.[23] Phaedrus

---

22. In fact, we do not need to suppose even that Socrates is represented in the *Euthyphro* as actually believing that this is the source of the accusation. He may say what he does only to express his doubts about such stories in such a way as ironically to underscore his own fallibility and vulnerability on such issues, thus emphasizing his "need" for Euthyphro's instruction. Certainly, nothing more is made of this issue regarding the actual legal case, in this or any other ancient source.

23. In general, we believe that middle and late period dialogues cannot be used to interpret earlier works except when they supplement or clarify positions already established as Socratic in the early period works (see nn. 7 and 8, above). We believe that this passage in the *Phaedrus* may be cited as evidence of the views of Plato's Socrates as opposed to the views of Plato because the passage fits

asks if Socrates really believes the old myth about Boreus, and Socrates responds by saying that he regards "the wise ones" (*Phdr.* 229c6) who attempt to explain away the old myths by providing rationalistic interpretations of them, as "clever, hard-working and not completely fortunate men" (*Phdr.* 229d4), for they find themselves in the position of having to go on to explain away all kinds of other mythical creatures and stories (*Phdr.* 229d4–e1). Socrates concludes his response in such a way as to betray an astonishing lack of intellectual interest in critical inquiry regarding religion.

> And if someone who doesn't believe in these things would seek to explain each of them in accordance with probability, by using a bumpkinish sort of wisdom, he will need much leisure. But I have no leisure for these things at all. And the reason, O friend, is this: I cannot yet, as the Delphic inscription has it, know myself. So it seems laughable to me, when I do not know these things—to investigate the still unknown—and purposeless. So I do not pursue these things, but in accepting what is believed about them, as I said just now, I investigate not these things but myself. . . . (*Phdr.* 229e2–230a3)

No twentieth-century philosopher could give this response to Phaedrus. So we should not look to Socrates as a model for the sort of religious criticism or rationalization we now take for granted among philosophers. Instead, we should understand that, for the most part, Socrates unreflectively accepted and intellectually ignored the jumble of myths that constituted the intellectual component of Greek religion, and even regarded the attempt to look critically at these myths as a vanity—a "bumpkinish sort of wisdom"—for which he had no leisure. It does not follow that he believed in the literal truth of these myths; indeed, the insistence that Socrates had to have some very specific and clearly defined commitment one way or the other is itself an anachronism. As he puts it in the passage just quoted, he follows the customary beliefs uncritically and without so much as the leisure or interest to pursue how much or whether he should believe in them. This sort of relation to religion is, we believe, quite common among unreflective people even now; religion has to become an intellectual issue before one even becomes aware of the degree or depth of one's religious beliefs.

6.3 Socrates and His *Daimonion*

6.3.1 Faith and Reason

At the beginning of this chapter, we noted that Socrates appears to hold a pair of incompatible beliefs: on the one hand, he professes a belief in various forms of divination, including "oracles and dreams and . . . every way in which any other divinity has ever commanded a human being to do anything whatsoever" (*Ap.* 33c4–7). The most notorious forms of such divinations Socrates claims to follow are those derived from the activity of his own "divine sign" (*Ap.* 40c3–4, 41d6; *Euthyd.* 272e4; *Rep.* VI.496c4; *Phdr.* 242b8–9) or "voice" (*Ap.* 31d3; *Phdr.*

---

the general principle we follow regarding the use of middle period works to help interpret the early period works.

242c2), the "something divine" (*Ap.* 31c8–d1, 40a4–6; *Euthphr.* 3b5–7; *Phdr.* 242b8–9) Socrates says he has had "since childhood" (*Ap.* 31d2–3). On the other hand, we find Socrates claiming to be a complete rationalist, one who follows only reason (*Cri.* 46b4–6). But surely it is not reason that tells us to obey "oracles and dreams," or signs and voices, but rather a very unsophisticated and superstitious sort of religious faith.

There are sharp differences of opinion among contemporary scholars on this issue. Some have argued that Socrates' trust in divination is wholly subordinate to his trust in ratiocination.[24] Others, ourselves included, have insisted that Socrates would count certain forms of divination—especially his own *daimonion*—as providing sources of information which are largely independent of Socrates' own ratiocination, and which he would follow in preference to his own ratiocination in cases of conflict.[25] Although this latter view has recently come under sharp attack,[26] there remains convincing evidence that there can indeed be conflict between Socrates' *daimonion* and Socrates' own powers of reasoning, and that, in such cases, Socrates would always follow the promptings of his *daimonion*.

Plato's Socrates is a man convinced that human reason is faulty and that his own wisdom—unsurpassed by any other mortal's—is "worth little or nothing," whereas "the god is truly wise" (*Ap.* 23a5–7). This obviously suggests that insofar as Socrates thought that some claim, monition, or command came from the god, it was more dependable than any claim, monition, or command from Socrates himself or from some other human being. So if we were to find a case in which Socrates was forced to choose between the conflicting directives of the products of his own—or any other human being's—reasoning, on the one hand, and the monition of his *daimonion*, on the other, we should expect Socrates to follow the directive of the *daimonion* in preference to the products of human ratiocination.

Another reason we believe that Socrates would allow his *daimonion* to "trump"[27] his own ratiocination stems from what Socrates himself says about the way the *daimonion* operates. At *Apology* 40a4–6, Socrates characterizes his *daimonion* as opposing him "quite frequently, even in little things, if I was going to do something wrong." And again at 40c2–3, Socrates says that surely his *daimonion* would have opposed him had he not been about to do something good. Earlier, at *Apology* 31d3–4, Socrates says his *daimonion* always operates in such a way as to oppose him when he is about to do something wrong, never in such a way as to guide him forward.

So the *daimonion* does not oppose Socrates when he merely considers courses of action; rather, it opposes him when he is about to take action. This certainly suggests that the opposition of the *daimonion* comes when Socrates' own deliberations are complete (if he did deliberate), and have aimed him at a course of action that turns out to be in some way or ways wrong or misguided. When Socrates,

---

24. Vlastos [1989b], [1990a], [1990b], [1991], ch. 6 and additional note 6.1, [1989a]; Reeve [1989], 62–73.

25. See Brickhouse and Smith [1990a] and [1990b]; McPherran [1991a].

26. See Vlastos [1989b], [1990a], [1990b], [1991], chapter 6 and additional note 6.1.

27. This is Vlastos's term ([1991], 286).

upon receiving his *daimonion*'s opposition, desists from the action in question—and not once do we find Socrates failing to desist after such opposition—he does so *in spite of whatever reasons he may have had for taking the action in the first place,* reasons which led him to be on the verge of taking the action, if only his *daimonion* had not intervened. This can be explained only if Socrates' *daimonion* is able to trump reason after all.

When Socrates says that his *daimonion* opposes him "quite frequently, even in little things" (*Ap.* 40a4–6), we must not assume that it opposes only actions he was about to take impulsively and without forethought. It often does oppose him "in little things," and it is not unreasonable to suppose that regarding many, if not most, of these "little things," Socrates had not engaged in careful deliberation. But Socrates does not say that the *daimonion* opposes him *only* in little things. For example, Socrates takes the fact that the *daimonion* did *not* oppose him in his speech or his preparation for the trial as a "great proof" (*Ap.* 40c1) that everything has turned out for the best at his trial (*Ap.* 40a2–c3). It seems reasonable to assume that the sorts of issues he confronted at his trial do not qualify as "little things." Yet Socrates' "great proof" works only if we assume that his *daimonion* might have opposed him at any moment during the trial or the events leading up to it, if what Socrates was doing or saying were in some way wrong. Moreover, we cannot assume that Socrates acted impulsively at his trial; yet Socrates' "great proof" works by an appeal to the fact that his *daimonion* did not oppose him in doing and saying these things, even though Socrates regarded it as thoroughly capable of opposing him at any time. We must conclude from this that Socrates considers it entirely possible that his *daimonion* could and might oppose him even when he has deliberated about the course of action in question, thus trumping his deliberation. It could and might have done so at or before the trial, but did not; so Socrates concludes that all has gone well. We do not see how to account for Socrates' "great proof" in this case, if the *daimonion* could only oppose Socrates when Socrates was acting without forethought.

6.3.2 A Critical Passage

A final reason for thinking that Socrates would permit his *daimonion* to "trump" his own ratiocinations comes from the passage at *Apology* 31c7–d5, in which Socrates says that his *daimonion* opposed his undertaking to engage in formal political activity (such as haranguing the Assembly). It is most implausible (and most uncharitable) to suppose that Socrates would undertake to engage in such political activity on a whim. Surely instead, we must suppose that when Socrates sought to engage in such activity—only to meet with the opposition of the *daimonion*—he did so on the basis of some rational consideration about the good he might do for his fellow citizens. The *daimonion,* of course, did not necessarily nullify Socrates' ideas about what would and what would not be good for the city or his fellow citizens. But it did nullify ("trump") Socrates' apparent commitment to the idea that he was in a position to do something worthwhile in the way of promoting his ideas in Athens' political institutions, an idea he surely did not come to purely impulsively.

Others have argued that this passage does not provide an example of the *daimonion* nullifying Socrates' own reasoning, on the ground that in the same passage Socrates goes on to show that he has reasons for thinking that the *daimonion*'s opposition was a good thing. So this is *not* a case, we are told, where the *daimonion* and Socrates' reasoning conflict.[28] But this reading of the passage seems to us to be plainly mistaken. Socrates does say that the *daimonion*'s opposition to his engaging in formal political activity was a good thing; but, then, of course, he is committed to the view that any such opposition—coming as it does from a divine source—is a good thing. After saying that the *daimonion* is what opposed his going into politics at 31d5, he does go on (at 31d5–6) to say he regards such opposition as having been a good thing. What Socrates does not say, but what he must be taken as implying, if this passage is not to be taken as a case of daimonic trumping of Socratic ratiocination, is that Socrates was well aware of these reasons *at the time* the *daimonion* signaled its opposition, such that those reasons *would have* sufficed to prevent Socrates from doing what the *daimonion* opposed. It seems more likely to us that the reasons Socrates adduces for supposing that the *daimonion*'s opposition was a good thing came *afterwards*, as Socrates considered why his *daimonion* would oppose his noble impulse to attempt to do some good for his city through political activity.

Surely, if Socrates already had sufficient reasons for avoiding institutional political activity (other than the minimum he would be expected as a citizen to perform),[29] then it seems obvious that there would have been nothing for the *daimonion* to *oppose*—Socrates would not have gone into politics anyway. But Socrates very plainly says that his *daimonion did* oppose his going into politics, and he is also clear in identifying, *not* his reasons for thinking the opposition was a good thing, but *the opposition of the daimonion* as what kept him from engaging in politics. *Apology* 31d2–5 can only be understood, then, as identifying a case in which the *daimonion* did in fact "trump" Socratic forethought.

6.3.3   *What Counts as a Reason for Socrates?*

If what we have argued so far is correct, Socrates' trust in his *daimonion* was more complete than his trust in his own ability to reason. But what, then, do we make of the unwavering commitment to reason Socrates expresses at *Crito* 46b4–6, in which Socrates claims to follow nothing but the reason (argument, or proposition—*logos*) that seems best to him when he reasons about an issue? In arguing, as we have, that Socrates would invariably follow the promptings of his *daimonion*—even when it opposed an inference which had led Socrates to the verge of some course of action—have we not violated the sense of this very important passage?[30] We think not. First, Socrates is not claiming, in the *Crito*

28. Vlastos [1991], 286.

29. Such as serving as a Prutanis when his tribe rotated into this position on the Council (see *Ap.* 32a9–b2).

30. Vlastos [1989b], and Reeve ([1989] 71–72) claim that this passage defeats our interpretation. The following argument is our reply to their objections. See also Brickhouse and Smith [1993]; Smith [1992].

passage, that he always follows arguments rather than the promptings of his *daimonion* or some other form of divination. Divination is not what Socrates has in mind as the alternative here; rather, in this passage Socrates is contrasting the opinion of the many with reason as it is reflected by the "one who knows" and is claiming that one should always reject the former in favor of the latter. Socrates does say that he would be persuaded by *nothing* but *logos,* but why must we assume that divination would fall into some category other than persuasive *logos,* for Socrates, and, hence, that Socrates would never put his faith in divination unless he had some (other) persuasive *logos* to do so? This assumption is not supported by the *Crito* passage, in which the reliability or justification of divination is not under consideration. Moreover, the *Crito* passage in no way excludes the possibility that his *daimonion*'s promptings would count as a *reason* for Socrates to be persuaded of something.

Second, we must not simply assume that Socrates would consider the monitions of his *daimonion* as non-rational signs. Indeed, surely Socrates' responses to the *daimonion* clearly bespeak his recognition of this "unpredictable little beast"[31] as providing Socrates with absolutely compelling reasons to cease and desist from the actions it opposes. When Socrates' *daimonion* opposes him, for example, which it does "very frequently even on very small matters" (*Ap.* 40a4–6), Socrates does not wait until he can concoct an *argument* to be persuaded that he must stop whatever he was about to do (*Ap.* 40a6). The opposition of his *daimonion* is itself Socrates' *reason* for stopping, though he will often attempt to discern subsequently, no doubt by reasoning about it, *why* that opposition was a good thing.

We never see Socrates dismissing someone else's point of view by saying only that his *daimonion* opposes that point of view. Because it reveals itself to Socrates alone, the *daimonion* can be of little use in Socrates' arguments with others. It might well oppose certain things Socrates finds himself about to say or argue; it might oppose Socrates' even associating with someone at all (see [Ps.-]Plato, *Alcibiades* I.103a1-b2). But because Socrates' interlocutor might not believe in Socrates' "sign," Socrates' citing the fact of its monition at some point in an argument might have little effect on his interlocutor. In *arguments* about something or other, then, Socrates cannot simply appeal to his *daimonion* as a reason for his interlocutor to concede some point or other.

Even this sort of consideration, however, does not mean that Socrates would not count the prompting of his *daimonion* as giving him a "reason" to think or to do something, as he deliberated about it. Rather, it only concedes that an appeal to his *daimonion* might not look like a plausible "reason" to someone else. But when Socrates says that he follows only the "reason" that seems best to him when he considers it, we must not suppose that he would not follow some consideration he finds plausible or compelling simply because others regarded that consideration as absurd or unlikely. In fact, Socrates is denying precisely this point in saying what he does in the *Crito:* he will follow the reason that seems best to him *in spite of* what would or would not count to others as reasonable or plausible.

31. This is Vlastos's expression [1989b].

So although Socrates is not talking about his *daimonion* in the *Crito* passage, and may not have it in mind as he speaks these words to Crito, we do not find his complete trust in the monitions of his "sign" exceptions to the rule he articulates to his concerned friend. Contemporary philosophers may be troubled by what Socrates says about his *daimonion* because they find trust in signs and voices irrational. But if we take the texts as our evidence, we see that it is a mistake to assume that Socrates' conception of the limits of rationality must coincide with our own on this point.

6.3.4 The Epistemological Limitations of Daimonic Opposition

Once the *daimonion* has stopped him as he was about to do something, Socrates would plainly count his doing of that action—at the time and place in question— as unquestionably and unambiguously wrong. The *daimonion* sounds its voice (or makes its sign, or whatever it does), so Socrates must stop, and the *reason* he must stop, he is absolutely convinced, is that what he was about to do—under these precise circumstances, at least—was wrong (*Ap.* 40a6, 40c2–3). This leaves a good deal for Socrates to reason about: What about this act-token is wrong, or is it the act-type? What about the current situation makes it wrong? In what does wrongness itself consist? and so on. The *daimonion* offers Socrates no rules of conduct, no general principles, no moral definitions; its activity seems always to be unexpected and it offers Socrates no explanations of its activity.[32] However slight the information he has received, it is enough to prevent Socrates from taking so much as another step in the undertaking he was considering. Socrates may not know the first thing about why he has been stopped, but he seems completely and unshakably certain that he must not do what he was about to do.

Now this certainty might itself be partly a product of reason. No doubt Socrates' own conviction that the *daimonion* stops him only when he was about to do wrong derives from Socrates' having wondered why his *daimonion* stops him when it does. The *daimonion* never tells Socrates *why* it stops him—it merely stops him. But it is the *daimonion*, and not reason, that stops Socrates cold in his tracks; it is not reason, for if it were, we should suppose that he would have stopped anyway if only he had thought about it for a moment. If his *daimonion* had not signaled its alarm, however, Socrates would neither stop nor say he had

32. For a detailed discussion of limitations on the epistemic value of the *daimonion*, see Brickhouse and Smith [1989b], sec. 5.5. In his review of our book, Vlastos brushes aside our careful discussion of the extent of these limitations by asking rhetorically, "But how could [what Socrates gets from his *daimonion*] be 'next to nothing' if by this means Socrates could count on getting, as they claim he does, access to some moral truths straight from God—truths which are 'logically independent of whatever beliefs he may have about the nature of virtue'?" The answer, of course, is in the conclusions we drew (already quoted): Socrates gets "next to nothing" from the *daimonion* regarding the sort of "truth which explains and defines, and which thus can be applied to the judgments and deliberations required for the achievement of the truly good life" (repeated verbatim from Brickhouse and Smith [1986] in Brickhouse and Smith [1989b], 253–54). "The problem" with the *daimonion*'s alarms, as we say on page 253 of Brickhouse and Smith [1989b], "is not fallibility but uninformativeness." Vlastos's rhetoric about "moral truths straight from God" is no refutation of our very cautious analysis.

reason to stop. That is why Socrates describes himself as being in the position, each time the *daimonion* acts, as "about to do something wrong" (*Ap.* 31d4, 40a4–6). So Socrates himself would cite, as his reason for stopping, that his *daimonion* had signaled its alarm (see, for example, *Ap.* 31d5).

Moreover, Socrates is not free to interpret his *daimonion*'s alarms in any way he might choose[33]—he may not, to say the least, interpret them as a sign of approval for the actions he was about to take. Reason certainly assists Socrates in assessing the significance of, or reason for, his *daimonion*'s alarms; but reason does not exhaust or fully explain the *daimonion*'s significance. The experience itself must tell part of the story. And the part it plays is to convey to Socrates at least this much information: he must desist from what he was about to do. This much is not a matter of interpretation. Moreover, *that* he must desist is treated by Socrates as beyond dispute, whereas his explanation of the ground for the *daimonion*'s command is open to alternative explanations. Hence, though reason does indeed play a role in Socrates' subsequent attempt to understand *why* the *daimonion* stopped him when it did, there remains at the core of the divinatory experience a kernel of indisputable truth, which is itself in no way either the product of or qualified by ratiocination. The kernel remains, as we have said, "virtually worthless" as a general guide to making judgments about right and wrong, for it provides "next to nothing" in the way of information, and nothing in the way of explanation of why the contemplated act is wrong. It simply says, in effect, "stop here and now."

6.4   Other Forms of Divination

6.4.1   "Oracles and Dreams"

A similar account to the one we have now given concerning Socrates' trust in his *daimonion* can and should be given for Socrates' response to a number of other forms of divination, to "oracles and dreams and . . . every way in which any other divinity has ever commanded a human being to do anything whatsoever" (*Ap.* 33c5–7). Each case stands in need of interpretation. But one avenue is not open to Socrates: he may provide no interpretation which counts the god's message as false (*Ap.* 21b6–7).

Moreover, it seems obvious that Socrates does regard divination as capable of providing a degree of confidence he cannot achieve any other way. In the *Apology*, for example, we find Socrates completely confident about the value of his own mission. He explains his confidence to his judges solely in terms of his understanding of certain divinatory experiences. All typically Socratic epistemological modesty is missing in this matter, which is simply inexplicable unless we suppose that Socrates' confidence derives at least in part from his faith in divination. For if it is explicable in other terms, we are left wondering why Socrates

---

33. Our point here is a response to a view Vlastos proposes in [1991], 170. McPherran offers a line of argument similar to ours on this point in his [1991a], 360–64.

himself did not explain it any other way. If we are to suspect Socrates' sincerity and honesty, we should be given compelling reasons for doing so.

6.4.2   Socrates and Seers

At *Apology* 22b8–c4, Socrates denies that seers have knowledge of what they say:

> Regarding the poets, I soon realized that it is not by wisdom that poets do what they do, but by some natural talent and by inspiration, like the diviners and oracle-givers, who also say many fine things, but know nothing of what they say.

The same claim is made about oracle-givers and diviners at *Meno* 99c2–5.

Some might be tempted to conclude that Socrates regards oracle-givers, seers, poets, and diviners as having no knowledge at all.[34] We think this is a misunderstanding of Socrates' claim. First, we would do well to note that in the *Ion* (538d7–e3) Socrates says that diviners have a *technē*.[35] Moreover, in the *Laches* 198e2–199a3, Socrates includes the seer in a subordinate role on the staff of the general. What is significant is that although the seer's role is subordinate to that of the general,[36] Socrates never disputes (or even questions) the qualifications of the seer to provide valuable information to the general.

So Socrates allows that real diviners have a *technē,* and it is because they are able to practice their craft that they are able to convey commands, judgments, or predictions, which are divinely certified (see *Ion* 534b3; *Meno* 99c4), and which are assuredly true (see *Ap.* 21b6–7). Nevertheless, Socrates also claims that diviners, in the practice of their craft, put themselves into a state in which they become inspired. In this state, they are "mad" (see *Phdr.* 244a6–d5), "out of their minds" (see *Ion* 534b5). As a result, they do not say what they say because of their own understanding of it, but rather because of the god's inspiration, which they receive through the practice of their craft. The commands, judgments, or predictions that real diviners bring to light are *not* the product of their own rational thought. What needs to be explained, then, is the relationship between diviners' craft and the knowledge which constitutes it and the truths or commands they divine when they are "mad" and "out of their minds."

6.4.3   Some Different Types of Knowledge

At *Politicus* 260c6 and following, Plato's Eleatic Stranger distinguishes two sorts of *technai* concerned with the giving of commands. One group initiates or pro-

---

34. This view has been defended by Gregory Vlastos, who writes: "For Socrates diviners, seers, oracle-givers, poets are all in the same boat. All of them in his view are know-nothings" ([1991], 170).

35. It is curious that despite the fact that he has obviously given the issue careful attention, Vlastos never mentions this passage. Vlastos rightly insists that in the *Ion* Socrates expresses the same view as the one (cited above) he offers in the *Apology* ([1991], 287–88). The *Phaedrus* repeats the *Ion*'s claim, as well; indeed, in the *Phaedrus*, divination is called "the noblest craft" (244c1).

36. In this connection, Vlastos admits only that "Socrates reminds his interlocutors that the law requires the diviner to obey the general" ([1991], 160, n.17).

duces the commands, whereas the other group only reproduces the commands of others. The king's craft belongs to the first group. To the second group, the Stranger assigns the crafts of "the interpreter, the boatswain, the diviner, the herald, and many other related crafts" (260d11–e2). Like Plato's Socrates in the early dialogues, then, the Eleatic Stranger counts divination among the crafts.

Included among the mediumistic *technai* in the Eleatic Stranger's list is the heraldic craft. To be a qualified herald, one must obviously first be able to determine what the king's commands are. This would presumably be a fairly trivial and straightforward process—the herald needs only to be able to learn what the king wishes to have commanded. He must then know how to convey the king's commands to the appropriate people, in the appropriate manner, and so forth. But plainly there is nothing about the herald's special expertise which requires that he know why the king makes the commands he does, whether the king's commands are good ones, or what it is that makes a command good or bad. Of course, the herald may happen, as a matter of fact, to know any of these things. But he could not know such things *qua* herald. *Qua* herald he merely announces the commands of the king, and may be said to "know nothing of what he says."

It seems reasonable to suppose that primary emphasis in the diviner's craft would be on knowing how to receive the god's commands or revelations or on how to determine precisely what the commands or revelations of the god are.[37] Like the heraldic craft, however, the issue of how to present the commands or revelations may also require a certain sort of skill. But, just like the herald, the diviner (*qua* diviner) is in no special position to know *why* the god commands or reveals what he does.

We find nothing in the Eleatic Stranger's account that Plato's Socrates, in the early dialogues, would not accept. For Socrates, it seems clear that the god would never say what is false or command what is evil. The diviner, *qua* diviner, however, has no privileged position from which to recognize the moral qualities of the gods. The diviner knows how to determine what the god wants to say and (perhaps) how best to say it on the god's behalf, but he "knows nothing of what he says"; that is, his craft puts him in no special position to *understand* the commands or revelations he divines.

Perhaps we can get clearer about what Socrates thinks the true diviner knows and does not know by imagining the following. Suppose a college freshman who is ignorant of logic were thumbing through an extremely technical article about some theorem of logic. Someone might ask him what is stated at line 13 of page 4, and—so long as he knows how to turn pages, count, and read—he is surely in a position to give the correct answer. Moreover, if these assumptions about his abilities are correct, he can be completely confident that he is in a position to report absolutely accurately on what the text says. So he knows what it says. But because he is ignorant of the subject matter, we may also say that he knows nothing of what the text says, even though he knows exactly what it says. A less

---

37. There were many different ways of divining familiar to the ancient Greeks. For detailed discussions, see Bouché-Leclerq [1975]; Burkert [1985], 109–18; Halliday [1913]; Mikalson [1983]; Nilsson [1971], 121–39.

paradoxical way to put it is that the freshman knows what the text says, but does not understand it.

The student may not know whether what the text says is true, however. But the same sort of case can be constructed in which the truth of what is read in ignorance is reasonably taken to be beyond question. We have often found ourselves in this position in looking at legal documents; because we can read, we may know what they say. We may even know that they state incontrovertible legal facts. But we do not understand what we read. Hence, our knowledge, such as it is, does not constitute legal understanding.

Like the student who knows how to read the theorem in the text, the practitioners of the divining craft are able to discover god-given truths or commands. However, the diviners are at a loss—as we are when we attempt to read a complicated legal document—to understand or explain the truths and commands they come to possess through their craft.

It is important to note that in claiming that there is a craft of divination, Socrates is not suggesting that, through his *technē*, the diviner necessarily even knows what divine truth or command he has discovered. On the contrary, recall that in the *Apology* (22b8–c2) Socrates says that the poets are like the diviners and oracle-givers in one important respect: they are able to do what they do, not by wisdom, but "by some natural talent and by inspiration." So Socrates thinks that some diviners at least are unable to look into the future or to grasp what the god's will is unless they become "mad" and "out of their minds."[38] While "out of their minds," diviners do not speak their own words, but merely cry out the words of the god. So the "fine things" such mediums say are not the product of *their own* wisdom, but, rather, the product of the divinity or divinities who inspire them—"the god," Socrates says only a bit later, "is really wise" (*Ap.* 23a5–6). The seers themselves "know nothing *of what they say.*" Their specific prophecies, then, cannot be the products of any rational state of their own, including a *technē*.[39] Like the herald, the diviner may serve as a conduit without knowing any of the rationale for what he conveys—or even so much as that there is some rationale. Indeed, the diviner, who can gain access to divinely certified truths only when he is "mad" and "out of his mind," may not even know *what* he has said

---

38. In the *Phaedrus*, Plato's Socrates distinguishes between a form of divination which requires divine inspiration and a form which does not involve divine inspiration. He is very clear in saying that he regards the latter sort as inferior (see *Phdr.* 244c1–d5).

39. The claim that the diviner need not even know what he has said may seem to be directly contradicted by a remarkable passage at *Charmides* 173c3–7, where Socrates characterizes genuine divination as "knowledge of the future" (173c4). Socrates may have in mind those forms of divination which do not require divine inspiration (see n.38). But, more likely, Socrates means that genuine diviners do indeed know what the future holds in the sense that they can predict it, even if only in a trance or state of ecstasy. Later, however, when they return to their normal conscious state, they may not have any idea what he have uttered. In any event, even if the genuine seer must become "out of his mind," it makes sense to say that they can "see into" and hence "know the future." Vlastos [1991] misses this passage altogether in his account of divination and what the diviner might be said to know. If he hadn't, it is difficult to imagine that Vlastos would have been able to conclude that a genuine diviner could be accurately described as a "know-nothing" ([1991], 170).

if the utterance is issued in a moment of "inspiration."[40] If he really is a diviner, however, he will know that whatever he has said is divine in origin.

But even if diviners need not understand their utterances, Socrates thinks that diviners do possess knowledge of some sort; otherwise they could not be said to have a *technē*. Moreover, even if their *technē* only enables them to enter into the state of receptivity to the god, a state in which they are out of their minds, the knowledge that constitutes their *technē* is hardly trivial. We would count it as a wonderful thing if we found someone who knew how to provide us with information of great value which we were not able to obtain for ourselves. The fact that our benefactor had no idea of what it is that he had gotten for us or whether it is a good thing or not would in no way diminish the value of the information, and hence, the value we place on his knowledge of how to get it.

But does not this show that, after all, Plato's Socrates would have to regard the gift of divination as even more wonderful for the one who had it than whatever benefits one could obtain from leading the examined life? If we are right, Socrates believes that the diviner's *technē* enables him to receive truths of extraordinary significance. Nonetheless, we are convinced that Socrates would not be much impressed with the diviner's knowledge. To see why, it will be helpful to look at a passage in the *Apology* in which Socrates explains what about the poets is to be valued and what disparaged.

> So, taking up those poems in which they seemed to me to have worked most diligently, I asked them what they meant, so that I might at the same time learn something from them. I am ashamed to tell you the truth, O men, but it must be told. There was hardly anyone of those present who could not speak better than they [the poets] could about the poems they themselves had composed. (*Ap.* 22b2–8)

The poets say "many fine things" (*Ap.* 22c2). But having subjected them to elenctic examination, Socrates discovers that the poets are utterly ignorant of what it is about what they say that makes it "fine." Socrates can say precisely the same thing of diviners.[41] Regardless of whether or not diviners even know what they

---

40. A passage in the *Phaedrus* might suggest that, at least in the middle period, Plato did give more knowledge to the diviner. At *Phaedrus* 242b8–d2, Socrates describes his *daimonion* as making him a diviner, though not a very good one. But it makes him good enough to *know* (242c6), or to *perceive* (242d1), that he had done wrong. In what follows, it is clear that Socrates believes that he is able to provide the meaning of his *daimonion*'s opposition and to explain why it had opposed him when it did. Socrates' description of this case, however, does not require us to understand his own ability to decipher and understand the divinatory experience of his *daimonion* as itself the product of divination. Rather, the fact that he has his "sign" or "voice" is what qualifies him as a diviner. His understandings of its prohibitions need not themselves have come from divination or inspiration; they may be the product of his own ratiocination after his attention was called to the problem by his "sign."

41. Socrates never identifies poets as having a *technē* by which they can bring about the relevant state of inspiration. From the early to the late period, Plato is fully consistent in this contrast. In the *Phaedrus*, too, diviners do (244c1), but poets do not (245a1–8), have a *technē*. Likewise, the Eleatic Stranger in the *Politicus* does not list poets, but does list diviners, among the craft-possessing mediums (*Pol.* 260d11–e2). The poet is said to be like the diviner in that each does what he does through

say when they become "mad," the gods do not give them any insight into what it is about what they say that makes it true, good, or beneficial.

We can see in what sense Socrates disparages the knowledge of diviners when we compare what they know with what he considers to be the greatest knowledge of all, moral wisdom. Moral wisdom, and the understanding that contributes to or constitutes it, requires one to know *why* each particular moral judgment is correct; it enables one to explain the judgment in a coherent and comprehensive way (see *Grg.* 465a2–6, 500e4–501b1; *La.* 189e3–190b1). Perhaps more importantly, it enables one to know how to use such judgments to improve others. Knowing *that* what real diviners say is true is no great feat: we need only to know that they are qualified in the craft. Of course, it may be difficult to know whether one really is able to receive messages from the gods, for as Socrates concedes in the *Charmides* (173c5–6), some are true diviners and others are only impostors. But unlike many of the intellectuals who were his contemporaries, Socrates does not seem to doubt that there can be qualified diviners, and he clearly accepts the divine origin of the "many fine things" such men say.[42] It does not follow, of course, that we can know why or how or in what sense what they say is true—and, hence, we cannot know what motivates what they say. Only the gods know this. Moreover, without moral wisdom, even if we know that a divination is accurate, we cannot thereby use what has been revealed in an systematic way to make ourselves or anyone else better, for we will not be able to determine the range of cases to which the revelation applies or how exactly to apply it in any specific case. As a result, like Socrates' human wisdom, the knowledge possessed by diviners is "worth little or nothing" (see *Ap.* 23a6–7) relative to divine wisdom, which motivates and formulates the judgments the diviners are able only to convey, but never to make for themselves.

It follows that neither poetry nor divination threatens or rivals the epistemological primacy of philosophical inquiry. That is, the knowledge possessed by and available through divination is a paltry thing, in no way superior to what reason reveals. The truths Socrates unrelentingly seeks are not matters for divination, but for philosophy; as Xenophon's Socrates says, "What the gods have granted to us to do by the help of learning, we must learn; what is hidden from mortals we should try to find out from the gods by divination: for to him that is in their grace the gods grant a sign" (*Mem.* 1.1.9). But, more importantly, we may assume that Socrates believed that whatever specific knowledge we may gain through divination—and whatever knowledge the diviners themselves may have—moral understanding can be achieved only through rational inquiry and thought. To pur-

---

inspiration. For some poets, the inspired state is very rare indeed (see *Ion* 534d4–535a1). The "fine" results poets do achieve, when they do, is due to inspiration, just as it is in the case of the diviners. And just like the diviners, the poets are not in a position to understand or to explain the results of their inspirations. Diviners, however, appear to be of some genuine value—either on military expeditions or in other consultations—no doubt because they have a certain "servile" craft. Poets cannot produce their results so predictably.

42. In this, Socrates may be contrasted with a number of other fifth-century intellectuals who expressed the gravest doubts about divination and diviners. For a discussion of such skepticism, and especially the nature of its representation in the comedies of Aristophanes, see Smith [1989].

sue this goal, then, no matter how many truths the gods might reveal to us, "the unexamined life is not worth living for human beings" (*Ap.* 38a5–6).

6.5   Socrates on Death and the Afterlife

6.5.1   *"The Most Disgraceful Sort of Ignorance"*

In the *Apology*, Socrates explains to the jury why he will not abandon his philosophic mission in Athens out of a fear of death:

> For the fear of death, O men, is nothing other than the belief one is wise when one is not; for it is to believe one knows what one does not know. No one knows whether death happens to be the greatest of all goods for a person, but people fear it as if they knew it were the greatest of evils. And is this not the most disgraceful sort of ignorance, that of thinking one knows what one does not know? I, O men, in this way am perhaps also different from most people, and if I am wiser in anything it is this: that not having adequate knowledge about what is in Hades, I do not think I know. (29a4–b6, see also *Grg.* 522e1–2)

Yet elsewhere Socrates makes a number of critical moral judgments that suggest he actually has sufficient confidence about what happens at death to compare it favorably to a variety of other fates that can befall a human being. For example, *Crito* 47e3–5 shows that Socrates is convinced that life is not worth living for one who suffers from a worn out and ruined body;[43] and at *Gorgias* 512a2–5, he plainly implies that anyone suffering from a severe and incurable disease would be better off dead. One who is incorrigibly vicious is even worse off than one who is wracked by illness, and thus has a life that is even less worth living (*Cri.* 47e6–48a4); for such a person death is an even greater benefit than it is for the chronically and terribly ill (*Grg.* 512a2–b2). In fact, Socrates' most famous pronouncement seems to rely upon an assessment of the value of death, for if indeed "the unexamined life is not worth living for humans" (*Ap.* 38a5–6), it appears to follow that those who lead unexamined lives would be better off dead. But how can Socrates know that anyone would be better off dead without knowing at least that death is not a great evil? In making judgments such as these, is he not guilty of "the most disgraceful sort of ignorance," for is he not supposing he knows that death is no great evil, when in fact he has "no adequate knowledge" of death at all?

In fact, we do not believe that Socrates' remarks comparing the relative value of various lives to death convict him of "the most disgraceful sort of ignorance." In this section, we shall first examine what Socrates says he believes about death, and reveal the degree to which these beliefs are grounded in evidence and the nature of that evidence. Next, we shall examine his justification for supposing that

---

43. Although Socrates constructs his arguments from Crito's answers to his questions, Socrates indicates that he has endorsed this very piece of reasoning before and, hence, that he himself agrees with Crito's answers. "I am not able to throw away the reasons I used to use, because this happenstance has befallen me; but they appear to me to be almost exactly the same as before, and I revere and honor them just as before" (*Cri.* 46b6–c1; see also 48b3–6).

various sorts of lives are not worth living. Finally, we shall apply the conclusions of each of these examinations to the values Socrates attaches to various lives and show precisely why he believes his evaluation in each case is justified. We shall not argue that Socrates' conceptions about death lead him to the moral convictions he finds consistent with his views of the afterlife. Rather, his views of what death and the afterlife might be like probably reflect moral convictions he holds as more secure. But if what we shall argue is correct, one surprising conclusion follows: although he never claims to be wise in this all-important matter, Socrates believes there is good reason to think everyone will be better off dead.

6.5.2 Death in the Apology

Only twice in Plato's early dialogues does Socrates discuss in detail what he thinks death might be like. One of these two passages occurs at *Apology* 39e1 and following, where Socrates attempts to console those of his jurors who voted for his acquittal. Though it has now become clear that he will be executed, Socrates has become convinced that his death will be no evil, for he says "a wonderful thing has happened": his *daimonion,* which would surely have opposed him if what he was doing was leading him astray, has never once interrupted him the entire day. From this, Socrates feels confident that the outcome of his actions—including the sentence of death—is a good thing for him (*Ap.* 40a2–c3). Even if we suppose that Socrates' inference in this case is sound,[44] this "great proof" (*Ap.* 40c1), as he calls it, that his death will be no evil, does not guarantee that death in general will be no evil. If it did, our problem would be solved, for then any evil life would be a fate worse than death. But Socrates' "great proof" only shows (at most) that Socrates' *own* death will be no evil; nothing is implied about what might be in store for other people by his *daimonion*'s silence, a fact of which Socrates is well aware.

As Socrates leaves the courtroom, he makes this final remark: "I go to die, and you to live; but which of us goes to the better thing is clear to none but the god" (*Ap.* 42a2–5). For all he can say based on his "great proof," his own death will not be an evil for him precisely because death is never an evil. But it may also be the case that death offers very different possibilities for different people. Thus, whatever Socrates' degree of confidence that his own death will be no evil for him, it may well be that the jurors' lot in continuing to live will nevertheless be better than the lot awaiting Socrates in death. If so, death would be at least a relative evil for his jurors,[45] since for them it would be a fate worse than life. Socrates supposes that his own death will be a boon, for he suspects that if he were to go on living his life would be a troubled one (*Ap.* 41d2–5).[46]

---

44. For a discussion of how this inference works, see Brickhouse and Smith [1989b], 237–57. We no longer hold the view we argued in Brickhouse and Smith [1986].

45. For a discussion of how Socrates employs the conceptions of both relative and absolute evils, see sec. 4.4.

46. Nowhere in the *Apology* does Socrates say what these "troubles" are. He may be referring to "the infirmities of old age," as Xenophon would have it (see Xen. *Ap.* 6). More likely, he is referring

What might death hold for Socrates, and what about it allows his *daimonion* to remain silent rather than warning him away from the legal proceedings that would end in his condemnation? In speculating about this, Socrates realizes that he goes considerably beyond the evidence provided by his *daimonion*'s silence. The fact that his *daimonion* did not oppose him at any point during the trial provides no hint of what it is about death that will make it preferable to what his life would have been like. But Socrates offers his jurors "much hope" (40c4; see also 41c8) by considering two possibilities about death and showing why neither is to be feared.

The logical form of Socrates' argument is a constructive dilemma, either side leading to the conclusion that death is a good thing. But many interpreters have found Socrates' argument unconvincing[47] on the ground that the alternatives he considers appear only to be the most commonly imagined ones; others surely exist. He begins by offering what appear to be the two general possibilities: when we die either our soul perishes and goes nowhere, or else it leaves here and goes somewhere else. Socrates understands the first alternative as being like a sleep from which one never wakes (*Ap.* 40c5–7), which he regards as a "wonderful gain" (*Ap.* 40d1–2): even the Great King (of Persia) could count few of his days more pleasant that a night of dreamless sleep (*Ap.* 40d2–e4).[48] A variety of accounts present themselves as possibilities under the second alternative; the Pythagorean conception of transmigration of which Plato himself later becomes convinced is but one example. Socrates considers only one of these possibilities: if Socrates' soul is to go to another place of which the poets sometimes speak, he will be able to spend eternity conversing with the souls of all the great mortals now in Hades, for no one can kill him for talking with others in Hades (*Ap.* 41c4–5). He would count this as "an inconceivable happiness" (*Ap.* 41c3–4).

Socrates does not pretend to be offering his jurors an exhaustive analysis of the possibilities. He does not say that death *can only* be one of the two things he sketches in this passage. Thus, he is careful, in exploring the second option, the migration of the soul to Hades, to stipulate that the account he offers derives from "what is said" about death, from the stories that are typically told about it (*Ap.* 40c7, 40e5–6, 41c7), and he is very clear in withholding judgment as to the truth of these stories (*Ap.* 41c6–7).

But does the fact that Socrates considers only one of many possibilities within the "migration option" defeat the logic of Socrates' argument? In fact it does

---

to his "service on behalf of the god." (See 22a7, where Socrates refers to his examination of others as "toil," and Burnet [1924], note on 41d4, 171.) He may also be referring to the difficulties in carrying out his mission that have arisen in connection with Meletus' prosecution.

47. See, e.g., Armleder [1966], 46; Roochnik [1985], 212–20. For more charitable (and to our minds, more plausible) accounts, see Ehnmark [1946], 105–22; Hoerber [1966], 92; and especially Rudebusch [1991]. In our own earlier analyses of this argument (in Brickhouse and Smith [1986], and [1989b], 257–62), we, too, underrated the logic of Socrates' argument. We have been persuaded by Rudebusch's criticism of our view, however, and the following analysis owes much to his formulation.

48. Socrates' assessment of the value of death on this option has been questioned by Roochnik ([1985], 214). Defenses of Socrates' assessment may be found in Brickhouse and Smith [1989b] 258–59, and Rudebusch [1991].

not,[49] since the only sort of possibility that would defeat Socrates' argument would be one in which the soul migrated to a place that would render the continued existence of that soul bad. Socrates, however, is a man committed to a theology according to which the gods are flawlessly good, and would, therefore, never do anything evil to one another or to human beings (see, for example, *Ap.* 41d1–2, and our discussion in 6.2.1, above). The possibility that the afterlife could be an evil place would appear to be ruled out in principle by Socrates' theology of divine benevolence. All that Socrates' argument requires is that either of the two options for death—total extinction or afterlife—is a good thing for the dead. Given his assessment of the extinction option, and his theology of divine benevolence, this result seems assured.

6.5.3   The Value of "What Is Said" about Death

In reviewing the afterlife option of his argument, as we have said, Socrates considers only one of what appear to be indefinitely many possibilities. Although it is clear from his careful use of "what is said" about death that Socrates does not regard such stories as warranting anything like complete confidence, it is also true that he does not regard them as wholly without epistemic merit; if they were, we would have to conclude that there was only rhetorical value in seeming to mull them over as Socrates does. Socrates does not and cannot know the truth about death, but he does have some ground for supposing that the gist of the stories is true.

The sources of the myths about the afterlife are the poets, men who lack wisdom without knowing that they do. But, as we have seen, Socrates is convinced that their poetry can be the product of divine inspiration (*Ap.* 22a8–c8; see also *Ion* 533c9–535a2). Not all poetry, to be sure, is divinely inspired; the "greatest proof" (*Ion* 534d4–5) of this is the case of Tynnichos of Chalcis, who was inspired but once in an undistinguished career as a poet (*Ion* 534d4–535a1). But the difference between Tynnichos' inspired work and his other inventions is so patent that Socrates is convinced the god has used poor Tynnichos as a sign that the source of great poetry is divine.

The best known stories about death and the afterlife come from Orpheus, Musaeus, Hesiod, and Homer. Because Socrates has not personally examined these men, of course, he cannot say authoritatively that they did not understand the real meaning of their divinely inspired works. But of the poets Socrates tells his jury he has examined, although they said "many fine and noble things," they "know nothing of what they say" (*Ap.* 22c2–3). Perhaps part of the explanation is that the form of expression divine inspiration takes is sometimes obscure and perhaps even muddled, thus making the proper interpretation difficult. And perhaps in some cases the sheer arrogance of the poets themselves blinded them to the true meaning of what they had written. But one thing is certain: where the ultimate

---

49. George Rudebusch [1991] has recently made a persuasive case that the logic of Socrates' position is not defeated by the fact that he considers only one of many possibilities within the "migration opinion."

source of the poetry is the god, the poetry does not lie; genuine dishonesty is not within the god's nature (see *Ap.* 21b6–7).

Socrates' own positive[50] assessment of the migration of his soul to some other place is perhaps only what we would expect from a man committed to divine beneficence. In fact, Socrates' idea that death might be a good thing, relative to life, is not particularly unusual;[51] it is clear that the picture he offers can legitimately be said to derive from "what is said" about death by the poets and mythographers.[52] And the fact that all of the most inspired poets generally agree that the soul migrates to another place in the afterlife could also be seen as evidence in favor of the divine origin of such stories. This is hardly compelling evidence, however, for surely the poets are not always right even when they generally agree on something. The poets seem generally to agree that the gods sometimes do wicked things, for example, which Socrates says he finds hard to accept (*Euthphr.* 6a6-8). But although Socrates believes he has some reason to reject stories about divine wickedness, he has no particular reason to suppose that the tales of the soul's migration are false.[53] And if they are false, it would appear the most likely alternative account is that death is like an endless sleep,[54] which, for the reasons he gives in the *Apology,* Socrates would consider no evil.

6.5.4 Death in the Gorgias

Socrates gives a strikingly similar account of death in the *Gorgias* (523a1–527a4). There, it appears that Socrates does not consider the migration story merely one of the two most likely accounts, but indeed, the account of whose truth he is

50. Certainly Homer cannot be said to depict this migration as an "inconceivable happiness." See, e.g., *Odyssey* 11.477–503. But more positive assessments of this migration can be found, especially regarding those among the dead who were good while alive. Excellent summaries of the many varieties of ancient Greek views of the afterlife may be found in Adkins [1960], 138–39, 146; Dover [1974], 243–46, 261–67; Mikalson [1983], 74–82; Richardson [1985], 50–66; Rohde [1966], 236–42, 539–44; Rudhardt [1958], 113–26.

51. See, e.g., Homer, *Iliad* 17.446–47, 24.525–533; Archilochus 58, 67 (Diehl); Simonides of Amorgos 1, 3 (Diehl); Lysias 6.20; and esp. Herodotus I.31.

52. See the works cited in n.50 for citations of pertinent texts. This is not to claim that Socrates does not provide his own especially optimistic interpretation of "what is said," but rather that his interpretation does not amount to a complete fabrication of a new myth about the afterlife.

53. Although the *Phaedrus* is a later dialogue and thus contains a number of doctrines that actually conflict with the views of the "Socrates" of the early dialogues, what is said at 229c6–230a2 may help illuminate the point of view Socrates articulates in the earlier works (see n.23). This passage explains why Socrates was willing to accept mythological stories for which he found he had no (serious) contrary evidence and why he was not at all disposed to look for contrary evidence. If this is correct, the problematic cases for Socrates seem to be only those in which the gods are portrayed as immoral, petty, or mean. For further discussion of Socratic religion and orthodoxy, see Brickhouse and Smith [1989b], esp. sec. 3.1.5, and sec. 6.2, this volume.

54. The connection between sleep and death is as old as Homer (see, e.g., *Iliad* 14.231, where Sleep is brother to Death, and 16.672 and 682, where they are said to be twins. A number of ancient sources seem to count total extinction as one of the possibilities for death; see, e.g., Plato, *Phd.* 69e7–70a6; Hyperides 6.43; Democritus fr. 297 (Diels); Xenophon, *Cyr.* 8.7.19–23. The alternative Socrates seems to have in mind in comparing death to everlasting sleep, then, would also appear to have its source in tradition and myth, if not inspired poetry.

convinced (*Grg.* 523a1–3, 524a8–b1, 526d3–4, 527a5–b2).[55] Dreamless sleep, a possibility mentioned in the *Apology* (40d1), while no doubt still a possibility, does not now seem to be as plausible as the other alternative. Socrates insists that despite all his (and Gorgias' and Polus') searching, he can nowhere find any account that was better and truer than the one concerning migration, which he frequently associates in this passage with the most inspired of all poets, Homer (*Grg.* 523a3, 525d7, 526d1).

In the *Apology*, Socrates says that he is convinced that "no evil comes to a good man either in life or in death, nor does the god neglect his [the good man's] affairs" (*Ap.* 41d1–2). The same conviction is evident in the great myth of the *Gorgias:* after death, the person who is judged to be good goes directly to the "Isles of the Blessed" (*Grg.* 523a7–b4, 526c1–5). Even the wicked person, whose evil is curable, is benefited through punishment (*Grg.* 525a6–c1). But the soul of the incurably evil person suffers the "greatest, most painful, and most frightening" (*Grg.* 525c5–6) punishments. By suffering such punishments, however, the incurably wicked are prevented from acting on their wickedness, and hence even in their suffering they are better off than wicked ones who are still alive and who commit their evil deeds with impunity. Moreover, by suffering these tortures, the incurably evil souls may even do some good, for their punishments provide an example for all others (*Grg.* 525c1–8).[56]

Socrates' belief in such stories is insufficiently justified to qualify as knowledge. His evidence is incomplete and may be interpreted in other ways. But it is the best evidence available, and given the support such stories receive from other views of which he is convinced, he considers himself to have good reason to accept them. The evidence provided by such stories is consistent with his view that that death is nothing to fear.

6.5.5 Bad Lives

Socrates consistently affirms that what *is* to be feared is a life of viciousness. To be vicious, Socrates insists, is to be wretched; worst of all, however, is being vicious and not being punished for it. This is so, Socrates thinks, because vice is to the soul what disease is to the body: a corruption. He also thinks that as we have reason to prize our health, so we have reason to prize virtue; in fact, Socrates is convinced that as the soul is so much more important than the body, so much

---

55. Socrates' use of full-blown myth in the *Gorgias* is striking, for mythology as this sort is more characteristic of the character "Socrates" in the middle dialogues. However, what Socrates says in the *Gorgias* merely embellishes the only possibility for what occurs at death considered in the *Crito* (54a7–c7), and, unlike the myths of the middle dialogues, is in no way inconsistent with any of the other doctrines associated with the early dialogues.

56. For stories involving judgment in the afterlife, see Dover [1974], 263–68; Mikalson [1983] 78–82. McPherran [forthcoming] takes the account of judgment and the potential for punishment in the afterlife in the *Gorgias* to be evidence that the *Gorgias* cannot be counted as representing Socrates' own view. But we also find judgments in the afterlife (and plainly therefore an implied threat of some form of sanction in their judgments—one must assume punishment, given the customs of ancient Greece) in the *Apology* (40e7–41a4) and in the *Crito* (54c6–7). See nn. 62 and 63.

more should we prize virtue than health. Considerations such as these lead Socrates to say that he would prefer death to wrongdoing, even though he does not know what death will bring (*Ap.* 29a4–30c1). But *why* does he think that vice and illness are so corrosive to happiness?

As we noted in section 4.3.2, Socrates uses the expressions "living well," "doing well," and "happy" as if they were synonyms.[57] We argued that each of these conditions requires not only the virtuous condition of the soul, but also the capacity to engage in virtuous activities (see section 4.3). Let us consider each of these requirements.

In Book I of the *Republic*, Socrates argues that the soul has the functions "management, rule, deliberation, and life" (*Rep.* I.353d2–354a2). The good soul will perform these functions well, and the evil soul will perform them poorly; in fact, this is the reason why good souls are good and evil souls are evil. But why does the failure to perform these functions well condemn one to wretchedness?

Like all "eudaimonists," Socrates identifies happiness as the highest good, and counts as goods all and only those things that promote or produce happiness. For anything to qualify as a benefit, it must promote or produce something good; so it follows trivially that whatever is good is beneficial, and vice versa. If the soul is to perform its function properly, then, it must not merely manage, rule, deliberate, and live; it must do these things in such a way as to promote or produce benefits for the one to whom the soul gives life. Accordingly, the good person lives a life managed by a soul whose management brings benefit; and the evil person lives a life managed by a soul whose management brings harm.

Now Socrates is convinced that no one does evil knowingly, for to do evil is necessarily to bring harm to oneself, and no one wants what he or she recognizes as harm (see section 3.4 for discussion). All evil, then, is some kind of ignorance. The ignorant person unknowingly obstructs his or her own pursuit of goods and benefits either by misevaluating what he or she pursues as goods when they are not, or by pursuing what is really good in an unfruitful or self-defeating way. Thus, the ignorant person brings harm upon himself or herself without actually willing that harm. For Socrates, procuring what is harmful is wretchedness. And, as we have seen, the worst wretchedness is suffered by the one who continues to bring harms to himself or herself unimpeded by intervention and corrective punishment.

Ignorance leads us to an incorrect evaluation not only of activities, but also of goals and principles. So leading the unexamined life is especially dangerous because it raises the likelihood that we will not only pursue unworthy and harmful activities, but also select unworthy policies by which our activities will be governed and according to which our pursuits will be even more certain to bring us harm. One benefit of an elenctic encounter with Socrates, thus, occurs when one is shown that within one's own beliefs lies (at least one) contradiction. The pur-

---

57. See *Rep.* I.354a1–2. At *Euthydemus* 278e3–279a2 Socrates uses the expression "to do well" to denote what we all desire. Later, at 280b6–7, he uses both "to do well" and "happiness" as if they were interchangeable. After 280b7, Socrates exclusively uses "happiness." The exchange of these two expressions in a continuous argument shows that Socrates regards them as synonyms.

suits that flow from such contradictory beliefs obviously cannot both be fulfilling. As valuable as this awareness is, however, it is not enough; one must then determine which of one's contradictory beliefs to abandon. Socrates is often helpful in targeting the belief to give up. But only by leading the examined life can one ensure that the "management and rule of one's life" will not be needlessly self-defeating. Pursuits governed by contradictory principles are bad enough; the proliferation of policies inimical to one's real goals is even worse. Both fates can be mitigated through the pursuit of the examined life (see sections 1.3.1–2 for discussion).

Vice, then, is ignorance. It is the condition of a soul that does not perform its functions of ruling and governing properly. Instead of managing one's life in beneficial ways, the evil soul leads one to do what is harmful. The way to gain relief from this condition of bad management is to treat the ignorance as if it were a disease by subjecting one's principles and commitments to the "medical" examination of the *elenchos*, and one can then "cure" one's soul of the contradictions and confusions the examination uncovers.[58]

What of the condition of one whose *body* is incurably diseased? Socrates is convinced that such a person, too, is condemned to live so badly as to make his or her life a fate worse than death. Socrates never tells us his reason for thinking this; he seems instead simply to assume it in the arguments in which it appears (*Cri.* 47e3–5, *Grg*; 512a2–b2). Perhaps Socrates has conditions in mind that involve so much direct suffering as to make the conclusion obvious.[59]

But in the *Apology*, Socrates tells his jurors of the mission by which he believes his life has been made worthwhile. The principal feature of this life is his daily examination of himself and others. Once he has been convicted, he refuses to offer any counter-penalty that would bring an end to his mission (37b7–38b1). In considering exile, he is particularly adamant; "a fine life that would be for me at this advanced age," he exclaims, "passing from city to city and always being driven out" (37d4–6). The reason he will consider none of these things, least of all voluntarily giving up philosophizing, is that he must "talk every day about virtue . . . examining myself and others . . . [for] the unexamined life is not worth living for a human being" (38a1–6). For Socrates to have any chance at happiness, it seems, not only must he examine himself, but he must examine others.[60]

Socrates never tells us how narrowly or broadly he conceives "the examined life." Does he mean to identify only those lives in which one "neglects all [one's] own affairs" (*Ap.* 31b1–3), as he has, and lives only to philosophize? Or might one lead an examined life who, dedicated largely to other activities (farming, for example), also took care to spend regular time in philosophical discussions with others? Because he chastises his fellow Athenians only for caring more about

58. For Socrates' comparison of the effects of philosophical discussion with those of medicine, see, e.g., *Charm.* 157a1–c6.

59. See Lysias, fr. 73 (Thalheim). The idea that death can be a relief from suffering is also found throughout the ancient sources (see Dover [1974], 267).

60. For an excellent discussion of just why Socrates thinks that he ought to engage himself and others in philosophy, see McPherran [1986], 541–60.

other things than "prudence, truth, and the soul" (*Ap.* 29e1–2), but not for not caring at all for these most important goods (see his reference to "the other goods" at *Ap.* 30b3–4), we believe he construes "the examined life" fairly broadly.

One's health, then, cannot be so bad as to preclude one from leading the examined life. So, because "the unexamined life is not worth living," the life of one so badly disabled as to make one unable to lead the examined life is not worth living either. And if other pursuits are necessary for a life worth living (though few, if any, seem to be so for Socrates), then one's health must be good enough to allow one to engage in those pursuits as well. The common cold, however annoying it may be, does not suffice to remove any hope one might have of leading a life worth living. Plainly, Socrates has a much graver condition in mind when he speaks of someone whose body is "worn out and ruined" (*Cri.* 47e3–5). So mere poor health does not suffice to make one's life not worth living; only when it becomes so poor as to leave one's body "ruined" would one be better off dead.

6.5.6   The Value of Death and the Value of Life

So not all disease makes one's life not worth living; certainly nothing curable does so. But what about vice? Surely *some* vice is curable, and Socrates' mission is designed to provide at least some treatment for this condition (among other things). Thus, one's life is worth living so long as one maintains the care of the soul that helps it to be free of the evil of complacent ignorance. Of course, one's ignorance may never be cured, but it can be mitigated, as Socrates' is;[61] if not, one's life will turn out to be wasted. But the quality of a mere moment is obviously not a sufficient measure of the quality of a whole life. So curable (or treatable) ignorance does not automatically consign one's whole life to worthlessness. It will only end up being worthless if one never (or inadequately) treats one's corrosive ignorance. And even if one's life is wholly wasted, one of Socrates' views of the afterlife—the one involving the migration of the soul to Hades— holds out some hope that a remedy can come later, so long as one's soul has not been irreparably damaged (*Grg.* 525b4–c1).

Socrates also seems to think, however, that some souls can become implacably and irremediably vicious. Such souls, it seems, cannot be cured of evil even in death. In the *Gorgias,* Socrates imagines that the only good they can serve is as an example to others, by "enduring forever for their transgressions the greatest, most painful, and most fearsome sufferings," for they are past hope of benefit themselves (*Grg.* 525c1–8). It might appear to follow from this that such people

---

61. In sec. 4.5.3, we contrasted Socratic ignorance with the disgraceful sort of ignorance from which others suffer. Socratic ignorance—even if suffered for an entire life—does not leave its sufferer with a life worse than death, and does not entail that its sufferer is evil in any way. So it is that Socrates, however profoundly ignorant, can without reservation consider himself a good man; see *Ap.* 41d1–2, where his reassurance to the jurors that "no evil comes to a good man" is plainly meant to apply to Socrates himself. Other forms of ignorance must be cured or mitigated, as we say here, to render one's life worth living.

would really be better off alive than dead. But because it is far better, Socrates believes, to suffer than to do evil, and because these people will no longer be able to engage in vicious action, it follows that they will still be better off dead than alive. Such souls, we may be assured, will no longer be free in death, as they had been in life, to pursue their evil goals. And if death is like endless sleep, the dead are plainly better off than the wicked who are alive: at least the dead do not continue to bring harm to themselves through an incorrect evaluation of what is in their interest. The dead, on this hypothesis, do not continue their evil ways; they merely sleep.

The view of the afterlife Socrates advocates in the *Gorgias* ensures that if a soul is curable, it shall be cured, and if it is incurable, it shall be thwarted from the doing of further evil and put to the best possible use. So it follows that both curably and incurably evil souls are better off in the afterlife. Of course living the upright life is itself rewarding, according to Socrates. But his view of the afterlife expressed at the end of the *Gorgias* also ensures that at death a further reward will be bestowed on a good soul. The good soul, we are assured, and especially the soul of the philosopher, is sent to the "Isles of the Blessed," where we can be sure that it enjoys the greatest conceivable happiness (*Grg.* 526c1–5). Thus, a good person, too, is better off dead, even though his or her life *had been* worth living.

6.5.7   An Objection Considered

It might be thought that the view of the afterlife found in the *Gorgias* must represent a different view from that expressed in the *Apology,* for if the "Socrates" whose views are expressed in the *Apology* had thought that the soul continues to exist after the death of the body, he would not have suggested "dreamless sleep" as a real possibility.[62] We must remember, however, first, that in the *Gorgias.* Socrates does not profess to *know* what happens at death. Thus, presumably even at the end of the *Gorgias* he regards dreamless sleep as a real possibility, although not as the most likely one. Second, in the *Apology,* Socrates is trying to provide the jurors with an argument which will give his jurors "good hope" (41c8) regarding what happens at death. Insofar as both alternatives Socrates presents are real possibilities and are seen as such by the jurors to whom he is speaking, he can achieve his goal of creating "good hope" by pointing out to them that on either possibility, the good man has reason to optimistic about what happens at death. Nothing requires that he try to convince them in the brief time he has left

---

62. See McPherran [forthcoming], who offers this as an argument for rejecting the *Gorgias* passage as reflecting a later Platonic view of the matter. Plainly, we are not persuaded by his argument, especially given the additional evidence from the *Crito* that Socrates did indeed accept the soul's migration to another place as the more likely (see next note). One problem for McPherran's view is that Plato himself seems to have accepted a Pythagorean form of reincarnation, but no trace of this can be found in the *Gorgias, Crito,* or *Apology*. In McPherran's view, the *Gorgias* does not accurately reflect either Socrates' or Plato's own mature view of death and the afterlife.

before being taken to prison that in fact transmigration is the *more likely* possibility.[63]

Socrates' view that everyone—regardless of the moral quality of his or her soul—is really better off dead is entirely consonant with a number of other traditional Greek views of the relative values of life and death, in which the suffering that pervades every person's life is relieved only at death.[64] But in Socrates' view, moral goodness makes the life of the upright person far more than a vale of tears; though he does say that few days of our lives are better than a night's dreamless sleep (*Ap.* 40c9–e2), he also equates happiness with "living well."[65] But if death is migration, it is even better than this for the good man: a "wonderful gain" (*Ap.* 40d1–2), or an "inconceivable happiness" (*Ap.* 41c3–4). So moral goodness can make one's life happy; but even so, death will still be better for the good person.

6.5.8 Concluding Remarks

If what we have argued is correct, Socrates believes that in some way or other, everyone will be better off dead.[66] This conclusion does not conflict with his view that certain lives are, and certain lives are not, worth living; for it does not follow from the fact that a life is worth living that the one living it will be worse off after his or her life ends. On the contrary: for Socrates, the more worth living one's life is, the more beatific one can expect one's afterlife to be. Our interpretation of what Socrates says about the values of life and death thus distinguishes between whether or not one has a life that is worth living, on the one hand, and whether or not one has a life that is worse than death. All of us have lives that are worse than what we have reason to expect in death; but some of us, if we work hard at it, will nonetheless have lives that are also worth living. In this sense, then, we are better off alive so long as we do what we can to make our lives worthy ones, for such a life is itself better than any other sort of life, and

63. There is reason to believe that Plato saw Socrates as holding the migration option all along to be more likely. In the *Crito*—a dialogue scholars generally agree to have been written in roughly the same period as the *Apology*—we find that "the Laws," speaking to Socrates, take it for granted that if Socrates chooses not to escape but to remain in prison, his soul "will go away and live in Hades" and that if he chooses to escape to Thessaly, when he does eventually die, "the laws in Hades will not receive [him] kindly" (54c6–7). McPherran [forthcoming] dismisses this as evidence for Socrates' own belief, on the ground that it is the Laws, and not Socrates, who express the view. But surely the actual laws of Athens do not state any such explicit commitment to a view of the afterlife (and surely Crito would be in a position to know this). So if Socrates is not expressing his own view here, he is attributing a view of the afterlife to the laws which is both unwarranted by the actual laws and misleading to his interlocutor (and to Plato's readers, who may reasonably assume that all of the other pronouncements by the Laws are accepted by Socrates).

64. See n.51 for references.

65. See n.57 for references.

66. Nothing in our argument, however, implies that Socrates would necessarily advocate taking the life of another or suicide, for, depending upon the particular circumstances, such acts might be unjust, and, hence, harm their agent(s). Socrates would never advocate injustice. Even the person who wrongfully takes a life will be better off in death, for as we have seen, whatever form relief from vice takes, death is a good for the vicious.

the rewards of having lived such a life are greater in the afterlife than the condition of one who did not lead such a life. (Socrates does not say that a curably evil soul, once cured in the afterlife, will then enjoy beatitude; he only says that it will be cured of its evil.) For Socrates, the greatest peril of all is to live a life that so corrupts one with evil that even one's afterlife is irredeemably spoiled. One's life, then, should be devoted to the care of that which continues after it—the soul. A life that follows this principle will not be lived in vain.

Finally, Socrates counts none of his beliefs about these matters as knowledge. So although he may fairly say that he is ignorant of the afterlife, he may nonetheless legitimately believe he has rational grounds for judging the relative value of various lives to death. And since his assessments are, as we have seen, also based upon various traditional views about the value of death, none is seen as particularly controversial or puzzling to Socrates' interlocutors, who accordingly challenge neither Socrates' profession of ignorance on this topic nor his confident assessment that certain lives are not worth living.

Bibliography

Adam, J. [1908] *Platonis Euthyphro*. Cambridge, England.

Adkins, A.W.H. [1960] *Merit and Responsibility*. Chicago and London.

———. [1970] "Clouds, Mysteries, Socrates and Plato." *Antichthon* 4: 13–24.

Allen, R. E. [1970] *Plato's Euthyphro and the Early Theory of Forms*. New York.

———. [1972] "Law and Justice in Plato's *Crito*." *Journal of Philosophy* 69, 557–67.

———. [1975] "The Trial of Socrates: A Study in the Morality of the Criminal Process." In, Martin L. Friedland, ed., *Courts and Trials: A Multi-Disciplinary Approach*, 3–21. Toronto and Buffalo.

———. [1976] "Irony and Rhetoric in Plato's *Apology*." *Paideia* (Buffalo) 5: *Special Plato Issue*, 32–42.

———. [1980] *Socrates and Legal Obligation*. Minneapolis.

Anderson, Daniel E. [1967] "Socrates' Concept of Piety." *Journal of the History of Philosophy* 5: 1–13.

Andrewes, Antony. [1974] "The Arginousai Trial." *Phoenix* 28: 112–22.

Armleder, P. J. [1966] "Death in Plato's *Apology*." *Classical Bulletin* 42: 46.

Arnim, H. von. [1914] *Platos Jugenddialoge*. Leipzig and Berlin.

Austin, Scott. [1987] "The Paradox of Socratic Ignorance (How to Know That You Don't Know)." *Philosophical Topics* 15: 23–34.

Barker, Ernest. [1951] *Greek Political Theory: Plato and His Predecessors*, 4th ed. New York.

Benson, Hugh. [1987] "The Problem of the Elenchus Reconsidered."*Ancient Philosophy* 7: 67–85.

———. [1989] "A Note on Eristic and the Socratic Elenchus." *Journal of the History of Philosophy* 27: 591–600.

———. [1990a] "Meno, the Slave-boy, and the *Elenchos*." *Phronesis* 35: 128–58.

———. [1990b] "Misunderstanding the 'What-is-F-ness?' Question." *Archiv für Geschichte der Philosophie* 72: 125–42.

———. [1990c] "The Priority of Definition and the Socratic *Elenchos*." *Oxford Studies in Ancient Philosophy* 8: 19–65.

———. (ed.). [1992] *Essays on the Philosophy of Socrates*. New York and Oxford.

Bers, Victor. [1985] "Dikastic *Thorubos*." In *Crux: Essays Presented to G.E.M. de Ste. Croix on His 75th Birthday*, Special Festschrift Edition of *History of Political Thought* 6: 1–15.

Beversluis, John. [1974] "Socratic Definition." *American Philosophical Quarterly* 11: 331–36.

———. [1987] "Does Socrates Commit the Socratic Fallacy?" *American Philosophical Quarterly* 24: 211–23.

Blundell, Mary Whitlock. [1987] "The Moral Character of Odysseus in *Philoctetes*."
    Greek, Roman and Byzantine Studies 28: 307–29.
Bolton, Robert. [1993] "Aristotle's Account of the Socratic Elenchus." Forthcoming, *Oxford Studies in Ancient Philosophy* 11.
Bonfante, L., and Raditsa, L. [1978] "Socrates' Defense and His Audience." *Bulletin of the American Society of Papyrologists* 15: 17–23.
Bonitz, H. [1966] *Platonische Studien*. Berlin.
Bouché-Leclerq, A. [1975] *Histoire de la divination dans l'antiquité*, vols. 1–4. Paris, 1879–1882; repr. New York.
Brickhouse, Thomas C. [1990] Review of Reeve [1989]. *Polis* 9: 198–209.
Brickhouse, Thomas C., and Smith, Nicholas D. [1983] "The Origin of Socrates' Mission." *Journal of the History of Ideas* 44: 657–66.
———. [1984a] "Irony, Arrogance and Sincerity in Plato's *Apology*." In E. Kelly, [1984], 29–46.
———. [1984b] "The Paradox of Socratic Ignorance in Plato's *Apology*." *History of Philosophy Quarterly* 1: 125–31.
———. [1984c] "Socrates and Obedience to the Law." *Apeiron* 18: 10–18.
———. [1984d] "Vlastos on the Elenchus." *Oxford Studies in Ancient Philosophy* 2: 185–95.
———. [1985] "The Formal Charges against Socrates." *Journal of the History of Philosophy* 23: 457–81.
———. [1986] "'The Divine Sign Did Not Oppose Me': A Problem in Plato's *Apology*." *Canadian Journal of Philosophy* 16: 511–26.
———. [1987a] "Socrates' Evil Associates and the Motivation for His Trial and Condemnation." In J. Cleary [1987], vol. 3, 45–71.
———. [1987b] "Socrates on Goods, Virtue, and Happiness." *Oxford Studies in Ancient Philosophy* 5: 1–27.
———. [1989a] "A Matter of Life and Death in Socratic Philosophy." *Ancient Philosophy* 9: 155–65.
———. [1989b] *Socrates on Trial*. Oxford and Princeton.
———. [1990a] Letter to the Editor. *Times Literary Supplement* Jan. 5–11: 11.
———. [1990b] Letter to the Editor. *Times Literary Supplement* Jan. 26–Feb. 1: 89.
———. [1990c] "What Makes Socrates a Good Man?" *Journal of the History of Philosophy* 28: 169–179.
———. [1993] Review of Vlastos [1991]. *Ancient Philosophy* (forthcoming).
Burkert, Walter. [1985] *Greek Religion*. Cambridge, Mass.
Burnet, John. [1924] *Plato's Euthyphro, Apology of Socrates, and Crito*. Oxford.
Burnyeat, M. F. [1971] "Virtues in Action." In Vlastos [1971a], 209–34.
———. [1977] "Examples in Epistemology: Socrates, Theaetetus, and G. E. Moore." *Philosophy* 52: 381–98.
Bury, J. B. [1926] "The Trial of Socrates." *Rationalist Press Association Annual*. London.
———. [1940] "The Life and Death of Socrates." *Cambridge Ancient History*, 3rd ed. vol. 5, ch. 13.4, 386–97.
———. [1962] *A History of Greece*. New York.
Chroust, Anton-Hermann. [1957] *Socrates, Man and Myth*. South Bend, Indiana.
Cleary, John (ed.). [1985, 1986, 1987, 1988, 1989] *Proceedings of the Boston Area Colloquium in Ancient Philosophy*, vols. 1 (1985), 2 (1986), 3 (1987), 4 (1988), and 5 (1989). Lanham, New York, and London.

Cohen, D. [1988] "The Prosecution of Impiety in Athenian Law." *Zeitschrift der Savigny-Stiftung für Rechtsgeschichte (Romanistische Abteilung)* 118: 695–701.

Colson, Darrel D. [1985] "On Appealing to Athenian Law to Justify Socrates' Disobedience." *Apeiron* 19: 133–51.

———. [1989] "*Crito* 51A-C: To What Does Socrates Owe Obedience?" *Phronesis* 34: 27–55.

Connor, W. R. [1991] "The Other 399: Religion and the Trial of Socrates." *Georgica: Greek Studies in Honour of George Cawkwell. Institute of Classical Studies Bulletin Supplement* 58: 49–56.

Cooper, John. [1975] *Reason and the Human Good in Aristotle.* Princeton.

Cornford, F. M. [1932] *Before and after Socrates.* Cambridge, England.

———. [1933] "The Athenian Philosophical Schools, I. The Philosophy of Socrates." *Cambridge Ancient History.* vol. 6, 302–9. Cambridge.

Crombie, I. M. [1962] *An Examination of Plato's Doctrines,* 2 vols. London.

Cushman, R. [1958] *Therapeia.* Chapel Hill.

Davidson, Donald. [1985] "Plato's Philosopher." *London Review of Books* August 1985: 15–17.

Davies, J. K. [1971] *Athenian Propertied Families: 600–300 B.C.* Oxford.

———. [1983] *Democracy and Classical Greece.* Stanford.

Dodds, E. R. [1959] *Plato: Gorgias.* Oxford.

Dover, K. J. [1974] *Greek Popular Morality in the Time of Plato and Aristotle.* Berkeley and Los Angeles.

———. [1975] "Freedom of the Intellectual in Greek Society." *Talanta* 7: 24–54.

Ehnmark, E. [1946] "Socrates and the Immortality of the Soul." *Eranos* 44: 105–22.

Ferejohn, Michael. [1984] "Socratic Thought-Experiments and the Unity of Virtue Paradox." *Phronesis* 29: 105–22.

Finley, M. I. [1968] *Aspects of Antiquity.* London.

Friedländer, P. [1964] *Plato,* 3 vols. New York.

Geach, Peter. [1966] "Plato's *Euthyphro:* An Analysis and Commentary." *Monist* 50: 369–82.

Gould, John. [1955] *The Development of Plato's Ethics.* Cambridge, England.

Grote, George. [1875] *Plato and the Other Companions of Socrates,* 3 vols. London.

———. [1888] *A History of Greece,* 10 vols. London.

Guardini, Roman. [1948] *The Death of Socrates,* trans. Basil Wrighton. New York.

Gulley, Norman. [1968] *The Philosophy of Socrates.* New York.

Guthrie, W.K.C. [1962, 1965, 1969, 1975] *A History of Greek Philosophy,* 5 vols. London. (The following entry [1971] is reprinted with some changes and additions from vol. 3.)

———. [1971] *Socrates.* Cambridge, England.

Hackforth, R. M. [1933] *The Composition of Plato's Apology.* Cambridge, England.

Haden, James. [1979] "On Socrates with Reference to Gregory Vlastos." *Review of Metaphysics* 33: 371–89.

Halliday, William R. [1913] *Greek Divination.* London.

Hanscn, Mogens Herman. [1980] "Hvorfor Henrettede Athenerne Sokrates?" *Museum Tusculanum* 40–43: 55–82.

Harrison, A.W.R. [1971] *The Law in Athens,* 2 vols. Oxford.

Hathaway, Ronald F. [1970] "Law and the Moral Paradox in Plato's *Apology.*" *Journal of the History of Philosophy* 8: 127–42.

Heidel, W. A. [1900] "On Plato's *Euthyphro.*" *Transactions of the American Philological Association* 31: 164–81.

Hoerber, Robert G. [1966] "Note on Plato, *Apologia* XLII." *Classical Bulletin* 42: 92.

Irwin, T. H. [1977] *Plato's Moral Theory*. Oxford.

———. [1979] *Plato's Gorgias*. Oxford.

———. [1986a] "Socrates the Epicurean?" *Illinois Classical Studies*, 11: 85–112.

———. [1986b] "Coercion and Objectivity in Platonic Dialectic." *Revue Internationale de Philosophie* 40: 49–74.

———. [1989] "Socrates and Athenian Democracy." *Philosophy and Public Affairs* 18: 184–205.

Jones, A.H.M. [1969] *Athenian Democracy*. London.

Jowett, B. [1953] *The Dialogues of Plato,* 4 vols. Oxford.

Kahn, Charles. [1988] "On the Relative Date of the *Gorgias* and the *Protagoras*." *Oxford Studies in Ancient Philosophy* 6: 69–102.

Kelly, Eugene (ed.). [1984] *New Essays on Socrates*. Lanham, New York, and London.

Keyt, David. [1978] "Intellectualism in Aristotle." *Paideia: Special Issue* 2 (*Aristotle*): 138–57.

Klosko, George. [1979] "Toward a Consistent Intepretation of the *Protagoras*." *Archiv für Geschichte der Philosophie* 61: 125–42.

Kraut, Richard. [1983a] "Comments on Gregory Vlastos, 'The Socratic Elenchus.' " *Oxford Studies in Ancient Philosophy* 1: 59–70.

———. [1983b] *Socrates and the State*. Princeton.

Laudan, Larry. [1977] *Progress and Its Problems*. Berkeley, Los Angeles, and London.

Lesher, James H. [1987] "Socrates' Disavowal of Knowledge." *Journal of the History of Philosophy* 25: 275–88.

Lipsius, J. H. [1905–1915] *Das attische Recht und Rechtverfahren*. Leipzig.

Loening, T. C. [1981] "The Reconciliation Agreement of 403/402 BC in Athens: Its Content and Applications." Ph.D. Dissertation, Brown University.

Lofberg, J. O. [1928] "The Trial of Socrates." *Classical Journal* 23: 601–9.

MacDowell, Douglas M. [1978] *The Law in Classical Athens*. Ithaca.

McPherran, Mark. [1985] "Socratic Piety in the *Euthyphro*." *Journal of the History of Philosophy* 23: 283–309.

———. [1986] "Socrates and the Duty to Philosophize." *Southern Journal of Philosophy* 24: 541–60.

———. [1990] Letter to the Editor. *Times Literary Supplement* Feb. 16–22: 171.

———. [1991a] "Socratic Reason and Socratic Revelation." *Journal of the History of Philosophy* 29: 345–73.

———. [1991b] Review of Brickhouse and Smith [1989b]. *Ancient Philosophy* 11: 161–69.

———. [forthcoming] "Socrates on the Immortality of the Soul." *Journal of the History of Philosophy*.

McTighe, Kevin. [1984] "Socrates on Desire for the Good and the Involuntariness of Wrongdoing: *Gorgias* 466a-468e." *Phronesis* 29: 193–236.

Mikalson, Jon D. [1983] *Athenian Popular Religion*. Chapel Hill.

Moline, Jon. [1981] *Plato's Theory of Understanding*. Madison, Wisconsin.

Montuori, Mario. [1981] *Socrates, Physiology of a Myth,* trans. J.M.P. Langdale and M. Langdale. Amsterdam.

Mulhern, J. J. [1968] "A Note on Stating the Socratic Paradox." *Journal of the History of Ideas* 29: 601–4.

Navia, Luis E. [1985] *Socrates: The Man and His Philosophy*. Lanham, New York, and London.

Nehamas, Alexander. [1986] "Socratic Intellectualism." In J. Cleary [1986], vol. 2, 275–316.

Nilsson, Martin. [1971] *Greek Folk Religion*. New York, 1940; repr. 1971.

O'Brien, M. J. [1967] *The Socratic Paradoxes and the Greek Mind*. Chapel Hill.

Panagiotou, Spiro. [1987] "Socrates' 'Defiance' in the *Apology*." *Apeiron* 21: 39–61.

Pappas, Nickolas. [1989] "Socrates' Charitable Treatment of Poetry." *Philosophy and Literature* 13: 248–61.

Penner, T. [1973] "The Unity of Virtue." *Philosophical Review* 82: 35–68.

———. [1992] "What Laches and Nicias Miss—And Whether Socrates Thinks Courage Is Merely a Part of Virtue." *Ancient Philosophy* 12: 1–27.

Plochmann, George Kimball, and Robinson, Franklin E. [1988] *A Friendly Companion to Plato's Gorgias*. Carbondale, Illinois.

Rabinowitz, W. G. [1958] "Platonic Piety: An Essay towards the Solution of an Enigma." *Phronesis* 3: 108–20.

Reeve, C.D.C. [1989] *Socrates in the Apology*. Indianapolis and Cambridge, England.

Richardson, N. J. [1985] "Early Greek Views about Life after Death." In P. E. Easterling and J. V. Muir, eds., *Greek Religion and Society*, 50–66. Cambridge.

Roberts, J. W. [1984] *City of Sokrates*. London, Boston, Melbourne, and Henley.

Robin, Leon. [1935] *Platon*. Paris.

Robinson, Richard. [1953] *Plato's Earlier Dialectic*. Oxford.

Rohde, E. [1966] *Psyche: The Cult of Souls and Belief in Immortality among the Greeks*; trans. W. B. Hillis from 8th ed. New York.

Roochnik, David L. [1985] "*Apology* 40c4–41e7: Is Death Really a Gain?" *Classical Journal* 80: 212–20.

Rudebusch, George. [1991] "Death Is One of Two Things." *Ancient Philosophy* 11: 35–45.

Rudhardt, J. [1958] *Notions fondamentales de la pensée religeuse et actes constitutifs du culte dans le Grece classique*. Geneva.

Santas, Gerasimos. [1979] *Socrates: Philosophy in Plato's Early Dialogues*. London and Boston.

Seeskin, Kenneth. [1987] *Dialogue and Discovery: A Study in Socratic Method*. Albany.

Shero, L. R. [1927] "Plato's *Apology* and Xenophon's *Apology*." *Classical World* 20: 107–11.

Shorey, Paul. [1933] *What Plato Said*. Chicago.

Sinclair, R. K. [1988] *Democracy and Participation in Athens*. Cambridge.

Smith, Nicholas D. [1987] Review of Seeskin [1987]. *Ancient Philosophy* 7: 215–19.

———. [1989] "Diviners and Divination in Aristophanic Comedy." *Classical Antiquity* 8: 140–58.

———. [1990] Review of Teloh [1986]. *Ancient Philosophy* 10: 105–12.

———. [1992] Review of Reeve [1989]. *Ancient Philosophy* 12: 399–407.

Stokes, Michael. [1986] *Plato's Socratic Conversations: Drama and Dialectic in Three Dialogues*. Baltimore.

Stone, I. F. [1988a] *The Trial of Socrates*. New York and London.

———. [1988b] "Was There a Witchhunt in Ancient Athens?" *New York Review of Books* 34 (Jan. 21, 1988): 37–41.

Strauss, Barry S. [1987] *Athens after the Peloponnesian War: Class Faction, and Policy, 403–386 B.C.* Ithaca, New York.

Tate, J. [1936] "Plato, Socrates and the Myths." *Classical Quarterly* 30: 142–45.

Taylor, A. E. [1927] *Plato: The Man and His Work*. New York.

———. [1933] *What Plato Said*. Chicago.

Taylor, C.C.W. [1976] *Plato's Protagoras*. Oxford.
———. [1982] "The End of the *Euthyphro*." *Phronesis* 27: 109–18.
Teloh, Henry. [1986] *Socratic Education in Plato's Early Dialogues*. Notre Dame.
Vatai, Frank Leslie. [1984] *Intellectuals in Politics in the Greek World*. London, Sydney, and Dover.
Vlastos, Gregory (ed.). [1971a] *The Philosophy of Socrates*. Garden City, New York.
———. [1971b] "Introduction: The Paradox of Socrates." In Vlastos [1971a], 1–21.
———. [1974] "Socrates on Political Obedience and Disobedience." *Yale Review* 63: 517–34.
———. [1976] "Editor's Introduction to Plato's *Protagoras*." *Protagoras*, vii–lvi. trans. M. Ostwald. Indianapolis.
———. [1978] "The Virtuous and the Happy." Review of Irwin [1977]. *Times Literary Supplement* Feb. 24: 230–31.
———. [1980] "Socrates' Contribution to the Greek Sense of Justice." *Arkaiognosia* 1: 310–324.
———. [1981] "What Did Socrates Understand by His 'What Is F?' Question." In G. Vlastos, *Platonic Studies*, 2nd ed. Princeton.
———. [1983a] "The Socratic Elenchus." *Oxford Studies in Ancient Philosophy* 1: 27–58.
———. [1983b] "Afterthoughts on the Elenchus." *Oxford Studies in Ancient Philosophy* 1: 71–74.
———. [1983c] "The Historical Socrates and Athenian Democracy." *Political Theory* 2: 495–516.
———. [1984a] "Reasons for Dissidence." Review of Kraut [1983b]. *Times Literary Supplement* August 24: 932.
———. [1984b] "Happiness and Virtue in Socrates' Moral Theory." *Proceedings of the Cambridge Philological Society* N.S. 30: 181–213.
———. [1985] "Socrates' Disavowal of Knowledge." *Philosophical Quarterly* 35: 1–31.
———. [1988] "Elenchus and Mathematics: A Turning Point in Plato's Philosophical Development." *American Journal of Philology* 109: 362–96; repr. in slightly revised form in Vlastos [1991] as chapter 4.
———. [1989a] "Socratic Piety." In Cleary [1989], vol. 5, 213–38.
———. [1989b] "Divining the Reason." Review of Brickhouse and Smith [1989]. *Times Literary Supplement* Dec. 15–21: 1393.
———. [1990a] Letter to the Editor. *Times Literary Supplement* Jan. 19–25: 63.
———. [1990b] Letter to the Editor. *Times Literary Supplement* Feb. 23–March 1: 197.
———. [1991] *Socrates: Ironist and Moral Philosopher*. Cornell and Cambridge.
Weiss, Roslyn. [1985] "Ignorance, Involuntariness, and Innocence: A Reply to McTighe." *Phronesis* 30: 314–22.
———. [1986] "Euthyphro's Failure." *Journal of the History of Philosophy* 24: 437–52.
Winspear, A. D., and Silverberg, T. [1960] *Who Was Socrates?* New York.
Wood, Ellen Meiksins, and Wood, Neal. [1978] *Class Ideology and Ancient Political Theory: Socrates, Plato, and Aristotle in Social Context*. New York.
Woodruff, Paul. [1982] *Plato, The Hippias Major*. Indianapolis.
———. [1986] "The Skeptical Side of Plato's Method." *Revue Internationale de Philosophie* 40: 22–37.
———. [1987] "Expert Knowledge in the *Apology* and *Laches:* What a General Should Know." In Cleary [1987], vol. 3, 79–115.
———. [1990] "Plato's Early Theory of Knowledge." In S. Everson, ed., *Companions to Ancient Thought I: Epistemology*, 60–84. Cambridge, England.

Woozley, A. D. [1971] "Socrates on Disobeying the Law." In Vlastos [1971a], 299–318.

———. [1979] *Law and Obedience: The Arguments of Plato's Crito*. Chapel Hill.

Zeller, Eduard. [1963] *Die Philosophie der Griechen in ihrer geschichtlichen Entwicklung*. vol. 1. Leipzig, 1922; repr. 1963.

Zeyl, Donald. [1982] "Socratic Virtue and Happiness." *Archiv für Geschichte der Philosophie* 64: 225–38.

Index of Passages

Titles of spurious or doubtful works are bracketed.

General Index